The Spectrum of Addiction

In loving memory of my parents. I have such gratitude for those precious pearls of wisdom you gave through deed and word to all of us in your ocean, ever reminding me that the world is indeed my oyster. And to all who left too soon for the Great Beyond, especially to M. L. "Little Mike" Boies and Sidney Jack.

—Laura J. Veach

This is dedicated to all the individuals, friends, and families that have been, and continue to be, affected by addiction, and specifically, by the opioid epidemic in our country.

—Regina R. Moro

The Spectrum of Addiction

Evidence-Based Assessment, Prevention, and Treatment Across the Lifespan

Laura J. Veach

Wake Forest School of Medicine

Regina R. Moro

Boise State University

Los Angeles | London | New Delhi
Singapore | Washington DC | Melbourne

FOR INFORMATION:

SAGE Publications, Inc.
2455 Teller Road
Thousand Oaks, California 91320
E-mail: order@sagepub.com

SAGE Publications Ltd.
1 Oliver's Yard
55 City Road
London EC1Y 1SP
United Kingdom

SAGE Publications India Pvt. Ltd.
B 1/I 1 Mohan Cooperative Industrial Area
Mathura Road, New Delhi 110 044
India

SAGE Publications Asia-Pacific Pte. Ltd.
3 Church Street
#10-04 Samsung Hub
Singapore 049483

Acquisitions Editor: Abbie Rickard
Editorial Assistant: Jennifer Cline
Production Editor: Bennie Clark Allen
Copy Editor: Terri Lee Paulsen
Typesetter: C&M Digitals (P) Ltd.
Proofreader: Rae-Ann Goodwin
Indexer: Maria Sosnowski
Cover Designer: Janet Kiesel
Marketing Manager: Jenna Retana

Printed in the United States of America

Library of Congress Cataloging-in-Publication Data

Names: Veach, Laura, author. | Moro, Regina, author.

Title: The spectrum of addiction : evidence-based assessment, prevention, and treatment across the lifespan / Laura Veach, Regina Moro.

Description: Los Angeles : Sage, [2018] | Includes bibliographical references and index.

Identifiers: LCCN 2017023015 | ISBN 9781483364834 (pbk. : alk. paper)

Subjects: | MESH: Substance-Related Disorders—diagnosis | Substance-Related Disorders—therapy | Substance-Related Disorders—prevention & control | Behavior, Addictive—psychology | Counseling—methods | Evidence-Based Medicine

Classification: LCC RC564 | NLM WM 270 | DDC 616.86—dc23
LC record available at https://lccn.loc.gov/2017023015

This book is printed on acid-free paper.

Certified Chain of Custody
Promoting Sustainable Forestry
www.sfiprogram.org
SFI-01268

SFI label applies to text stock

17 18 19 20 21 10 9 8 7 6 5 4 3 2 1

Brief Contents

Detailed Contents ❖

Preface

When most of us hear the term *spectrum*, we often visualize a rainbow. These are popular symbols used for a variety of reasons, one of which is to convey hope to those who see it. Instilling hope is a key therapeutic factor in professional counseling, particularly when working with clients struggling with addiction. In the same way that rainbows emerge following the gloomiest of days, the feeling of hope for those struggling with addiction often emerges after the stormiest of times in their lives.

In this book, we will be presenting a new vision of the spectrum, modeled after a rainbow. The spectrum means to expand your understanding of addictions counseling work. We propose that there are four stages (early use, risky use, severe-risk use, and addiction) to understanding where an individual client may be when we encounter them. These clients will not come into counseling with a neon sign above their heads flashing "risky user," but it is our job to discern where along the spectrum these individuals may lie.

Looking at Figure P.1, you will see the proposed spectrum graphic utilized as a foundation for the rest of this book. You will note the stages and also the ages—0 to 60. We certainly understand that the average lifespan of Americans is much higher than 60 years old; however, we also want to recognize that an individual diagnosed with a substance use disorder is more likely to have a reduced lifespan, just as many individuals with other medical disorders. It is with this conceptual consideration that we have utilized the age of 60. When looking at Figure P.1 you will also note that alongside the

Figure P.1   Spectrum Graphic Overview

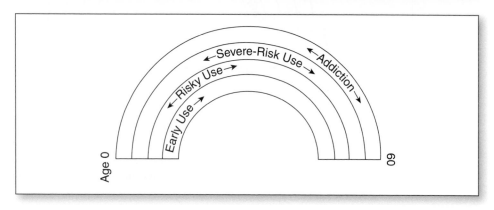

stages are arrows signaling that the stage may shift either earlier or later in an individual client's life. This graphic is not permanent; it will constantly change based upon the individual sitting before you.

This sounds like a good time for an example. You begin working with a client who initially presents to you with concerns related to her job. Her name is Shaylah, and she states that she is not feeling as passionate as she once did about her career as a high-level advertising executive. She lets you know that she felt called to do this work; she excelled in her courses in college and quickly moved up through the ranks in her agency. When you do your intake form, you discover that Shaylah is not enjoying many of the things she once did. She has not gone to a yoga class in over 2 years, a drastic change from her five times a week regimen, and she has been living alone since her partner left last year. During the biopsychosocial interview, you learn that Shaylah has been an active user of alcohol for the past 20 years. She reports that she did not find her use abnormal when she was in college or shortly thereafter, but that yes, her alcohol intake has increased substantially in recent years. She reports drinking about one bottle of wine every evening, and experiencing the shakes when she has tried to cut back on her drinking (a signal of physical dependence). We certainly would want to learn more about Shaylah's own unique experience before labeling her, but for this example, let's look at Figure P.2. You can see how we can conceptualize Shaylah's personal spectrum.

Figure P.2 Shaylah's Personalized Spectrum

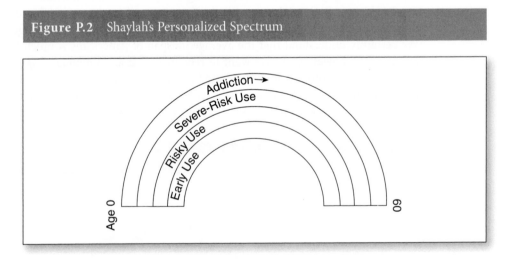

Brayden is another client you see in your practice just weeks after Shaylah. Brayden was referred to you because his granddaughter Rebecca was concerned about his use of medication. Brayden is a 58-year-old male, recently retired from the public-school system. He served over 30 years as a teacher. Brayden was in a car accident

15 years earlier, and he had struggled with back pain ever since. The doctor had him on a strict pain reliever regimen, which he was diligent about. In the past few months, Brayden's granddaughter has found that her grandfather has been running out of his medication earlier than it is able to be refilled. The first couple of times this happened she shrugged it off, but after speaking with other family members, she confronted Brayden. When you have a chance to speak with him, you find that he has used alcohol throughout his life, but "no more than my one beer at night." He states that he has never used illicit drugs, but he has been on pain medicine for quite some time. You learn that Brayden finds the pills help him relax, and he admits "yes, maybe I do take a few too soon, but they help me sleep and forget how useless I am now." Throughout your work with Brayden, you find that he is struggling with his transition to retirement, that there is a loss for him, and he is filling that void with his medications. You can see the difference in Brayden's spectrum graphic in Figure P.3 compared to Shaylah's, which we previously reviewed. For Brayden, the early-use period lasted much longer, and he may never enter the addiction stage.

Figure P.3   Brayden's Personalized Spectrum

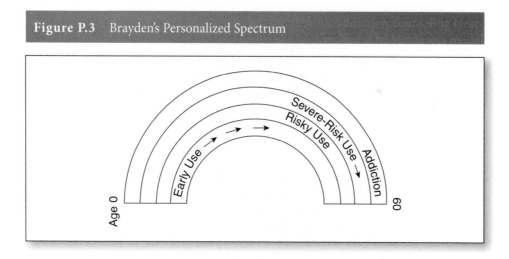

As professional counselors, we can intervene at a variety of points in this spectrum. We traditionally are active in the prevention phase, which is prior to the initiation of use. We are also active for those that seek treatment much further along the phase toward the addiction stage. As seen in Figure P.4, we are encouraged as counselors that we are able to work more along the full range of the spectrum, as depicted by the treatment stars. Not only is the spectrum constantly changing for the clients that we are working with, but so is the placement of the stars (our work with clients). Our hope is that you can use this graphic to not only consider where your client may be, but also where you are in your activities with them.

Figure P.4 Counselors Intervening Along the Spectrum

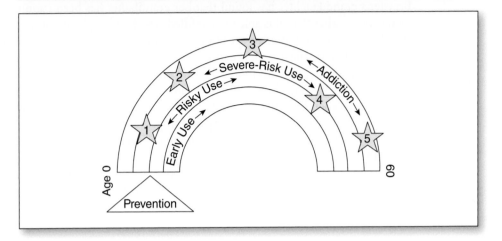

Purpose of the Book

Perhaps the most distinctive purpose of this text is the suggestion to counselors-in-training to view addiction on a spectrum ranging from experimentation to physical addiction and recovery, as described in the most recent edition of the *Diagnostic and Statistical Manual* (DSM-5; APA, 2013). There is an emphasis on the importance of assessing clients not just for addiction, but also for risky, mood-altering behaviors, continually across the lifespan. With this emphasis, our aim is to empower counselors-in-training with the knowledge and tools to intervene with clients who fall all along the spectrum of addictive behaviors. For instance, adolescents engaging in experimentation may benefit most from psychoeducational interventions, while adolescents who have moved along the spectrum to psychological and/or physical dependence may benefit most from brief counseling interventions focused upon increasing their motivation to change and seek intensive treatment. This knowledge is directly applicable to all counseling students, not just to those seeking an addictions counseling specialty.

Features of the Book

- Timely information is presented with a unique concentration on the 2009 CACREP Accreditation Standards for Addictions Counseling.
- Counselor perspectives from those that are working in the trenches are integrated throughout the text.
- The DSM-5 (APA, 2013) Substance Use Disorder diagnostic and statistical information is incorporated in the text.

- Evidence-based and culturally informed counseling—including prevention, intervention, and intensive treatment—is emphasized throughout the text to provide the addictions counselor with effective and applicable sociocultural knowledge and skills.

Structure of the Book

The structure of this text is intended to follow the spectrum, as best we could conceive. The first three chapters help lay the ground work for later chapters, providing foundational knowledge of the field of addictions counseling, the research and evidence-based practice world, and knowledge of substance and neurobiological systems of importance. The spectrum is elucidated through the next four chapters: Chapter 4 covers experimentation; Chapter 5 examines elements and patterns of risky use; Chapter 6 discusses brief screening and assessment; and Chapter 7 details diagnosis of process and substance use disorders. Chapter 8 introduces brief counseling interventions, an idea that can be utilized at multiple points along the spectrum, as can the family interventions detailed in Chapter 9. Chapter 10 examines multiple societal systems that are affected by the full-addiction spectrum, and Chapter 11 discusses the far right range of the spectrum by discussing intensive addictions counseling. Chapter 12 examines the growing issue of cross-addictions and comorbidities that complicate care and recovery pertaining to process and substance use disorders. Chapter 13 discusses the issues of continuing care and relapse prevention. Chapter 14 concludes this text with a discussion of future directions for the field, particularly research.

We wish this organization was a clear overlay of the spectrum, however, the concepts being discussed are not as easily organized. We also recognize that we do not work in a linear field. It is important for us as counselors to be flexible; how we proceed should be based upon the person or persons sitting across from us.

The chapters (excluding Chapter 1) have a three-part structure to them: Knowledge, Evidence-Based Practices, and Skills in Action. The knowledge section provides background information related to the topic being covered. The evidence-based practice section details evidence-based practices, and includes information about locating these programs. The skills-in-action section is intended to assist the reader with building their skills in relation to the chapter topic. These may be skills related to counseling, or related to finding evidence-based practices, but all are related to the readers' development as professional counselors in our continual quest to improve care for those impacted by process and substance use disorders

Reference

American Psychiatric Association. (2013). *Diagnostic and statistical manual of mental disorders* (5th ed.). Washington, DC: Author.

Acknowledgments

We are indebted to the leadership at SAGE: Kassie Graves who began this project with us, Abbie Rickard for her hope and optimism during the grueling stages, Nathan Davidson for seeing us to the finish line, and all of the other members of the valuable team. It truly took a village.

I, Regina, need to first thank my coauthor, Laura, for this opportunity. There are a million and one different experiences that I have gained as a result of our relationship—each and every one of them making me a better counselor and supervisor. I cannot imagine where I would be without your support and guidance. To Jennifer, this work would really not have been possible without you. We've grown in so many different ways since we first met one another, and I am honored to call you a friend.

I also would be remiss if I did not thank the faculty members in the departments of counseling at Syracuse University and the University of North Carolina at Charlotte. Not only did I gain a great education in counseling and supervision from these institutions, they helped me gain a clearer sense of who I am and what I was meant to do in this world. For that I will be forever grateful.

To my colleagues at Barry University and Boise State University, thank you for the support and kindness you have always shown me. And to the students who have been in classrooms with me, I feel honored to have been a part of your educational experience. Every time I see a lightbulb go on, I know I'm doing what I was meant to do. All of you have a passion and excitement I hope you are always able to retain.

And to my family, thank you. Many of you did not know that this book was being written, just another task of my life as an academic. But your continuous support and love helped me to keep going. Lastly, my best friend and partner, Ryan, your unwavering support and cheerleading helped me in ways that cannot be measured. You are my rock.

I, Laura, echo gratitude to my coauthor Regina for her creative designs anchored by the intensely researched content, both of which give strength to our teaching throughout this text. Her dedication to preparing counseling professionals, assisting those celebrating recovery, and those seeking help to prevent or recover from harmful use or processes, is steadfast and inspiring.

Next, the visionary trauma surgeons, specialists, and administrative professionals at Wake Forest School of Medicine, led by Dr. Wayne Meredith, are amazing in their clarity and commitment to care for the whole person. They all deserve the utmost appreciation for bringing addiction counselors into this stellar Level I trauma team. The commendable writing support and integration (especially guided by the business acumen of Veronica Getz and Cindy Warlick) of addiction services within an academic medical center are at the forefront of U.S. healthcare in intensive hospital trauma/burn/pediatric trauma centers and medicine hospital units.

Key mentors in my research and writing, notably, Dr. Barry Williams, Rev John Shields, Drs Ted Remley, Don Super, Barbara Herlihy, Coach Harris and Jim Sorg, all shaped my path of delving into pragmatic research and sparked quests to discover even better ways to help our world so impacted by risky use and addiction. I would also like to show my appreciation for the guidance that Dr. Geri Miller and Deb Weiner provided. Gratitude also for Dr. Viktor Frankl's profound work, which continually shows me the way to meaningful leaps of faith, such as writing a textbook while providing addiction counseling in a very busy trauma center! Heartfelt appreciation is also extended to the many clients and fellow recovering individuals who taught me so much about the power of addiction and the miracles of recovery—that is where this book began. In addition, much honor is given to the master's and doctoral counseling students who embraced learning new skills using novel counseling approaches with hospital patients in critical, life-changing days.

Lastly, for my wonderful circle of professional counseling colleagues, unicorns, fast friends, and steadfast family (George and Alana Harrelson, Nancy V. Solomon, and Dan Veach), who mean so much to that little girl who grew up "emotionally gifted"—you genuinely accepted and nurtured me unconditionally in the writing of this text as you do throughout the spectrum of life.

SAGE would like to think the following reviewers:

Maria A. Avila, *University of Miami*

Derrick E. Crim, *Metropolitan State University*

Kevin Curtin, *Alfred University*

Kathryn Dziekan, *New Mexico Highlands University*

Dian Jordan, *University of Texas of the Permian Basin*

Densie D. Lucas, *Fayetteville State University*

Arlene Saum, *Daytona State College*

Robert Scholz, *Pepperdine University*

Nancy Sherman, *Bradley University*

Michelle Kelley Shuler, *Texas A&M University–Central Texas*

Historical Foundations of Addiction Counseling

LEARNING OBJECTIVES

Upon completion of reading this chapter and participating in the guided exercises, the learner will be able to

- understand and distinguish between the numerous professional organizations representing the addictions counseling field;
- identify significant historical events related to the field of addictions counseling; and
- discuss and explain the professionalization of the addictions counseling field.

Examining the history of addiction within the United States is a multifaceted endeavor. A variety of different issues of focus come into awareness that one may never had considered before, such as looking at substance use trends, examining the person who has provided services to those struggling with addiction, and attending to legal issues of relevance. This history is extensive and long. To fully examine the history of addictions counseling, we will be covering five general historical foci: (1) the use of substances/addictions over time, (2) the treatment of addiction over time, (3) the legislative history of substance/behavior regulation, (4) the professionalization of addictions counselors, and (5) an introduction to the research foundations of the profession. The research foundations will be further elaborated upon in Chapter 2.

In addition, the chapter will conclude with a comprehensive timeline highlighting

- dates in history and trends related to substance use and addiction;
- the evolution of the treatment of addiction;
- legal regulations of substances/behaviors;
- the professional regulation of the addictions counseling profession; and
- the establishment of a research base in addictions treatment.

Historical Use of Chemical Substances

Historically, the use of substances has evolved over time. Alcohol, being the "oldest child" per se has dominated the landscape over time; however, there have been times in history that the use of other drugs has claimed prime popularity status. The following section will examine the trends of substance use, primarily focusing within the United States.

The use of mood-altering substances is not a new phenomenon, with findings going as far back as the Old Stone Age, as anthropological discoveries include stone pots that contained mild beer or wine (Kinney & Leaton, 1983). Other archaeological evidence of alcohol use dates back to 7000 BC in Japan and 3500 BC in Iran (Inaba & Cohen, 2007). It was during the 10th century that Rhazes, an Arabian physician, first discovered the distillation process, primarily to be used as medicine (Kinney & Leaton, 1983). During the early years of alcohol use it was mainly for these medicinal properties that Rhazes found, as well as nutritional purposes (Doweiko, 2012), as the alcohol was deemed safer than water.

In the 1500s, distilled spirits (e.g., vodka, whiskey) became popular as a beverage of choice (Kinney & Leaton, 1983). According to Inaba and Cohen (2007), the mood-altering benefits of the substance helped bolster its popularity. In 1640, the Dutch opened the first distillery in the United States, on Staten Island (Kinney & Leaton, 1983). The use of alcohol was so widespread that by 1790 all rations for soldiers of the United States included liquor (i.e., brandy, rum, or whiskey) at the rate of a ¼ pint (Kinney & Leaton, 1983). As America was forming as a country, the history of substance use, primarily alcohol, was firmly rooted in the soil.

In 1806, morphine was discovered and used heavily in the decades following (Field, 2002). During the American Civil War (1861–1865) addiction to morphine was referred to as the Army disease (Field, 2002); considering the devastation, and physical and emotional pain associated with war, it is not surprising that such rates were found during this time. It was also during this time, the 19th century, that alcohol and other drugs were used as medicines (Briggs & Pepperell, 2009). These drugs went by the names of Godfrey's Cordial (to treat colic), Laudanum (for women's menstruation), and Coca-Cola, and included cannabis (for headaches and women's menstruation).

The 20th century saw a rise and fall of numerous drugs of popularity. Many of you reading this can probably name a few, as drug trends are often deeply rooted within decades. If someone was to ask you about the 1960s and corresponding "Hippie Years" you may immediately think of marijuana and psychedelic use. If questioned about the 1990s and "Punk Rock/Grunge" days, you may think Kurt Cobain and of heroin. When someone imagines an addiction treatment center, they may even envision clients engaged in tobacco smoking via cigarettes, also an addictive substance. These connections are not random, as our history is constructed by stories, which are transmitted through a variety of media. Drug trends are no different from other movements (e.g., women's rights, civil rights) and have become woven into the historical fabric of our country.

Synthetic Drugs

In recent times a particularly dangerous trend has been the rise in drugs of abuse that are classified as synthetic. *Synthetic* implies the creation of the drug via a chemical process (i.e., in a laboratory) as opposed to other substances (e.g., cannabis, cocaine, opiates) that are derived from plants. This process is not new; in 1887 amphetamines were first synthesized, and in the following decades they were used to keep pilots awake during long hours of war (Inaba & Cohen, 2007). What is new is the creation of substances in man-made laboratories. Commonly referred to as "meth labs," these sites have become commonplace, with over 9,240 being found in 2014 (U.S. Department of Justice, Drug Enforcement Administration [DEA], 2015). In addition to methamphetamine, individuals are also creating substances such as "bath salts." These substances are not the bath salts used to aid relaxation during a bath, but are substances synthetically created, and sold legally (i.e., until regulations were passed) under the name "bath salts" (i.e., not for human consumption) to avoid FDA regulation. Word on the street spread fast that Ivory Wave, Bloom, and Vanilla Sky (National Institute on Drug Abuse, 2012) were not the traditional relaxation bath salts but instead were mood-altering substances you could purchase at your local corner shop or gas station. The latest drug of abuse synthetically made is known as "Flakka" and is becoming increasingly identified as a danger to the public, particularly due to the low cost of the substance.

This historical review of substance use is limited, and we suggest anyone who has a desire to work in the field of addictions counseling acquire a comprehensive knowledge of substances and associated histories. There are great resources available, such as Inaba and Cohen's (2007) *Uppers, Downers, All Arounders,* and also William White's (1998) *Slaying the Dragon.* The purpose of our review here was to lay the foundation of substance use/abuse in our history. Humans have been using mood-altering substances for an unknown period of time. What is known, as highlighted in the historical review, is that humans have and will continually use substances, and create new ones to advance the mood-altering effects. It is for this reason that treatment has continually evolved over time. We will review this history in the following section.

History of the Treatment and Recovery Movement

The following section will discuss the history of recovery in the United States. One caveat is needed when discussing the concepts of recovery, as there are multiple avenues for an individual. The following section will include information about mutual aid societies, as well as formalized treatment modalities. Mutual aid societies are not a primary treatment mechanism, but they are an adjunct for support and are typically thought of as groups. Treatment is designated as formalized and professional endeavors at helping individuals enter into a recovery program. Each individual's pathway to recovery is as unique as the individual.

The official beginning date for the treatment of addiction issues is unknown, however one may speculate that the initial attempts involved familial efforts to restrict an individual's substance use. There is formal documentation of Native American recovery circles in the 1700s (White, 2000a). These recovery circles were initiated by tribal leaders who themselves had overcome an addiction, and began these abstinence-based programs firmly rooted in native tribal traditions (Coyhis & White, 2002). While the recovery circle represented the beginnings of mutual aid support groups, they were also the beginnings of formalized treatment. Formalized treatment options during the late 1700s to early 1800s included religiously oriented inebriate homes, medically oriented inebriate asylums, for-profit private addiction cure institutes, and bottled home cures for the use of alcohol, drugs, and tobacco (White, 2000a). These options represent a wide variety of attempts at curbing the issue of addiction and were due, in part, to a lack of understanding of addiction.

In 1784, Dr. Benjamin Rush outlined the effects of alcohol on the body and mind in his landmark manuscript (Thombs, 2006). This writing also included a list of "remedies for the evils which are brought on by the excessive use of distilled spirits" (Rush, 1823, p. 28). Dr. Rush's work has been acknowledged as the first recognition of alcoholism as a disease (Inaba & Cohen, 2007; Thombs, 2006). In 1823, Dr. Rush published *An Inquiry Into the Effects of Ardent Spirits Upon the Human Body and Mind* (Kinney & Leaton, 1983). This book included information about the current attitudes toward alcohol at the time, as well as information related to scholarly treatment of the time. For example, Dr. Rush referred to the importance of religion on fostering sobriety along with the powerful feelings of guilt and shame. He further identifies that for some it is the recognition of medical problems that are a result of alcohol use, and even making a commitment as productive treatment mechanisms that helps one achieve sobriety, and he further comments on the power of a vegetable-based diet. Many of Dr. Rush's recommendations related to treatment were based upon anecdotal evidence from one or two patients. The recommendations by Dr. Rush represent a common theme of the time: go see a physician and *try whatever works.*

In addition to formal treatment modalities and support systems, societal concern over addiction was increasing, which led to the founding of organizations focused on abstinence messages. First, in 1840, the Washingtonian Total Abstinence Society was formed (White, 1998). As the name of the organization implies, the organization focused on the exclusive use of abstinence to eliminate the societal problems attributed to alcohol. Throughout the rest of the decade (1842–1850) fraternal order of temperance societies emerged across the country (White, 1998). These all had different names (e.g., The Sons of Temperance, Good Templars, and Good Samaritans), however they all had a similar mission, which also corresponded to the Washingtonians': to eliminate the destruction from alcohol through an abstinence movement.

The 1870s saw the beginnings of mail-order treatment. One business owner, Sam Collins, sold a bottled "cure" via the postal service to users looking to cure their addiction (Morgan, 1981). These bottle home cures were often used to cure alcohol, tobacco, and other drug use, yet were found to have high levels of substances (e.g., cocaine, marijuana, alcohol) early in the 20th century (White, 2004). The very thing individuals were hoping to be free from was exactly what they were ingesting.

If there is any single decade that is crucially important in the history of the recovery movement, it is the 1930s, specifically the year 1935. The Porter Narcotic Farm Act (Field, 2002) was a piece of legislation that provided the first federal funding for addiction treatment. As a result, two treatment centers opened, one in Lexington, Kentucky, and the other in Fort Worth, Texas. The 1930s was also when Dr. Richard Peabody reportedly applied the first psychological methods to the treatment of individuals struggling with addiction to alcohol (Kinney & Leaton, 1983). For current recovery issues, 1935 represented a significantly important year, as the popular organization Alcoholics Anonymous (AA) was formed by Bill Wilson ("Bill W") and Dr. Robert Smith ("Dr. Bob") (White, 1998). AA has become synonymous with the recovery movement through the years, relying not on professional treatment but on the power of individuals struggling with their addiction to alcohol coming together in fellowship to support one another. Today, AA has over 2 million members worldwide (Alcoholics Anonymous, 2014), and has contributed to the founding of other like-minded organizations. The well-known Narcotics Anonymous (NA), a group for those struggling with other drug addictions, was founded in California in 1953 (White, 1998). Although there was an emergence of multiple organizations for the narcotic addict, the California-based organization formed the roots of the organization as it is known today.

The Minnesota model of treatment for alcoholics followed closely behind the creation of AA (Spicer, 1993). Addiction treatment following the Minnesota model embraces the disease concept and provides individuals with tools to assist as they embark on a journey of recovery. In addition to attending lectures about the 12 steps of AA (the guiding principles), participants in Minnesota model–type treatment receive medical care and clinical counseling—creating a multidisciplinary and multimodal treatment approach. This model was reminiscent of the treatment provided at the Emmanuel Clinic, founded in 1906 (White, 1998). This treatment effort combined multiple disciplines (i.e., medicine, religion, and psychology) to offer well-rounded treatment, very similar to the success of the Minnesota model. However, the Emmanuel Clinic was not able to sustain following the death of one of their founders.

Box 1.1: The Florida Model

The Florida model grew on the success of the Minnesota model in terms of integrating multiple services. According to Caron (2014), the model integrates treatment in both clinical and residential settings. The programs typically offer residential facilities that have a home-life feel, much different from traditional dormitories of inpatient facilities (Palm Beach Institute, 2013). In addition, treatment is often more comprehensive, offering differing levels of care with transitional housing nearby. Although these services are often recommended upon discharge from a treatment center, the Florida model differs by integrating that into the entire treatment program. From medical detoxification to halfway houses, the Florida model represents a comprehensive program of care.

In stark contrast to the legacy that Alcoholics Anonymous and the Minnesota model have forged, the organization Synanon was founded in 1958 (White, 2000b). Synanon was formed by Charles Dederich and early on was composed of a group of individuals struggling with alcohol addiction who attended AA meetings, while the group also met three times per week at Dederich's home (White, 1998). These early meetings set the groundwork for the legacy of confrontational treatment that Synanon has been known for. Dederich, with no formal training, was leading groups and experimenting with different techniques such as ridicule and shaming (White, 1998). Synanon has gone through transitions as an organization, with the second shift moving away from solely focusing on meetings to the rise of the therapeutic community model (Oshe, 1980), which is recognized as the first such model for treatment. Within this model, communities were organized with clients living on site, and oftentimes becoming workers (Oshe, 1980). This shift is also where the confrontational style became more prominent and relied on the staff (who were themselves in recovery) to enforce the rules of the communities (White, 2000b). Although the organization claimed significant rates of rehabilitation, there was little documented evidence of these claims (Oshe, 1980). The founding and resulting evolution of Synanon has contributed to the field of addiction treatment, particularly in regard to the therapeutic community model, while at the same time has produced many cautionary tales for the field (White, 1998). For a more thorough review of the Synanon organization, including the final transformation into an organized religion, please refer to the work of Richard Oshe (1980).

The later part of the 20th century involved two parallel movements: one of integration, one of diversification/separation. It was during the 1980s that Dr. Ottenberg, of the Eagleville Hospital and Rehabilitation Center in Pennsylvania, called to integrate alcoholism and drug treatment (White, 2000b). During this time, there was also a recognized importance of attending to systemic issues of clients (i.e., family, support systems) and family members began being integrated into treatment (White, 2000b). Another significant change included the diversification of the background of treatment providers. Previously the professional membership included those who were solely in recovery themselves, however during the 1980s there was a surge in family members of addicts seeking training, as well as academically trained professionals (Hagedorn, Culbreth, & Cashwell, 2012; White, 2000b).

There was an emergence of mutual aid groups offering alternatives to AA. Dr. Jean Kirkpatrick founded Women for Sobriety in 1975, Secular Organization for Sobriety was formed in 1985, and Rational Recovery was founded in 1986 (White, 2000b). These organizations separated themselves from AA for a variety of reasons and are but a small representation of such alternatives.

In addition to attending to the treatment process, the later part of the century also saw attention shift to relapse prevention. Relapse prevention is precisely as it sounds: helping clients learn to prevent the use of substance or act of behavior after a period of abstinence. One of the most well-known authors and researchers on the topic of relapse prevention is Gordon Marlatt, who developed a specific model for clinicians and centers to use (see Marlatt & George, 1984). Other relapse prevention models include the CENAPS model by Gorski (1989) and the Recovery Training and Self Help model specifically for opiate addiction (McAuliffe & Ch'ien, 1986).

Managed Care, Placement, and Diagnosis

Managed care entities began during the 20th century, with the primary goal to offer alternative forms of health care to those who may not be able to afford medical costs (Miller, 2015). The growth of inpatient residential programs was stymied during this time (Spicer, 1993). In addition to the goal of providing care, the managed care organizations (i.e., health maintenance organizations, preferred provider organizations) were also seeking to reduce health care costs, and therefore became much less likely to pay for inpatient treatment if there was an alternative outpatient care program available.

The American Society of Addiction Medicine (ASAM, 2015) published its first Patient Placement Criteria manual in 1991. These criteria are used by managed care entities to determine the level of care a patient requires (e.g., outpatient, inpatient, intensive outpatient). Since the first publication, the ASAM criteria have been revised, most recently in 2013. The ASAM also furthered the mission of the organization in 2007 when it created the American Board of Addiction Medicine. The ABAM offers specific addiction-related training to physicians seeking to be board certified in addiction medicine (ABAM, 2015).

In May 2013, *The Diagnostic and Statistical Manual, 5th edition*, was released by the American Psychiatric Association (APA, 2014). The release of this edition was not without controversy. The fifth edition of the manual had significant changes for the sections pertaining to substance use and addictions counseling. The diagnostic categories of "Abuse" and "Dependence" were removed, and instead the language of a severity spectrum was implemented to diagnose "Substance Use Disorders." Some critics suggested that the new diagnostic possibilities would increase the amount of substance use disorder diagnoses via false positives. An alternative viewpoint is that more individuals in need of treatment would be able to seek such without being labeled as an abuser or dependent. A recognized strength of this edition was the integration of ICD-9 and ICD-10 coding systems into the manual. These codes are used worldwide for health conditions, where the DSM is solely focused for use in the United States. This shift helps create a uniform language for professionals to utilize; more about this will be explored in Chapter 7 when we discuss diagnosis in detail.

Treatment Today

In reviewing the history of the recovery initiatives, it is obvious that the focus of attention has been directed to one of two issues. The first is direct attention to the prevention of addiction by emphasizing abstinence. This was commented on above with the creation of abstinence societies (e.g., Washingtonian Temperance Society). The second focus of attention has been on the individual who is struggling with the more debilitating disease of addiction. When considering these two foci, it is obvious there is a large gap between when an individual is abstinent, to when they are struggling with the disease. This gap is the target of this text, as we will be examining many more points to intervene with clients than has previously been examined.

In addition to the greater emphasis on the gap between prevention and intensive treatment that has been occurring in recent years, there has also been a surge of initiatives to integrate recovery into educational settings, both at the secondary and collegiate level. The Association of Recovery Schools (2016) has identified 38 recovery high schools in existence in the United States, with five more in planning stages. In addition to high school initiatives, there are many college campuses embracing the recovery movement. At the time of this writing, the Association of Recovery in Higher Education (2016) estimates there are 72 college campuses across the United States with collegiate recovery programs, each unique to the campus culture and population. This number is ever changing as more programs are identified by the association, and as more programs are created. These recovery education programs symbolize a shift away from the tradition of isolation among individuals in treatment and recovery to integrating the many parts of our clients' lives.

Many of the workers working on the front lines of addiction treatment, whether in inpatient settings or manning prevention efforts, will report on the increased importance of evidence-based practices for the work that is being conducted. Evidence-based practices are treatments that are rooted in scientific evidence. The rationale for using these practices is logical; the more evidence a treatment has the more likelihood it would work for an individual. This has become increasingly important for a variety of reasons, including the recognized impact of dual-diagnosed clients (e.g., mental disorder and substance use disorder) and the complexities associated with treatment. We will explore these treatments in depth in Chapter 2 and throughout the text.

The above history of recovery in the United States is certainly not fully comprehensive. The purpose was to familiarize readers with the process individuals seeking recovery may take, via the many different mediums (e.g., mutual aid support groups, professional treatment). For a full history of addiction treatment we would like to refer readers to *Slaying the Dragon* and *The History of Addiction Counseling in the United States*, both authored by William L. White, and *Learning the Language of Addiction Counseling* (4th edition), authored by Geri Miller.

History of Addiction-Related Research

There are multiple accounts for who is recognized as the founding researcher concerning the concepts of addiction. As mentioned previously, Dr. Benjamin Rush has received credit for being the first to give recognition to alcoholism being a disease. However, Dr. Thomas Trotter has also received credit as being the first to fully describe the concept of alcoholism, in 1804, and is considered by Kinney and Leaton (1983) to have offered the first published scientific formulation of drunkenness. As we do not have an available time machine to fully examine the historical timeline, we will regard both Dr. Rush and Dr. Trotter as the pioneers of the scientific evaluation of the concept of addiction.

The Congressional Research Service (CRS) was formed in 1914. Among many other issues and topics, the CRS conducts research on drug trends, treatment needs, and uses the findings to inform U.S. Congress members with information relevant to legislation. This is crucially important research in terms of addiction when considering legalization of drugs of abuse and professional regulation.

The Yale Center of Alcohol Studies, the first academic center to do research on alcoholism, was founded in the 1930s at Yale University (Spicer, 1993). This center became a hub of research activity related to alcoholism. In 1940, the first academic journal was published, the *Quarterly Journal of Studies on Alcohol*, now known as the *Journal of Studies on Alcohol and Drugs* (Kinney & Leaton, 1983). Dr. E. Morton Jellinek was a researcher at the Yale Center and published the book *The Disease Concept of Alcoholism* in 1952. Within this publication was the Jellinek curve, a proposed model to understand alcohol addiction, represented by a downward curve. The model was expanded in the 1960s by including an upward part of the curve, symbolizing the recovery process (Hazelden Betty Ford, 2016). Although the model has remained popular for explanatory purposes, questions concerning the research methodology and supporting evidence have emerged over the years (Ward, Bejarano, Babor, & Allred, 2016). The Summer School of Alcohol Studies was founded in 1943, which provided a professional platform for dissemination of addiction-related research (Center of Alcohol Studies, 2014). The activities of the Yale Center are still alive and active today, however they have been relocated to Rutgers University, located in New Brunswick, New Jersey.

The disease concept of addiction was formally recognized by the American Medical Association via a publication in the *Journal of the American Medical Association* in 1956 (Merta, 2001). Not only did this scholarly publication have implications for future research, but it also had implications for treatment. This theory of addiction differed to the popular moral model theory of addiction, which viewed addictive behavior as a choice, and the user, a sinner. This new theory removed the judgment from the person and allowed the use to be conceptualized as a symptom of the greater disease. From this viewpoint, individuals that live with addiction are told they are *not responsible for the disease, but they are responsible to the disease.*

The National Institute on Drug Abuse (NIDA), a branch of the U.S. National Institutes of Health (NIH), initiated the Monitoring the Future survey in 1975 (NIDA, 2015). This annual survey examines national use and longitudinal trends concerning substance use among youth and activity in other risky behaviors. The following year, an infamous report titled "Alcoholism and Treatment" but better known as the "Rand Report was published (Armor, Polich, & Stambul, 1976). This report was conducted by the Rand Corporation and upon its release was highly controversial. All nationally funded treatment programs were required to collect intake and follow-up (6 months) data from patients. Among other findings, the study reported that some of the participants reported controlled drinking (in contrast to abstinence only) at follow-up. The study also found no difference in treatment in the form of halfway houses, hospitals, or group counseling.

In 1992, the U.S. Congress passed legislation creating the Substance Abuse and Mental Health Services Administration (SAMHSA, n.d.). The mission of this organization is to "reduce the impact of substance abuse and mental illness on America's communities" (SAMHSA, n.d., p. 1). In addition, the organization aims to make information, services, and research related to substance use more available to the public.

Toward the end of the century, the main findings of Project MATCH were released (National Institute on Alcohol Abuse and Alcoholism [NIAAA], 1996). Project MATCH is a landmark study examining a variety of variables related to treatment of alcohol-specific addiction. The project's main aim was to identify if matching patients to treatment based upon patient characteristics would increase treatment outcomes. At the 1-year follow-up, the hypothesis of patient placement was not supported. This was important as it identified cognitive behavioral therapy, motivational enhancement therapy, and Twelve-Step Facilitation to all be just as effective in reducing alcohol consumption. Lastly, in 1997, SAMHSA launched the National Registry of Evidence-based Programs and Practices (NREPP, 2012), a clearinghouse of treatments. Chapter 2 will include more attention to this national registry, and the history of research within addiction counseling will be rounded out via the examination of evidence-based treatments throughout the remaining chapters.

Historical Legislation Efforts Impacting the Field

Although discussing politics is not always the best way to make friends, we are hopeful we will not alienate you all through this discussion. Legislation related to drug use/addiction has had a profound impact on our profession. We will examine some of the most critical legislative activities in our history as related to addictions counseling.

Regulation primarily began in the beginning of the 20th century. The Pure Food and Drug Act was passed in 1906 (Morgan, 1981), which created the Food and Drug Administration. The significance of this act is that it limited the mail-order bottle cure industry. (Remember our previous discussion of Mr. Collins?) The Harrison Act was passed in 1914, which regulated narcotics distribution and prescriptions (Briggs & Pepperell, 2009).

The 18th Amendment may be the most well-known piece of legislation to be passed by Congress during the 20th century. This amendment is commonly referred to as *Prohibition*, which made the production and distribution of alcohol illegal (Kinney & Leaton, 1983). Prohibition lasted 13 years, from 1920–1933, when it was repealed through the passing of the 21st Amendment. In 1929, Congress passed the first piece of legislation to formalize treatment for Americans, specifically, those in prison. The Porter Narcotic Farm Act authorized the Public Health Service to open federal hospitals specifically focusing on addiction treatment (Field, 2002). The two facilities, one in Fort Worth, Texas, and one in Lexington, Kentucky, were opened in 1935. Although alcohol prohibition was over, in 1937 the Marijuana Tax Act was passed (WGBH Educational Foundation, 2014). This law restricted possession of marijuana solely to individuals who paid a tax for authorized uses (medical and industrial), which in effect criminalized marijuana in the United States.

The 1960s were not only filled with flower children and love-ins, but the decade also represents a period of time in which there were significant legislative efforts to expand treatment for addiction issues. President Lyndon Johnson made a statement in which he discussed the disease concept of alcoholism in 1965, which marked the first presidential speech attending to addiction issues (White, 1998). In 1966, Congress passed the Narcotic Addict Rehabilitation Act that created a federal compulsory treatment program (Field, 2002). The 1968 Amendments to the 1963 Community Mental Health Centers Act established treatment grants for local areas specifically focusing on addiction (Field, 2002). It was clear that the U.S. government was not taking the issue of drug use and addiction lightly. This was even more evident in 1968 with the creation of the Bureau of Narcotics and Dangerous Drugs (formed via a merger of the Federal Bureau of Narcotics and the Bureau of the Dangerous Drugs of the Food and Drug Administration).

The Controlled Substance Act was passed in 1970, which created a drug classification system (Moore, 2013). The schedule is still in use, and consists of five categories, each rated in intensity of abuse potential (taking into account medical use considerations) (Inaba & Cohen, 2007). Schedule V is the least severe, consisting of drugs that are very low in abuse potential, mainly because they contain low levels of narcotics, some of which are sold over the counter. Schedule IV drugs also have a low abuse potential, however just slightly more so than Schedule V drugs. Schedule III drugs have a moderate abuse potential, and are sometimes drugs that are compounds containing Schedule II drugs. Schedule II drugs have a high potential for abuse, however they also have acceptable medical uses (e.g., pain killers, ADHD stimulant medication). Schedule I drugs are those deemed highly addictive and have no accepted medical use. Of relevance toward legislation is that as of the writing of this textbook, marijuana is classified as a Schedule I substance.

Legislation in the early 1970s created the National Institute for Alcohol Abuse and Alcoholism (via the Comprehensive Alcohol Abuse and Alcoholism Prevention and Treatment Act), and the National Institute on Drug Abuse (via the Drug Abuse Treatment Act of 1972). The NIAAA and NIDA are two leading organizations focusing on researching addiction and educating the public. The Drug Enforcement Agency (DEA) was also created in the early 1970s due to a merger of the Bureau of Narcotics and Dangerous Drugs and the Office of Drug Abuse Law Enforcement (WGBH Educational Foundation, 2014).

President Ronald Reagan may be known for his history as a famous actor, but he also played a significant role in the history of our field. In 1984, he signed the National Minimum Drinking Age Act into law, raising the legal age of alcohol consumption to 21 years of age (Hanson, 2015). He also signed the Anti-Drug Abuse Act into law in 1986. This law created mandatory sentences for drug-related crimes (WGBH Educational Foundation, 2014). The hard-hitting ways of President Reagan were upheld by his successor, President George H. W. Bush, who declared a new *War on Drugs* in a nationally televised speech (WGBH Educational Foundation, 2014).

Although the voice from the presidential office was clear, along with the legislative efforts of Congress, the people's voice rang loud in 1996 when California became the first state to legalize medical marijuana by passing Proposition 215 (WGBH Educational Foundation, 2014). Following the passage in California, 22 additional states, the District of Columbia, and Guam passed similar legislation. Although these states and districts approved of the legal usage of medical marijuana, the federal prohibition is still in effect.

If you have had a cold and gone to a pharmacy in the last decade, you may have been surprised to be asked for your driver's license to purchase a particular type of cold medicine. As discussed in the above historical use section, one recent trend has been the use of synthetic drugs, of which one is methamphetamine ("meth"). Meth has drastically risen in popularity, primarily due to the ability to manufacture the substance at home. In 2005, the Combat Methamphetamine Act was signed to regulate the sale of retail over-the-counter medication used in the manufacture of methamphetamine (U.S. Department of Justice, Drug Enforcement Administration, 2007). Over-the-counter medicines that contain pseudoephedrine are required to be kept behind the pharmacy counter, require purchasers to show ID, and are entered into a database to limit the quantities an individual is able to purchase.

Three pieces of legislation have had significant impacts on the treatment of addiction within the past decade. In 2008, Congress passed the Mental Health Parity and Addiction Equity Act (U.S. Department of Labor, 2010). In sum, this act puts mental health and substance abuse treatment on par with medical/surgical treatment. In 2010, President Barack Obama signed the Affordable Care Act into law. This law requires all U.S. citizens to have medical insurance, and created a national medical insurance program to offer low-cost insurance. Although controversial, this law has expanded medical insurance coverage, and as a result has increased treatment availability. The latest piece of legislation having a significant impact on the field of addictions counseling is the 21st Century Cures Act. According to NAADAC (National Association for Alcoholism and Drug Abuse Counselors, 2016), this act provides over $1 billion to help states with opiate prevention and treatment services. Also, the act provides funding to establish federal drug courts and encouragement for integration of substance use disorders within primary care (NAADAC, 2016).

The most recent legislative efforts are in relation to substance use, specifically marijuana. Although it was in 1996 that California passed the medical-marijuana law, it was in 2012 that two states, Washington and Colorado, successfully became the first two states to legalize recreational use of marijuana (Moore, 2013). Although the federal ban is still in existence, and marijuana is still considered a Schedule I drug under the 1970 Controlled Substance Act, the U.S. Department of Justice issued a statement in 2013 that no federal efforts would block the legalization process in states that seek to legalize marijuana (Moore, 2013). Although not a piece of legislation, this was a significant statement made by a powerful organization.

The Evolving Addiction Treatment Professional

The professional identity of addictions counselors is multifaceted and has been referred to as a "patchwork system" (Mitchell, 1981, cited in White, 2000b). There is not one pathway to become an addictions counselor, which leads to confusion among students as they attempt to navigate the complexities related to education requirements, practice standards, assessment requirements, state regulations, and even personal sobriety requirements. The following will outline the historical evolution of the helping professions, particularly attending to the emergence of addiction counseling as a particular field of practice.

The initial years of addiction treatment predominantly relied on services provided by individuals who were in recovery themselves. The mid-20th century saw a rise in government-funded training initiatives through the Office of Economic Opportunity, Department of Labor, the National Institute of Mental Health, NIAAA, and NIDA (Hagedorn et al., 2012). Not only was the substance abuse field establishing a professional identity through these training programs, but the counseling profession was also solidifying during this time (West, Mustaine, & Wyrick, 1999). The Association for Counselor Education and Supervision presented the first set of counselor preparation standards in 1973 (Hagedorn et al., 2012), and in 1981 the Council for the Accreditation for Counseling and Related Educational Programs (CACREP) was founded (Hagedorn et al., 2012). The National Commission for Credentialing Alcoholism Counselors, the first national body seeking to implement uniform credentialing standards for addiction treatment providers, was founded in 1977 (West et al., 1999).

In 1989, the National Certification Reciprocity Consortium/Alcohol and Other Drug Abuse (NCRC/AODA) was formally named (West et al., 1999) although it was really a combination of early efforts of a wide variety of organizations that began around 1977. Throughout the years, the organization has evolved and is now formally known as the International Credentialing & Reciprocity Consortium (IC&RC). IC&RC is the largest credentialing organization and represents the "gold standard for competency in the field" of addictions counseling (IC&RC, n.d.a, para. 3). One major initiative the IC&RC undertook in the late 20th century was clarification of the role of an addictions counselor. After examining more than 2,000 duties a counselor may perform, the IC&RC identified 12 core functions (e.g., intake, assessment, counseling, crisis intervention) an addictions counselor can be expected to perform (IC&RC, n.d.a.). The functions allow for consistency between international credentialing and competency expectations.

The IC&RC has eight standardized credentials that allow reciprocity opportunities once earned (IC&RC, n.d.b, para. 2). The eight credentials are (1) Alcohol & Drug Counselor (ADC); (2) Advanced Alcohol & Drug Counselor (AADC); (3) Clinical Supervisor (CS); (4) Prevention Specialist (PS); (5) Certified Criminal Justice Addictions Professional (CCJP); (6) Certified Co-Occurring Disorders Professional (CCDP); (7) Certified Co-Occurring Disorders Professional Diplomate (CCDPD); and (8) Peer Recovery (PR). Although there is consistency within the larger organization, each individual nation, state, and territory of member organizations may use different professional titles (e.g., Licensed Clinical Addiction Specialist, Certified Addiction Professional). The following table highlights the variety in credentialing language as demonstrated by the two authors' credentials.

Table 1.1 IC&RC Credentials of Authors

Regina R. Moro			Laura J. Veach		
IC&RC State	Credential	IC&RC Equivalent	IC&RC State	Credential	IC&RC Equivalent
N. Carolina	Licensed Clinical Addiction Specialist	Advanced Alcohol and Drug Counselor	N. Carolina	Certified Clinical Supervisor	Clinical Supervisor
Idaho	Advanced Certified Alcohol/Drug Counselor	Advanced Alcohol and Drug Counselor	N. Carolina	Licensed Clinical Addiction Specialist	Advanced Alcohol and Drug Counselor

In 2009, CACREP became the first graduate-level mental health training accreditation body (i.e., among the counseling, social work, and psychology professions) to adopt the inclusion of addiction-related content knowledge requirements for all students, regardless of their scope of practice (Hagedorn et al., 2012). This inclusion indicated that in order to receive a master's degree in counseling, all students in CACREP-accredited programs now have to learn about the "theories and etiologies of addictions and addictive behaviors, including strategies for prevention, intervention, and treatment" (CACREP, 2009, p. 11). National requirements mostly require substance abuse counselors to have the equivalent of a high school degree, whereas the majority (i.e., 97%) of states require mental health counselors are required to hold a master's degree (Kerwin, Walker-Smith, & Kirby, 2006). West et al. (1999) pondered the question of why the professional standards of substance abuse counselors are so much less than that of professional counselors.

One other certification board that should be acknowledged is the National Certification Commission for Addiction Professionals (NCCAP), a member organization of NAADAC, the Association for Addiction Professionals. This organization has three main credentials, with a variety of other certificates it offers. The credentials are The National Certified Addictions Counselor Level I and Level II, and the Master Addiction Counselor (MAC) (NCCAP, 2013). The MAC credential was initiated in the 1980s by three different organizations (i.e., the National Board for Certified Counselors [NBCC], NAADAC and the Commission on Rehabilitation Counselor Certification [CRCC]). All three organizations have MAC credentials today, although each requirement is specific to the organization (e.g., NBCC requires those seeking the MAC credential through their organization to be certified as a National Certified Counselor).

The complexity associated with the title of addictions professional makes the process quite complex for those seeking this professional pathway. As outlined, there are numerous organizations that provide credentials for individuals to seek certification and/or licensure, as well as complexities in relation to educational standards. Individuals are encouraged to peruse the certification and/or licensure requirements of their state for additional guidance related to the necessary background to practice in the addiction field.

Conclusion

The historical evolution of addictions counseling is multifaceted and complex. As we highlighted in this chapter, not only is it important to consider trends of use in relation to substances, but also the evolution of treatment modalities over time. In addition, legislative efforts have had a significant impact on the profession, as well as the changing landscape of the addiction counselor over time. The historical research base of the profession has been established and will be expanded upon in Chapter 2.

Box 1.2: Case Illustration of Malini's Exploration of the Addiction Counseling Profession

Hi, my name is Malini, and I am entering my senior year of college. I have been a pre-med major, doing well academically, however I have decided that a career in medicine is not what I want to pursue. I originally decided on medicine primarily because it is a typical career path for others in my family. I was born and raised in the United States, and my parents immigrated here from New Delhi, India, to attend medical school. They excelled and are both currently practicing—my mother an anesthesiologist and my father a neurosurgeon. It has been expected that I will also follow in their footsteps, yet my passions are being ignited elsewhere. For many years, my father has struggled with an addiction, although

(Continued)

(Continued)

this was well hidden. He has a very stressful job, and he has up until about 5 years ago, managed very well. Five years ago, things went south really fast. My father has always been a drinker, but with my brother and I both being in college, my mom would call and say how much more Dad was drinking in the evenings coming home from work. Then one night when Dad was on call, he decided to have a few drinks. Although he was never called to go in for surgery, my mother was extremely distressed by this. She was concerned that if he was called, he would have gone in and performed surgery. It was then that my mom decided he needed an intervention. My whole family was there and we went through the process; my dad entered a treatment program that was specifically tailored for medical professionals, and my mom, brother, and I entered our own counseling. My dad has been sober for the past 3 years, and I have been incredibly grateful for the support of our counselor as well as the support group, Al-Anon, that I joined during that time. All of this has led to me wanting to give back in some way to other families struggling with addiction. My dream is to now become an addictions counselor, yet I'm having a hard time understanding how to live out my dream.

Questions for Reflection

What advice do you have for Malini?

What organizations would you recommend Malini look into?

How would you describe the difference between certification and licensure to Malini?

Table 1.2   Comprehensive Timeline of Events Related to Addiction Counseling

Date	Event
Stone Age	Archaeological evidence of pots that contained a mild beer or wine
900s	Rhazes, an Arabian physician, discovered distilled spirits
1500s	Distilled spirits became a popular drink
1640	Dutch opened first distillery in Staten Island
1700s	Native American recovery circles were in existence
1790	All rations for U.S. soldiers included ¼ pint of brandy, rum, or whiskey
1800–1880	Recognized widespread drug patterns
1804	Dr. Thomas Trotter describes the "disease concept" of alcoholism
1806	Morphine was discovered

Date	Event
1861–1865	American Civil War; morphine addiction is known as the "Army Disease"
1823	Dr. Benjamin Rush authors a book on addiction as a disease
1840	Founding of the Washingtonian Total Abstinence Society
1842–1850	Founding of Fraternal Order of Temperance Societies (e.g., The Sons of Temperance, Good Templars, and Good Samaritans)
1870s	Clinical concepts of addiction solidified
1870s	Emergence of the mail-order bottled cures
1877	*The New York Times* published an article including reference to addiction as "a disease which [requires] proper medical aid and systematic treatment"
1800s	Use of alcohol and other drugs as medicines: • Godfrey's Cordial ("Mother's Helper") used to treat colic • Laudanum (women for pain) • Coca-Cola (with cocaine) for energy • Cannabis (feminine pain and headaches)
1800s	Emergence of alcoholic mutual aid societies
1892	The American Psychological Association was founded
1906	Congress passed the Pure Food and Drug Act
1914	Congress passed the Harrison Act
1914	Congressional Research Service formed
1919	Congress passed the 18th Amendment, aka Prohibition
1920–1933	Prohibition was in effect
1929	Congress passed the Porter Narcotic Farm Act
1930	The Federal Bureau of Narcotics was founded
1933	Congress passed the 21st Amendment, repealing Prohibition
1930s	The Yale Center of Alcohol Studies was founded at Yale University
1935	Alcoholics Anonymous was formed
1935	A treatment facility opened in Lexington, Kentucky, under the Porter Narcotic Farm Act
1936	"Reefer Madness" released
1937	Marijuana Tax Act passed

(Continued)

Table 1.2 (Continued)

Date	Event
1938	A second treatment facility opened in Fort Worth, Texas, under the Porter Narcotic Farm Act
1940	Yandell Henderson, Howard Haggard, Leon Greenberg, and later E. M. Jellinek founded the *Quarterly Journal of Studies on Alcohol*
1943	The Summer School of Alcohol Studies was founded at Yale University's Center of Alcohol Studies
1948	Disulfram (brand name Antabuse) first used in the United States to treat alcoholism by Dr. Ruth Fox
1949	Founding of the first group called "Narcotics Anonymous" in New York City, NY
1951	Formalization of Al-Anon
1951	New York City Medical Committee on Alcoholism formed (founding organization of the American Society of Addiction Medicine)
1952	The Council on Social Work Education was formed
1953	Narcotics Anonymous was founded in California
1958	Founding of Synanon
1964	Methadone maintenance began as a research initiative at Rockefeller University
1965	President Lyndon Johnson addressed the disease concept of alcoholism
1966	Congress passed the Narcotic Addict Rehabilitation Act (NARA)
1966–1972	Training initiatives were developed by the Office of Economic Opportunity, the Department of Labor, and the National Institute on Mental Health
1967	American Medical Association's disease concept was first published
1968	Amendments are made to the 1963 Community Mental Health Centers Act in order to support specialized addiction treatment grants
1968	The Bureau of Narcotics and Dangerous Drugs was formed
1970	Controlled Substance Act is passed
1970	Comprehensive Alcohol Abuse and Alcoholism Prevention and Treatment Act passed (created the NIAAA)
1970s	NIAAA and NIDA created training programs
1972	Drug Abuse Treatment Act passed (created NIDA)

Date	Event
1972	National Association of Alcoholism Counselors and Trainers was formalized (now NAADAC)
1973	The U.S. Drug Enforcement Agency was formed
1973	ACES introduced the first set of counselor preparation standards
1970s–1908s	Call to integrate alcohol and drug abuse treatment by Dr. Donald Ottenberg
1975	Women for Sobriety Founded by Dr. Jean Kirkpatrick
1975	Monitoring the Future Survey initiated
1976	The Rand Report "Alcoholism and Treatment" was published
1977	National Commission for Credentialing Alcoholism Counselors was formed, the first national body seeking to implement uniform credentialing standards
1981	CACREP was established (premier accrediting body for the training of professional counselors)
1980s	Emergence of including family members in treatment
1980s	Diversification of treatment provider backgrounds increased
1982	The National Board for Certified Counselors was established
1984	National Minimum Drinking Age Act of 1984 was signed into law by President Ronald Reagan
1985	Secular Organization for Sobriety was founded
1986	Rational Recovery was founded
1980s	NBCC, NAADAC, and CRCC create the "Master Addictions Counselor" (MAC) credential
1986	Anti-Drug Abuse Act signed into law by President Reagan; instituted mandatory sentences for drug-related crimes
1988	The American Medical Association approves the American Society of Addiction Medicine as a national medical specialty
1989	The National Certification Reciprocity Consortium/Alcohol and Other Drug Abuse (NCRC/AODA) was formally named
1989	President George H. W. Bush declares a new *War on Drugs* during televised speech
1990	Drug Abuse Treatment Outcome Studies initiated by NIDA 1990 –Drug Abuse Reporting Program (data collection from 1969–1972) –Treatment Outcome Perspective Study (data collection from 1979–1981)

(Continued)

Table 1.2 (Continued)

Date	Event
1991	ASAM published the first Patient Placement Criteria
1992	Congress passed legislation creating the Substance Abuse and Mental Health Services Administration (SAMHSA)
1994	Federal funds were allocated to explore the use of drug courts
1996	California becomes the first state to legalize medical marijuana
1996	Project MATCH main findings released
1997	National Registry of Evidence-based Programs and Practices launched
2005	Combat Methamphetamine Act signed to regulate the sale of retail over-the-counter medication used in the production of methamphetamine
2009	CACREP became the first graduate mental health training accreditation body to adopt the inclusion of addiction-related content knowledge requirements
2008	Congress passes the Mental Health Parity and Addiction Equity Act
2010	President Barack Obama signs the Affordable Care Act into law
2012	Congress passed the Synthetic Drug Abuse Prevention Act
2012	Washington and Colorado become the first two U.S. states to legalize personal, recreational use of marijuana
2013	*The Diagnostic and Statistical Manual, 5th edition*, was released by the American Psychiatric Association
2016	The 21st Century Cures Act was signed into law by President Obama

RESOURCES FOR FURTHER LEARNING

Websites

Center of Alcohol Studies

http://alcoholstudies.rutgers.edu/history

International Credentialing & Reciprocity Consortium Credentials

http://internationalcredentialing.org/creds

National Board for Certified Counselors Master Addictions Counselor Credential

http://www.nbcc.org/Certification/MAC

National Certification Commission for Addiction Professionals Credentials

http://www.naadac.org/certification

Webinar

History of Recovery in the United States and the Addiction Profession

Presented by William L. White

Sponsored by NAADAC

http://www.naadac.org/thehistoryofrecoveryintheunitedstatesandtheaddictionprofession

REFERENCES

Alcoholics Anonymous. (2014). *Estimated worldwide AA individual and group membership.* Retrieved from http://www.aa.org/assets/en_US/smf-132_en.pdf

American Board of Addiction Medicine (ABAM). (2015). *About ABAM.* Retrieved from http://www.abam.net/about/

American Psychiatric Association (APA). (2014). *DSM-5 implementation and support.* Retrieved from http://www.dsm5.org/Pages/Default.aspx

American Society of Addiction Medicine (ASAM). (2015). *ASAM historical timeline.* Retrieved from http://www.asam.org/about-us/about-asam/asam-historical-timeline

Armor, D. J., Polich, J. M., & Stambul, H. B. (1976). *Alcoholism and treatment* (Report No. R- 1739-NIAAA). Santa Monica, CA: The Rand Corporation.

Association of Recovery in Higher Education. (2016). *Programs.* Retrieved from http://collegiaterecovery.org/programs/

Association of Recovery Schools. (2016). The state of recovery schools, 2016 biennial report. Denton, TX: Author. Retrieved from http://www.recoveryschools.org

Briggs, C. A., & Pepperell, J. L. (2009). *Women, girls, and addiction: Celebrating the feminine in counseling treatment and recovery.* New York, NY: Routledge.

Caron. (2014). *Florida treatment model.* Retrieved from https://www.caronrenaissance.org/about/history/florida-treatment-model

Center of Alcohol Studies. (2014). *The history of the center of alcohol studies.* Retrieved from http://alcoholstudies.rutgers.edu/history

Coyhis, D., & White, W. L. (2002). Addiction and recovery in Native America. *Wellbriety! 3*(5), 4–8. Retrieved from http://www.whitebison.org/magazine/2002/fall/vol3no5.html

Doweiko, H. E. (2012). *Concepts of chemical dependency.* Belmont, CA: Brooks/Cole.

Field, G. D. (2002). Historical trends of drug treatment in the criminal justice system. In C. G. Leukefeld, F. Tims, & D. Farabee (Eds.), *Treatment of drug offenders: Policies and issues* (pp. 9–21). New York, NY: Springer.

Gorski, T. T. (1989). The CENAPS model of relapse prevention planning. *Journal of Chemical Dependency, 2*(2), 153–169.

Hagedorn, W. B., Culbreth, J. R., & Cashwell, C. S. (2012). Addiction counseling accreditation: CACREP's role in solidifying the counseling profession. *The Professional Counselor: Research and Practice, 2*(2), 124–133.

Hanson, D. J. (2015). *The national minimum drinking age act of 1984.* Retrieved from http://www.alcoholproblems andsolutions.org/YouthIssues/1092767630.html#.VXsvPWB xKF4

Hazelden Betty Ford Foundation. (2016). *What is the Jellinek curve?: A classic tool with present-day usefulness.* Retrieved from http://www.hazeldenbettyford.org/articles/jellinek-curve

Inaba, D. S., & Cohen, W. E. (2007). *Uppers, downers, all arounders: Physical and mental effects of psychoactive drugs.* Medford, OR: CNS Publications.

International Credentialing & Reciprocity Consortium (IC&RC). (n.d.a). *About IC&RC.* Retrieved from http://internationalcredentialing.org/about

International Credentialing & Reciprocity Consortium (IC&RC). (n.d.b). *About IC&RC's credentials.* Retrieved from http://internationalcredentialing.org/creds

Kerwin, M. E., Walker-Smith, K., & Kirby, K. C. (2006). Comparative analysis of state requirements for the training of substance abuse and mental health counselors. *Journal of Substance Abuse Treatment, 30*(3), 173–181. doi:10.1016/j.jsat.2005.11.004

Kinney, J., & Leaton, G. (1983). *Loosening the grip: A handbook of alcohol information.* St. Louis, MO: The C. V. Mosby Company.

Marlatt, G. A., & George, W. H. (1984). Relapse prevention: Introduction and overview of the model. *British Journal of Addiction, 79,* 261–273.

McAuliffe, W. E., & Ch'ien, J. M. (1986). Recovery training and self help: A relapse-prevention program for treated opiate addicts. *Journal of Substance Abuse Treatment, 3*(1), 9–20.

Merta, R. J. (2001). Addictions counseling. *Counseling and Human Development, 33*(5), 1–24.

Miller, G. (2015). *Learning the language of addiction counseling* (4th ed.). Hoboken, NJ: John Wiley & Sons.

Moore, L. (2013). *Milestones in U.S. marijuana laws.* Retrieved from http://www.nytimes.com/interactive/2013/10/27/us/marijuana-legalization-timeline.html?_r=0

Morgan, H. W. (1981). *Drugs in America: A social history, 1800–1980.* Syracuse, NY: Syracuse University Press.

NAADAC. (2016). *Press releases: NAADAC applauds the passage of the 21st century cures act.* Retrieved from http://www.naadac.org/Default.aspx?p=110609&naid=22950

National Certification Commission for Addiction Professionals (NCCAP). (2013). *Certification.* Retrieved from http://www.naadac.org/certification

National Institute on Alcohol Abuse and Alcoholism (NIAAA). (1996). *NIAAA report Project MATCH main findings.* Retrieved from http://www.nih.gov/news/pr/dec96/niaaa-17.htm

National Institute on Drug Abuse (NIDA). (2012). *DrugFacts: Synthetic cathinones ("bath salts").* Retrieved from http://www.drugabuse.gov/publications/drugfacts/synthetic-cathinones-bath-salts

National Institute on Drug Abuse (NIDA). (2015). *Monitoring the future.* Retrieved from http://www.drugabuse.gov/related-topics/trends-statistics/monitoring-future

National Registry of Evidence-based Programs and Practices (NREPP). (2012). *Legacy programs.* Retrieved from http://www.nrepp.samhsa.gov/SearchLegacy.aspx

Oshe, R. (1980). The social development of the synanon cult: The managerial strategy of organizational transformation. *Sociological Analysis, 41*(2), 109–127.

Palm Beach Institute. (2013). *The Florida treatment model actually works.* Retrieved from http://www.pbinstitute.com/florida-treatment-model-actually-works-2/

Rush, B. (1823). *An inquiry into the effects of ardent spirits upon the human body and mind* (8th ed.). Boston, MA: James Loring.

Spicer, J. (1993). *The Minnesota model: The evolution of the multidisciplinary approach to addiction recovery.* Center City, MN: Hazelden Educational Materials.

Substance Abuse and Mental Health Service Administration (SAMSA). (n.d.). *About us.* Retrieved from http://www.samhsa.gov/about-us

Thombs, D. L. (2006). *Introduction to addictive behaviors* (3rd ed.). New York, NY: Guilford.

U.S. Department of Justice, Drug Enforcement Administration. (2007). *General information regarding the combat methamphetamine epidemic act of 2005.* Retrieved from http://www.deadiversion.usdoj.gov/meth/cma2005.htm

U.S. Department of Justice, Drug Enforcement Administration. (2015). *Combat meth epidemic act: Assessment of annual needs.* Retrieved from http://www.dea.gov/resource-center/meth-lab-maps.shtml

U.S. Department of Labor. (2010). *The mental health parity and addiction equity act of 2008.* Retrieved from http://www.dol.gov/ebsa/newsroom/fsmhpaea.html

Ward, J. H., Bejarano, W., Babor, T. F., & Allred, N. (2016). Re-introducing Bunky at 125: E. M. Jellinek's life and contributions to alcohol studies. *Journal of Studies on Alcohol and Drugs, 77,* 375–383.

West, P. L., Mustaine, B. L., & Wyrick, B. (1999). State regulations and the ACA code of ethics and standards of practice: Oil and water for the substance abuse counselor. *Journal of Addictions & Offender Counseling, 20*(1), 35–47.

WGBH Educational Foundation. (2014). *Marijuana timeline.* Retrieved from http://www.pbs.org/wgbh/pages/frontline/shows/dope/etc/cron.html

White, W. L. (1998). *Slaying the dragon: The history of addiction treatment and recovery in America.* Bloomington, IL: Chestnut Health Systems.

White, W. L. (2000a). *Toward a new recovery movement: Historical reflections on recovery, treatment and advocacy.* Retrieved from http://www.fead.org.uk/docs/toward_new_recovery.pdf

White, W. L. (2000b). The history of recovered people as wounded healers: II. The era of professionalization and specialization. *Alcoholism Treatment Quarterly, 18*(2), 1–25.

White, W. (2004). History of drug problems and drug policies in America. In R. Coombs (Ed.), *Addictions counseling review: Preparing for comprehensive certification exams* (pp. 81–104). Boston, MA: Lahaska Press.

2

Understanding the Importance of Evidence-Based Practices for Professional Counselors

❖

LEARNING OBJECTIVES

Upon completion of reading this chapter and participating in the guided exercises, the learner will be able to

- explain the professional and ethical importance of evidence-based practices;
- define and identify evidence-based programs and practices in addictions counseling; and
- identify key stakeholders involved in treatment of addictions counseling.

"If we knew what we were doing, it would not be called Research.*"—Albert Einstein*

The quote from Albert Einstein is one that has resonated with many of us who have embarked on the journey of conducting research. We believe it is also true for students as they begin learning about the research process and consider the implications for their future as professional helpers. Research is an important process in many different ways, and we will explore the overall impact research has to the field of addictions counseling in this chapter.

Overview of Evidence-Based Practices

Whether you are a student working on the coursework component of your education, or a student/trainee who has begun your clinical experience, it is likely you have been introduced to the buzzword *evidence-based*. Reed and Reed (2008) found a dramatic increase in the cited use of the word *evidence-based* over a 20-year period in scholarly papers, and more specifically from 1997 to 2007, with findings of fewer than 250 publications in 1997 to more than 3,000 publications in 2007. We also conducted a review of the literature via scholarly databases and found a similar rise in publications pertaining to evidence-based practices (EBPs).

The Google Scholar database was utilized for the ease of accessibility for the public. The other database that was identified was PsycINFO, a database owned by the American Psychological Association. The PsycINFO database is well known for the comprehensive nature of peer-reviewed publications. The first search was conducted in the Google Scholar platform, examining the presence of citations using the search words "evidence based practice" and returned over a million and a half hits. The time frame was narrowed in the second analysis, and the results are displayed in Figure 2.1. There was a 394% increase in publications identified by the search words, with 6,060 citations during the year 2000, to 23,900 citations in the year 2014. This search alone exemplifies the buzz surrounding evidence-based practices.

The next search examined the presence of citations within the PsycINFO database, particularly related to the search words "evidence based practice." Again, you will notice a sharp steady rise over the past 15 years (see Figure 2.2).

The last search (see Figure 2.3) also examined the PsycINFO database, searching for the key phrases "evidence based practice" AND "addiction." The results of this search also demonstrate an upward trajectory for publications dedicated to this topic. There is a noticeable difference between the two searches within the PsycINFO database, with the search that also includes the keyword of addiction having more fluctuation. Although there may be a variety of factors, we wonder about the impact of the economic recession during the late 2000s, and the access to funding for grant opportunities specifically for addiction-related research.

Figure 2.1   Google Scholar Database: "Evidence Based Practice AND Addiction"

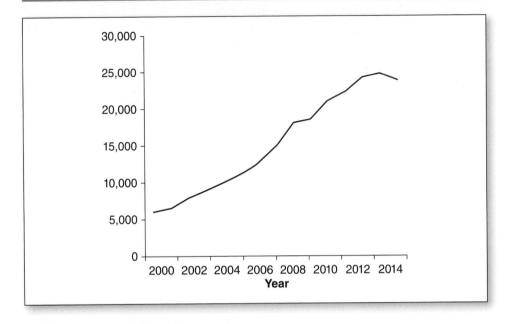

Figure 2.2   PsycINFO Database: "Evidence Based Practice"

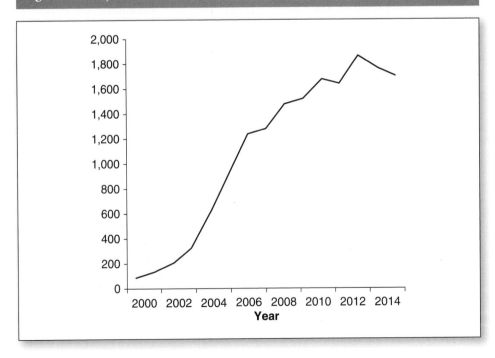

Figure 2.3 PsycINFO Database: "Evidence Based Practice AND Addiction"

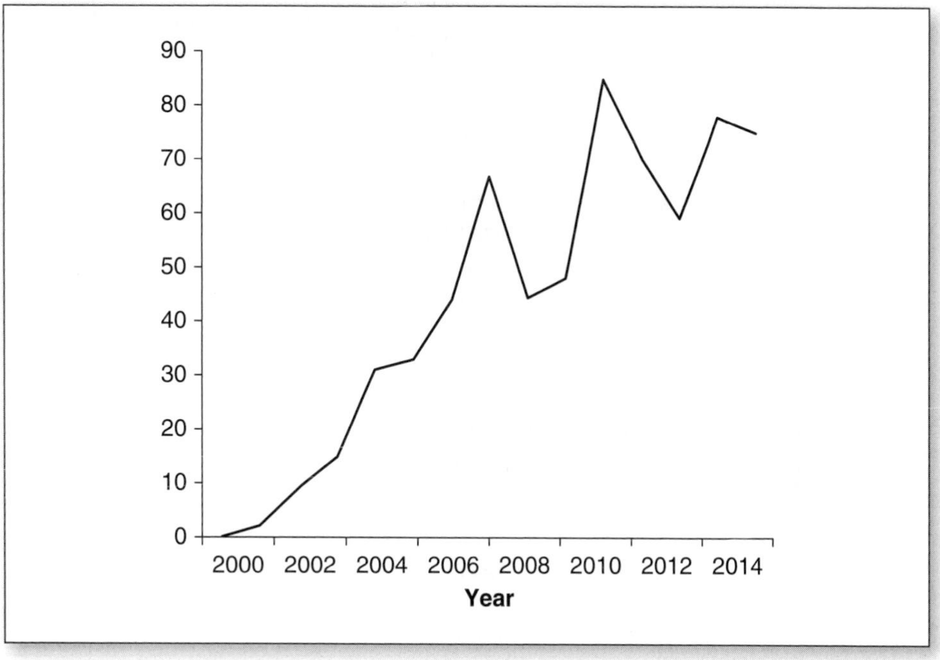

Defining Evidence-Based

Throughout our writing we have chosen to use the language of *evidence-based* as we believe it is the most comprehensive and relevant to our discussion. In order to move forward on our journey through this text, we would like to provide you all with a guiding definition of *evidence-based*. We will be following the definition provided by the Institute of Medicine (IOM; 2001) as it is commonly used in the literature as the guiding definition (Glasner-Edwards & Rawson, 2010; Prendergast, 2011):

> Evidence-based practice is the integration of best research evidence with clinical expertise and patient values. *Best research evidence* refers to clinically relevant research, often from the basic sciences of medicine, but especially from patient-centered clinical research into the accuracy and precision of diagnostic tests (including the clinical examination); the power of predictive markers; and the efficacy and safety of therapeutic, rehabilitative, and preventive regimens. *Clinical expertise* means the ability to use clinical skills and past experience to rapidly identify each patient's unique health state and diagnosis, individual risks and benefits of potential interventions, and personal values and expectations. *Patient values* refers to the unique preferences, concerns, and expectations that

are brought by each patient to a clinical encounter and must be integrated into clinical decisions if the patient is to be served. (IOM, 2001, p. 47)

The Substance Abuse and Mental Health Services Administration (SAMHSA) provides further clarification (see Table 2.1) for professionals to determine what qualifies specific programs as evidence-based by meeting at least one of the following outlined categories.

Table 2.1   SAMHSA's Criteria for Evidence-Based Practices

Category	Description	
1	The intervention is included in Federal registries of evidence-based interventions; OR	
2	The intervention is reported (with positive effects on the primary targeted outcome) in peer-reviewed journals; OR	
3	The intervention has documented evidence of effectiveness, based on guidelines developed by SAMHSA/CSAP and/or the state, tribe, or jurisdiction. Documented evidence should be implemented in accordance with the four recommended guidelines, all of which should be followed. The guidelines are below:	
	Guideline 1	The intervention is based on a theory of change that is documented in a clear logic or conceptual mode; AND
	Guideline 2	The intervention is similar in content and structure to interventions that appear in registries and/or the peer-reviewed literature; AND
	Guideline 3	The intervention is supported by documentation that it has been effectively implemented in the past, and multiple times, in a manner attentive to scientific standards of evidence and with results that show a consistent pattern of credible and positive effects; AND
	Guideline 4	The intervention is reviewed and deemed appropriate by a panel of informed prevention experts that includes well-qualified prevention researchers who are experienced in evaluating prevention interventions similar to those under review; local prevention practitioners; and key community leaders as appropriate, e.g., officials from law enforcement and education sectors or elders within indigenous cultures.

Adapted from source: Substance Abuse and Mental Health Services Administration (SAMHSA). (2009). *SAMHSA Criteria*. Retrieved from https://captus.samhsa.gov/prevention-practice/defining-evidence-based/samhsa-criteria

It is important to note that there are other organizations that also provide definitions for what qualifies as evidence-based, however we have chosen to focus on the SAMHSA criteria due to the appreciation to diverse ways of helping by attending to indigenous healing practices. For further information concerning other organizational criteria, interested individuals are encouraged to look at Glasner-Edwards and Rawson's (2010) review of evidence-based practices relating to addiction treatment, in which they provide a comprehensive comparison between the organizations and their specific requirements.

Research Concepts

The purpose of this text is not to teach you about reading and digesting empirical research, yet we do feel it necessary to provide you with a few definitions to guide our work together. We have already defined evidence-based as we will use it in this text, and believe the following terms are beneficial for you to be familiar with:

Efficacy. The model or program under investigation has been found to have statistically significant results within the limits of conducting a clinical trial (i.e., research setting) but is not known whether this can be adapted to the "real world."

Effectiveness. Implies that the model or program under review has been shown to be successfully adapted to the real world, while maintaining consistency to the model.

Fidelity. Refers to consistency with the standardized way of carrying out an intervention.

Peer-reviewed. In order to be identified as a peer-reviewed publication, the writing must go through a review process in which it is examined and deemed worthy of dissemination by identified experts.

Randomized clinical trial. A type of research study in which there is random assignment of participants to groups (i.e., treatment vs. control group, or multiple treatment groups). This is considered the gold standard of evidence-based research.

Statistical significance. Whether the chance of attaining the result is more than chance alone. Typically set at a .05 or .01 level. Therefore, if the result is less than .05 or .01, then the result is statistically significant, stating it was more than just chance alone that produced the finding.

Understanding Research in Action

The adoption of evidence-based practices initially began in the medical field (Reed & Reed, 2008; Wampold & Bhati, 2004). There was a strong interest in maximizing patient outcomes by translating the evidence from research into clinical application.

Clearly, with the focus on achieving the best outcomes for the patient this makes sense for addiction counselors to also be interested in utilizing modalities rooted in research.

The Research Process: Remembering the Scientific Method

There are variations of the actual amount of steps and names of the parts of the scientific method, particularly depending upon the discipline in which the research is being conducted. The following discussion will utilize the more open language of phases as opposed to the traditional more linear language of steps or stages to capture the fluid nature of the process.

The first phase of the research process is when an individual (or group) first begins thinking about a problem. This individual has identified that there is an issue that needs to be explored further and may begin to do this themselves or may seek out further assistance via professional researchers. This further exploration is the second phase of the process. This involves collecting information about the problem that is currently in the literature. The researcher actively examines the literature, finding references to scholarly work, and critically reviews the studies. Digesting this information may provide the researcher with information about the identified problem, or a gap may be identified. If the individual identifies information relevant to the identified problem, the research process may be discontinued.

When a gap is identified, there is room to expand the current literature via the following research process phases. One must identify the hypothesis they will be examining. This is based upon his or her experience of the phenomenon they have identified, as well as the literature that has been reviewed. The next phase is when data is collected and examined, following permission of a review board to protect human subjects. Lastly, the findings are explored by the researcher and are disseminated to a wider audience. This process helps fill the gap, so that the next individual to experience the problem and who also has questions about it will be able to conduct a search of the literature and learn from the previous person's data collection, analysis, and dissemination.

It is important to note that throughout these identified phases, individuals may decide to write publications concerning the identified problem. If the writing occurs in the earlier-identified phases, before data are collected, this is commonly referred to as a conceptual piece, that is, conceptualizing the issue, and posing hypotheses for the problem. If the writing occurs after the analysis of the collected data, this is typically thought of as an empirical research publication.

Although there is a strong interest in evidence-based practices for addiction counseling, this does not come without controversy (Glasner-Edwards & Rawson, 2010). One identified difficulty the field of addiction counseling has is translating research findings into clinical practice. Many of the skills needed to review and implement research findings are often learned during graduate education, which many addictions counselors are not required to have in order to work clinically by current state practice requirements (Glasner-Edwards & Rawson, 2010; Kerwin, Walker-Smith, & Kirby, 2006). Therefore, if one were not able to critically review research study descriptions and findings, they would most likely not be able to implement the model as required.

Another concern is time. First, there is a large gap between when empirical studies are conducted to when the results become available, and further when the practice can be adopted (Prendergast, 2011). Counselors often cite time constraints as a barrier to implementing evidence-based practices (Hartzler & Rabun, 2014), as there is more of a demand to be providing clinical services to clients, yet caseloads are increasing as staff cuts are made. It also takes time to digest research findings, and further, to make the systemic change required of implementing a new treatment modality.

Importance and Demand for Evidence-Based Practice

The use of evidence-based practices can demonstrate a commitment to excellence for an individual and/or organization. This excellence has implications for the clients being served, mainly that they are receiving a high level of quality care. Many organizations, specifically in the health care industry, have quality improvement programs that aim for continuous actions to improve the delivery of services for a targeted group (Health Research and Services Administration [HRSA], 2011).

Quality improvement (QI) programs have four key principles: the improvement program is understood to work as systems and processes operate; the focus is on patients; the focus is on being part of a team; and there is a focus on the use of data (HRSA, 2011). The focus on data is that of making decisions, therefore before a decision is made to adopt a new treatment modality, data are gathered about the need for the new treatment within the system. If this is a consideration whether to adopt an evidence-based practice, there may be data collected concerning the need for the program, the cost associated with acquiring the program and/or training for the counselors to implement the program, and potential benefits of the adoption. The data gathered may result in the program being adopted or not, all with the aim of improving patient services. In considering evidence-based practice adoption, it is crucial that there is a visible benefit for the organization and ultimately, the recipients of the care.

Key Stakeholders

Stakeholders are individuals and/or organizations that have a vested interest in an outcome. For example, if the discussion were examining key stakeholders regarding the professional sports industry, we would identify stakeholders as the players, players' families, coaches, athletic trainers, managers, owners, fans, and others as all having a vested interest in the decisions of the professional sports team.

In the addiction counseling world, these individuals and organizations typically have an interest in the individual's recovery, although this may be for a variety of reasons. To examine the stakeholders, it is helpful to utilize a framework for which we have chosen Bronfenbrenner's (1977) ecological systems theory. This is a comprehensive systemic model to examine the individual client systems and stakeholders as they relate to addictions counseling.

Bronfenbrenner's Ecological Systems Theory

Urie Bronfenbrenner's (1977) theory describes multiple levels of systemic involvement. According to the model, there are four levels involved in systems represented by four circles nested in one another. The center of the model is the immediate system containing an individual at the center of examination. This level is named the *microsystem*, and it is characterized by the individual involved in a particular role, in a particular activity. For example, this may be a female client, who is actively involved in her immediate system of home and is in the particular role of daughter.

The next level according to Bronfenbrenner is the *mesosystem*. The *meso* level is characterized by interactions among the systems found in the micro level. An example is that if the *micro* level is the female client, the *meso* level would be the interaction between the client's home system, her peer system, and her school system. In other words, "a mesosystem is a system of microsystems" (Bronfenbrenner, 1977, p. 515). Outside the *meso*system level is an extension, known as the *exosystem*. This system does not contain the person identified in the *micro*system yet has influence on the systems an individual is in. To continue with our example, the female client is actively involved in her school system, and the governing school board influences this school system without directly influencing the client. The last level is the *macrosystem*, representing the identified example for how things should operate (i.e., societal rules). This could also be referred to as social norms, and have an influence, similar to that of the meso level, however on a much larger scale. Given our female client example, the macrosystem may include gender role stereotypes firmly held within the dominant culture.

Key Stakeholders Related to Addictions Counseling Research

As we examine evidence-based practice, quality of care, and stakeholders, it is important to translate the discussion to the potential adoption of researched intervention services. Here is a non-exhaustive list of specific entities that may have a vested interest in the results of a research study's outcome (i.e., results).

Grant Funders

Grant foundations typically have a guiding mission for the organization. Grants are awarded that are strongly aligned with the mission, in order to strengthen the organization. Therefore, the organization has an interest in successful outcomes for the funded grant projects (i.e., research studies) that uphold the mission of the organization at large.

Managed Care Entities

We discussed managed care entities in Chapter 1. These organizations have a vested interest in research study outcomes, as these provide insight into understanding the support for specific treatments. The managed care entities are highly interested in cost-saving approaches, and ultimately may recommend or even require specific treatments over others.

Public Policy

Much of the world of addiction counseling is guided by the legislative actions in our state and federal governments. Legislatures often do not have experience in the addiction counseling world and as a result rely on statistics and empirical data to make decisions concerning their constituents. These decisions also directly impact state and federal agencies that rely on funding from our legislative bodies.

Accrediting Bodies

Accreditation bodies have a vested interest in the research process, as they are constantly examining what education should be required of students. As such, if a research study provides sound empirical support for one treatment over another, it would be wise for accreditation bodies to examine whether education in the differing treatments would be important for their students.

Ethical Support for Evidence-Based Practices

Not only is it important to use evidence-based practices for the reasons cited above, but professional counselors also have an ethical responsibility to provide services that have empirical support. The ethical codes and specific items listed in Tables 2.2, 2.3, and 2.4 are relevant for counselors working in addictions settings when considering whether to adopt an evidence-based program.

Table 2.2 American Counseling Association Code of Ethics	
Specific Ethics Code Item	**Description**
C.7.a.	Scientific Basis for Treatment – When providing services, counselors use techniques/procedures/modalities that are grounded in theory and/or have an empirical or scientific foundation. (p. 10)
C.7.b.	Development and Innovation – When counselors use developing or innovative techniques/procedures/modalities, they explain the potential risks, benefits, and ethical considerations of using such techniques/procedures/modalities. Counselors work to minimize any potential risks or harm when using these techniques/procedures/modalities. (p. 10)
C.7.c.	Harmful Practices – Counselors do not use techniques/procedures/modalities when substantial evidence suggests harm, even if services are requested. (p. 10)

Adapted from source: American Counseling Association. (2014). *2014 ACA Code of Ethics.* Retrieved from http://www.counseling.org/docs/ethics/2014-aca-code-of-ethics.pdf?sfvrsn=4

Table 2.3 National Board for Certified Counselors Ethics Code

Specific Ethics Code Item	Description
26	National Certified Counselors (NCCs) shall demonstrate multicultural competence and shall not use techniques that discriminate against or show hostility towards individuals or groups based on gender, ethnicity, race, national origin, sexual orientation, disability, religion or any other legally prohibited basis. Techniques shall be based on established theory. NCCs shall discuss appropriate considerations and obtain written consent from the client(s) prior to the use of any experimental approach.
73	NCCs shall work collaboratively with clients in the creation of written plans of treatment that offer attainable goals and use appropriate techniques consistent with client's psychological and physical needs and abilities.
83	NCCs shall not employ deceptive techniques in research unless there are no alternatives and there is significant prospective scientific, educational or clinical value. In all cases, NCCs shall review potential techniques and shall not use any that can be reasonably expected to cause harm, as well as provide an explanation to participants during the debriefing.

Adapted from source: National Board for Certified Counselors. (2012). *National Board for Certified Counselors (NBCC) Code of Ethics.* Retrieved from http://www.nbcc.org/Assets/Ethics/NBCCCodeofEthics.pdf.

Table 2.4 The Association for Addiction Professionals, NAADAC, Ethics Code

Specific Ethics Code Item	Description
I	It is the responsibility of the addiction professional to safeguard the integrity of the counseling relationship and to ensure that the client is provided with services that are most beneficial. The client will be provided access to effective treatment and referral giving consideration to individual educational, legal and financial needs.
IV	The addiction professional espouses objectivity and integrity and maintains the highest standards in the services provided. The addiction professional recognizes that effectiveness in his or her profession is based on the ability to be worthy of trust. The professional has taken time to reflect on the ethical implications of clinical decisions and behavior using competent authority as a guide.

Adapted from source: NAADAC. (2011). *Ethical standards of alcoholism and drug abuse counselors.* Retrieved from http://www.naadac.org/assets/1959/naadac_code_of_ethics_brochure.pdf.

In addition to the above-referenced codes of ethics and items, it may be important to look at state licensure boards, or professional boards that govern the practice of counselors and addiction professionals in the state that one practices. Now that we have covered the importance of EBP, we will transition to talking about where to find these approaches.

Locating Evidence-Based Practices

In order to practice from an evidence-based model, a counselor must first locate the information about the approach. While we have discussed many of the characteristics of EBP and provided a definition, it is important to know there are existing databases that have already sorted through the research findings for the public. SAMHSA has compiled one of the largest databases, titled the National Registry of Evidence-based Programs and Practices (NREPP). This can be found at the following website: www.nrepp.samhsa.gov. There are many filters to use in order to find an EBP, such as whether it is for mental health, substance use or for comorbid disorders, which ages the program has been evaluated for, and which races/ethnicities it has been studied with. These are just a few of the search filters available to help a counselor locate the best program for them. The NREPP is a user-friendly, comprehensive service that all counselors working in the field of addictions should be familiar with.

A Caveat: The Common Factors Model and Evidence-Based Practice

The past 20 years has seen a rise in evidence-based practice, not only in addictions counseling, but also in a wide array of mental health services. There is an important consideration to address when it comes to evidence-based practices: the common factors model.

The earliest thought concerning the idea of examining the common factors that are responsible for psychotherapy outcomes was by Saul Rosenzweig in 1936 (as cited in Luborsky et al., 2002). Rosenzweig was interested in examining outcomes within psychotherapy research and hypothesized that across the variety of psychotherapy approaches there would only be small differences in outcomes. This original hypothesis coined the term "Dodo Bird Verdict," derived from *Alice in Wonderland*, when the Dodo Bird character declared all participants were winners following the big race (Luborsky et al., 2002). It was in 1975 that Luborsky, Segal, and Luborsky reviewed 100 studies and found support for Rosenzweig's original hypothesis (as cited in Luborsky et al., 2002).

In the late 1990s, Asay and Lambert (1999) conducted research and found continued support for identifying broad key categories that are associated with client outcomes. Four distinct elements of therapeutic change, and their corresponding percentages, were discovered: (1) client/extratherapeutic (40%); (2) therapeutic relationship (30%); (3) placebo effect, hope, and expectancy for change (15%); and (4) therapeutic models and techniques (15%). These common factors suggest it is more of what the client brings to the process, or what the client experiences outside the therapeutic encounter, and the relationship between the counselor and the client, which account for the most significant change. The models/techniques account for approximately 15% of the outcomes. In other words, the evidence-based practice accounts for 15% of change. Certainly, any change is important to consider, and due to the variability involved not only with clients, but also with the therapeutic relationship, it makes sense that external stakeholders would seek to have the most effective 15% possible via implementing evidence-based models/techniques.

Counseling Theories and EBP

Understanding and practicing from an established counseling theory is crucially important for professional counselors, as emphasized in the above excerpt from the ACA Code of Ethics. It is important to note that some counseling theories can be rigorously researched via clinical trials due to the ability to create standardized treatment manuals from them; this is particularly true with Beck's (1979) cognitive therapy (now commonly known as cognitive behavior therapy), and derivatives such as dialectical behavior therapy (Linehan, 1993), and acceptance and commitment therapy (Hayes, Strosahl, & Wilson, 1999). This is in contrast with counseling theories from other traditions, such as humanistic theories like person-centered counseling (Rogers, 1961). One notable difference between these theories is that the latter is less focused on standardized use of assessments and specific interventions. Clear interventions are a core component of manualized treatments, and these manuals can then be easily studied and translated into evidence-based practices. This is an important acknowledgment, as it does not then mean one counseling theory is better than another, but that the intervention (and overarching theory) is easier to translate into clinical research.

Conclusion

Throughout this chapter the discussion has focused on understanding the concept of evidence-based practice. There was an overview on the rise in popularity of evidence-based practices, specifically in the last 15 years. The discussion further focused on understanding key concepts associated with research in general, and more specifically on understanding stakeholders. A model was presented for considering systemic involvement and interest in research. Overall, we are hopeful you are finishing this chapter with an appreciation and interest in further examining evidence-based practice as it relates to addiction counseling. The following sections will give you an opportunity to practice your new learning, in case study format, as well as an activity to help solidify your learning. The next chapter will examine the foundation principles of brain science that are important for addiction counselors to be familiar with.

Skills in Action

Box 2.1: Case Illustration of Application of Bronfenbrenner's Model to Robert

My name is Robert, and I am sitting here with you today because I just got busted big time. I'm 22 years old, and I graduated from college 4 months ago. I was a history major; that has really been the only subject that I have always done well in. Mostly, I think, it is because it is like one big story. It makes sense to me, and I decided I wanted to be a history teacher. Unfortunately, as you probably know, the job market hasn't been the best for me, so I'm back at home living with my parents, something I thought would never happen to me. It has been a big adjustment after being away at school for 4 years, to then being back. It is like my parents still think of me like I was when I graduated from high school, but they just do not understand how much I've grown and that I am actually an adult now. They keep harping on me when I come home late on the weekends, but to me it's like #1, I'm legally able to be out at bars now, and #2, what do they want me to do, sit and watch old reruns of *Friends* with them? Despite being unemployed and well, living in my old bedroom, things were going well, until last week. I've been substitute teaching at the high school that I went to until hopefully a full-time job opens up. But the problem is that my best friend Josiah's little brother, Judah, is a senior there. I completely forgot that he was still in high school; I mean, I'm so used to being at his house and even partying with him when we are home for break. Because of my space brain, I was not thinking and sold Judah a gram of pot in the parking lot of the school. And of course with it being 2015, there was a video camera that caught the whole thing on camera. A school security guard watched the whole thing and called the police immediately. And now, here I am, talking to you.

- As Robert described his story, were you able to identify the different levels of Bronfenbrenner's model? Describe those below.

  Micro Level:

  _____

  _____

  Meso Level:

  _____

  _____

  Exo Level:

  _____

  _____

  Macro Level:

  _____

  _____

- If you were unable to identify the levels, what further information would you want to gain from Robert? How would you plan to elicit that information?

Box 2.2: Case Illustration of Helping Meghan Search for Research Articles

Hey, Sheila, it's Meghan. I'm wondering if you can help me with an assignment I have for grad school. I'm taking this class called Research in Clinical Work, and since you already have a master's degree in counseling I was hoping you could answer some questions. My professor has asked me to find a research article from the last 5 years on a topic that I'm interested in. As we have talked about, I'm becoming really interested in working with females who identify as sex addicts. So, I need to find an article and then critique it. But the problem is that I'm not sure what that means. Here are some questions that I have:

- Where can I find an article like this? I'm so used to my professors having them on our course webpages that I've never had to search for one before.
- How do I know if it is a good article? What are specific things I should be looking for?
- Thank you for any help you can offer me!

Experiential Skills Learning Activity

The following activity will help you find and critique a research article of choice.

a. Identify a database to search for empirical research studies (e.g., Google Scholar, PsycINFO, PubMed, Medline).

b. Identify a topic you are interested in. An example may be an interest in the nonmedical use of prescription medications among college students. If this was the subject, you may search for "Stimulant use and college student" or "Nonmedical prescription pain use among college students."

c. Next, examine your results list. It is important to note that your search may not provide any results, in which case it would be important for you to revisit the keywords you used in your search. A possible cause of this is that you were too specific in your search (e.g., Adderall use by college students at ABC University). To expand your results, identify a broader search word.

d. Once you have selected an article, you are able to begin critically reviewing it. Questions to ask yourself as you explore:

   i. When was this article published?

   ii. Is this a research article or a conceptual article?

   iii. If this is a research piece:

      1. Who are the participants?

      2. How are the participants described?

      3. What measurement tools were used, and how were they described?

      4. How do the authors describe the findings?

      5. What claims do the authors make concerning the findings?

e. Following your participation in this activity, what implications does this have for your future as an addictions counselor?

f. What did you learn about the literature search process by engaging in this activity?

RESOURCES FOR FURTHER LEARNING

Substance Abuse and Mental Health Services Administration

Defining Evidence-Based

https://captus.samhsa.gov/prevention-practice/defining-evidence-based

Substance Abuse and Mental Health Services Administration

National Registry of Evidence-based Programs and Practices

http://nrepp.samhsa.gov/01_landing.aspx

REFERENCES

American Counseling Association. (2014). *2014 ACA Code of Ethics*. Retrieved from http://www.counseling.org/docs/ethics/2014-aca-code-of-ethics.pdf?sfvrsn=4

Asay, T. P., & Lambert, M. J. (1999). The empirical case for the common factors in therapy: Quantitative findings. In M. A. Hubble, B. L. Duncan, & S. D. Miller (Eds.), *The heart and soul of change: What works in therapy* (pp. 23–55). Washington, DC: American Psychological Association.

Beck, A. T. (1979). *Cognitive therapy and the emotional disorders*. New York, NY: Meridian.

Bronfenbrenner, U. (1977). Toward an experimental ecology of human development. *American Psychologist, 32*(7), 513–531.

Glasner-Edwards, S., & Rawson, R. (2010). Evidence-based practices in addiction treatment: Review and recommendations for public policy. *Health Policy, 97*(2–3), 93–104. doi:10.1016/j.healthpol.2010.05.013

Hartzler, B., & Rabun, C. (2014). Training addiction professionals in empirically-supported treatments: Perspectives from the treatment community. *Substance Abuse, 35*(1), 30–36. doi:10.1080/08897077.2013.789816

Hayes, S. C., Strosahl, K. D., & Wilson, K. G. (1999). *Acceptance and commitment therapy: An experiential approach to behavior change*. New York, NY: Guilford.

Health Research and Services Administration (HRSA). (2011). *Introduction and overview: The HRSA quality toolkit*. Retrieved from http://www.hrsa.gov/quality/toolbox/introduction/index.html

Institute of Medicine (IOM). (2001). *Crossing the quality chasm: A new health system for the 21st century*. Washington, DC: National Academy Press.

Kerwin, M. E., Walker-Smith, K., & Kirby, K. C. (2006). Comparative analysis of state requirements for the training of substance abuse and mental health counselors. *Journal of Substance Abuse Treatment, 30*(3), 173–181. doi:10.1016/j.jsat.2005.11.004

Linehan, M. M. (1993). *Cognitive-behavioral treatment of borderline personality disorder*. New York, NY: Guilford.

Luborsky, L., Rosenthal, R., Diguer, L., Andrusyna, T. P., Berman, J. S., Levitt, J. T. . . . Krause, E. D. (2002). The dodo bird verdict is alive and well—mostly. *Clinical Psychology: Science and Practice, 9*(1), 2–12.

NAADAC. (2011). *Ethical standards of alcoholism and drug abuse counselors*. Retrieved from http://www.naadac.org/assets/1959/naadac_code_of_ethics_brochure.pdf

National Board for Certified Counselors. (2012). *National Board for Certified Counselors (NBCC) Code of Ethics.* *Retrieved* from http://www.nbcc.org/Assets/Ethics/NBCCCodeofEthics.pdf

Prendergast, M. L. (2011). Issues in defining and applying evidence-based practices criteria for treatment of criminal-justice involved clients. *Journal of Psychoactive Drugs, Suppl 7,* 10–18.

Reed, F. D. D., & Reed, D. D. (2008). Towards an understanding of evidence-based practice. *Journal of Early and Intensive Behavior Intervention, 5*(2), 20–29.

Rogers, C. (1961). *On becoming a person: A therapist's view of psychotherapy.* New York, NY: Houghton Mifflin Company.

Substance Abuse and Mental Health Services Administration (SAMHSA). (2009). *SAMHSA criteria.* Retrieved from https://captus.samhsa.gov/prevention-practice/defining-evidence-based/samhsa-criteria

Wampold, B. E., & Bhati, K. S. (2004). Attending to the omissions: A historical examination of evidence-based practice movements. *Professional Psychology: Research and Practice, 35*(6), 563–570.

3

Understanding the Brain in the Addictive Process

LEARNING OBJECTIVES

Upon completion of this chapter, the learner will be able to

- describe two key brain pathways involved in the addictive process;
- list at least one neurobiological aspect important for understanding the treatment of a substance use disorder; and
- discuss the importance of the brain in understanding chemical and process addictions.

Knowledge: Enhanced Understanding and Brain Research

Addiction as a Brain Disorder

At no time in the history of substance abuse and addictions counseling has it been clearer about the role of the brain in addiction and what happens when individuals use mood-altering substances and the effects they have on the brain. We still have a long way to go to better understand the full spectrum of substance use, misuse, and addictions, yet we have gained an incredible amount of knowledge within recent decades about the major role of the brain in understanding euphoria, risky use, and addiction. With ever more understanding of our brain functions, importantly what the National Institute of Neurological Disorders and Stroke (NINDS) refers to as the most productive decade of brain research than all preceding centuries (NINDS, 2015), more addiction professionals can add to the understanding of harm reduction in increasingly neuroscientific ways. The National Institute on Drug Abuse (NIDA) is a leader in the United States regarding brain research, especially as it relates to drug use, abuse, addiction, and prevention. Looking at research from NIDA, (2014) we know that the brain is a central organ in understanding the full spectrum of substance use and disordered use. In fact, NIDA director Nora Volkow notes that addiction must be defined in terms of a brain disorder. Many addiction specialists agree with the explanation of addiction as a disease that is also equated with the current criteria for diagnosing a severe substance use disorder as described by addiction specialists:

> Addiction is defined as a chronic, relapsing brain disease that is characterized by compulsive drug seeking and use, despite harmful consequences. It is considered a brain disease because drugs change the brain—they change its structure and how it works. These brain changes can be long-lasting, and can lead to the harmful behaviors seen in people who abuse drugs. (NIDA, 2014, p. 5)

While the brain is a key organ involved in addiction, it is not the only factor that should be considered in enhancing our understanding of addiction and substance misuse. As shown in other risk factors contribute substantially toward improving our understanding. Research helps identify our genetic makeup; environments in our home, school, and community; in combination with the drug(s) used; and how they are used that affect brain function.

The Basics: The Brain

The human brain is an amazing organ that weighs a mere three pounds, yet it is responsible for operating hundreds of functions simultaneously in the human body. The origins of connecting the importance of the brain's work with how human beings function can be traced back 2,500 years. An important researcher, Alcmaeon of Croton, is noted for his revolutionary notions that "conscious experience originates in the stuff of the brain" (as cited in Schwartz & Begley, 2002, p. 23). Hippocrates is credited with placing additional attention on the brain, concluding "it is the brain that is the messenger to the understanding [and] the brain that interprets that understanding" (as cited in Schwartz & Begley, 2002, p. 23). Scientists add new knowledge about the brain each day. A basic understanding of brain science,

Figure 3.1 Risk Factors

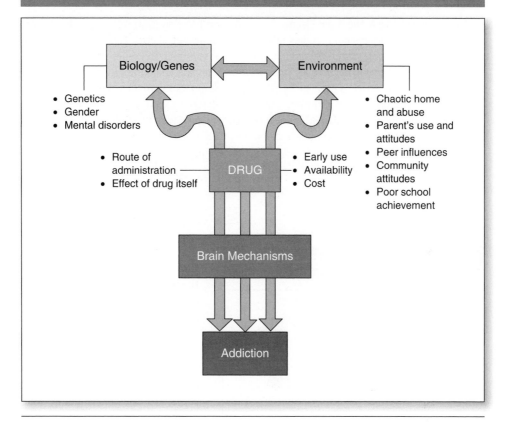

SOURCE: NIDA, 2014, p. 8.

therefore, adds to the professional helper's ability to provide effective care and is reviewed in this chapter.

Currently, brain researchers, also known as neuroscientists, document new findings that include *neurogenesis*, the brain's ability to generate new brain cells; *neuroplasticity*, the brain's ability to produce new functions and undergo a transformation involving "rewiring of the brain" (Schwartz & Begley, 2002, p. 15); and new brain imaging technology, such as positron emission tomography (PET) or functional magnetic resonance imaging (fMRI) scanning equipment, which allows neuroscientists to uniquely see into the living brain at work processing information, revealing the brain's electrical energy exchange in motion, and helping neuroscientists map the brain and how it functions. It is also important to delve into the newest foci in the field of helping and the brain: How can we help a person heal a brain that has been damaged by neurotoxic substances, stressors, genetics, or trauma?

Box 3.1: Brain Imaging Studies

A division of NIAAA, the Brain Electrophysiology and Imaging (BEI) section conducts both functional and structural brain-imaging studies related to alcoholism to better able look inside the living brain while under the influence of alcohol. For functional scanning, BEI relies on functional magnetic resonance imaging (fMRI) techniques and positron emission tomographic (PET) studies to work with human brains in action. Research by BEI also includes brain volume measurements using MRI as well as newer tools, such as diffusion tensor imaging (DTI). Exciting and amazing techniques, such as nuclear magnetic resonance (NMR) spectroscopy, are even able to study different brain metabolites. Newer studies using fMRI technology examines emotions, feelings, and motivational functions specifically pertaining to risky use and abuse. Pharmacological fMRI studies highlight research looking at ways alcohol is taken in by the body and the brain.

Figure 3.2 Neuron

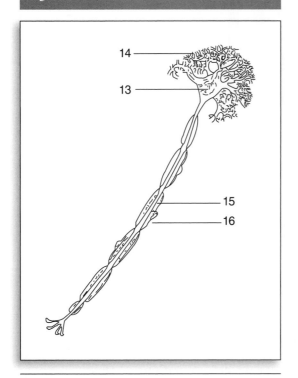

SOURCE: NIDA, 2015.

First, an overview of the brain can assist the substance abuse clinician to understand the importance of certain functions within the brain. Let's look at how the brain deals with information. One can examine the brain and see it is a powerful command center that is responsible for communication and coordinating literally billions of nerve cells—neurons—as an enormous volume of messages are constantly being sent throughout our bodies. Every nerve cell sends and receives this information by electrical pulsations that send the messages to the next nerve cell and then repeats the cycle to the next neuron. Each neuron connects with other neurons at a junction that is the empty space between neurons called the synapse (NIH, 2010). It is thought that one neuron forms at least 1,000 synapses with other nerve cells (NIH, 2010).

Each nerve cell is made up of three important structures. First, the cell body, shown in Figure 3.2 and labeled number 13, consists of the nucleus at the center of manufacturing (NINDS, 2015). Next, as indicated by number 14, dendrites are shown branching out just like tree branches and are critical for receiving messages from other neurons. The axon, labeled number 15, is like the trunk of the tree and is very involved in carrying a number of messages simultaneously

(NINDS, 2015). For example, instructions generated in the brain to operate our hearts, lungs, and blood flow are constant and automatic; we do not have to consciously remember to tell our lungs to inflate and then deflate as we breathe, on average, 15–20 respirations per minute. Our brains generate the messages using neurons to ensure that this happens on a consistent basis.

Addiction research scientists now know much more about the communication within the brain by looking at neurotransmission, especially examining the synapse—the open area where the electronic signal passes from the nerve cell to another nerve cell. Networks of these neurons (nerve cells) form to better handle the information traffic more efficiently.

Each neuron also constantly generates electrical energy to send and receive messages. In order to more efficiently send messages, for example, to breathe, the electrical

Figure 3.3 Neurotransmission Synapse

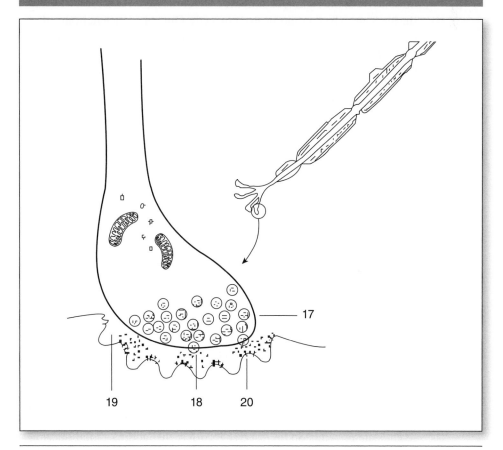

SOURCE: NIDA, 2012.

energy gets transportation help in the form of chemicals called neurotransmitters, shown in Figure 3.3 as number 18 (NINDS, 2015). A simplistic way of conceptualizing neurotransmitters might be to think of them like the fuel for our automobiles in our mobile culture—fuel in the vehicle helps us get where we are going faster, more efficiently, and more accurately than if we were traveling by pedaling a car like Fred Flintstone. The neurotransmitter serves a very important function in getting our messages transported efficiently by traveling down the axon into tiny sacs at the end of the axon (Figure 3.3, no. 17) that then release their contents (messages) into the synapse (Figure 3.3, no. 19), the gap at the end of the neuron where the message actually crosses over to another nerve cell (NINDS, 2015). Once the neurotransmitter begins to transport the important brain message, it is critical that it is able to deliver that message to the proper location—we want to keep breathing without having to think about it, so these receptors are vital to help all those billions of messages get to the right place. Brain messages need to get to a specialized location on each receiving brain cell, also called a receptor (Figure 3.3, no. 20). Many brain specialists equate this receptor that is accepting a message, for example, as a lock and key—the neurotransmitter (the key) must arrive at the right location, the correct receptor (lock for its message) in order for the message to be communicated correctly. Our very efficient brains then recycle those used neurotransmitters with chemical *transporters* that bring the used neurotransmitter back to the cell, thereby shutting off the electrical energy generated in the neuron since the message was delivered (NIDA, 2014). And remember, our brains have billions of neurons. The electrical activity and messages exchanged involve an amazing network of communication that allows us to breathe, run, see, move, touch, sense, talk, feel, and so much more. In addition, our precious neurons that are so important in all of our physical functioning are uniquely protected. The structure of a blood–brain barrier (BBB) is tightly constructed with endothelial cells to protect our neurons by keeping many substances out of the brain (BSCS, 2010). This important BBB is responsible for keeping toxins that can damage our cells away from the neurons in our brains. Drugs of abuse that penetrate the BBB have to be fat-soluble to be able to penetrate the barrier to affect our brain cells and neurotransmission (BSCS, 2010).

The Basics: Euphoria-Seeking Altered States

Individuals are often described as being "hard-wired" to seek an altered state. That altered state may range from a state of relaxation, stimulation, distraction, competition, or contemplation. Human beings over the centuries are known to have engaged in the pursuit of an altered state and for many, that occurs without harmful consequences or damage to brain functioning. Much has been written about achieving various states of enlightenment that are part of many individual's aspirations and dreams. Weil (2014) writes about observing young children who seek altered states as a natural activity. Activities such as twirling until dizzy, running fast, or laughing hard enough to cause belly pain are just a few examples of how humans, even at the earliest ages, seek a different state of being. Some researchers argue that adding mood-altering substances or mood-altering processes such as running a marathon or winning at the racetrack are part of the natural progression of seeking altered states. The experience of euphoria is often pleasant and brings about changes in one's mood that many people find rewarding. Much of the chemical effect is experienced in one major organ, the brain. Many people remain puzzled as to why only a limited percentage of individuals develop the brain disorder of addiction. Research into evidence-based neuroscience to explore addiction and its effect on the brain is a later focus in this chapter. Next, we examine a number of the commonly abused drugs that individuals use to seek euphoria.

Chemicals: Alcohol and Other Drugs

As can be seen in the Commonly Abused Drugs chart in Table 3.1 (NIDA, 2012), various drugs in 10 different categories have been used for decades as a way to experience euphoria and to achieve the desired effects. In the case of drugs that were originally prescribed to treat a medical condition such as opiates for extreme pain, the associated experience of euphoria may be an incidental secondary effect that later becomes the primary desired effect. Additional focus will highlight various drugs of abuse throughout the text, but growing concerns also include behaviors that are increasingly seen as addictive processes. In addition to mood-altering drugs, a number of processes are also associated with euphoria and are purported to lead to nonsubstance-related disorders, also called process or behavioral addictions, for a certain percentage of individuals. Next, process addictions will be reviewed with a focus on brain research.

Process Addictions: Gambling, Online Gaming, Sex, and Food

Debates remain within the addictions counseling professional field regarding the prevalence of process or behavioral addictions such as gambling disorders, sexual addiction, online gaming disorders, or food addictions (Kor, Fogel, Reid, & Potenza, 2013; Sussman & Sussman, 2011). For the purposes of clarity and consistency in this debate, the term process addiction will be used in this text to describe non-chemical addictions. Increasingly, more neuroscience points out that the brain chemistry and functioning seen in process addictions are similar to that which occurs in drug addiction (Ahmed, Guillem, & Vandaele, 2013). In addition, firsthand accounts and personal stories from gambling addicts, for example, emphasize the "high" that is often experienced in placing a bet or playing slot machines at a casino. Other accounts describe gambling as an addiction that is much worse to recover from than heroin addiction (Lee, 2005). In the most recent diagnostic manual, the *Diagnostic and Statistical Manual of Mental Disorders* (*DSM-5*), gambling is classified for the first time within the Substance-Related and Addictive Disorder category (American Psychiatric Association [APA], 2013). Closely related to gambling is online, or Internet, gaming, another process addiction often considered within the technology addiction umbrella. At present, the *DSM-5* highlights consideration for future inclusion of an Internet gaming disorder and suggests related diagnostic criteria that closely resembles addictive-use disorder symptoms; however, at this time there is no approved category

Table 3.1 Commonly Abused Drugs

NIDA NATIONAL INSTITUTE ON DRUG ABUSE

Commonly Abused Drugs
Visit NIDA at www.drugabuse.gov

National Institutes of Health
U.S. Department of Health and Human Services
NIH...Turning Discovery Into Health

Substances: Category and Name	Examples of Commercial and Street Names	DEA Schedule*/How Administered**	Acute Effects/Health Risks
Tobacco			
Nicotine	Found in cigarettes, cigars, bidis, and smokeless tobacco (snuff, spit tobacco, chew)	Not scheduled/smoked, snorted, chewed	*Increased blood pressure and heart rate/chronic lung disease; cardiovascular disease; stroke; cancers of the mouth, pharynx, larynx, esophagus, stomach, pancreas, cervix, kidney, bladder, and acute myeloid leukemia; adverse pregnancy outcomes; addiction*
Alcohol			
Alcohol (ethyl alcohol)	Found in liquor, beer, and wine	Not scheduled/swallowed	*In low doses, euphoria, mild stimulation, relaxation, lowered inhibitions; in higher doses, drowsiness, slurred speech, nausea, emotional volatility, loss of coordination, visual distortions, impaired memory, sexual dysfunction, loss of consciousness/increased risk of injuries, violence, fetal damage (in pregnant women); depression; neurologic deficits; hypertension; liver and heart disease; addiction; fatal overdose*
Cannabinoids			
Marijuana	Blunt, dope, ganja, grass, herb, joint, bud, Mary Jane, pot, reefer, green, trees, smoke, sinsemilla, skunk, weed	I/smoked, swallowed	*Euphoria; relaxation; slowed reaction time; distorted sensory perception; impaired balance and coordination; increased heart rate and appetite; impaired learning, memory; anxiety; panic attacks; psychosis/cough; frequent respiratory infections; possible mental health decline; addiction*
Hashish	Boom, gangster, hash, hash oil, hemp	I/smoked, swallowed	
Opioids			
Heroin	*Diacetylmorphine:* smack, horse, brown sugar, dope, H, junk, skag, skunk, white horse, China white; cheese (with OTC cold medicine and antihistamine)	I/injected, smoked, snorted	*Euphoria; drowsiness; impaired coordination; dizziness; confusion; nausea; sedation; feeling of heaviness in the body; slowed or arrested breathing/constipation; endocarditis; hepatitis; HIV; addiction; fatal overdose*
Opium	*Laudanum, paregoric:* big O, black stuff, block, gum, hop	II, III, V/swallowed, smoked	
Stimulants			
Cocaine	Cocaine hydrochloride: blow, bump, C, candy, Charlie, coke, crack, flake, rock, snow, toot	II/snorted, smoked, injected	*Increased heart rate, blood pressure, body temperature, metabolism; feelings of exhilaration; increased energy, mental alertness; tremors; reduced appetite; irritability; anxiety; panic; paranoia; violent behavior; psychosis/weight loss; insomnia; cardiac or cardiovascular complications; stroke; seizures; addiction*
Amphetamine	*Biphetamine, Dexedrine:* bennies, black beauties, crosses, hearts, LA turnaround, speed, truck drivers, uppers	II/swallowed, snorted, smoked, injected	*Also, for cocaine*—nasal damage from snorting
Methamphetamine	*Desoxyn:* meth, ice, crank, chalk, crystal, fire, glass, go fast, speed	II/swallowed, snorted, smoked, injected	*Also, for methamphetamine*—severe dental problems
Club Drugs			
MDMA (methylenedioxymethamphetamine)	Ecstasy, Adam, clarity, Eve, lover's speed, peace, uppers	I/swallowed, snorted, injected	*MDMA—mild hallucinogenic effects; increased tactile sensitivity, empathic feelings; lowered inhibition; anxiety; chills; sweating; teeth clenching; muscle cramping; sleep disturbances; depression; impaired memory; hyperthermia; addiction*
Flunitrazepam***	*Rohypnol:* forget-me pill, Mexican Valium, R2, roach, Roche, roofies, roofinol, rope, rophies	IV/swallowed, snorted	*Flunitrazepam—sedation; muscle relaxation; confusion; memory loss; dizziness; impaired coordination/addiction*
GHB***	*Gamma-hydroxybutyrate:* G, Georgia home boy, grievous bodily harm, liquid ecstasy, soap, scoop, goop, liquid X	I/swallowed	*GHB—drowsiness; nausea; headache; disorientation; loss of coordination; memory loss/ unconsciousness; seizures; coma*
Dissociative Drugs			
Ketamine	*Ketalar SV:* cat Valium, K, Special K, vitamin K	III/injected, snorted, smoked	*Feelings of being separate from one's body and environment; impaired motor function/anxiety; tremors; numbness; memory loss; nausea*
PCP and analogs	*Phencyclidine:* angel dust, boat, hog, love boat, peace pill	I, II/swallowed, smoked, injected	*Also, for ketamine—analgesia; impaired memory; delirium; respiratory depression and arrest; death*
Salvia divinorum	*Salvia, Shepherdess's Herb, Maria Pastora, magic mint, Sally-D*	Not scheduled/chewed, swallowed, smoked	*Also, for PCP and analogs—analgesia; psychosis; aggression; violence; slurred speech; loss of coordination; hallucinations*
Dextromethorphan (DXM)	Found in some cough and cold medications: Robotripping, Robo, Triple C	Not scheduled/swallowed	*Also, for DXM—euphoria; slurred speech; confusion; dizziness; distorted visual perceptions*
Hallucinogens			
LSD	*Lysergic acid diethylamide:* acid, blotter, cubes, microdot, yellow sunshine, blue heaven	I/swallowed, absorbed through mouth tissues	*Altered states of perception and feeling; hallucinations; nausea*
Mescaline	Buttons, cactus, mesc, peyote	I/swallowed, smoked	*Also, for LSD and mescaline—increased body temperature, heart rate, blood pressure; loss of appetite; sweating; sleeplessness; numbness; dizziness; weakness; tremors; impulsive behavior; rapid shifts in emotion*
Psilocybin	Magic mushrooms, purple passion, shrooms, little smoke	I/swallowed	*Also, for LSD—Flashbacks, Hallucinogen Persisting Perception Disorder*
			Also, for psilocybin—nervousness; paranoia; panic
Other Compounds			
Anabolic steroids	*Anadrol, Oxandrin, Durabolin, Depo-Testosterone, Equipoise:* roids, juice, gym candy, pumpers	III/injected, swallowed, applied to skin	*Steroids—no intoxication effects/hypertension; blood clotting and cholesterol changes; liver cysts; hostility and aggression; acne; in adolescents—premature stoppage of growth; in males—prostate cancer, reduced sperm production, shrunken testicles, breast enlargement; in females—menstrual irregularities, development of beard and other masculine characteristics*
Inhalants	Solvents (paint thinners, gasoline, glues); gases (butane, propane, aerosol propellants, nitrous oxide); nitrites (isoamyl, isobutyl, cyclohexyl); laughing gas, poppers, snappers, whippets	Not scheduled/inhaled through nose or mouth	*Inhalants (varies by chemical)—stimulation; loss of inhibition; headache; nausea or vomiting; slurred speech; loss of motor coordination; wheezing/cramps; muscle weakness; depression; memory impairment; damage to cardiovascular and nervous systems; unconsciousness; sudden death*

SOURCE: National Institute on Drug Abuse (NIDA). (2012). *Commonly abused drugs.* Retrieved from https://www.drugabuse.gov/sites/default/files/cadchart.pdf

for an Internet gaming disorder (APA, 2013). Of note, the massively multiplayer online role-playing games (MMORPGs) are considered prominent in online gaming and concern increases for addictive properties in these online games involving large numbers of players (Hsu, Wen, & Wu, 2009). Additional attention is being given to proposing a new term, technology addiction, that encompasses compulsive and obsessive use in online gaming, Internet, social media, and other technological devices (Acosta, Lainas, & Veach, 2013). Efforts to understand addictive components and brain implications continue to stress the importance of clarity and treatment implications for those who suffer from gambling and online gaming losses.

Another area of focus in process addictions involves sexual addiction. Healthy experiences with sexual acts and orgasms, for example, often produce euphoria and are considered to be a beneficial part of being human. However, for those individuals who self-identify as sex addicts, there are accounts of obsessive and compulsive sexual acts accompanied by increasingly negative consequences, such as reports of physical injury or criminal arrests related to illegal sexual activities, such as indecent exposure (Sexaholics Anonymous, Inc., 2001). Increasingly, terminology related to sexual addiction and compulsivity include the term hypersexuality (Politis et al., 2013). Recent brain research with Parkinson's disease patients and hypersexual behaviors conducted by Politis and colleagues (2013) may also help addiction professionals begin to better understand specific areas of the brain that are involved in sexual compulsivity and addictive patterns. In essence, brain-imaging study findings show pronounced sexually disinhibited behaviors and brain activity in the ventral striatum, cingulate, and also the orbitofrontal cortex area when the individual is on dopamine-type medicines commonly used in treating Parkinson's disease (Politis et al., 2013). It can be further underscored, with substantial implications for addictive disorders particularly, that drugs that target the neurotransmitter dopamine may change the circuitry in the cerebral cortex in such a way that compulsive sexual behaviors begin to occur that had not previously occurred. Important research findings, such as those described, continue to add substantial support that when the brain changes, increases in risky and addictive use or processes such as compulsive sexual behaviors may be more likely to occur due to the measurable changes in brain functioning and chemistry (Voon et al., 2014). Moreover, counselors can help educate their clients in knowledge that clarifies why the addict behaves in ways that are often counter to the person's values and beliefs due to substantial brain changes associated with addiction.

Last, in the brief overview of prominent process addictions and key brain research, the area of food addiction is examined. Increased research attention explores popular and anecdotal terms used to describe compulsive, obsessive, and impairing behaviors that involve food as a process addiction (Ahmed et al., 2013; Clark & Saules, 2013; Gearhardt, White, Masheb, & Grilo, 2013; Sinha & Jastrehoff, 2013). Findings in research studies suggest, for example, that sugar causes a release in neurotransmitters associated with the euphoria-producing results similar to mood-altering drugs. Ahmed and colleagues continue examining addictive qualities in sugar and other foods with high fat and sugar (2013). Many experts continue to grapple with the addictive process in eating patterns (National Eating Disorders Association, 2014). Binge eating disorder (BED) is an example of the challenges in understanding food addiction. In the most recent *DSM-5*, it is clear that this new diagnostic classification, BED, lists symptoms that are also seen in substance use disorders such as compulsivity, obsessiveness, and loss of control over bingeing patterns, yet BED is not listed in the category containing addiction disorders (APA, 2013).

Other areas of concern pertaining to process addictions include workaholism, compulsive shopping, compulsive exercising, or self-injurious/cutting behaviors, to name only a few. Extensive research in the next decade promises to help counselors advance the neuroscience of process addictions and more effective ways to provide clinical care. Examining key areas of neuroscience and addiction to better equip the counselor is addressed in the following section as we explore more evidence-based neural information.

Evidence-Based Practice

Recent Discoveries

Reward Pathway

Some scholars view the brain disorder of addiction basically as disrupted neurotransmissions that occur between neurotransmitters and receptors. Other neuroscientists examine the basic structure of the brain. Early in addiction brain research, scientists believed they had identified the key area of the brain responsible for addictive behavior, the pleasure center, or limbic system (NIDA, 2014). Much attention was given to help clinicians understand the basic actions of the limbic system when mood-altering substances crossed the BBB. It was widely touted in the early 1990s in many addiction treatment settings that the key to understanding addiction was revealed in understanding the mechanisms of the limbic system in response to drugs like heroin, cocaine, marijuana, and alcohol, for example. It was clearly documented that a flood of one particular type of feel-good neurotransmitters, dopamine, was released in abundance, which causes euphoria, or in the vernacular, a high, when these drugs were consumed and then present in the brain.

To better understand how drugs can have such a profound effect on the brain, it is valuable to consider that the chemical structure of many drugs of abuse have very similar chemical structure to our naturally occurring brain chemicals that help alleviate pain, for example, or help stimulate energy production (NIDA, 2014). Next, scientists point out that drugs of abuse primarily act on the brain's reward circuitry, increasing the specific neurotransmitter dopamine in larger than normal amounts. Dopamine, remember, is considered to be one of the principle neurotransmitters to create feelings of well-being and the euphoric experiences associated with mood-altering drugs of abuse. Figure 3.4 illustrates the major reward pathway in the brain and the importance of the neurotransmitter dopamine.

To further explain this action in the brain, one must consider the individual who takes a mood-altering substance into the body. The substance can be any of the

Figure 3.4 Reward Pathway

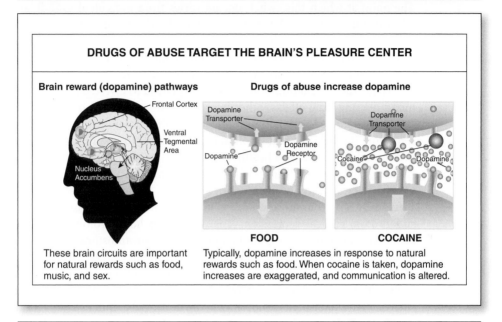

DRUGS OF ABUSE TARGET THE BRAIN'S PLEASURE CENTER

Brain reward (dopamine) pathways

Frontal Cortex
Ventral Tegmental Area
Nucleus Accumbens

These brain circuits are important for natural rewards such as food, music, and sex.

Drugs of abuse increase dopamine

Dopamine Transporter
Dopamine
Dopamine Receptor

FOOD

Dopamine Transporter
Cocaine
Dopamine

COCAINE

Typically, dopamine increases in response to natural rewards such as food. When cocaine is taken, dopamine increases are exaggerated, and communication is altered.

SOURCE: NIDA, 2014, p.18.

mood-altering chemicals including alcohol, heroin, cocaine, marijuana, prescribed pain relievers, or anti-anxiety medications—the brain does not differentiate whether it is legal, illegal, prescribed, or purchased in some back alley or reputable pharmacy (Kühn & Gallinat, 2011). Once the mood-altering chemical crosses into the brain, many actions occur. Dopamine is released in larger than normal quantities, upward of 2 to 10 times the amount released in natural functioning (NIDA, 2014). This extra dopamine delivers an overwhelming number of messages via the receptor cells to unlock a flood of pleasurable sensations (NIDA, 2014). In a simplistic explanation, this abundance of dopamine bathes the brain in a powerful neurotransmitter that signals many other neurons to get excited, thus bringing about a cascade of well-being, superior sensations of joy, relaxation, empowerment, confidence, strength, and many other pleasurable sensations that comprise euphoria. For the first-time user, these sensations can result in a positive association with the chemical and a return to the use of it. Certain mood-altering drugs and the amount taken can influence the amount of dopamine released and thus, the amount of pleasure experienced for any user. One does not have to be addicted to activate the brain's response to the presence of mood-altering drugs. Many individuals who misuse drugs, including alcohol or prescription drugs, do so in an effort to seek the euphoric effects of the chemicals. Unfortunately, we have not identified ways to determine which brains will develop an addictive response to these mood-altering drugs since it is known that not all individuals who use mood-altering drugs become addicted.

Brain studies show that the difference for those who develop an addictive disorder is much like a figurative "switch" in the brain that "flips" at some point (NIH, 2005). The point at which this switch occurs varies from individual to individual, but "the effect of this change is the transformation of a drug abuser to a drug addict" (NIH, 2005, p. 5). Early research examined ways to interrupt that release of dopamine to counteract the euphoric effects of the mood-altering drugs, experimenting with ways to try to reset the switch to counter the addictive cycle.

While substantial time and foci were expended to investigate the limbic system and mood-altering drug effects, other neurotransmitters were also identified in substance use, misuse, and addiction. One of those identified as an important neurotransmitter is serotonin. It is believed that serotonin is responsible for many other good feelings, positive moods, appetite, and healthy sleep patterns (National Institute of Mental Health [NIMH], 2014). Other studies show a clear connection of clinical depression in those who have lower than normal levels of serotonin. Many antidepressants are made to act specifically on serotonin receptors to increase amounts of serotonin in the brain if one suffers from clinical depression. It is yet unclear how serotonin might influence the addictive cycle. Glutamate is another important neurotransmitter being studied to learn its role in the addictive cycle and damage to the brain (NIDA, 2014).

Moreover, neuroscientists now know that in addition to the dopamine and serotonin effects in our limbic system—the pleasure center, certain mood-altering drugs such as PCP can also block not only neurotransmitters but also key receptor sites that act to stop important brain messages from getting messages through to the receptor, thus changing the brain's chemistry and messages that might be trying to say "stop," or "that is enough of that drug." Cocaine is another drug that also blocks and alters the transporting of important information back to the releasing neuron (NIH, 2005), thereby causing major disruption to the brain's normal functioning. Cocaine and methamphetamine, both classified as stimulants, "can cause the neurons to release abnormally large amounts of natural neurotransmitters or prevent the normal recycling . . . this disruption produces a greatly amplified message, ultimately disrupting communication channels" (NIDA, 2014, p. 17). Brain damage, including damage to important receptors, is particularly seen with prolonged abuse of methamphetamine.

For researchers to get a closer look at the importance of receptors by looking at opiates, for example, they know that there are certain specialized receptors in the brain that work to naturally help an individual cope with pain. Again, think of a keyhole in a door as a brain receptor. The unique keyhole will only work when the correct key is used to turn the lock. The specialized keyhole, such as an opiate-specific brain receptor, varies considerably in the "shape" and "size" in the brain. We also have naturally occurring types of pain blockers, or keys, in our brains, called endorphins. Our brains literally make these pain-relieving key chemicals, endorphins, naturally as a response to coping with pain. These special receptors, or keyholes, work to accept natural endorphins when we are in pain from an injured arm, for example. However, the brain is conservative and only makes enough endorphins and specialized receptors to help us cope with the pain. Opiates such as heroin, morphine, or prescription pain relievers are able to also use these same specialized receptors to unlock messages in our body to cope with pain. The brain does not differentiate the naturally produced endorphins from the synthetic, manufactured opiates. The heightened risk associated with the use of opiates for pain management can lead to the specialized receptors being used repeatedly, thereby disrupting the pain response and providing ways for the individual to become accustomed to increasing amounts of opiates in an effort to try to achieve baseline functioning to feel normal; thus, due to unnatural overuse of the specialized receptors, for the addict the euphoria is never as intense as it is during early use of the drug. In addition, with continued use, or more importantly misuse, the receptors' normal conservative functioning is compromised and it ceases operation with important neurotransmitters such as in dopamine suppression. These opiate receptors thus become damaged and overly dependent on opiates. Scientists have named the specialized receptor sites delta, mu, and kappa receptors (NIH, 2005). In addition to the understanding of the limbic system, receptors, and the reward pathway, yet another pathway relevant to understanding addiction has been identified in newer neuroscience research.

Inhibitory Pathway

In addition to the concept of the reward pathway, research findings now suggest another important brain pathway that may be central to understanding the aspect of loss of control, obsessive and compulsive features that are hallmarks of severe substance use disorders (Morein-Zamir & Robbins, 2014). This additional pathway is described as the inhibitory pathway. Described in layman's terms, something structural is wrong with the brain that prevents the regulation of overuse; both rodent and human research suggest important findings regarding the brain's architectural inhibitory malfunction (Morein-Zamir & Robbins, 2014). If we turn back to the analogy of an automobile to analyze the inhibitory pathway of the brain that malfunctions, one can see that if the addicted brain was an automobile, we would say that there was something wrong with the braking system of the vehicle. At first it seems to be an intermittent problem with some random incidences of braking problems, then increasingly, there is complete brake failure that results in no stopping. It is thought that the usual components in the brain that regulate use of mood-altering substances for many users do not operate in a typical manner any longer and are not able to stop the use with reliability or predictability. Other types of obsessive-compulsive behaviors and impulse-control disorders such as obsessive-compulsive disorder are also possibly related to malfunctions in this inhibitory pathway. Neurobiologists suggest the prefrontal cortex (PFC), the orbitofrontal cortex (OFC), and the anterior cingulate cortex (ACC) comprise the inhibitory pathway (Feil et al., 2010). One major analysis of multiple dominant research studies that examine brain biology and addiction found that "preliminary studies provide consistent evidence of a relationship between prolonged drug administration, neuroadaptations of the PFC (specifically the three PFC-striatothalamic circuits, the DLPFC [dorsolateral prefrontal cortex], OFC and ACC), and the persistence of drug-seeking behaviors" (Feil et al., 2010, p. 270).

The brain and receptor sites are not limited to opiates and their effects. In addition, we have been able to identify other mood-altering drug actions in various parts of the brain. Table 3.2 briefly highlights some of the important neural discoveries thus far.

Table 3.2 Select Drugs and Brain Effects

Drug	Brain Actions	Associated Effects
Marijuana	Cannabinoid and anandamide receptors; Cerebellum (balance, posture, and coordination movement); Hippocampus (memory, short- and long-term memory); Sensory cortex (visual and depth perception); amygdala (emotions and stress response); adolescent brain-development problems, specifically damaged neural connections and lower number of neural fibers in precuneus (brain area in charge of awareness and synthesizing information), fimbria (brain area important for learning and memory), and prefrontal cortex (PFC) also involved in inhibiting behaviors. (Volkow, Baler, Compton, & Weiss, 2014)	Alters areas of the brain responsible for memory, coordination, thought, concentration, time and depth perception, less ability to determine risk and behave in risk-averse manner due to prefrontal cortex damage, particularly problematic for adolescents. Lower IQ if frequent marijuana use begins in adolescence and continues into adulthood.
Cocaine	Prevents reabsorption of dopamine back into neuron, which causes a build-up of dopamine in the brain; fewer dopamine receptors available in the brain; blocks reuptake of serotonin and norepinephrine; prefrontal cortex and amygdala damage.	Strong cravings, memory, mood swings; eventual severe cocaine use disorder can lead to paranoid psychosis, tactile hallucinations.
Alcohol	Scattershot effect on a number of areas of the brain; dopamine surges further disrupt neurotransmissions, overwhelm the dopaminergic system and receptors; other neurotransmitters such as sertonin and glutamate are disrupted. Volkow and Baler (2013) found studies detecting "relapsers show increased atrophy in bilateral orbitofrontal cortex and in the right medial prefrontal cortex and ACC, brain areas associated with error monitoring" (p. 663).	Severe alcohol use disorder in advanced stage brain damage can be as severe as Alzheimer's patient and can lead to dementia—some estimate approximately 10 million alcoholics show brain damage to a detectable degree (Oscar-Berman & Marinkovic, 2003).

Drug	Brain Actions	Associated Effects
Hallucin-ogens: LSD, MDMA (Ecstasy), Molly	Serotonin receptors (help in normal brain functioning); depletion of serotonin levels (Inciardi & McElrath, 2011)	Visual, auditory, and tactile hallucinations; at times, severe mood swings; sleep problems; severe anxiety; confusion; or depression.
Metham-phetamine	Dopamine (chemically similar) production; cell death particularly in frontal cortex, amygdala, and striatum (movement center); mycaglia cells die; cell regeneration damaged for over 1 year after ceasing meth use.	Semipermanent loss of dopamine even after years of discontinuing use; 2013 studies show brain impairment continues long after stopping meth use (NIDA, 2013).

Addiction and Brain Challenges

Developing Brain in Youth

Much attention has also been given to brain development in youth. In the area of substance abuse and risky use, there are particular worries about the use of drugs by adolescents. The brain undergoes such radical development during adolescence that it is particularly vulnerable to mood-altering substances (Volkow et al., 2014). For the addiction specialist working with youth, we provide a number of resources in this chapter that can aid understanding about brain functions and how drugs affect the young brain. Counselors working in treatment settings may also want to utilize selected resources due to the accessibility of the material at no cost. In particular, the National Institutes of Health (NIH) Curriculum Supplement Series for Grades 9–12 has up-to-date teaching materials, online materials, lesson planning, handouts, and complete modules to supplement instruction to optimize understanding the brain and addiction (NIH, 2010).

Many neuroscientists agree that new brain cells develop, hone, and create important neural pathways during adolescence. In fact, research shows that the brain continues rapid development well into an individual's twenties (Gogtay et al., 2004). Previously, the period of substantial brain development was thought to decrease notably by adolescence. Yet, science has clearly confirmed that drugs change how neurons behave and communicate important information (NIH, 2010). Once again, the area of the brain called the prefrontal cortex (PFC) is key: "the part of the brain associated with higher level cognitive functions such as judgment, decision making, long-term planning and impulse control—the prefrontal cortex—undergoes dramatic changes that allow the brain to develop into a fully matured state" (CASAColumbia, 2011, p. 12). As noted earlier, the PFC includes important inhibitory, braking, and regulating circuitry in the brain and is key to developing better judgment, refusal skills, moderating behaviors, and improved future goal-planning (CASAColumbia, 2011). In light of the key architectural building of the brain circuitry that is crucial in the adolescent years, it is particularly important for counselors working with youth to understand the risks associated with experimental and risky use during the teen and younger years. What others have incorrectly deemed as a passing phase may inadvertently be contributing to marked brain changes. Note the importance of how casual use of drugs by teens, for example, can cause changes in just one of the important neurotransmitters:

> "For teens who continue to use these substances, the pleasure associated with the dopamine release that results from the ingestion of an addictive substance can become overvalued by the brain over time to the point where the value of most other natural rewards fade in comparison." (CASAColumbia, 2011, p. 14)

In other words, activities that were previously enjoyable increasingly fade from the teen's routine, replaced by the artificial euphoria from mood-altering substances or processes—online gaming, for example. The importance of the role of the counselor in educating teens and families about the brain's role in substance use cannot be stressed enough. One recent study reported that substance use disorders were considered by the vast majority "as a problem of willpower or self control (62.9 percent of students and 53.8 percent of parents)" as compared to only one-third of those surveyed identifying substance use disorders as a physical or mental illness (CASAColumbia, 2011, p. 14).

Other neurological research findings substantiated detectable brain damage to key areas of memory, learning, executive functioning, and synthesizing information in marijuana-smoking adults who began frequent marijuana use in adolescence, especially when compared with adults who had not smoked marijuana in their adolescence (Volkow et al., 2014). Further studies strongly suggest an increased vulnerability for developing various addictions in the regular marijuana adolescent user due in part to dopamine regulation problems. Moreover, tetrahydrocannabinol (THC) "can prime the brain for enhanced responses to other drugs" (Volkow et al., 2014, p. 2221). Notably, the concentration of THC in marijuana has increased from approximately 3% in the 1980s to over 12% as reported in 2013 (Mixed Signals: The Administration's Policy on Marijuana, Part Four, 2014). In essence, the more study given about the young brain and the impact of mood-altering drugs, the greater the concerns.

Gender and Brain Research

Only recently has attention turned to gender differences in the brain pertaining to use of mood-altering substances. With improved technology, recent studies suggest that female brains react differently to alcohol, for example. Studies suggest that the female brain suffers greater damage from abusing alcohol than is seen in the male brains (Fahlke et al., 2012). A groundbreaking study determined that women with alcohol dependence who consumed alcohol at volumes similar to alcoholic men had similar disruption in brain chemistry yet had significantly less time of heavy drinking—an average of 4 years for women but 14 years for men (Fahlke et al., 2012). Newer findings confirm further that women often experience more damaging effects from alcohol in a shorter period of time. More research into the female brain's response to risky use of mood-altering substances is needed.

Future Directions

Neuroplasticity and Generating New Brain Cells

Research done in the late 1990s that looked at the brain's capacity to basically rewire injured areas revealed encouraging findings. One finding led to new revelations that suggest the uninjured parts of the brain were being used to compensate when areas of the brain had been injured, such as occurs with a stroke. Moreover, therapies aimed at reusing weakened areas of the body impacted by a stroke could be drastically helped. One remarkable area of treatment showed "a marked enhancement in the cortical areas that become active during movement of an affected limb . . . the brain had recruited healthy motor cortex tissue in the cause of restoring movement to the stroke-affected hand" (Schwartz & Begley, 2002, p. 194). What had been seen as permanently set in the brain was now viewed as cross-modal functional plasticity, meaning that the brain could retrain and take on new functions in parts of the brain previously thought to be hard-wired (Schwartz & Begley, 2002). The implications of neuroplasticity for many individuals who suffer from brain disorders, then, was nothing short of miraculous. For the substance abuse and addiction field, new hope was generated in "seeing evidence of the brain's ability to remake itself throughout adult life, not only in response to outside stimuli but even in response to directed mental effort" (Schwartz & Begley, 2002, p. 223). These findings provide new directions for recovery-oriented research and treatment due to the prevalent defining feature of addiction, a brain disorder.

Restoring Brain Health

Different medications have been tried in attempts to alter the high, reduce the brain's response, and prevent the reinforcing effect of the euphoria. When harm-reduction methods such as methadone were developed it was with this key attention to altering or dampening the high experienced in the limbic system of the brain, often referred to as drug agonists. Medications that functioned as antagonists were also developed in an effort to completely block euphoric effects. Antagonists such as Naltrexone or Naloxone continue to be used, often reverse opiate overdoses, and have shown utility in other recovery efforts. Researchers and addiction clinicians believed this lack of a high would reduce drug-seeking behaviors, cravings, and related criminal behaviors, thus reducing harm to the individual, loved ones, and communities. Since the mid-1990s, public health officials in the United States expressed urgent calls for scientifically based harm-reduction policies and programs, such as had been developed in Europe and Australia (Des Jarlais, 1995). Increasing attention to brain functions and drug responses continue to add important research evidence that a scientific approach to developing harm-reduction alternatives benefits the public health. Now, recommendations written 20 years ago for our public health and addiction professionals continue to have these yet unaccomplished goals to take "current botanical, chemical, and neuroscience methods . . . to produce safer products than those currently available, both licit and illicit" (Des Jarlais, 1995, p. 11). In current treatment principles of effective treatment, research indicates that combining newer medication-assisted therapies with addiction-specific counseling is optimal (NIDA, 2014). Medications with beneficial support toward recovery include Naltrexone and Acamprosate for alcohol addiction, Methadone and Buprenorphine for opioid addiction, or Bupropion and Varenicline for nicotine addiction (NIDA, 2014).

Individuals who suffer from addictive disorders often benefit from current knowledge that explains how addiction is classified as a brain disorder; therefore, addiction and substance abuse-helping professionals need to understand basics of neuroscience in order to communicate effectively the advances made in this important area of research and counseling.

Sources available for free at NIAAA, NIDA, SAMHSA, and NINDS are all valuable educational resources that can be made readily available for psycho-educational tools that the addiction specialist can use to help increase understanding and reduce shame with individuals who seek help for risky use, problematic illicit use, and the chronic debilitating disease of addiction.

Skills in Action

Box 3.2: Case Illustration: How Does the Counselor Explain About the Brain?

Case Study

This is my first time ever talking with a counselor, but I am here because I just graduated from college where I jokingly tell people that I majored in partying where I got all As. I really decided I would slow down on my partying, especially my drinking, after graduation. So I have really been working on just that. But here's what I do not understand. I tell myself I am only going to have two beers and then switch to Diet Sprite and stay with that the rest of the night. So I get a Sprite, then find that just one more beer would be okay, then I lose count and spend the rest of that night drinking way more than I promised myself. Please help explain what is going on with me. I am a smart person and I just cannot figure this out.

As an addiction counselor, how would you explain what is happening in your client's brain if you have diagnosed a severe alcohol use disorder? How does your counseling response change if you consider multicultural factors such as age, gender, ethnic/racial identity, and so on?

Experiential Skills Learning Activity

1. Explore the resources in the Sara Bellum Blog found online at http://teens.drugabuse .gov/blog and discuss at least four ways counselors can use the information seen in the blog.

2. Act as if you are the addiction counselor explaining the brain and substance use. Practice at least two different ways of explaining how the brain works when mood-altering drugs are taken. Have an observer review both ways and provide feedback to you about the strengths of each practice session. Consider video and audio recording your explanations; review these recordings with the following questions to guide you.

   a. Are your explanations clear? Are you using terms that your client understands? Would you change your explanation for a different age client? Different gender client? Different education background of the client? Different drug being used by your client? Different pattern of use by your client, for example, a risky drinker as compared to an opiate addict who is using drugs intravenously?

   b. Do you have any visual materials that you are using to illustrate your explanations? If not, where could you go to find free materials? (Hint: Online resources might be found in the website list at the end of this chapter.)

   c. Is your explanation too short? Too long? Are you lecturing or preaching at the client? Are you giving enough time for questions by the client?

   d. What is your plan if you are asked something and you do not have an answer?

Consider practicing this explanation on a regular basis to improve your ability to be clear to your clients. If you reject the need to explain this to clients, explore your reluctance. How confident are you in providing information about the brain and its role to your clients? Explore your concerns with addiction professionals.

3. Interview at least two addiction counseling specialists to learn about their views of the brain and substance use, misuse, and disorders.

4. Take the quiz at the end of this section to review your brain knowledge.

Quiz: Brain and Addiction

These materials are produced by the National Institute on Drug Abuse, National Institutes of Health. They are in the public domain and may be reproduced without permission.

Instructions: See **Facts on Drugs: Brain and Addiction** on the *NIDA for Teens* website (http://teens.drugabuse.gov/), then take this short to test. (NIDA, 2012. Retrieved from https://www.poehealth.org/wp-content/uploads/2012/03/Brain-Addiction-Quiz.pd.)

1. The human brain weighs about as much as a _____.
   a) doughnut
   b) 12-pack of soda
   c) Chihuahua

2. Neurons in the brain communicate with each other by _____.
   a) passing axons
   b) releasing chemicals
   c) instant messaging

3. When you do something you enjoy, like watch a good movie, your _____ system gets activated.
   a) limbic
   b) digestive
   c) nervous

4. When someone uses drugs repeatedly, their brain _____.
   a) becomes trained to crave the drug
   b) becomes smaller than before
   c) is not changed

5. After a prolonged period of drug abuse, the brain_____.
   a) needs less drug to get the same effect
   b) needs more drug to get the same effect
   c) experiences increasing amounts of dopamine

6. The brain's reward system is part of the _____.
   a) sensory cortex
   b) limbic system
   c) spinal cord

7. Brain cells or neurons turn electrical impulses into _____.
   a) chemical signals
   b) movement
   c) axons

8. Drugs work in the brain because they have similar _____
   a) electrical charges as brain cells
   b) size and shape as natural brain chemicals
   c) nerve cells as the brain

9. Drugs of abuse create intense feelings because they _____.

   a) depress the nervous system

   b) shut off receptors in the occipital lobe

   c) cause a rise in dopamine in the limbic system

10. Drug abusers develop "tolerance" for drugs, meaning they need _____.

    a) more drug to get the same effect

    b) less drug to get the same effect

    c) neither A or B

Answer Key: Brain and Addiction Quiz

1. **C:** The human brain weighs about 3 pounds, about the size of a Chihuahua. A doughnut only weighs a few ounces, and a 12-pack of soda weighs 9 pounds.

2. **B:** The transfer of a message from one neuron to another occurs by releasing chemicals called neurotransmitters into the spaces called synapses between the neurons. The axon is the long, threadlike fiber that transmits the message.

3. **A:** The "reward" system is part of the limbic system, which gets activated when you do something you like. Dopamine is a brain chemical that is released, producing feelings of pleasure and letting you know that something important is happening.

4. **A:** The brain is wired to remember feelings of pleasure, including those produced by drugs unnaturally. The brain then strives to repeat those feelings, which the drug user experiences as a craving for the drug.

5. **B:** At first, drug use may cause floods of dopamine. But prolonged drug abuse causes the brain's dopamine levels to decrease. That means the brain might need more of the drug just to get the dopamine levels back to normal and even more to produce the high that it craves.

6. **B:** The limbic system is involved in emotions, learning and memory, and other functions necessary for survival. The reward circuit is part of the limbic system and is activated by pleasurable activities, such as hanging out with friends and by drugs of abuse.

7. **A:** A message travels down a neuron as an electrical impulse. To pass the message to another neuron, the electrical impulse triggers the chemical signals called neurotransmitters, which flow into the synapse (the gap between the two neurons) and trigger an electrical impulse in the next neuron. Axons are the branches of a neuron that release the neurotransmitter.

8. **B:** Drugs "fool" the brain because they are similar in size and shape to the natural brain chemicals called neurotransmitters.

9. **C:** Drugs of abuse cause the brain's limbic system to release dopamine, the neurotransmitter that produces feelings of pleasure.

10. **A:** Drug tolerance results in people needing more and more of the same drug to get the same effect because, over time, drugs can cause the brain to produce less dopamine, the neurotransmitter that produces feelings of pleasure. Drug abusers may need more of the drug than before to reach the same level of dopamine to get the same "high."

RESOURCES FOR FURTHER LEARNING

International Congress on Technology Addiction

www.technologyaddiction.org/en

National Clearinghouse for Alcohol and Drug Information (NCADI)

www.addiction.com/a-z/samhsas-national-clearinghouse-for-alcohol-and-drug-information/

National Council on Alcoholism and Drug Dependence, Inc. (NCADD)

www.ncadd.org

National Institute on Alcohol Abuse and Alcoholism (NIAAA)

www.niaaa.nih.gov

National Eating Disorders Association

www.nationaleatingdisorders.org

National Institute on Drug Abuse (NIDA)

www.drugabuse.gov

Resources for teachers and teens at NIDA

http://teens.drugabuse.gov/educators/lesson-plans-and-materials

National Institute of Neurological Disorders and Stroke (NINDS)

www.ninds.nih.gov

Office of National Drug Control Policy (ONDCP)

www.whitehousedrugpolicy.gov

Substance Abuse and Mental Health Services Administration (SAMSHA), Department of Health and Human Services

www.samhsa.gov

For website interactive tools, go to http://science.education.nih.gov/supplements/nih2/ addiction/default.htm for views of brain-imaging tools depicting varying brain activity.

REFERENCES

Acosta, K. M., Lainas, H., & Veach, L. J. (2013). An emerging trend: Becoming aware of technology addiction. *NC Perspectives, 8*, 5–11.

Ahmed, S. H., Guillem, K., & Vandaele, Y. (2013). Sugar addiction: Pushing the drug-sugar analogy to the limit. *Current Opinion in Clinical Nutrition and Metabolic Care, 16*, 434–439.

American Psychiatric Association (APA). (2013). *Diagnostic and statistical manual of mental disorders* (5th ed.). Washington, DC: Author.

BSCS. (2010). *The brain: Understanding neurobiology through the study of addiction* (NIH Pub. No. 09-4871). Retrieved from http://science.education.nih.gov/supplements/nih2/Addiction/guide/pdfs/Entire.pdf

CASAColumbia. (2011). *Adolescent substance use: American's #1 public health problem.* Retrieved from http://www.casacolumbia.org/addiction-research/reports/adolescent-substance-use

Clark, S. M., & Saules, K. K. (2013). Validation of the Yale Food Addiction Scale among a weight-loss surgery population. *Eating Behaviors, 14*, 216–219.

Des Jarlais, D. C. (1995). Harm reduction: A framework for incorporating science into drug policy. *American Journal of Public Health, 85*, 10–12.

Fahlke, C., Berggren, U., Berglund, K. J., Zetterberg, H., Biennow, K., Engel, J. A., & Balldin, J. (2012). Neuroendocrine assessment of serotonergic, dopaminergic, and noradrenergic functions in alcohol-dependent individuals. *Alcoholism: Clinical & Experimental Research, 36*, 97–103. doi:10.1111/j.1530-0277.2011.01598.x

Feil, J., Sheppard, D., Fitzgerald, P. B., Yucel, M., Lubman, D. I., & Bradshaw, J. L. (2010). Addiction, compulsive drug seeking, and the role of frontostriatal mechanisms in regulating inhibitory control. *Neuroscience and Biobehavioral Reviews, 35*, 248–275.

Gearhardt, A. N., White, M. A., Masheb, R. M., & Grilo, C. M. (2013). An examination of food addiction in a racially diverse sample of obese patients with binge eating disorder in primary care settings. *Comprehensive Psychiatry, 54*, 500–505.

Gogtay, N., Giedd, J. N., Lusk, L., Hayashi, K. M., Greenstein, D., Vaitucis, A. C., . . . Thompson, P. N. (2004). Dynamic mapping of human cortical development during childhood through early adulthood. *Proceedings of the National Academy of Sciences, USA, 101*, 8174–8179. doi:10.1073/pnas.0402680101

Hsu, S., Wen, M., & Wu, M. (2009). Exploring user experiences as predictors of MMORPG addiction. *Computers & Education, 53*(3), 990–999. doi:10.1016/j.compedu.2009.05.016

Inciardi, J. A., & McElrath, K. (2011). The evolution of drug taking and drug seeking in America. In J. A. Inciardi & K. McElrath (Eds.), *The American drug scene: An anthology* (6th ed., pp. 4–27). New York, NY: Oxford Press.

Kor, A., Fogel, Y. A., Reid, R. C., & Potenza, M. N. (2013). Should hypersexual disorder be classified as a sexual addiction? *Sexual Compulsivity & Disorders: Treatment and Prevention Journal, 40*, 27–47.

Kühn, S., & Gallinat, J. (2011). Common biology of craving across legal and illegal drugs–a quantitative meta-analysis of cue-reactivity brain response. *European Journal of Neuroscience, 33*(7), 1318–1326.

Lee, B. (2005). *Born to lose: Memoirs of a compulsive gambler.* Center City, MN: Hazelden.

Mixed signals: The administration's policy on marijuana, part four: Hearings before the Subcommittee on Government Operations of the House Committee on Oversight and Government Reform, 113th Cong. (2014).

Morein-Zamir, S., & Robbins, T. W. (2014). Fronto-striatal circuits in response-inhibition: Relevance to addiction. *Brain Research.* Retrieved from http://www.sciencedirect.com/science/article/pii/S0006899314011998

National Eating Disorders Association. (2014). Retrieved from http://www.nationaleatingdisorders.org

National Institute of Mental Health (NIMH). (2014). *Brain basics.* Retrieved from http://www.nimh.nih.gov/health/educational-resources/brain-basics/brain-basics.shtml

National Institute of Neurological Disorders and Stroke (NINDS). (2015). *Brain basics: Know your brain.* (NIH Publication No. 11_3440a). Retrieved from http://www.ninds.nih.gov/disorders/brain_basics/know_your_brain.htm?css=print#Image%207

National Institutes of Health (NIH). (2005). *Mind over matter: Teacher's guide.* (NIH Publication No. 05-3592). Retrieved from http://www.drugabuse.gov/publications/mind-over-matter/teachers-guide

National Institutes of Health (NIH). (2010). *The brain: Understanding neurobiology through the study of addiction.* (NIH Publication No. 09-4871). Washington, DC: Author.

National Institute on Drug Abuse (NIDA). (2012). *Commonly abused drugs.* Retrieved from https://www .drugabuse.gov/sites/default/files/cadchart.pdf

National Institute on Drug Abuse (NIDA). (2013). *Methamphetamine.* Retrieved from https://www.drugabuse .gov/publications/research-reports/methamphetamine

National Institute on Drug Abuse (NIDA). (2014). *Drugs, brains, and behavior: The science of addiction (Revised).* (NIH Pub. No. 14-5605). Rockville, MD: Author.

Oscar-Berman, M., & Marinkovic, K. (2003). *Alcoholism and the brain: An overview.* Retrieved from http://pubs .niaaa.nih.gov/publications/arh27-2/125-133.pdf

Politis, M., Loane, C., Wu, K., O'Sullivan, S. S., Woodhead, Z., Kiferle, L., . . . Piccini, P. (2013). Neural response to visual sexual cues in dopamine treatment-linked hypersexuality in Parkinson's disease. *Brain, 136,* 400–411. doi:10.1093/brain/aws326

Schwartz, J. M., & Begley, S. (2002). *The mind and the brain: Neuroplasticity and the power of mental force.* New York, NY: HarperCollins.

Sexaholics Anonymous, Inc. (2001). *What is a sexaholic and what is sexual sobriety?* Retrieved from http://www .sa.org/sexaholic.php

Sinha, R., & Jastrehoff, A. M. (2013). Stress as a common risk factor for obesity and addiction. *Biological Psychiatry, 73,* 827–835.

Sussman, S., & Sussman, A. N. (2011). Considering the definition of addiction. *International Journal of Environmental Research and Public Health, 8,* 4025–4038. doi:10.3390/ijerph8104025

Volkow, N. D., & Baler, R. D. (2013). Brain imaging biomarkers to predict relapse in alcohol addiction. *JAMA Psychiatry, 70,* 661–663.

Volkow, N. D., Baler, R. D., Compton, W. M., & Weiss, S. R. B. (2014). Adverse health effects of marijuana use. *The New England Journal of Medicine, 370,* 2219–2227.

Voon, V., Mole, T. B., Banca, P., Porter, L., Morris, L., Mitchell, S., Lapa, T. R., . . . Irvine, M. (2014). Neural correlates of sexual cue reactivity in individuals with and without compulsive sexual behaviours. *PLoS ONE.* doi:10.1371/journal.pone.0102419

Weil, A. (2014). *Why people take drugs.* In J. A. Inciardi & K. McElrath (Eds.), *The American drug scene: Readings in a global context* (7th ed., pp. 72–80). New York, NY: Oxford Press.

4

Experimentation and Seeking Altered States

❖

LEARNING OBJECTIVES

Upon completion of this chapter, the reader will be able to

- understand and describe the factors related to seeking altered mental states;
- demonstrate the ability to search for prevention programs; and
- describe the importance of protective factors in prevention work.

Knowledge

Social and Cultural Factors

Seeking Altered States

Chapter 3 outlines the brain's response to mood-altering substances, and this chapter examines other factors that influence the use of substances in the pursuit of altered states of being. Drug use has long been studied to better understand why the human condition seems hard-wired to seek mood-altering states, particularly euphoria, or in the current vernacular, getting high. It is also clear that a "drug-free" society is not realistic and has not ever existed (Hart, Ksir, & Ray, 2009). Evidence in archeology shows that substances have been used for religious, social, academic, economic, political, or medical purposes from the early days of mankind in every society (Aines, 2012; McGovern, 2009; Smith, 2008). Speculation and scientific analysis of the earliest artifacts show an important role for one drug—alcohol: dietary benefits include hunger suppressant, extra calories converting to fat, and a way to withstand the harsh demands of survival. McGovern, a foremost biomolecular archeological authority on alcohol, notes that artifacts suggest fermented beverages, such as grog, were available as early as 100,000 B.P. as early man was migrating out of Africa (2009). It follows that early man used fermented beverages to add to "social rituals that bring the community together, artwork that symbolizes the working of the mind and nature, and religious rituals that give human experience meaning and coherence" (McGovern, 2009, p. 22). Important spiritual rituals and the use of mood-altering substances were regulated in accordance with the reverence shown rather than being used for hedonistic purposes (Guerra-Doce, 2014). Further, records indicate wine was valued over beer by Greek, Chinese, Egyptian, and Roman societies (Aines, 2012).

The *Urban Dictionary* (Get high, n.d.), a popular U.S. web-based dictionary with definitions of slang terms created by readers, lists at least 20 words that relate to getting high, such as blazed, stoned, wasted, ripped, drunk, toking, toasted, getting ill, baked, or lit. It can be said that the majority of descriptors of a euphoric mood are often negative in connotation and are normally looked upon as an experience to avoid. For example, the words blazed, toasted, or lit normally connote an experience related to burning, which, as it relates to the human condition, is usually painful, yet, when related to euphoria as caused by mood-altering drugs, is generally seen in terms that connote a euphoric experience. And often, the more extreme the descriptor, the more profound the euphoria, such as getting totally toasted is equated with an exceptional euphoric mood. The positive descriptors attribute endorsement by those who are describing their euphoric experience. Group norms and peer pressure to experiment with euphoria-producing drugs are often influenced by language that is reflective of a drug-seeking culture.

National findings further examine first-time user, or initiate, trends and patterns to better forecast prevention and treatment planning, and in 2013, an important survey that began to be used in 1971, the National Survey on Drug Use and Health (NSDUH), indicated that by far, marijuana is the most frequently reported illicit drug of first use (70.6%), with nonmedical use of prescription drugs as the next most frequent illicit drug of experimentation (SAMHSA, 2014).

To get a better understanding of American patterns of experimentation, consider additional findings from SAMHSA's *2013 National Survey on Drug Use and Health*. For example, from 2013 data it is estimated that every day in the United States there is an average of 12,500 new drinkers and 7,800 new users of other addictive drugs; these results are also similar to figures for 2012 (SAMHSA, 2014). Findings list important statistics for first-time use of illicit drugs such as marijuana or prescription drugs used in non-prescribed ways. For a majority of first users of illicit drugs excluding alcohol (representing approximately 2.4 million individuals), the chosen drug is marijuana. Additionally, one-fifth of new addictive drug users (representing approximately 1.5 million individuals) used prescription medications in non-prescribed ways, primarily taking medicines for pain relief (SAMHSA, 2014), which has also been identified as a gateway to the use of the highly addictive opiate heroin (NIDA, 2015). Another drug of first use, inhalants, is selected by approximately 6% of first users. Of the remaining drugs surveyed, hallucinogens such as bath salts or ecstasy are first used by approximately 2.6% of first users. Lower use is attributed to drugs such as cocaine (601,000 first users), crack cocaine (53,000 first users), and heroin (169,000 first users). However, when alcohol first use is included, alcohol consistently remains higher than the other substances described, with an estimated 4.6 million first-time users, nearly twice the number of first-time marijuana users (SAMHSA, 2014).

Further, for youth aged 12–17, the survey findings show ongoing use as shown in estimated patterns, such as almost 9% of youth currently use illicit drugs, approximately 7% currently smoke marijuana (the most abused substance other than alcohol), and slightly more than 2% use prescription medications in a nonmedical manner; other drugs, such as hallucinogens, inhalants, cocaine, and heroin, are used by less than 1% of youth aged 12–17 (SAMHSA, 2014).

Cigarette smoking continues to decline for first-time users, yet overall numbers yield continued concern because of the estimated 2.1 million first-time smokers. It is noted that tobacco use by youth remains an important predictor of alcohol and marijuana misuse (Van Ryzin, Fosco, & Dishion, 2012). Another important survey in 2013 of American youth, "Monitoring the Future," asked about electronic cigarette use (also referred to as e-cigarettes) for the first time in national surveys, and found a much higher rate of reported recent use by 8.7% of eighth graders, 16.2% of 10th graders, and 17.1% of senior high school students smoking e-cigarettes within the recent month (NIDA, 2014). Of greater concern in these 2013 findings from senior high school students is that only 14.2% of youth surveyed indicated that e-cigarettes are harmful, even though e-cigarette use can involve nicotine, and the health consequences of e-cigarettes are far from known. Smoking a hookah also showed increasing use by high school seniors by nearly 23% (NIDA, 2014). Prevention researchers note that any substance use before the age of 17 is a compelling predictor of more misuse and even dependence in later years (Van Ryzin et al., 2012). Other prevention research regarding substance use by youth in America cites heightened public health concerns and concludes that "risky substance use is a major public health problem that can be ameliorated through evidence-based public health measures, including education about the disease and its risk factors, screenings, and clinical interventions" (Feinstein, Richter, & Foster, 2012, p. 431). In summary, it is clear that experimentation with mood-altering substances is evident in American culture and prompts curiosity as to factors that contribute to experimentation.

What social and cultural factors seem to propel a user into seeking an altered state? Thombs (2006) highlights four main influences in American culture that contribute to seeking altered states. The first, and perhaps the most important, suggests that the experience of interacting with others is eased when one is in an altered state. Since humans are considered social beings, any experiences that contribute to socialization and social interaction would be valued. A second influence cited by Thombs is connected to experiences of when one is in an altered state that can allow the alcohol or other drug user to "provide a release from normal social obligations" (p. 232). This can relate to a relaxing, for example, of the acute awareness of parenting roles and responsibilities when the parent is under the influence of a mood-altering substance. The substance may make it easier for the individual to forget or be less aware of role obligations and expectations, thus enhancing the attraction to experiencing an altered state. Advertising campaigns seem to use this connection, for example, when advertising a loosening of one's role obligations and social expectations. Catchy campaigns from Las Vegas come to mind with the adage "What happens in Vegas, stays in Vegas," suggesting that the usual social role expectations may lead to behavior that would be embarrassing in normal social circles in one's hometown. Thombs notes a third outcome of altered states that also influences group cohesion within the group. Group identity can be further seen with groups that choose not to drink or abstain, conversely, those who drink heavily might also adopt a group identity related to heavy drinkers. The social identification with the group may continue to influence patterns around seeking altered states. Thombs concludes that the use of mood-altering substances can serve as a way to reject the social and cultural mores by the dominant group, especially the middle class. More emphasis can then be placed on hedonism, freedom from responsibilities, and an overall rejection of values perpetuated by the American middle class.

When one explores certain mood-altering substances, alcohol again leads the discussion primarily due to its prolific use in mainstream America. Since trends were documented beginning in 1850 regarding the use of alcohol in the United States, beer has been the alcoholic beverage most prevalent and, overall, the general trend for 150 years shows that consumption of alcohol has remained steady at an approximate average of slightly over two gallons per person per year (Nephew, Williams, Stinson, Nguyen, & DuFour, 1999). According to the National Institute on Alcohol Abuse and Alcoholism (NIAAA), the leading national resource for professionals regarding research pertaining to alcohol, free publications, facts, and videos, as of 2012 nearly 90% of individuals 18 or older noted they had consumed alcohol at least once in their lifetime, 71% had done so in the recent year, and over half (56.3%) drank alcohol in the past month (2014).

For one to understand more about first experimentation with drugs, including alcohol, it may be helpful to examine additional data. The reporting year of 2013 looked at smaller age segments and found that 2.1% of individuals aged 12 or 13 reported current use of alcohol, 1.3% used prescription drugs for nonmedical reasons, 1% used marijuana, and 0.6% used inhalants (SAMHSA, 2014a). By the ages of 14 and 15, there is a notable increase in use trends: 5.8% used marijuana, 2.2% reported nonmedical use of prescription medications, 0.6% used inhalants, and 0.4% used hallucinogens (SAMHSA, 2014a). Reports from NIAAA (2014) show two out of five teens aged 15 have had at least one drink; 9.3 million youth aged 12 to 20 (approximately 24%) consumed alcohol within the recent month. Additional national survey findings report that between 2002 and 2013 there have been decreases in binge drinking frequencies from 28% in 2002, yet the numbers show an estimated 5.4 million young people aged 12 to 20 comprise the majority of binge drinkers (SAMHSA, 2014a). Perhaps of more concern for the helping professional are the creation of effective helping strategies in the area of treating substance use disorders for the estimated 15% of youth aged 12 to 20 who are engaged in binge drinking with almost equal distribution between males (16.5%) and females (14.0%). Of concern related to the incidence of addiction in youth is the unacceptably elevated rate of teens who need addiction care as compared with the approximately 6% who receive that care (Feinstein et al., 2012). As is highlighted in Chapter 3, the adolescent brain is still developing, and the use of alcohol, especially in binge patterns, can put the young person at additional risk to develop harmful substance use disorders with more alcohol-related complications in legal, educational, health, and family areas.

Box 4.1: Experimenting and Other High-Risk Behaviors: All-Terrain Vehicle Injury, Youth, and Underage Alcohol Use

In the United States, all-terrain vehicle (ATV) riding has increased dramatically in recent years. ATV-related injuries disproportionately involve youth. Approximately 25,000 youth under the age of 16 were treated in hospital departments, ranging from the emergency department to the trauma center in 2013 (U.S. Consumer Product Safety Commission [U.S. CPSC], 2015). In addition, since recordkeeping began in 1982, almost one-fourth of ATV-related fatalities occurred to those less than 16 years of age (U.S. CPSC, 2015). Other studies indicate that youth are twice as likely to be hospitalized for ATV injuries than youth injured in motor vehicle collisions (Shults, West, Rudd, & Helmkamp, 2013). Too many young children, often less than 6 years old, are injured by ATV riding, with the average age between 9 and 13 years (Hagopian, Burkhalter, & Foglia, 2014). A variety of factors contribute to the severe injuries, especially brain injuries, in youth riding ATVs, such as infrequent use of helmets, riding on pavement—which enables the ATV to travel at higher rates of speed, operating the ATV while underage (younger than 16 years of age), and the more powerful, recent model ATVs (Shults et al., 2013). However, by far, the use of alcohol in underage drinkers contributes significantly to ATV while fatalities in youth (Hall, Bixler, Helmkamp, Kraner, & Kaplan, 2009). The combination of an underdeveloped frontal cortex and executive functioning in the young developing brain to exercise good judgment, the all-powerful ATV machines, and the euphoric-producing use of alcohol create major risks for even the first-time underage drinker. Information and resources regarding safety with ATVs combined with facts about the effects of alcohol may help reduce the number of ATV and alcohol-related injuries and deaths in American youth.

SOURCE: Dr. Andrea Doud, MD, a pediatric surgeon, served as a fellow with the Childress Institute of Pediatric Trauma and completed her surgery residency at Wake Forest Baptist Medical Center.

Social Pressures: Theories

When one examines the long history of the use of mood-altering substances such as alcohol across the lifespan, one can begin to question and explore how these patterns of use have emerged. As long ago as the earliest Greek society, alcohol-related social behavior began to be addressed in legal proceedings. It is known, for instance, that

Plato, one of the leading Greek philosophers, established guidelines at professional gatherings to further ensure that social behavior would be best governed by a sober leader of the proceedings (Thombs, 2006). It seems no accident that sobriety in a social setting was important in ancient societies. Sociological theories such as the examination of marijuana use in the 1950s by Howard S. Becker (as cited in Hirsch, Conforti, & Graney, 2004) or the work that examines tobacco social rituals by Nichter (2004) stress the role of learning about pleasurable effects of substances as central to initiation and continued use, especially related to social influences. Other theories offer varying explanations as to the reason humans seek altered states. Weil (2014), for example, began writing in the 1980s that we are all innately driven from birth to seek altering experiences and feelings. He attributes this drive, even apparent in young children who enjoy twirling to the point of dizziness, to biological reasons that are not related to cultural or social reasons, and genetically related differences in sensation-seeking continue to be explored. For many, however, the dynamic research of social influences around initiating substance use is central to much of our understanding of concepts regarding peer, community, marketing, or family influences.

Theories abound about our social patterns and social development. When one reviews theories about the pursuit of altered states, one particular theory stands out: social learning theory. Prominent American theorist Albert Bandura developed his ideas about how people behave and learn, and how we do so in a social context (1977). His key concepts are that we learn through observation, we imitate role models, and that we self-observe; these concepts are attributed to many human behaviors, including why people begin to drink, use other drugs, or seek altered states. In essence, it is theorized that the person seeks an altered state because they have *learned* by observing others who seek and experience altered states. McGovern adds that the brain development in early man included the Broca's area, which contains "mirror neurons, which, as the phrase implies may record any action that we observe, and then call it up again, like a photograph, to imitate it" (2009, p. 23). A number of substance use specialists cite social learning theory as an important explanation for early use, continued use, and even addiction (Marlatt, 1985). Bandura further adds contributions to our understanding that yield a more developed theory, social cognitive theory, and its tenets continue to be tested and inform a vast variety of helping professionals and specialists.

Social cognitive theory constructs, including self-efficacy, explain how people learn, particularly when knowledge is combined with observational learning and repeated actions (behavior) of the observed task; Bandura posits that "self-efficacy" or a sense of mastery is the desired result. McLernen (2014) notes that the same principles can apply to risky behaviors such as aggressive driving. One example related to experimental use of mood-altering substances is to observe people in a social setting who are using mood-altering substances such as alcohol, followed by the observer then experimenting with alcohol and experiencing euphoria. This leads one to believe that they have mastered drinking behaviors. For example, social cognitive theory suggests that risky drinking without an adverse outcome, such as having an accident, likely results in increased self-efficacy related to future drinking, which leads to repeated actions of risky drinking amid heightened self-efficacy. A resource of the National Library of Medicine, the Consumer Health Informatics Research Resource (CHIRr) offers an in-depth explanation of the importance of the concept of self-efficacy (2013). In social cognitive theory, further definition of the concept of self-efficacy and its prominent role in understanding health issues is provided. To clarify the term, Bandura (2007) defined self-efficacy as a

> belief in what *someone can do* with whatever resources one can muster—rather than with what *someone has.* Individuals are not asked to rate the *abilities they possess,* but rather the strength of their assurance they *can execute* given activities. (p. 646)

Self-efficacy, then, has become an important area to examine. As Jenkins (2014) notes, it can be vital in promoting health behaviors with adolescents. Information from CHIRr (2013) points out that self-efficacy is an important measure to determine effective health-promotion strategies and offers numerous examples. One example is noted regarding optimizing the U.S. health care system, particularly suggesting the importance of self-efficacy for traumatized individuals who believe they can recover from traumas due to natural disasters, terrorism, military combat, or assaults (Benight & Bandura, 2004; Rimal, Lapinski, Cook, & Real, 2005). The complicated duality of self-efficacy can also result in greater risk-taking, thus leading to behavior that can be detrimental to health (Livingstone, Haddon, & Gorzig, 2012; Llewellyn, Sanchez, Asghar, & Jones, 2008). More research with adolescents could help clinicians better understand the concept of self-efficacy, which can foster healthy behaviors such as deferring substance misuse and experimentation.

Particularly in the work of prevention of alcohol and other drug experimentation by underage youth, the concepts of social cognitive theory are useful to understand why individuals begin to use mood-altering substances. Most substance abuse specialists agree that approximately 70% of adults in the United States drink alcohol in some manner, which provides the most common model of those who use mood-altering substances.

Social Pressures: Peer, Family, and Community Influences

It is important to focus on social and cultural influences to see how drinking adults can have a substantial impact on individuals who view alcohol use as a socially acceptable behavior. If one considers social cognitive theory and observational learning, one can more easily understand how observing adults who consume alcohol could be a behavior to emulate and engage. Marketing and advertising efforts, particularly as reflected in alcohol pricing, further demonstrate the power of modeling socially promoted use of alcohol. Powerful influences of selling alcohol are noted in multiple studies that show that young people are particularly vulnerable to advertising that shows risky behaviors, likable animal characters, and elevated social status that consequently shape more favorable attitudes toward purchasing and consuming alcohol (CASAColumbia, 2011; Center on Alcohol Marketing and Youth [CAMY], 2008; Feinstein et al., 2012). Further data analyzed from 2006 indicate that for every ad seen by youth, an additional 1% of drinking was estimated (Snyder, Milici, Slater, Sun, & Strizhakova, 2006). Other researchers' findings suggest that if alcohol advertising was banned, approximately 7.609 young lives would be saved annually from alcohol-related deaths (Hollingworth et al., 2006). Even the presence of a greater number of stores selling alcohol or tobacco products has been associated with increased risks of smoking and drinking (CASAColumbia, 2011).

Many advocates have called on the alcohol industry to greatly decrease advertising when underage youth are in the market (CAMY, 2008). One report highlighted a rate of nearly one-quarter of television ads that promote alcohol were violating the voluntary alcohol industry standards established to decrease alcohol advertising when programs have young audiences (Parsons, 2013). Newer findings underscore the power of advertising, as Ross and colleagues (2014) point out in their study, along with 14 other long-term studies (Samuels, 2015) that show a strong pattern in underage drinkers who consume alcohol brands advertised on television programs popular with a young audience as compared with drinking alcohol brands not advertised. Additional research shows that increased drinking by youth is associated when more alcohol advertising exists (Snyder et al., 2006). However, the Federal Trade Commission (FTC) in its latest report highlights alcohol sales of nearly $60 billion in 2011 for the 14 major alcohol companies, which accounts for nearly 80% of all alcohol sold in the United States (FTC, 2014). Moreover, these 14 major alcohol companies spent considerably less on traditional marketing in 2011 than in 2008, but substantially more alcohol advertising dollars, nearly 8% of the total advertising budget, were spent on digital and online advertising in 2011 (4 times greater than in 2005) for a total of $3.45 billion for all alcohol advertising combined (FTC, 2014). Accounting of alcohol advertising dollars expended "noted that in 2006, the alcohol industry still ran ads on 14 of the 15 television shows most popular with teens, according to a CAMY analysis: 1,722 ads at a cost of more than $8.7 million" (CAMY, 2008, p. 4).

It is further interesting to note that only 2.9% of the total advertising dollars spent in 2011 were allocated to "social responsibility programs and messages," such as designated driver or underage drinking reduction campaigns, whereas nearly one-third of the advertising dollars were spent in sports often involving youth (FTC, 2014). National 2013 findings indicate further decreasing trends with regard to prevention messages: 72.6% of 12- to 17-year-old youth indicated that they had seen or heard drug or alcohol prevention messages from community sources other than schools. This finding was much lower than in 2002 (83.2%), and even 1 year prior, in 2012 (75.9%) (SAMHSA, 2014). Whereas the FTC has continued to monitor alcohol advertising to youth and reports improved data for the 14 major companies that produce and market alcohol, there remains substantial effort needed to better understand links among alcohol marketing, prevention messages, and underage drinking.

Additional social pressures in the community as examined by Xu and Chaloupka (2011) outline multiple studies that demonstrate clear impacts on use and abuse of alcohol related strongly to the pricing of alcoholic beverages. The review of major research found that "studies have reported consistent evidence that higher prices (and/or taxes) of alcoholic beverages are negatively associated with adverse consequences of drinking" (Xu & Chaloupka, 2011, p. 242). Further, more studies found that federal and state taxes on alcohol are well below other taxed categories and "had little impact on public policy, with the Federal Government and most State governments allowing the inflation-adjusted value of their alcoholic beverage taxes to fall as demonstrated by the infrequent and modest increases in these taxes" (p. 242). Conversely, if taxes were increased, such as has been done with cigarettes, and if they were more in line with expected taxation, a pronounced reduction in harmful use would be evident (Xu & Chaloupka, 2011). In addition, the reduction of use is especially noted in teens and young adults when prices for alcohol are higher, as shown in multiple studies, yet U.S. policy does not reflect this clear evidence (Xu & Chaloupka, 2011).

Additional examination of media exposure to drugs other than alcohol has yet to be fully explored. For example, it remains unclear about the impact of increased advertising of prescription medications on the patterns of first nonmedical use of prescription drugs. Mainstream America has seen a substantial increase in the number of television and print ads for various prescription drugs. How much these ads influence our social acceptance of prescription medications has yet to be fully explored. The modeling of improved health and enhanced well-being as described in advertising prescribed medications may be depicting models of prescription medications that further normalize the taking of pills, whether they are mood-altering or not (Feinstein et al., 2012). Wider acceptance of the use of prescribed medications, less stigma associated with medications, and increased availability may combine to present a message that goes beyond the sale of the particular medicine being advertised. Van Zee (2009) highlights the aggressive marketing for opiate prescriptions; for example, OxyContin sales exceeded $1 billion in 2000 and by 2004 the drug was a major factor in alarming overdose deaths and accelerated addiction rates. Many current policies and prevention campaigns are underway in the United States to combat early experimentation and deter using prescription opiates to seek altered states; future decades will reveal if these public health initiatives can be as successful as past cigarette use campaigns to deter initial use.

It is also yet to be understood about the impact of media depiction of marijuana use and new legislation in various American states on influencing use of marijuana for first-time users. In national surveys there is evidence that points to more favorable attitudes toward marijuana in addition to less perceived harm related to marijuana use: In 2013, slightly over one-third of high school seniors had concerns about regular marijuana use as compared with responses 5 years previously, when over half of high school seniors indicated that regular marijuana use could put the user at greater risk (NIDA, 2014). It comes as no surprise then that national surveys see a pattern of increased use of substances like marijuana and prescription medications when data trends show less perception of harm when experimenting and regularly using these same substances. High school seniors, for example, have shown a decreasing perception of harm from smoking marijuana over the past 20-plus years. In 1991, nearly 80% of high school seniors indicated concern for harm; by 2014, that percentage showing concern had dropped to 36% (NIDA, 2014). Added to the heightened availability and legalizing trends in the United States, a different drug, synthetic marijuana, has been a formidable drug used experimentally, especially in the last decade. While marijuana is part of the name, few scientists find any marijuana contained in the drug. Conversely, the illegal drug is often a combination of random plant material often sprayed or treated with a chemical compound that does not contain marijuana or any of the active ingredients of cannabinoids, such as THC (tetrahydrocannabinol). The American Association of Poison Control Centers (AAPCC) notes poisoning alerts for synthetic marijuana, also known as spice or K2, began in 2009. Nearly 8,000 adverse events such as seizures, psychotic episodes, collapse, or deaths were reported in 2015 due to use of synthetic marijuana (AAPCC, 2016). In addition, poison alerts also exist for experimental drugs known as "bath salts," which also have nothing in common with soap or soaking products one might use in their bath (AAPCC, 2016). Again, chemical compounds that have euphoric properties in addition to unknown chemicals with adverse and unpredictable side effects, such as disturbing hallucinations that last for multiple days, are the main ingredients in bath salts and contribute to a vast array of drugs that are used to seek an altered state, particularly by youth.

Continued awareness within the substance abuse counseling community is an important part of our work to help our communities as we examine factors that lead to experimentation and the pursuit of altered states. Continued focus is also needed for other behaviors that can also contribute to seeking altered states, such as gambling.

Family Influences

The efforts of the researchers who conduct national surveys regarding alcohol and other drug use have expended considerable effort to try to understand the important risk and protective factors, especially when looking at patterns and influences of first-time users. Findings show encouraging trends when it comes to the influence of family on experimentation with alcohol and other drugs. Clearly, more research findings support the protective factors from parenting: "parental monitoring and family relationships are powerful platforms from which to create lasting suppressive effects on substance use in middle and high school" (Van Ryzin et al., 2012, p. 1321). In 2013 findings, it is clearly shown that a large majority of youth aged 12 to 17 (88.4%) knew that their parent(s) would strongly disapprove of their experimentation with marijuana, even if only experimenting once or twice (SAMHSA, 2014). Further, the findings go on to illuminate the strength of family influence since current marijuana use is greatly lower in youth who know of a disapproving stance by their parent(s) at 4.1% use of marijuana as compared with youth who did not indicate parental disapproval of marijuana experimentation at 29.3%. Further studies support these important parental influences, suggesting the quality of the family relationship has a substantial effect on a lower probability of substance misuse into the youth's high school years, even when examining the influence of problematic peer influence (Van Ryzin et al., 2012). An example from North Carolina shows results from a study conducted in 2014 commissioned by the North Carolina Alcohol Beverage Control Commission (NCABCC). Findings from parental input indicate "although 4 in 5 (84%) think underage drinking in their community is a problem, the plurality (47%) think it's only a minor problem" (NCABCC, 2014, p. 2), whereas students ranked underage drinking as a more urgent problem. Further, it was noted

> if parents think underage drinking in their community is a serious problem, the conversations are more common (frequently 41%, sometimes 46%, and rarely 13%) than among parents who think underage drinking in their community is only a minor problem (frequently 26%, sometimes 52%, and rarely 22%). (NCABCC, 2014, p. 2)

For another state perspective, we can look at a recent North Carolina report regarding a state comparison to the national findings. Each state's report can be searched at the SAMHSA.gov website. From the report for North Carolina, we can see, for example, that individuals aged 12 or older are receiving treatment for alcohol abuse issues with similar findings as in the United States. Chapter 3 outlines the brain's response to mood-altering substances, and this chapter examines other factors that influence the use of substances in the pursuit of altered states of being. Unfortunately, 91.3% did not receive the needed treatment in North Carolina and only 9% received the necessary alcohol use treatment (SAMHSA, 2013).

When cigarette smoking influences from parents are examined, not only is the effect of the role model influential on youth behaviors with first use of cigarettes, the physical effects are increasingly seen in the negative effects of secondhand smoke. One recent study, for example, notes a pronounced increase in youth affected by attention deficit hyperactive disorder if they were in homes with secondhand smoke (Padron et al., 2015).

Gender Influences and Altered States

Recent studies began to focus on gender considerations and use of mood-altering substances to seek altered states. A number of researchers who observe alcohol use, for example, see a narrowing of the gap between genders in terms of current use (Wilsnack, Wilsnack, & Kantor, 2013). Briggs (2016) notes a growing concern with the prevalence in risky drinking patterns of women as she points out that in the

1980s there were approximately five alcoholic men for every alcoholic woman; however, in the 1990s that ratio changed to an alarming 2.5 alcoholic men for every alcoholic woman. Further, national trends as reflected in SAMHSA surveys indicate early drinking behaviors for youth aged 12 to 17 mirror increasing trends of use by females: alcohol use is currently slightly higher for young females (11.9%) than for males (11.2%) (2014). In terms of other illicit use of substances, survey results show young boys (aged 12 to 17) use illegal drugs other than alcohol at slightly higher rates than young girls (9.6% for young males, 8% for young girls) yet reported addiction rates for both genders in that age range are the same at just over 5% (SAMHSA, 2014). Patterns of consumption of alcohol in 2013, for example, showed that nearly 57% of males aged 12 or older were considered current drinkers (having had at least one alcoholic beverage within the past month), which was slightly higher than the rate of females, which indicated that nearly half were considered current drinkers (SAMHSA, 2014).

Women and fetuses are at particular risk if the mother drinks when pregnant; new studies highlight risks even for women trying to conceive who drink or use other mood-altering substances. For example, a 1996 report indicated that there were approximately 0.5 to 3.0 cases of fetal alcohol syndrome per 1,000 births in the United States; recent reports have adjusted the prevalence of alcohol-related complications and birth defects upward to two to seven cases per 1,000, with an even broader range for fetal alcohol spectrum disorders at 20 to 50 cases per 1,000 births (NIAAA, 2014). National findings show a prevalence of just over 9% of pregnant women who report current alcohol use; alarmingly 2.3% report binge drinking patterns, and 0.4% report heavy drinking (SAMHSA, 2014). Increasingly, studies point to patterns of drinking prior to pregnancy may be linked to drinking during pregnancy; this is especially noted with binge drinking pre-pregnancy, as binge patterns of consumption are known to be linked to heavier drinking during pregnancy (Skagerstrom, Chang, & Nielsen, 2011; Wilsnack et al., 2013).

Cultural Influences

Examination of national trends shows a pattern of use of alcohol predominantly by white Americans more than any other racial or ethnic group. For individuals aged 12 or older, almost 60% of whites reported current use of alcohol, whereas slightly over 40% of blacks or Hispanics reported current use, 38% of Native Hawaiians or Other Pacific Islanders, 37% of American Indians or Alaskan natives, and 34% of Asian individuals reported current alcohol use (SAMHSA, 2014). More research is needed to add to our knowledge of cultural influences upon substance use initiation and experimentation. Clark, Doyle, and Clincy (2013) found that biracial youth, for example, showed differences in initiation use patterns. White-Asian biracial youth were found to start marijuana use and risky alcohol use at much younger ages than whites; additionally, rates of first use were greater for all substances when one examines rates of first use by Asian youth.

School Influences

The percentage of school-enrolled youths who report that they had seen or heard prevention messages at school also declined during this period, from 78.8% in 2002 to 73.5% in 2013 (CASAColumbia, 2011). The prevalence of past-month illicit drug use in 2013 was lower among youth who reported having such exposure to prevention messages compared with youth who did not have such exposure. One survey notes that school personnel also contributed to mixed messages about use of addictive substances, especially by teens. The findings highlight that teachers "generally view binge drinking as more dangerous than the misuse of controlled prescription drugs which, in turn, is seen as more risky than marijuana use" (CASAColumbia, 2011, p. 67). It goes on to describe responses from teachers who indicate that of all the concerns in schools, and ranking the top three concerns, only 46% of teachers would include preventing alcohol use in the top three; only 27.5% would put prevention of illicit drug use excluding marijuana in the top three; only 25.2% would identify prevention of marijuana use in the top three concerns; only 15.7% would identify prevention of cigarette smoking in the top three concerns; and only 4.5% would include prevention of prescription drug misuse in the top three concerns (CASAColumbia, 2011).

Other Influences and College Youth

Some literature suggests that youth in first experimentation with mood-altering substances are more inclined to experiment if they experience self-perceived social or personal failures. Certain affective education approaches that try to equip the individual with other success-oriented experiences, it is believed, will help offset the experience of failure, thus thwarting a quest for mood-altering experiences (Hart & Ksir, 2012). A college professor when writing about young college students drinking to excess commented,

> You think it's a coincidence that it's in college that most Americans do their most serious falling-down drinking and drugging . . . those naked boys hanging upside down out of their frat house's windows on Friday night are simply trying to get a few hours' escape from the stuff that any decent college has forced them to think about all week. (Wallace, 1998, p. 27)

Goodman (2014) offers further lessons about drinking to intoxication by college students; in essence, much can be learned from looking back into earliest writings such as *The Bacchae*, which depicts a young man struggling with the Greek god of wine, Dionysus, and intoxication, control, and power: "Euripides' play still matters after some 2,500 years because it is the product of a culture and a poet who were far better than we are at imagining themselves into a time when drunkenness was still new" (p. 22). Drunkenness in the American culture is no longer new; there are large numbers of studies that show particularly problematic patterns of intoxication on college campuses and minimal learning about what can effectively reduce alcohol-related harms, which is examined in Chapter 5. Campus systems model was created in 2007 as part of *Assessing Comprehensiveness and Quality of Alcohol Screening, Treatment, and Prevention Systems for Young Adults within Educational Systems*, funded by the Robert Wood Johnson Foundation's Substance Abuse Policy Research Program (RWJF #63118). Principal investigator Traci Toomey and co-investigators Darin Erickson, Toben Nelson, and Ken Winters developed a comprehensive framework for considerations on college campuses that influence college student drinking patterns. Their model shows that significant and targeted changes work most effectively. Part of the answer as to why young people use mood-altering substances, especially in high-risk consumption patterns, has to do primarily with access to the substances. From the rigorous studies conducted thus far, increasing stricter enforcement of laws currently in place and enhanced community intervention with bar owners and liquor stores does produce measurable benefits to reduce high-risk drinking behaviors as is highlighted in Chapter 5.

Next, the use of other mood-altering drugs has led to attention ranging from youth to senior adults. *VICE*, an investigative television program, in 2014 highlighted a series on heroin addicts and a government-sponsored Netherland program begun in the 1990s that provided heroin addicts with the means to use heroin three times per day in a health facility (Roes & Smith, 2014). The program describes a downward trend of heroin use and addiction in addition to surprisingly low criminal behavior in the Netherlands, which is directly opposite of the substantially increasing use in the United States. One insightful comment from a health care practitioner in a heroin clinic in Amsterdam noted the following:

> If you get the dope for free, your only problem is that you're addicted to the dope. It seems like a paradox, but it's true. All that's left when everything else is taken care of is the question: do I really want to keep on using this? (Roes & Smith, 2014, television show).

American Culture

Finally, it is important to understand more about *why* we believe it is important to look carefully at first use and experimentation. Is it just a normal rite of passage for youth? Is it a "phase" that will pass and is just a routine part of adolescence? These attitudes can be important to examine, particularly if there is implicit approval communicated to the young person. And the question remains for the professional clinician: what if that attitude is erroneous? What are the risks associated with experimental use? In 2011, the National Center on Addiction and Substance Abuse at Columbia University, CASAColumbia, produced an extensive report on adolescent substance use in America. The analyses underscored the conclusion by the researchers that adolescent substance use is the number one health problem in America (2011). Further, the major emphasis in the report notes that substance use preventive work could help cut the onset of addiction from one in four to one in 25 if clinicians and health professionals use resources collaboratively to address substance use by youth (CASAColumbia, 2011). It is highlighted that "nine out of 10 people who meet the clinical criteria for substance use disorders began smoking, drinking or using other drugs before they turned 18" (CASAColumbia, 2011, p. ii) as compared with individuals who did not use until they were 25 or older and have substantially reduced addiction rates of one in 25 (0.04%).

In addition, there are compelling arguments that attribute American culture as a powerful influence and risk factor for initiating substance use, especially among youth: "While adolescence itself increases the chances that teens will use addictive substances, American culture further increases that risk" (CASAColumbia, 2011, p. 3). The focused report on teens from CASAColumbia stresses that teens especially are "vulnerable to the wide-ranging social influences that subtly condone or more overtly encourage their use of these substances" (p. 3). The report further adds, "the media's tendency to present substance use as glamorous, fun and stress relieving, coupled with limited regulation of the advertising of tobacco and alcohol products, contribute to a culture of pervasive pro-substance use messages that bombard teens every day" (p. 81). Listing the major influences for youth initiating substance use include acceptance of use by parents, peers, schools, celebrities, health care practitioners, communities, and manufacturers of alcohol, medications, and other addictive substances as often depicted in media through entertainment, social media, and advertising. For example, research points to strong indicators of risk for those parents who communicate to their children that they allow them to drink at home, suggesting that "allowing teens to drink at home actually increases the likelihood that they will drink outside of the home" (CASAColumbia, 2011, p. 65). A number of findings show that when parents' or caregivers' disapproval is clearly communicated, the less likely the teen is to use addictive substances.

When parental role modeling is examined as it pertains to initiating and continuing use of addictive substances, it is even more important for parental actions (what is done) to be examined as compared with verbal statements (what is said). In other words, teens and children are very influenced by what parents and adults *do* more than what parents or adults *say*. For example, the report notes nearly half of American youth—34.4 million of youth 17 years of age or younger—live in a home with an influential adult who is using addictive substances in a risky manner, including cigarettes, alcohol, pain pills, or other addictive drugs (CASAColumbia, 2011). In surveys, slightly over one in five youth indicate that marijuana is a harmless drug, for example, and this adds to its reputation as a gateway drug that leads to greater susceptibility to experiment with other mood-altering drugs (CASAColumbia, 2011). Additional initiatives have been implemented to deter use of other gateway drugs, such as prescription drugs that can lead to use of illicit opiates such as heroin. A national movement led by the Centers for Disease Control and Prevention (CDC) is underway that has identified 10 top areas of prevention focus; three of those key areas relate to substance use and include alcohol-related harms, prescription drug overdose, and tobacco use (CDC, 2016). Overall, continued work at every level is needed to better understand contributing factors of experimental use and effective ways to prevent and reduce risky use and addiction.

Protective Factors

Enhancing Refusal Skills

Effects of Protective Factors

In a circular fashion, the question at the beginning of this chapter with only a slight modification remains: Do I really want to use this mood-altering substance? If so, why? We reviewed a number of contributing factors, and we can clearly see that there is no one reason but rather a complex combination of factors that influence that initial experimental substance use. Working with individuals to actively study effective ways to address experimental use of mood-altering substances can be an important area for substance use specialists, some of whom will specialize in prevention work exclusively. Reports also concur that protective factors include parents or caregivers who model a vibrant health focus and healthy behaviors within a nurturing home environment, engaged adults in the youth's life and activities, clear and frequent communication about expectations of substance-free choices by youth, other positive adult role models, healthy attachment in home and community by the young person, and future-oriented goals (CASAColumbia, 2011; Van Ryzin et al., 2012). As such, helpful interventions by the substance abuse specialist, especially those counselors working in prevention specialities, can target parental models of effective communication, trust-building exercises, and conflict management/mediation skills to enhance the protective factors of parents and important caregivers. As one example, the National Highway Traffic Safety Administration (NHTSA) offers a sample contract (see Figure 4.1) for parents or caregivers that provides a clear message about teen alcohol use which can then serve as a written and signed contract between the teen and the parent(s). It addresses other safety issues but includes alcohol use restrictions and is on a document that addresses teen driving, which is a very important area for many teens looking forward to driving a car independently. At the time of reviewing this contract, it can also be an important tool for the parents and teen to have a conversation about drinking. In addition, this document can serve as a therapeutic tool for clinicians to introduce in family sessions as a way to add and underscore clear messages about restricting underage drinking.

Successful Community-Based Prevention

As highlighted in Chapter 2, a key resource for evidence-based prevention is the National Registry of Evidence-based Programs and Practices (NREPP), which is maintained as a part of the Substance Abuse and Mental Health Services Administration (SAMHSA). On the list in the NREPP are over 300 different models of prevention programs with specific contact, audience, outcome, and other important informational

Figure 4.1 Parent–Teen Driving Contract

Parent-Teen Driving Contract

ONE TEXT OR CALL COULD WRECK IT ALL

Young, inexperienced drivers, die too often in fatal crashes largely because of immaturity and inexperience. Three-stage GDL laws reduce these factors by gradually introducing driving tasks and privileges through controlled exposure to high-risk situations. All States and the District of Columbia have GDL laws with these three stages:

- Learner's Permit,
- Intermediate (Provisional) License, and
- Full Licensure

Make sure you and your teen drivers know and understand your State GDL laws before they get behind the wheel.

DISTRACTED DRIVING: In 2013, for drivers 15-19 years old involved in fatal crashes, 15 percent of the distracted drivers were distracted by the use of cell phones.

1. **RULE: NO CELL PHONES.**

   AGREEMENT: ______________________________
   CONSEQUENCES: ______________________________

2. **EXTRA PASSENGERS:** The risk of fatal crashes goes up in direct relation to the number of teens in the car. **RULE: NO EXTRA PASSENGERS.**

   AGREEMENT: ______________________________
   CONSEQUENCES: ______________________________

3. **SPEEDING:** In 2013, speeding was a factor for 42% of teen (15-19) drivers in fatal crashes. **RULE: NO SPEEDING.**

   AGREEMENT: ______________________________
   CONSEQUENCES: ______________________________

4. **ALCOHOL:** In 2013, 1,164 teen drivers were killed in motor vehicle traffic crashes. Twenty-five percent (289) of these drivers had alcohol in their system. **RULE: ABSOLUTELY NO ALCOHOL!**

   AGREEMENT: ______________________________
   CONSEQUENCES: ______________________________

5. **SEATBELTS:** In 2013, almost half (49%) of teen (15-19) drivers of passenger car and light trucks killed in crashes were unrestrained. **RULE: ALWAYS BUCKLE-UP.**

   AGREEMENT: ______________________________
   CONSEQUENCES: ______________________________

TEEN: ______________________________

PARENT/GUARDIAN: ______________________________
DATE: ______________________________

NHTSA
www.nhtsa.gov

SOURCE: National Highway Traffic Safety Administration (2015). Washington, DC: United States Department of Transportation. Retrieved from http://www.distraction.gov/take-actiondownloads.html.

items to help equip professionals who are working toward prevention with best practices in the prevention field. While the registry is not all-inclusive of all prevention models, it does offer one more important resource for helping professionals as evidence-based models are explored and examined. Below are only two samples from the NREPP and its relevant descriptors for those who are interested in searching the registry and to provide an opportunity to demonstrate what to expect when searching for a prevention program.

Evidence-Based Practice

Examining Effective Prevention Programs

Positive Action. Positive Action is a fully developed program that is focused on improving achievement and attendance in schools and problems with substance misuse, violence, school suspensions and dropping out, and risky behaviors. Another goal is to help with parent–child bonding challenges and family distress. The primary focus is helping individuals see positive actions as a way of family and self-improvement with four key focus areas: positive actions for the physical, intellectual, social, and emotional. The program is designed to help prekindergarten through 12th grade, using very short scripted lessons (see Table 4.1). Also available are helpful kits for issues such as drug education, conflict resolution, improvement for elementary and secondary schools, school counselor resources, family resources, and community resources (SAMHSA, 2014b).

Table 4.1 NREPP: Positive Action Evidence-Based Example

Areas of Interest	Substance Abuse Prevention
Outcomes	**Review Date: November 2014** 1: Substance Use 2: Social-Emotional Mental Health 3: Problem Behaviors (violence, substance use, disciplinary referrals, suspensions, and bullying) 4: Academic Achievement 5: Absenteeism **Review Date: December 2006** 1: Academic Achievement 2: Problem Behaviors (violence, substance use, disciplinary referrals, and suspensions) 3: School Absenteeism 4: Family Functioning

Areas of Interest	Substance Abuse Prevention
Outcome Categories	Alcohol Crime/Delinquency Drugs Education Family/Relationships Social Functioning Tobacco Violence
Ages	6–12 (Childhood) 13–17 (Adolescent) 18–25 (Young Adult) 26–55 (Adult)
Races/Ethnicities	American Indian or Alaskan Native Asian Black or African American Hispanic or Latino Native Hawaiian or Other Pacific Islander White
Settings	School
Geographic Locations	Urban Suburban Rural and/or Frontier
Implementation History	Positive Action, Inc., was founded by Dr. Carol Gerber Allred in Twin Falls, Idaho, in 1982. Since then, the company's program has serviced approximately 5 million individuals in more than 15,000 settings in all 50 states, internationally, and in various contexts, including 15,000 schools/districts and school-related sites (such as alternative schools, detention centers, and before- and after-school programs), mental health centers, adult and juvenile courts, welfare and other social services, probation and corrections, businesses, family services, law enforcement, affordable housing, and others. Positive Action has been implemented with a wide variety of ethnic, cultural, and socioeconomic groups. The duration of implementation has varied, with some customers having used the program for as long as 17 years.

(Continued)

Table 4.1 (Continued)

Areas of Interest	Substance Abuse Prevention
NIH Funding/ CER Studies	Partially/fully funded by National Institutes of Health: Yes Evaluated in comparative effectiveness research studies: No
Adaptations	Positive Action currently offers a Spanish-language version of most of the grade-level kits, including kindergarten through 4th grade, 7th and 8th grade, Secondary Drug Education, Conflict Resolution Kit, Family Kit, Family Classes, and Parenting Classes.
Adverse Effects	No adverse effects, concerns, or unintended consequences were identified by the developer.
IOM Prevention Categories	Universal Selective Indicated

SOURCE: SAMHSA's National Registry of Evidence-Based Programs and Practices, 2014.

Across Ages: Across Ages provides a substance abuse prevention program for youth ages 9 to 13. The key focus of Across Ages pairs older adult mentors (55 years and older) with young adolescents heading into middle school (see Table 4.2). The major aim is to target and enhance protective factors for students to interrupt risk factors associated with substance use (SAMHSA's National Registry of Evidence-based Programs and Practices, 2008).

Table 4.2 NREPP: Across Ages Evidence-Based Example

Areas of Interest	Substance Use Disorder Prevention
Outcomes	**Review Date: June 2008** 1: Reactions to situations involving drug use 2: Attitudes toward school, future, and elders 3: School attendance 4: Knowledge about and attitudes toward older adults
Outcome Categories	Alcohol Education Family/Relationships Tobacco
Ages	6–12 (Childhood) 13–17 (Adolescent)

Areas of Interest	Substance Use Disorder Prevention
Genders	Male Female
Races/Ethnicities	Asian Black or African American Hispanic or Latino White Race/Ethnicity Unspecified
Settings	School Other Community Settings
Geographic Locations	Urban
Implementation History	Across Ages was first funded in 1991 by the Center for Substance Abuse Prevention as a 5-year research and demonstration project. Since 1996, 85 sites have been trained on the program, representing urban, suburban, and semirural communities in 37 states. Approximately a third of these sites have sustained implementation, with funding from a variety of sources, for two or more funding cycles. Approximately 8,300 youth have participated in the program.
NIH Funding/ CER Studies	Partially/fully funded by National Institutes of Health: Yes Evaluated in comparative effectiveness research studies: Yes
Adaptations	Some Across Ages program materials have been adapted for Native American populations and translated into Spanish.
Adverse Effects	No adverse effects, concerns, or unintended consequences were identified by the developer.
IOM Prevention Categories	Selective

SOURCE: SAMHSA's National Registry of Evidence-Based Programs and Practices, 2008.

Skills in Action

Box 4.2: Case Illustration: Experimental Use or Problematic Use?

My name is Carey. I don't even know why the teacher asked me to come see a counselor. I don't have much to say. The teacher just said you could talk with me about how things are going for me. I guess she got really mad when she saw me with a beer can this morning at the bus stop as she was driving in to school. It's no big deal and it was really only my first sip I'd ever had. One of the other guys dared me to do it. So I did.

Experiential Skills Learning Activity

First, explore the NREPP website and select two evidence-based interventions that might help Carey, review important findings, and write a summary indicating strengths and weaknesses in possible substance abuse counseling settings you might imagine working. Select your top choice and share your recommendations. Would cost be a factor? If so, how would you advocate for the funding needed to implement your top choice. What are five other important considerations that you would want to discuss? Rank them in order of importance, 1 is the top importance and 5 the least important. Share your findings.

Next, imagine yourself as a helping professional in a substance use disorders counseling setting and consider these possible professional counseling responses to Carey to foster a caring and listening nonjudgmental response.

Possible counseling responses to begin the session:

Counselor: *It seems you're not clear why you're here seeing me. Sounds like you are wondering if it might be somehow connected to your teacher being concerned when she saw you at the bus stop this morning with a beer.*

Counselor: *Having a beer in your hand at the bus stop this morning seems like no big deal for you as it was after a dare to drink it . . . yet, the concern from your teacher prompted her to ask you to meet with me.*

Counselor: *Coming in to meet with me today isn't something you can see is needed since the beer you were holding came about after you were dared to drink it.*

Counselor: *It seems like I sense mixed reactions to you talking with me about having a beer at the bus stop.*

In small groups, discuss the following:

Do you worry your counseling responses may be giving the client more permission to continue underage drinking? Why? Why not?

List at least three emotions that you each experience when you read these counseling responses. Discuss in your small group how you imagine your feelings may influence your professional counseling responses while working with your client.

Practice taking turns using the counseling responses with each member of the group in a role-play activity. Stop after the initial opening responses and discuss how you as the counselor in the role play are reacting. What are the top two challenges? What are your top two indicators that your responses are helpful? (And gently remind yourself that there are no absolute right answers to these thought-provoking questions. Rather, these are designed to help foster greater self-awareness of what types of issues and feelings this work with an underage drinker might bring out in your work.)

RESOURCES FOR FURTHER LEARNING

American Association of Poison Control Centers (AAPCC)

http://aapcc.org

Center for the Application of Prevention Technologies (CAPT)

http://captus.samhsa.gov

Community Anti-Drug Coalitions of America (CADCA)

http://www.cadca.org

Stop Medicine Abuse

This group of five women is spreading the word about cough medicine abuse.

http://stopmedicineabuse.org

NASPA—Student Affairs Administrators in Higher Education, Alcohol and Other Drug (AOD) Knowledge Community

http://www.naspa.org

National Inhalant Prevention Coalition (NIPC)

http://www.inhalants.org

National Parent Teacher Association (PTA) Drug and Alcohol Abuse Prevention Project

http://www.pta.org/parents

The Network Addressing Collegiate Alcohol and Other Drug Issues

http://www.thenetwork.ws

Partnership for Drug-Free Kids

http://drugfree.org/

Partnership for Prevention (PFP)

http://www.prevent.org

Society for Adolescent Health and Medicine

http://www.adolescenthealth.org

Substance Abuse and Mental Health Services Administration (SAMHSA), Behavioral Health Treatments and Services

http://www.samhsa.gov/treatment

SAMHSA, Center for Substance Abuse Prevention (CSAP)

http://beta.samhsa.gov/about-us/who-we-are/offices-centers/csap

Society for Prevention Research

http://www.preventionresearch.org

REFERENCES

Aines, E. D. (2012). *Carousing with the ancients.* Retrieved from http://www.eaines.com/archaeology/the-archaeology-of-ancient-alcohol/

American Association of Poison Control Centers. (2016). *Synthetic cannabinoids.* Retrieved from http://www.aapcc.org/alerts/synthetic-cannabinoids/

Bandura, A. (1977). *Social learning theory.* Upper Saddle River, NJ: Prentice Hall.

Bandura, A. (2007). Much ado over faulty conception of perceived self-efficacy grounded in faulty experimentation. *Journal of Social and Clinical Psychology, 26*(6), 641–658.

Benight, C. C., & Bandura, A. (2004). Social cognitive theory of posttraumatic recovery: The role of perceived self-efficacy. *Behaviour Research and Therapy, 42*(10), 1129–1148. http://doi.org/10.1016/j.brat.2003.08.008

Briggs, C. (2016). Gender, sex, and addictions. In D. Capuzzi & M. D. Stauffer (Eds.), *Foundations of addictions counseling* (3rd ed., pp. 406–427). New York, NY: Pearson.

CASAColumbia. (2011). *Adolescent substance use: American's #1 public health problem.* Retrieved from http://www.casacolumbia.org/addiction-research/reports/adolescent-substance-use

Center on Alcohol Marketing and Youth (CAMY). (2008). *Alcohol marketing and youth: An overview.* Retrieved from http://www.camy.org/_archive2015/research/Summary_Brochures/brochure0305.pdf

Centers for Disease Control and Prevention (CDC). (2016). *Prevention of Prescription Overdoses.* Retrieved from https://wwwn.cdc.gov/psr/NationalSummary/NSPDO.aspx

Clark, T. T., Doyle, O., & Clincy, A. (2013). Age of first cigarette, alcohol, and marijuana use among U.S. biracial/ethnic youth: A population-based study. *Journal of Addictive Behaviors, 38,* 2450–2454. http://dx.doi.org/10.1016/j.addbeh.2013.04.005

Consumer Health Informatics Research (CHIRr). (2013). *Variable: Self efficacy.* Retrieved from http://www.chirr.nlm.nih.gov/self-efficacy.php

Federal Trade Commission (FTC). (2014, March). Self-regulation in the alcohol industry: Report of the Federal Trade Commission. Retrieved from http://www.ftc.gov/system/files/documents/reports/self-regulation-alcohol-industry-report-federal-trade-commission/140320alcoholreport.pdf

Feinstein, E. C., Richter, L., & Foster, S. E. (2012). Addressing the critical health problem of adolescent substance use through health care, research, and public policy. *Journal of Adolescent Health, 50,* 431–436.

Get high. (n.d.). Retrieved from http://www.urbandictionary.com/define.php?term=get+high

Goodman, R. (2014, December). How to be intoxicated. Alcohol's hold on campus (Special Report). *The Chronicle of Higher Education.* Retrieved from http://www.chronicle.com/article/How-to-be-intoxicated/150239/?cid=cr&utm_source=cr&utm_medium=en

Guerra-Doce, E. (2014). The origins of inebriation: Archaelogical evidence of the consumption of fermented beverages and drugs in prehistoric Eurasia. *Journal of Archaeological Method and Theory,* 1–32. doi:10.1007/s10816-014-9205-z

Hagopian, M. M., Burkhalter, L., & Foglia, R. P. (2014). ATV injury experience at a pediatric trauma center: A 5-year review. *Trauma, 16*(2), 99–102. doi:10.1177/1460408613515804

Hall, A. J., Bixler, D., Helmkamp, J. C., Kraner, J. C., & Kaplan, J., A. (2009) Fatal all-terrain vehicle crashes: injury types and alcohol use. *American Journal of Preventative Medicine, 36,* 311–316.

Hart, C. L., & Ksir, C. (2012). *Drugs, society, and human behavior* (15th ed.). Boston, MA: McGraw Hill.

Hart, C. L., Ksir, C., & Ray, O. (2009). *Drugs, society, and human behavior* (13th ed.). Boston, MA: McGraw Hill.

Hirsch, M. L., Conforti, R. W., & Graney, C. J. (2004). The use of marijuana for pleasure: A replication of Howard S. Becker's study of marijuana use. In J. A. Inciardi & K. McElrath (Eds.), *The American drug scene: An anthology* (pp. 27–35). Los Angeles, CA: Roxbury Publishing Company.

Hollingworth, W., Ebel, B. E., McCarty, C. A., Garrison, M. M., Christakis, D. A., & Rivara, F. P. (2006). Prevention of deaths from harmful drinking in the United States: The potential effects of tax increases and advertising bans on young drinkers. *Journal of Studies on Alcohol, 67*, 300–308.

Jenkins, M. (2014). A concept analysis of self-efficacy and adolescent sexual risk-taking behavior. *Nursing Forum.* doi:10.1111/nuf.12070

Livingstone, S. M., Haddon, L., & Gorzig, A. (2012). Children, risk and safety on the internet: Research and policy challenges in comparative perspective. Bristol: The Policy Press.

Llewellyn, D. J., Sanchez, X., Asghar, A., & Jones, G. (2008). Self-efficacy, risk taking and performance in rock climbing. *Personality and Individual Differences, 45*, 75–81. doi:10.1016/j.paid.2008.03.001

Marlatt, G. A. (1985). Relapse prevention: Theoretical rationale and overview of the model. In G. A. Marlatt & J. R. Gordon (Eds.), *Relapse prevention: Maintenance strategies in the treatment of addictive behaviors* (pp. 3–70). New York, NY: Guilford.

McGovern, P. E. (2009). *Uncorking the past: The quest for wine, beer, and other alcoholic beverages.* Los Angeles: University of California Press.

McLernon, M. Y. (2014). *Risk propensity, self-efficacy and driving behaviors among rural, off-duty emergency services personnel* (Doctoral dissertation, Southern Illinois University Carbondale). Retrieved from http://opensiuc.lib.siu.edu/cgi/viewcontent.cgi?article=1840&context=dissertations

National Institute on Alcohol Abuse and Alcoholism (NIAAA). (2014). *Alcohol facts and statistics.* Retrieved from http://www.niaaa.nih.gov

National Institute on Drug Abuse (NIDA). (2014). *Monitoring the Future Survey 2014: Overview of findings.* Retrieved from https://www.drugabuse.gov/related-topics/trends-statistics/monitoring-future/monitoring-future-survey-overview-findings-2014

National Institute on Drug Abuse (NIDA). (2015). *Heroin: How heroin is linked to prescription drug abuse.* Retrieved from https://www.drugabuse.gov/publications/research-reports/heroin/how-heroin-linked-to-prescription-drug-abuse

Nephew, T. M., Williams, G. D., Stinson, F. S., Nguyen, K., & DuFour, M. C. (1999). *Apparent per capita alcohol consumption: National, state, and regional trends, 1977–1997.* (Surveillance Report No. 51). Rockville, MD: U.S. Department of Health and Human Services.

Nichter, M. (2004). Smoking: What does culture have to do with it? In J. A. Inciardi & K. McElrath (Eds.), *The American drug scene* (4th ed., pp. 41–49). Los Angeles, CA: Roxbury Publishing Company.

North Carolina Alcohol Beverage Control Commission (NCABCC). (2014). *The state of underage drinking in North Carolina: Executive summary.* Retrieved from http://www.talkitoutnc.org/wp-content/uploads/2014/09/State-of-Underage-Drinking-in-NC-Quantitative-Executive-Summary.pdf

Padron, A., Galan, I., Garcia-Esquinas, E., Fernandez, E., Ballbe, M., & Rodriguez-Artaljo, R. (2015). Exposure to secondhand smoke in the home and mental health in children: A population-based study. *Tobacco Control.* doi:10.1136/tobaccocontrol-2014-052077d

Parsons, T. (2013). *Alcohol ads reaching too many young people in TV markets across the United States.* Retrieved from http://www.camy.org/press/Press_Releases/Alcohol_Ads_Reaching_Too_Many_Young_People_in_TV_Markets_across_the_United_States.html

Rimal, R. N., Lapinski, M. K., Cook, R. J., & Real, K. (2005). Moving toward a theory of normative influences: How perceived benefits and similarity moderate the impact of descriptive norms on behaviors. *Journal of Health Communication, 10*, 433–450.

Roes, T., & Smith, S. (2014). Only in the Netherlands do addicts complain about free government heroin [Television series episode]. In B. Maher, *VICE.* Los Angeles, CA: HBO.

Ross, C. S., Maple, E., Siegel, M., DeJong, M., Naimi, T. S., Ostruff, J., & Jernigan, D. (2014). The relationship between brand-specific alcohol advertising on television and brand-specific consumption among underage youth. *Alcoholism: Clinical and Experimental Research, 38*, 2234–2242. doi:10.1111/acer.12488

Samuels, A. (2015, January). Brand-specific television ads a significant predictor of brand consumption among underage youth. Retrieved from http://www.camy.org/press/Press_Releases/Brand-Specific%20 Television%20Alcohol%20Ads%20a%20Significant%20Predictor%20of%20Brand%20Consumption%20 Among%20Underage%20Youth

Shults, R. A., West, B., Rudd, R., & Helmkamp, J. (2013). All-terrain vehicle-related nonfatal injuries among young riders in the United States, 2001–2010. *Pediatrics, 132*, 282–289.

Skagerstron, J., Chang, G., & Nielsen, P. (2011). Predictors of drinking during pregnancy: A systematic review. *Journal of Women's Health, 20*, 901–913.

Smith, F. H. (2008). *The archaeology of alcohol and drinking.* Gainesville: University of Florida Press.

Snyder, L. B., Milici, F. F., Slater, M., Sun, H., & Strizhakova, Y. (2006). Effects of alcohol advertising exposure on drinking among youth. *Archives of Pediatric and Adolescent Medicine, 160*, 18–24.

Substance Abuse and Mental Health Services Administration (SAMHSA). (2008). National Registry of Evidence-based Programs and Practices. "Across Ages." *NREPP.SAMHSA.gov*, pp. 1–6, accessed April 27, 2015. http:// legacy.nreppadmin.net/ViewIntervention.aspx?id=138

Substance Abuse and Mental Health Services Administration (SAMHSA). (2013). *Behavioral health barometer: North Carolina.* (HHS Publication No. [SMA] 13-4796NC). Rockville, MD: Author.

Substance Abuse and Mental Health Services Administration (SAMHSA). (2014a). *Results from the 2013 National Survey on Drug Use and Health: Summary of national findings* (HHS Publication No. [SMA] 14-4863). Rockville, MD: Author. Retrieved from http://www.samhsa.gov/data/sites/default/files/NSDUH resultsPDFWHTML2013/Web/NSDUHresults2013.pdf

Substance Abuse and Mental Health Services Administration (SAMHSA). (2014b). National Registry of Evidence-based Programs and Practices. "Positive Action." *NREPP.SAMHSA.gov*, pp. 1–2, accessed April 27, 2015. http://legacy.nreppadmin.net/ViewIntervention.aspx?id=400

Thombs, D. L. (2006). *Introduction to addictive behaviors.* New York, NY: Guilford.

U.S. Consumer Product Safety Commission (CPSC). (2015). *2013 Annual report of ATV-related deaths and injuries.* Bethesda, MD: Author.

Van Ryzin, M. J., Fosco, G. M., & Dishion, T. J. (2012). Family and peer predictors of substance use from early adolescence to early adulthood: An 11-year prospective analysis. *Addictive Behaviors, 37*, 1314–1324. doi:10.1016/j.addbeh.2012.06.020

Van Zee, A. (2009). The promotion and marketing of OxyContin: Commercial triumph, public health tragedy. *American Journal of Public Health, 99*(2), 221–227. http://doi.org/10.2105/AJPH.2007.131714

Wallace, D. F. (1998, July). Laughing with Kafka. *Harper's Magazine.* Retrieved from http://harpers.org/ archive/1998/07/laughing-with-kafka/

Weil, A. T. (2014). Why people take drugs. In J. A. Inciardi & K. McElrath (Eds.), *The American drug scene: Readings in a global context* (7th ed., pp. 72–80). New York, NY: Oxford Press.

Wilsnack, S. C., Wilsnack, R. W., & Kantor, L. W. (2013). Focus on: Women and the costs of alcohol use. *Alcohol Research: Current Reviews, 35*(2), 219–228.

Winters, K. C., & Kaminer, Y. (2008). Screening and assessing adolescent substance use disorders in clinical populations. *Journal of American Academy of Child and Adolescent Psychiatry, 47*, 740–744.

Xu, X., & Chaloupka, F. J. (2011). The effects of prices on alcohol use and its consequences. *Alcohol Research and Health, 34*(2), 236–245. Retrieved from http://search.proquest.com/docview/912160784?accountid=14868

5

Understanding Risky Use Patterns ❖

LEARNING OBJECTIVES

The learner will be able to

- define risky use;
- list at least three important factors counselors should consider in understanding risky use patterns; and
- discuss two main contributors to binge drinking by college students.

Knowledge

For a number of years, precious resources in the substance abuse field were mainly used for primary prevention efforts or intensive addiction treatment. Research, too, focused on work to prevent substance use, especially in youth in elementary schools, or on counseling services after addiction took its toll on the individual and family. Imagine on the spectrum of use, one end representing prevention of first use and, at the far end of the spectrum, intensive inpatient specialized addiction treatment. Sparse attention was given to the area in the middle of that vast spectrum between prevention and intensive treatment. Yet, in recent years, addiction specialists have begun to understand the greater issue for those who use mood-altering substances in risky ways but are not yet addicted. The college student who binge drinks for perhaps their first time ever and then engages in unsafe sex, for example, typifies a risky drinker. Another example might include the woman prescribed pain medication after a minor surgery who then takes one extra pill from her prescription because she has noticed it has relieved her focus on work and family, allowed her to put her cares aside, and she wants that particular type of escape. Attention by more researchers and counselors has begun to expand to this middle part of the spectrum, the risky user. You might ask why. The person does not meet criteria for a substance use disorder. The person is still quite functional, does not exhibit symptoms of clinically significant impairment, is not seeking help for substance use, and is not considered chemically dependent. The questions of why to examine and why address risky users are increasingly important and some of the recent research studies help us look at the answers.

Risky Drinking

The substance abuse field has learned of the volume of those who are considered risky users. In examining risky drinkers, for example, calculations by the National Institute on Alcohol Abuse and Alcoholism (NIAAA) show approximately 28% of alcohol use by adults in the United States is putting risky drinkers at increased risk for alcohol use disorders, liver complications, and other problems (NIAAA, 2013). It is also noted that approximately 37% of drinkers in the United States consistently drink at low-risk levels and are not the focus of risky drinker interventions. Additionally, 35% of adults in the United States do not drink at all. Of the 28% who are drinking at risk, 9% exceed both daily and weekly limits as outlined by the NIAAA and are at highest risk to develop an alcohol use disorder; the American Psychiatric Association (APA) calculates that approximately 8.5% of adults in the United States currently meet criteria for an alcohol use disorder (2013). The approximately 19% of drinkers who exceed either daily or weekly limits consume alcohol in risky patterns, yet have largely been ignored since their drinking often did not meet the level of concern as did those seen with alcoholic drinking patterns. However, we have learned that drinking at risky levels can be hazardous to health, well-being, and longevity.

For a number of individuals who use mood-altering substances, their use of mood-altering chemicals could be best categorized as risky use when they do not meet the *Diagnostic and Statistical Manual of Mental Disorders* (5th edition, *DSM-5*) criteria for a diagnosis of a substance use disorder yet drink in ways that are a risk to health, such as infrequent binge drinking putting the drinker at increased risk of injury, for example. In recent years increasing attention has been given to risky users and how to best define a pattern of risky use. According to NIAAA, a leading national resource for helping professionals regarding information pertaining to alcohol research, "for healthy adults in general, drinking more than the single-day or weekly amounts . . . is considered 'at-risk' or 'heavy' drinking" (2013, p. 4). Single-day advisories include for men less than 65 years of age and in good overall health, no more than four standard alcoholic beverages on any one day and no more than 14 standard drinks total per week; for women (and men over age 65 or in poor health), no more than three standard alcoholic beverages on any one day and no more than seven standard drinks total per week (NIAAA, 2013).

Information, as of 2012 regarding lifespan drinking prevalence, indicated that nearly 90% of individuals 18 or above noted they had consumed alcohol at least once in their lifetime, 71% had done so in the recent year, and over half (56.3%) drank alcohol in the past month (NIAAA, 2017). Of particular concern when examining first use and experimentation, more information is added to that picture when examining patterns of use among youth. Any use, even alcoholic beverages, by youth can be considered risky as that use is illegal, therefore, risks of negative consequences are a given but regular use is of particular concern. Reports from NIAAA show two of five teens aged 15 have had at least one drink, yet 9.3 million youth aged 12 to 20 (approximately 24%) consumed alcohol within the recent month (SAMHSA, 2014). Perhaps of more concern for the professional who is learning effective helping strategies in the area of treating substance use disorders pertains to an estimated 15% of youth aged 12–20 reporting risky drinking with almost equal distribution between males (16.5%) and females (14%). Further, it is estimated that almost 1 million youth had already developed a diagnosable alcohol use disorder—that is approximately 4.6% of youth aged 12 to 17 (APA, 2013). For comparison, those aged 65 years and beyond have approximately 1.5% with a diagnosable alcohol use disorder (APA, 2013). These statistics make efforts to intervene with risky users more compelling in helping staunch the incidence of addiction in youth.

For the most abused drug, alcohol, definitions of risky use include information about patterns of use. For example, for adults without other health problems, risky drinking exceeds standards developed from research conducted in the National Institutes of Health, particularly the NIAAA. Based on recent recommendations, risk levels increase, for men 65 years of age and younger, if they drink five or more drinks on any day and if they consume a total of 15 or more standard alcoholic drinks per week. In reviewing standard drink definitions, as this text utilizes measurements, one standard drink equals a 12-ounce beer, 8 ounces of malt liquor, 5 ounces of wine, or 1.5 ounces of 80-proof liquor, such as vodka (NIAAA, 2013). For women, risky drinking involves lower amounts of alcohol due to physiological differences as women have less water in their bodies than men, leading to higher concentrations of alcohol when consumed. Risky drinking for women involves drinking four or more drinks on any given day, eight or more drinks in a week, or exceeding both the daily and weekly limits (NIAAA, 2013).

The example in Figure 5.1 depicts information that is shared with individuals who may be exploring their alcohol use patterns. It is important to note that this publication highlights that 70% of Americans typically drink at low-risk levels or not at all. Focus on the 30% who are drinkers has been an added area of work in the field of substance use.

Additional findings suggest risk is heightened when mixing alcohol with high-energy drinks, especially in relation to medical care involving traumatic injuries from falls, motor vehicle collisions, or pedestrians being struck due to an observed dulling of awareness when energy drinks (acting as a stimulant) serve to mask the level of alcohol intoxication to the drinker, often providing an inaccurate sense of alertness, attention, and coordination (O'Brien, McCoy, Rhodes, Wagoner, & Wolfson, 2008). Based on knowledge gained when studying risky drinkers, it is highlighted that by intervening before a person develops addiction but while a person may be exhibiting risky drinking patterns, it is believed that the number of individuals who may become addicted can be substantially reduced. Further, certain studies have shown a reduction in related health risks such as reinjury in an alcohol-related car crash or subsequent driving-while-impaired (DWI) behaviors when alcohol screening and brief interventions have been

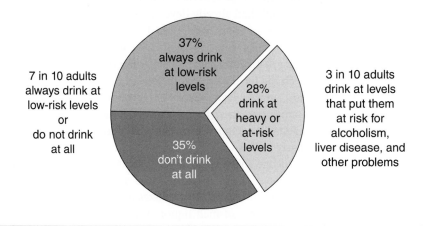

Figure 5.1 Rethinking Drinking

Do you enjoy a drink now and then? Many of us do, often when socializing with friends and family. Drinking can be beneficial or harmful, depending on your age and health status, the situation, and, of course, how much you drink.

Do you think you may drink too much at times? Do you think "everyone" drinks a lot? See below for results from a nationwide survey at 43,000 adults by the National Institutes of Health on alcohol use and its consequences.

Alcohol Use by Adults in the United States*

7 in 10 adults always drink at low-risk levels or do not drink at all

37% always drink at low-risk levels

35% don't drink at all

28% drink at heavy or at-risk levels

3 in 10 adults drink at levels that put them at risk for alcoholism, liver disease, and other problems

SOURCE: NIAAA, 2013, p. 1.

*Although the minimum legal drinking age in the U.S. is 21, this survey included people aged 18 or older.

conducted with risky drinkers (Gentillelo et al., 1999; Schermer, 2005). Data that are reviewed showed that drinking is associated with 60% of fatal burn injuries, 60% of drownings, and 60% of murders; approximately half of all traumatic injuries and sexual assault cases; and approximately 40% of fatal motor vehicle collisions, completed suicides, or fatal falls (NIAAA, 2013).

Box 5.1: Alcohol Use and PTSD

In a recent National Epidemiologic Survey, the lifetime prevalence of co-occurring posttraumatic stress disorder (PTSD) and alcohol dependence was 1.59% (Blanco et al., 2013). These diagnoses are believed to have a bidirectional relationship where the presence of PTSD increases the risk for substance abuse and vice versa (Lockwood & Forbes, 2014). The theory is that individuals abuse substances to alleviate PTSD symptoms and, by abusing substances, increase their chances of being exposed to traumatic events. This is due to the fact that accidents are more likely to happen when individuals are under the influence. Medical providers are becoming increasingly aware of the existence of PTSD in their patients, and of the cost to the medical system of delayed diagnosis and treatment (Love & Zatzick, 2014). Beyond considering patients who may walk in the door with PTSD, medical care can be traumatizing in and of itself, particularly in more critical cases where intensive care is needed, as is the case with significant burn injuries (McKibben, Bresnick, Wiechman Askkay, & Faurbach, 2008). One example of a strategy for addressing this issue is a program that was developed by mental health counselors working at the Burn Center at Wake Forest Baptist Hospital, which has made screening patients for PTSD part of the standard of care. This program ensures that patients who screen positive are visited by a mental health counselor who can offer debriefing, psychoeducation, and referral for ongoing care. By addressing PTSD that results from medical care or that is worsened by medical care, patients face less risk of abusing substances and thereby less risk of ending up back in the hospital from an accident.

Lindsay M. Shearer, MS, LPC, LCMHC, NCC, PhD candidate, is a licensed professional counselor and is completing her doctoral studies in counselor education and supervision at the University of North Carolina at Charlotte.

Risky Use of Other Mood-Altering Substances

Looking at other mood-altering substances and use, in 2014 the Substance Abuse and Mental Health Services Administration (SAMHSA) produced their 2013 National Survey on Drug Use and Health in the United States (NSDUH); the report noted that almost 10% of the U.S. population 12 years of age and older had used an illegal mood-altering substance within the previous month; further, nearly double the number of 18- to 20-year-old individuals (19.9%) reported using such substances within the previous month (2014). From a risk perspective, 39% of youth 12–17 years old who were surveyed perceived a greater risk if drinking five or more drinks on a weekly basis or smoking marijuana weekly; however, in 2007, the perception of risk was much greater at 54.6% when gauging weekly marijuana use (SAMHSA, 2014). As was highlighted in Chapter 3, the adolescent brain is still developing and the use of alcohol or other drugs, especially in binge patterns, can put the young person at additional risk for developing substance use disorders and having more alcohol-related complications in legal, educational, health, and family areas.

Risky Use of Prescription Medication

Another type of risky use that has gained national attention involves prescription drugs used in non-prescribed ways. Taking medication in prescribed ways can then change to using the medication in non-prescribed ways to achieve a desired effect, such as euphoria. Often, the term non-medical prescription drug use (NMPD) is the term given to this type of risky use. This risky use pattern can include, for a few examples, taking medications that were prescribed to someone else, taking more than was prescribed to achieve a desired mood change, or combining medications in ways that were not advised. Too often the naïve person may develop a preference for taking prescription medication in increasing amounts without awareness about the risky patterns that may develop in as little as 10–14 days of prescribed use, especially regarding opiates. The opiate-naïve individual, then, may begin to develop more reliance on the associated mood changes without an understanding of the physical impact and begin to use the medication in increasing amounts thereby developing a pattern of risky use. More recent studies suggest that youth, especially college-age youth, may be at higher risk for NMPD use of stimulants and pain medicines particularly if they are regular users of energy drinks (Arria et al., 2010). Further, risks may be minimized or poorly understood by the risky user due to perceptions of the NMPD use as "utilitarian (e.g., as a study aid) or status-oriented, such as among the 'self-treatment' subtype of nonmedical users" (Arria et al., 2010, p. 77). A link between NMPD use and other high-risk behaviors is evident as one of many studies highlights increasing NMPD use as over one-third of participants indicated NMPD use among a survey of undergraduate college students (Benotsch, Koester, Luckman, Martin, & Cejka, 2011). The study findings also included higher risky use rates of alcohol, marijuana, ecstasy, cocaine, methamphetamine, and other stimulants by those who engaged in NMPD use. The study authors noted particular concerns seen in risky use patterns that increase the potential for addiction as well as increased risk of sexually transmitted disease due to increased rates of unprotected sex by NMPD users (Benotsch et al., 2011). It is also important to note that there appears to be less negative risk associated with NMPD use (stimulants) by college students as suggested in one study: "negative consequences may be seen as unlikely or if they are expected to occur, they are not considered overly bad" (Lookatch, Dunne, & Katz, 2012). Risky use is associated with additional risks to health behaviors.

Risk of death is another heightened concern related to risky use of NMPDs. For the 11th year in a row, overdose deaths in the United States showed an increasing trend. In the United States in 2010, according to a review of death certificates by Jones, Mack, and Paulozzi (2013), 38,329 drug overdose deaths occurred. On average, 105 individuals died from overdoses every day, and of the 16,451 pharmaceutical-related overdose deaths, nearly 73% were unintentional/accidental overdoses, primarily because of opiates (Jones et al., 2013). Additionally, it was noted that individuals with mental health treatment are at a higher risk of overdose. A pattern of binge use may be involved in these risks of overdose, but much more research needs to be conducted to ascertain key factors related to increasing NMPD overdoses. An additional concern centers on risky use related to overdoses involving alcohol. Recent data from the Centers for Disease Control and Prevention (CDC) in 2015 describe an alarming increase in deaths by alcohol poisoning. It is estimated by the CDC that on any given day in the United States at least six people die due to alcohol poisoning (2015a). In addition, unlike other trends discussed in this chapter that pertain to young adults, increasingly alcohol poisoning is associated with older adults. It is reported that 3 out of 4 (76%) alcohol poisoning-related deaths in the United States are adults aged 35–64, primarily non-Hispanic white males (CDC, 2015a). While the reader might suspect that alcoholism is the cause of the poisoning, the CDC notes that alcoholism is a factor in only 30% of the deaths related to alcohol poisoning; risky binge drinking is a primary contributing factor (2015a).

Other categories of risky drug use include hallucinogens, such as ecstasy; heroin; marijuana; stimulants, like cocaine or methamphetamine; and other designer drugs as noted in earlier chapters. Most health problems, such as overdose, are related to the inexperienced user taking larger-than-planned amounts of these types of mood-altering drugs.

Box 5.2: Violence and Alcohol

Only in the 1990s has violence become a public health problem that could be addressed through the social and behavioral sciences. Additionally, the first trauma centers in San Francisco and Chicago became prominent organizations in urban centers that cared for those injured by high urban violence. Today many trauma centers recognize the need to intervene and prevent future violent injury during hospital stays. Cornwell et al. (1998) reported that 67% of the patients admitted to a Level I Trauma Center had consumed alcohol prior to a stab wound and 47% prior to a gunshot wound. Cherpitel found that those injured by violence were more likely to have drunk alcohol an hour before injury, 35% indicated drinking more than seven drinks, and nearly half of the violently injured participants feeling drunk (1993).

Studies indicate that perhaps addressing violence alone is not enough. Without intervention, alcohol misuse and abuse can become alcohol dependence and leave individuals more vulnerable to injury or even death (Dischinger, Mitchell, Kufera, Soderstrom, & Lowenfels, 2001). Moreover, injury recidivism is twice as likely in those patients that misuse alcohol than those who do not consume alcohol (Dischinger et al., 2001; Worrell et al., 2006). In a 2006 study researchers found that females involved in gun violence were also associated with high-risk alcohol use (Erickson, Butters, Cousineau, Harrison, & Korf, 2006). Within the emergency care setting, Choo and colleagues (2014) proposed that the most effective approach to reduce violent injury is by also addressing substance use simultaneously. Since alcohol misuse and abuse is such a prominent mitigating factor in violent injury, it is important to continue to investigate the ways to address the reduction of alcohol consumption, thereby reducing violent injury.

Youth and Violent Injury

Each day in the United States, 16 youths between the ages of 10 and 24 are murdered. Nearly half of youth who die annually from trauma die from violence-related injuries. Health services are challenged to address this public health crisis by reducing future violence-related incidents, recidivism, and retaliation. Youth that have sustained a previous intentional injury have an approximately 20% chance of dying due to violence. Likewise, victims with previous violent injuries will have a 10% to 50% chance of being reinjured through violent means. Youth violence is described as "the intentional use of physical force or power, threatened or actual, exerted by or against children, adolescents or young

(Continued)

(Continued)

adults, ages 10–19, which results in or has a high likelihood of resulting in injury, death, psychological harm, maldevelopment, or deprivation" (Butchart, Farrington, & Cerda, 2002). Violence might include community violence, gang violence, dating violence, and bullying. Researchers believe that increasing resources such as brief intervention can serve to support these youth and thereby reduce violent injury recidivism (Goins, Thompson, & Simpkins, 1992; Shibru et al., 2007).

In recent years, youth violence has become a monumental concern in health care. Medical institutions have been encouraged to provide violence prevention and intervention into the medical care of youth. Also, views on youth violence have shifted from being viewed as a justice system problem to a medical issue (Cunningham et al., 2009). Accordingly, medical institutions, such as emergency departments, trauma centers, and primary care offices, have taken action. In a randomized control trial conducted at an urban emergency department, researchers studied if brief intervention for youth who reported alcohol use and violence in the past year would be effective and feasible. Brief intervention effectiveness was based on behavioral changes such as attitude, self-efficacy, and readiness to change alcohol consumption and violent acts. The researchers determined that the brief interventions were effective in attitudes and self-efficacy. However, readiness to change alcohol use and violence was not statistically significant (Cunningham et al., 2009). Further examination of the relationship between age and alcohol brief counseling intervention with counselors in a trauma center is needed.

SOURCE: Leigh Zick Dongre, PhD, LPCA, LCASA, completed her doctoral studies at the University of North Carolina at Charlotte.

College Students and Binge Patterns: Chemical and Process

The culture as a college student within a center of higher learning, such as undergraduate, graduate, or community college setting, is often described as its own special culture. Increasingly, attention has been directed at a better understanding within the college culture about risks to the learner's health. It is no surprise that mood-altering drugs capture an important amount of focus in this examination of college culture and health. Statistics show a higher than average amount of experimentation, misuse, and harmful, risky use of mood-altering substances than in the average American culture. For the college student, for example, an Internet search can produce a number of sites that explain how to get drunk very fast or unexpected learnings from being a heroin addict. Hingson, Zha, and Weitzman (2009) conducted research specifically looking at the alcohol-related problems associated with 18- to 24-year-old college students and found disturbing trends: *every year* almost 2,000 students die from alcohol-related injuries, almost 700,000 are assaulted by another intoxicated student, and 97,000 report sexual assault that is specifically alcohol related. Often, this type of alcohol use pertains to even riskier binge drinking patterns. Binge drinking as defined by the CDC consists of rapid consumption in a concentrated time period: for males, five or more standard drinks are consumed; with females, binge drinking involves consuming four or more standard drinks at one drinking episode (CDC, 2015a). It is important to note that the lesser volume of alcohol designated as a binge limit for females is lower than males. Research has substantiated that females process alcohol differently and an increased effect is achieved with lower amounts of alcohol (NIAAA, 2013). Further, it is noted that the average amount of standard drinks consumed during a binge drinking episode is approximately eight drinks (CDC, 2015a).

McMurtrie (2014) highlights findings that try to explain the *why* in these disturbing trends among college students. Her work notes that studies consistently show environmental factors are important, such as proximity of bars and liquor stores and alcohol enforcement of legal identification and age verification. When the bars surrounding campuses make drink specials and drink discounts enticing, this pattern leads to overindulgence. In addition, binge drinking was often found with membership in fraternities and sororities, and a history of binge drinking prior to entering college. Attempts to harness expertise led to the development of many resources for universities including, but not limited to, the Higher Education Center for Alcohol, Drug Use, and Violence Prevention, with extensive research projects and resources to identify ways to intervene effectively to reduce harm to college students seeking mood-altering substances. From findings at 10 different universities that were being studied to see what might be effective at reducing binge drinking on campus, the Harvard Public Health researchers noted small changes at five of the 10 universities: "small improvements in alcohol consumption and related harms at colleges . . . changing alcohol-related policies, marketing, and promotions" (Weitzman, Nelson, Lee, & Wechsler, 2004). Whereas effective measures can help reduce binge drinking, McMurtrie (2014) points out that 750 college presidents, when surveyed, indicated a lack of evidence-based changes that instead showed a reliance on past approaches that did not show efficacy. The University of Minnesota produced an approach using Brofenbrenner's social ecological theoretical approach (as outlined in Chapter 2). The approach used provides a comprehensive way of coordinating the amount of work and breadth of foci involved in working to reduce high-risk drinking by college students. Perhaps the conclusions reached by Weitzman and colleagues sum it up best: "Changing conditions that shape drinking-related choices, opportunities, and consequences for drinkers and those that supply them with alcohol appear to be key ingredients to an effective public health prevention program" (2004, p. 195).

Evidence-Based Practices

Predisposing Factors

Evidence has identified certain predisposing factors, or aspects that contribute to risky use, that continues throughout the lifespan. It can be helpful when working with clients to highlight these factors that may place the person at even higher risk of developing problems with addictive substances or processes. Genetics and family history are seen as important factors that contribute to health risks around substance use (National Institute on Drug Abuse [NIDA], 2003). Past research highlights negative childhood events as particularly indicative of future substance use problems, such as a parent with a substance use disorder and substantial dysfunction in the family can put the young child at greater risk for future problems with risky use of alcohol, other drugs, and other addictive behaviors. Aggressive behaviors in early childhood can lead to escalating problems that, without intervention, can spiral further into patterns of addiction (NIDA, 2003). Major life transitions, experimentation at an early age, peers engaging in risky use of substances, increasing family stressors such as poverty or chronic illness, and traumatic experiences add to factors that can predispose an individual to problems in their situation. Even older adults, when facing major life stressors such as retirement or loss of a life partner, are predisposed to develop substance misuse patterns as a maladaptive means of coping if, for example, they are in a retirement community where peers engage in risky use of substances. Hence, throughout the lifespan, factors can predispose individuals to be more at risk for misuse of substances and addictive processes. While predisposing factors are important to explore with clients in order to better identify heightened patterns of risk, it is also important to help clients begin to explore and identify protective factors as discussed in the following section.

Protective Factors

In efforts to have an impact on the estimated 6 million teens, young adults, and adults born between 1983 and 2000 who are projected to die from smoking-related causes, the Office of Adolescent Health (OAH) has gathered data on protective factors that might have a positive influence to reduce those projections (2015). Since cigarette smoking, including e-cigarette use with nicotine, is considered a risk factor for other substance misuse, it is even more important to examine protective factors that inhibit the use of cigarettes. Several factors are highlighted as protective and hence are important for the substance abuse counselor to explore and assess.

Parental influence remains important; when parents are modeling a tobacco-free home environment, that behavior is protective for the young person in their care. Likewise, if a parent chooses abstinence from tobacco or seeks counseling for smoking cessation, important health decisions are then modeled to the young person. Next, conversations about smoking and parent disapproval are considered important and impactful. Having regular conversations about healthy choices to avoid cigarette use and other drug abstinence are considered effective protective tools. The CDC reports recent trends, such as nearly one-quarter of high school students (24.6%) indicated current use of some form of tobacco, and for the first time e-cigarettes were the leading method by which tobacco was used (2015b). Whereas, those youth who refrain from smoking until the age of 26 are less likely to ever smoke (CDC, 2015b). Intervention with youth who are engaging in risky use of tobacco is an especially important consideration for the counselor. With one-fourth of high school students using tobacco in some form, particularly e-cigarettes, major strategies that address this age group and risk pattern are important. While prevention of first use or experimentation is important, it is the young user who is demonstrating risky use that is of particular concern and who might best benefit from more focused intervention prior to nicotine dependency being triggered. For example, a sophomore in high school who indicates no harmful side effects of using e-cigarettes, uses e-cigarettes when socializing with other smokers in his or her age group 1–2 times per week, and has not developed nicotine dependency is the very individual a brief intervention by a knowledgeable counselor or health care professional trained in specialized brief intervention techniques might benefit. More in-depth information and examination of clinical tools of brief interventions will be reviewed in later chapters examining clinical interventions.

Additional protective factors throughout the lifespan include better access to health care and evidence-based approaches to cope with adverse childhood events, improved PTSD and trauma-focused care, effective strategies to manage bullying, support for identifying sexual orientation, healthy relationship skills, improved communication at home or schools or workplaces, media guidelines around advertising, pricing guidelines in communities for alcohol markets, and healthy coping resources to manage stress such as mindfulness approaches. All of these protective factors can involve counselors and advocacy work on behalf of clients engaging in risky substance use. Screening early is stressed as noted by Feinstein and colleagues "given the link between age of initiation and lifetime incidence of addiction, identification and early intervention are vital" (Feinstein, Richter, & Foster, 2012, p. 433).

Identifying Protective Factors and Advocacy

While a number of protective factors can be identified, far greater research is needed to create effective implementation of enhancing the known protective factors. Clearly, "more research is needed on the effectiveness of promising prevention programs, early interventions, and treatments tailored to teens of high school age, and of best practices for implementation" (Feinstein et al., 2012, p. 434). Additional community and national recommendations to identify protective factors and align care with effective tools involves expansion of billing and reimbursement for counselors providing effective screening and interventions, prevention services that are available to youth and adults at no charge, increased federal funds to provide integrated health care and qualified health centers, and guidelines for equity in care for substance-related issues (Feinstein et al., 2012). Further, improved screening and care of mental health disorders is important to reduce overdose deaths (Jones et al., 2013). Recommendations for protective initiatives and advocacy for effective prescription drug monitoring programs and sharing of electronic health records can help detect and decrease more risky NMPD use, especially for opioids and benzodiazepines.

In summary, as noted in the beginning of this chapter, it is an important time as a counselor to begin to provide much-needed services for those who have been using substances in risky ways but are not yet addicted. Risky use is an important and evolving area of counseling focus at present and for the foreseeable future, especially as an important key to prevent and reduce the incidence of substance use disorders. Further exploration of assessment of risky use and addictive use follows in Chapter 6. Questions about diagnosing and the criteria of substance use disorders and process addiction are further detailed in Chapter 7.

Skills In Action

Box 5.3: Case Illustration of Questioning Risky Use

My name is Nikki. I am here to see you because a friend was injured in a camping trip after we had set up camp for the night. We built a wonderful campfire, grilled dinner over the fire, and continued our night with a few drinks. My friend maybe had more drinks than usual and stumbled getting up to go get a last drink for the evening. Unfortunately she stumbled into the fire, and was burned on her arms and on her chin. We immediately took her to the emergency room at the nearest hospital. During the nurse's assessment, my friend was asked about the amount of alcohol she had consumed and then she was asked if her burn injury might be related to alcohol use. That really got my attention. I wondered about that for a long time. Then, the nurse asked the last question about whether she or anyone else had been injured as a result of drinking in the past year. My heart tumbled then because I was the one who brought the drinks, I was the one who had talked all about us getting super relaxed and partying by the campfire, and I was the one who then began to wonder about my own patterns and what all this means. And most importantly, do I have a drinking problem?

Experiential Skills Learning Activity

If you were the counselor for Nikki, how would you go about responding to her last question?

What facts or resources would you want her to explore?

1. Imagine being a counselor working with risky substance users and finding yourself in an elevator with your state senator. Identify at least three talking points from this chapter that you want to be sure to convey to the senator. Practice giving this elevator speech with classmates; reflect on strengths of your speech and changes you want to make.

2. Go to www.rethinkingdrinking.niaaa.nih.gov and practice with the interactive screening tools on the website. Share with classmates your first reactions. How would you prepare a client to go to the same site if they were worried about their alcohol use? List strengths of the website for future clients. List areas of concern.

RESOURCES FOR FURTHER LEARNING

Centers for Disease Control and Prevention

http://www.cdc.gov

Higher Education Center for Alcohol and Drug Misuse Recovery and Prevention

http://hecaod.osu.edu

Office of Adolescent Health

http://www.hhs.gov/ash/oah

REFERENCES

American Psychiatric Association (APA). (2013). *Diagnostic and statistical manual of mental disorders* (5th ed.). Arlington, VA: American Psychiatric Publishing.

Arria, A. M., Caldeira, K. M., Kasperski, S. J., O'Grady, K. E., Vincent, K. B., Griffiths, R. R., & Wish, E. D. (2010). Increased alcohol consumption, nonmedical prescription drug use, and illicit drug use are associated with energy drink consumption among college students. *Journal of Addiction Medicine, 4*(2), 74–80. doi:10.1097/ADM.0b013e3181aa8dd4

Benotsch, E. G., Koester, S., Luckman, D., Martin, A. M., & Cejka, A. (2011). Non-medical use of prescription drugs and sexual risk behavior in young adults. *Journal of Addictive Behaviors, 36*, 152–155.

Blanco, C., Xu, Y., Brady, K., Pérez-Fuentes, G., Okuda, M., & Wang, S. (2013). Comorbidity of posttraumatic stress disorder with alcohol dependence among US adults: Results from National Epidemiological Survey on Alcohol and Related Conditions. *Drug and Alcohol Dependence, 132*(3), 630–638.

Butchart, M., Farrington, D., & Cerda, M. (2002). Youth violence. *The world report on violence and health.* Geneva (Switzerland): World Health Organization.

Centers for Disease Control and Prevention (CDC). (2015a). Alcohol poisoning deaths. *CDC Vital Signs.* Retrieved from http://www.cdc.gov/vitalsigns/pdf/2015-01-vitalsigns.pdf

Centers for Disease Control and Prevention (CDC). (2015b). Tobacco use among middle and high school students—United States, 2011–2014. *Morbidity and Mortality Weekly Report, 64*(14), 381–385. Retrieved from http://www.cdc.gov/mmwr/preview/mmwrhtml/mm6414a3.htm?s_cid=mm6414a3_e

Cherpitel, C. J. (1993). Alcohol and violence-related injuries: an emergency room study. *Addiction, 88*(1), 79–88.

Choo, E. K., Benz, M., Rybarczyk, M., Broderick, K., Linden, J., Boudreaux, E. D., & Miner, J. (2014). The Intersecting roles of violence, gender, and substance use in the emergency department: A research agenda. *ACEM Academic Emergency Medicine, 21*(12), 1447–1452.

Cornwell, E. E., Belzberg, H., Velmahos, G., Chan, L. S., Demetriades, D., Stewart, B. M. . . . Berne, T. V. (1998). The prevalence and effect of alcohol and drug abuse on cohort-matched critically injured patients. *The American Surgeon, 64*(5), 461–465.

Cunningham, R. M., Walton, M. A., Goldstein, A., Chermack, S. T., Shope, J. T., Raymond Bingham, C., & Blow, F. C. (2009). Three-month follow-up of brief computerized and therapist interventions for alcohol and violence among teens. *Academic Emergency Medicine, 16*(11), 1193–1207.

Dischinger, P., Mitchell, K., Kufera, J., Soderstrom, C., & Lowenfels, A. (2001). A longitudinal study of former trauma center patients: The association between toxicology status and subsequent injury mortality. *The Journal of Trauma: Injury, Infection, and Critical Care, 51*(5), 877–886.

Erickson, P. G., Butters, J. E., Cousineau, M. M., Harrison, L., & Korf, D. (2006). Girls and weapons: An international study of the perpetration of violence. *Journal of Urban Health, 83*(5), 788–801.

Feinstein, E.C., Richter, L., & Foster, S. E. (2012). Addressing the critical health problem of adolescent substance use through health care, research, and public policy. *Journal of Adolescent Health, 50*, 431–436. doi:10.1016/j.jadohealth.2011.12.033

Gentilello, L., Rivara, F., Donovan, D., Jurkovich, G. J., Daranciang, E., Dunn, C. W., . . . Ries, R. R. (1999). Alcohol interventions in a trauma center as a means of reducing the risk of injury recurrence. *Annals of Surgery, 230*, 473–483.

Goins, W. A., Thompson J., & Simpkins, C. (1992). Recurrent intentional injury. *Journal of the National Medical Association, 84*(5), 431–435.

Hingson, R. W., Zha, W., & Weitzman, E. R. (2009). Magnitude of and trends in alcohol-related mortality and morbidity among U.S. college students ages 18–24, 1998–2005. *Journal of Studies on Alcohol, 16*, 12–20. Retrieved from http://www.ncbi.nlm.nih.gov/pubmed?cmd=search&term=19538908

Jones, C. M., Mack, K. A., & Paulozzi, L. J. (2013). Pharmaceutical overdose deaths, United States, 2010. *Journal of American Medical Association, 309,* 657–659. doi:10.1001/jama.2013.272

Lockwood, E., & Forbes, D. (2014). Posttraumatic stress disorder and comorbidity: Untangling the Gordian knot. *Psychological Injury and Law, 7*(2), 108–121.

Lookatch, S. J., Dunne, E. M., & Katz, E. C. (2012). Predictors of nonmedical use of prescription stimulants. *Journal of Psychoactive Drugs, 44,* 86–91. doi:10.1080/02791072.2012.662083

Love, J., & Zatzick, D. (2014). Screening and intervention for comorbid substance disorders, PTSD, depression, and suicide: A trauma center survey. *Psychiatric Services, 65*(7), 918–923. doi:10.1176/appi.ps.201300399

McKibben, J. B. A., Bresnick, M. G., Wiechman Askay, S. A., & Fauerbach, J. A. (2008). Acute stress disorder and posttraumatic stress disorder: A prospective study of prevalence, course, and predictors in a sample with major burn injuries. *Journal of Burn Care & Research: Official Publication of the American Burn Association, 29*(1), 22–35.

McMurtrie, B. (2014, December 2). Why colleges haven't stopped binge drinking. *The Chronicle of Higher Education.* Retrieved from http://chronicle.com/article/Why-Colleges-Haven-t-Stopped/150229/

National Institute on Alcohol Abuse and Alcoholism (NIAAA). (2013). *Rethinking drinking.* (NIH Pub No. 10-3770). Rockville, MD: National Institute on Alcohol Abuse and Alcoholism.

National Institute on Alcohol Abuse and Alcoholism (NIAAA). (2017). *Alcohol facts and statistics.* Retrieved from https://www.niaaa.nih.gov/alcohol-health/overview-alcohol-consumption/alcohol-facts-and-statistic

National Institute on Drug Abuse (NIDA). (2003). *Preventing drug abuse among children and adolescents: A research-based guide for parents, educators and community leaders* (2nd ed.) (NIH Pub No. 04-4212A). Retrieved from https://www.drugabuse.gov/publications/preventing-drug-abuse-among-children-adolescents/chapter-1 -risk-factors-protective-factors/what-are-early-signs-

O'Brien, M. C., McCoy, T. P., Rhodes, S. D., Wagoner, A., & Wolfson M. (2008). Caffeinated cocktails: Energy drink consumption, high-risk drinking, and alcohol- related consequences among college students. *Journal of Academic Emergency Medicine, 15,* 453–460.

Office of Adolescent Health (OAH). (2015). *Risk and protective factors.* Retrieved from http://www.hhs.gov/ash/ oah/adolescent-health-topics/substance-abuse/tobacco/tips-for-parents.html

Schermer, C. R. (2005). Feasibility of alcohol screening and brief intervention. *The Journal of Trauma: Injury, Infection, and Critical Care, 59*(3), S119–S123.

Shibru, D., Zahnd, E., Becker, M., Bekaert, N., Calhoun, D., & Victorino, G. P. (2007). Benefits of a hospital-based peer intervention program for violently injured youth. *Journal of the American College of Surgeons, 205*(5), 684–689.

Substance Abuse and Mental Health Services Administration (SAMHSA). (2014). *Results from the 2013 National Survey on Drug Use and Health: Summary of National Findings,* NSDUH Series H-48, (HHS Publication No. 14-4863). Rockville, MD: Author.

Weitzman, E. R., Nelson, T. F., Lee, H., & Wechsler, H. (2004). Reducing drinking and related harms in college: Evaluation of the "A Matter of Degree" program. *American Journal of Preventive Medicine, 27,* 187–196.

Worrell, S. S., Koepsell, T. D., Sabath, D. R., Gentilello, L. M., Mock, C. N., & Nathens, A. B. (2006). The risk of reinjury in relation to time since first injury: A retrospective population-based study. *The Journal of Trauma: Injury, Infection, and Critical Care, 60*(2), 379–384.

6

Assessment of Risky Use and Addictive Disorders

LEARNING OBJECTIVES

Upon completion of reading this chapter and completing the suggested activities, the learner will

- describe the specific elements in releasing confidential information;
- list key considerations in an informed consent process;
- discuss at least two counseling skills recommended for assessment;
- describe empathy as it relates to building rapport and trust; and
- practice screening in a role play with at least one screening tool.

Risky Use

In the previous chapter, information was provided in a brief overview of risky use of addictive substances for which the field has gained better knowledge. In this chapter, we examine various counseling-related elements, such as empathy, involved in assessing various types of use and misuse over the vast spectrum of problematic substance use. Assessment is often a multilayered dynamic process, not just completed in one session, and includes looking at the whole person, especially substance abuse issues as they may interact with other mental disorders. The following graphic in Figure 6.1 can help you visualize the process as a whole with arrows demonstrating how it is a continually fluid process and, often, additional mental health conditions may become apparent. Emphasis in this chapter will also highlight the person-centered approach as an important counseling goal. Keep in mind there is no one-size-fits-all approach to assessment. Consider the following tenets when reviewing assessment for each client: (1) Cultural identity is often significant and is key to consider with each client's assessment, (2) culture may also include various treatment cultures such as 12-step groups or alternative healing approaches that may be very important in the assessment process, and (3) counselors should seek clinical supervision as assessment expertise is developed.

Figure 6.1 Relationships Among Screening, Assessment, and Treatment Planning

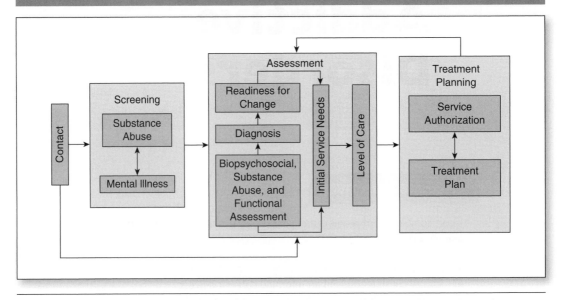

SOURCE: Center for Substance Abuse and Treatment, 2006. Retrieved from https://store.samhsa.gov/shin/content/PHD1131/PHD1131.pdf.

These next three chapters provide an expanded look at the use of screening and brief interventions covering the spectrum of misuse to addictive abuse of mood-altering substances and processes. For this chapter, we will first focus on assessment involving screening and then on more extensive evaluation tools. The following chapter will focus on forming a diagnosis and consideration of treatment planning, looking at level of care needs. Chapter 8 will explore brief counseling interventions.

Knowledge

The Continuum of Assessment

In substance-related counseling, it is important to evaluate where on the spectrum of experimental use, misuse, or addictive use a client's pattern of using, drinking, or behaving would be found. Increasingly, it becomes very important for assessment to be conducted in a professional manner utilizing professional counseling assessment tools. Assessment, according to the *Diagnostic and Statistical Manual of Mental Disorders* (5th ed., *DSM-5*) (American Psychiatric Association [APA], 2013), reminds clinicians that when assessing, especially with new *DSM-5* cross-cutting symptom assessment tools, that these tools help to view the issues being assessed as dimensional. In other words, in a dimensional approach the counselor views many more aspects from various dimensions of the person's health and symptoms incorporating how severe the symptoms may be with types of symptoms and other features. This dimensional assessment is then included with the traditional categorical assessment, yes/no approach. This can lead to future assessment that incorporates "basic disease mechanisms based on pathophysiology, neurocircuitry, gene-environment interactions, and laboratory tests . . . to supplement and enhance the accuracy of the diagnostic process" (APA, 2013, p. 733). These dimensional concepts are fitting for the assessment and evaluation actions by the professional counselor working with individuals whose patterns range from risky use to severely disordered. In addition, counselors using assessment tools for those whose behaviors range from risky to severe addictive behaviors, such as gambling or any of the various process addictions, should also carefully use the tools to enhance clinical decisions. Process addiction-related disorders continue to be evaluated for assessment and diagnosis purposes as seen in Internet gaming disorder that is under consideration in the *DSM-5* as a condition for further study (APA, 2013).

Next, we are reminded of the importance of assessment as part of counseling. Miller and Rollnick (1991) emphasized the importance of using "evaluation results as part of motivational counseling" (p. 89). Assessment can also involve diagnosing, which will be discussed in greater depth in the following chapter. Counselor training, especially in an addiction counseling accredited specialty, requires specific knowledge, skills, awareness, and clinical internships in practice areas that meet quality accreditation standards approved by the Council for Accreditation of Counseling & Related Educational Programs (CACREP) for counselor preparation programs including substance use screening, assessment, and diagnosis (CACREP, 2016). For the focus of this chapter it is important to examine the full spectrum of assessment. Currently, assessment, as highlighted in this chapter, can range from a brief phone screening to a lengthy multiday, multidisciplinary full psychosocial evaluation.

Important Considerations: Laying the Groundwork for Assessment

Addressing Informed Consent

Another important aspect of building trust and gaining rapport pertains to informed consent, in other words, helping the client understand better what it is they are consenting to and what to expect in a professional counseling session. Another important consideration of the informed consent carefully provides information on confidentiality, especially as tied to the Federal Confidentiality Regulations as noted in the following section. In a careful approach to helping connect with the client, especially related to substance use issues, there are several steps recommended, including a review of what diagnoses, if any, will be made; recommendations for further treatment, if indicated; risks and benefits of addiction or risky use counseling; monetary costs involved; options if recommendations are rejected by the client; and the important issue of client choice (Walker, Logan, Clark, & Leukefeld, 2005). Often these issues are addressed in a written document called Informed Consent, which is provided to the client at the beginning of services, reviewed, and then signed by both the client and counselor (Remley & Herlihy, 2007). It is also recommended that if the assessment session may lead to a diagnosis, such as when utilizing insurance benefits for the session, the counselor is expected to "disclose to clients (or their parents or guardians) their diagnosis when the diagnosis is recorded" (Remley & Herlihy, 2007, p. 262). The process of reviewing what is to be expected in a professional counseling setting can begin to assist clients with building trust. Another important area that helps build trust is in reviewing client confidentiality and specific consents for the release of any confidential information.

Counselors working with clients misusing alcohol and other drugs have special guidelines pertaining to confidentiality that are governed by federal laws, uniquely different from confidentiality and mental disorders. It is strongly recommended that the counselor become familiar with these laws in order to answer questions the client may present. The specific federal law that addresses substance abuse counseling is *Federal Regulation 42 CFR Part 2*, and it applies to any program that has a role in providing substance abuse or addiction education, treatment, counseling. or prevention, and importantly, receives any funding from the federal government such as Medicaid reimbursement, for example (Kunkel, 2012). These laws supersede state laws when it pertains to protecting clients with alcohol or other drug issues and are receiving services as outlined above. There are exceptions to maintaining confidentiality such as those that are ordinarily utilized if child or elder abuse is reported, medical emergencies, or if the client is determined to be suicidal or homicidal. In addition, confidential information may be released when the provider of the services obtains a specific written consent (Kunkel, 2012). The national organization Center for Substance Abuse Treatment (CSAT) offers treatment improvement manuals regarding various issues in substance abuse care. These manuals can be downloaded or mailed at no charge, cover many key issues in substance-related counseling, and can be vital resources for beginning counselors, especially if the client has any requests that assessment results be provided to any others. Below, in Figure 6.2, is one example of a sample consent for release of information provided by CSAT (2000).

It may be important to include the confidential information reminder, as shown in the following, on any screening tools that are utilized in the program. Information may include a footer at the bottom of the page for information that is released stating, for example,

Figure 6.2 Sample Consent Form

Consent for the Release of Confidential Information

I, _____, authorize XYZ Clinic to receive
(name of client or participant)

from/disclose to _____
(name of person and organization)

for the purpose of _____
(need for disclosure)

the following information_____
(nature of the disclosure)

I understand that my records are protected under the Federal and State Confidentiality Regulations and cannot be disclosed without my written consent unless otherwise provided for in the regulations. I also understand that I may revoke this consent at any time except to the extent that action has been taken in reliance on it and that in any event this consent expires automatically on _____ unless otherwise specified below.
(date, condition, or event)

Other expiration specifications:

_____
Date executed

_____
Signature of client

_____
Signature of parent or guardian, where required

From: Figure 7-3: Sample Consent Form

SAMHSA/CSAT
Treatment
Improvement
Protocols

Integrating Substance Abuse Treatment and Vocational Services.
Treatment Improvement Protocol (TIP) Series, No. 38.
Center for Substance Abuse Treatment.
Rockville (MD): Substance Abuse and Mental Health Services Administration (US); 2000.

Any information noted on this document has special protection by Federal Confidentiality Regulations (42 CFR Part 2) that prohibits disclosure or redisclosure without specific written consent. General consent for release of medical information is NOT acceptable for disclosure of this client's information.

In the box below, practice creating a sample consent for release of information that you could imagine using with a client who is seeing you for alcohol screening. If you have a practice partner, next practice how you might present this information to your client. Make notes of possible changes you believe would be helpful for this informed consent.

Box 6.1: Exercise for Developing an Informed Consent Form

Develop your own informed consent document.

Once informed consent procedures have been completed with your client, it is time to focus on further building rapport and trust with the client. This is greatly enhanced by professional counselors who are being intentional with active listening, use of foundational reflective counseling skills, and efforts to create a psychologically safe environment that conveys warmth, genuineness, congruence, care, positive regard, and perhaps, most importantly, nonjudgmental understanding.

Rapport-Building and Trust Issues

Throughout this text, emphases on motivational considerations are key. Gaining trust, understanding your client better, building rapport, and helping your client are fostered by key concepts first identified in the 1940s by Carl Rogers as "empathic listening," also known as "active listening" interventions (Kirschenbaum, 2009) and the emphasis on person-centered counseling skills (Rogers, 1957; Young, 2012) emphasizing rapport-building and enhanced empathy with reflective listening is important in the counseling work with a client, and one might argue, especially in the screening stage with a client. Much has been written about building the optimal counseling relationship and its importance in the working alliance (Parsons & Zhang, 2014). Rogers challenged the field of counseling in many ways and in the area of diagnosing clients he indicated the following: "It is not stated that it is necessary for psychotherapy that the therapist have an accurate psychological diagnosis of the client" (1957, p. 101). The addiction counselor, then, is encouraged to rely more on the therapeutic foundational skills rather than emphasize diagnosing. The student is encouraged to review basic counseling skills texts to incorporate many of the teachings about foundational counseling skills in the work as a substance abuse counselor. Empathy has continued to be recognized as an important therapeutic element in helping any client; Bill Miller incorporated Rogers's empathic concepts into his motivational interviewing (MI) model (Miller, 2014) and noted "this [Rogers's] style of empathic warmth and reflective listening is employed from the very beginning and throughout the process of motivational interviewing" (Miller & Rollnick, 1991, p. 55).

Key points to remember about empathic listening are summarized as follows:

- Listen carefully *without* blaming, judging, criticizing, or fault-finding, rather *warmth and understanding*;
- Acceptance of the person differs from approval of addictive behaviors and fosters trust; often referred to as unconditional positive regard for the client from Rogerian theory and Stanley Standal's work (Kirschenbaum, 2009);

- Reflective listening is an essential foundation to effective counseling, especially with substance use issues;
- Genuineness on the part of the counselor, in other words, "being real" (Parsons & Zhang, 2014); this is an especially important core condition for therapeutic work with clients struggling with substance abuse and related negative stigmas, expressing concern for the client is beneficial primarily when shared from a genuine concern by the counselor; with screening, it has been our experience that expressing concern for the client's health helps diminish defensiveness regarding alcohol and other drug abuse; and
- Congruence as seen with the counselor who, for example, persistently doubts the truthfulness of the client—it is better for the counselor to own and voice these feelings therapeutically than pretend a false acceptance; "nondefensive genuineness." (Kirschenbaum, 2009, p. 194)

As an added resource, the following graphic (see Figure 6.3) developed by the coauthor, Dr. Veach, may help remind counselors-in-training of the importance of rapport-building, especially with a nontrusting client such as one struggling with stigmas around alcohol and other drug-related disorders. In order to best reach our clients, remember REACH: Relate, Reflect with Empathy, and Affirm Concern for Health. Especially in the early beginning of the session, the professional addiction counselor is able to skillfully vary reflections and affirmations to build a therapeutic counseling relationship before moving into a formal assessment process.

Figure 6.3   REACH

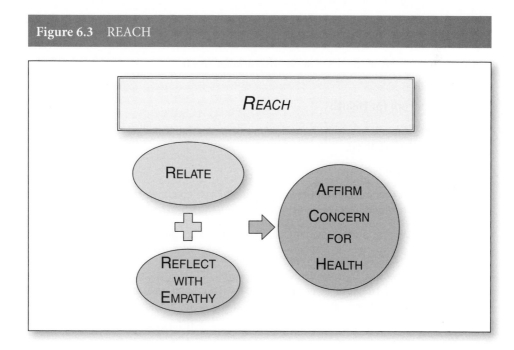

Box 6.2: Exercise for Enhancing Empathy and Understanding With Clients

REACH Case Illustration (Session begins after informed consent has been reviewed)

Relate

Counselor: It can sometimes be hard to make the choice to come in to talk with a counselor; thank you for making that choice today.

Client: I'm not even sure why I'm here; I didn't want to be here, but it's my boss who started all this mess making me come get an assessment about my drinking.

Reflect With Empathy

Counselor: You're upset about being here and feel like you are pressured by your boss to be here today.

Client: Yeah, it's just too much to do—I really don't want to talk to anyone.

Counselor: I sense a lot of frustration.

Client: You are so right—it's nobody's business how much I drink, I do my job!

Counselor: Doing your job is important to you.

Client: Yes, it is! I work hard every day, always there on time, been there for years. Now all of a sudden, I have a problem at work. It's not fair—why am I being picked on? Other people go out and have a beer or two at lunch. The one time I do it, somebody tells the boss.

Counselor: You see yourself as a dedicated worker now dealing with a new challenge around drinking. It's hard to understand, "Why me?"

Client: Yeah, it's hard; I'm not hurting anyone, so what?

Affirm Concern for Health

Counselor: Sounds like when your drinking isn't harmful, it makes you question a lot about this whole thing.

Client: Yeah!

Counselor: It sounds important to you to explore more about whether your drinking patterns might be harmful or within health limits.

Client: Well, that might be interesting . . . but I'm not an alcoholic. I don't have a problem!

Counselor: So, looking briefly at your regular use to explore if any health risks might be present might give you some more information as you decide how you're going to move forward. These brief 10 questions can help us see whether some risky use might be present. These questions are not about telling you that you are or are not an alcoholic. These 10 questions look more deeply into the spectrum of risky drinking and your health—low risk, moderate risk, or severe risk. Let's see your health risks and begin with the first question; then we will look at your results in a few minutes, and go over how or if risky use may be something you want to look at further.

It is expected then that addiction counselors care for clients in a professional manner with understanding and empathy. Lewis (2014) noted that empathy is the most important component of MI according to Miller; further, empathy is best "demonstrated through reflective listening" (p. 92). Carl Rogers is viewed by many as a key theorist to first highlight empathy as a very important and necessary condition for effective counseling to occur (Kirschenbaum, 2009). His theory evolved into tenets that stressed "the [therapy or counseling] methods are not nearly as important as the attitudes of the therapist" (Kirschenbaum, 2009, p. 195) or what we more often refer to now as the therapeutic alliance. Kirschenbaum adds a concluding highlight as cited about Rogers while in South Africa: "When I can be very present in the group, fully present, without façade, without any white coat, either real or imaginary, that seems to initiate the process" (2009, p. 505). Miller and Rollnick (2012) highlight research findings since 1980 that underscore the major importance of empathic listening that has been emphasized for effective MI. With MI being researched in more than "200 clinical trials . . . MI is often associated with beneficial outcomes when compared with no intervention or brief advice, or when added to other active treatment" (Miller & Rollnick, 2012, p. 379). Further, when compared with more direct confrontational-type approaches, Miller and Rollnick (2012) note substantial benefits and improved outcomes when MI is used: "[A] therapeutic approach that is empathic, compassionate, respectful, and supportive of human strengths and autonomy is likely to shine" (p. 381). For example, one major analysis of multiple studies noted that "the effect size of MI was twice as large when those treated came primarily from U.S. minority groups rather than from the majority white population" (Hettema et al., 2005 as cited by Miller & Rollnick, 2012, p. 381), leading to conclusions that active listening had such an effect since it was more unusual in interactions with professionals. Continued research into the particular ingredients of MI that are most effective remains a goal of Miller and Rollnick (2012), as it is not yet clear the exact specific actions that bring about positive results with MI. Addiction clinicians are encouraged to seek specific training in MI with credentialed MI trainers and supervisors if pursuing models that exhibit MI fidelity. However, addiction counselors can begin to focus on important preliminary work toward empathic responses as next discussed.

Importantly then, this key area in the learning goals of the addiction counselor relates to the counselor's attitudes; work on self-awareness to change attitudes of blaming, criticizing, or judging the client; and reminders of power differentials, such as presenting oneself in white coats. In essence, negative stigma is often present around issues of substance or process addictions and is often a major barrier to developing trust with the professional counselor (Lloyd, 2013). Keyes and colleagues (2010) found troubling trends in individuals needing counseling for an alcohol use disorder: the worse the perceived stigma around addiction, the less likely the person was to seek counseling, no matter how severe the alcohol use disorder. Consider, then, how difficult it must be for the client to even enter the counselor's doorway for brief screening.

Box 6.3: Exercise for Exploring Empathy

EMPATHY QUESTIONS

To clarify further, empathy is not to be confused with sympathy. Take a moment and list qualities associated with sympathy; next list qualities associated with empathy. Reflect on the differences between sympathy and empathy.

- How would you describe the differences between empathy and sympathy to one of your counseling student peers?
- Discuss why it is important to be very clear in your professional counseling skills about the differences.
- Why is it important for the addict or alcoholic to be treated with empathy and not sympathy?
- How will you work toward being empathetic? List at least five goals you have toward enhancing your empathy with individuals affected by substance-related disorders or risky use.

The importance of the counselor's increasing awareness, then, of the negative effects of stigma adding to judgmental attitudes by counselors, is critically important toward enhancing rapport and trust-building. Remember, the client is coming in to the counselor's office, often for their very first counseling experience, and many are worried about being judged harshly. The first impression the client has of you may likely remain with them for any future services they seek. See Box 6.4 to examine counselor attitudes.

Empathy can be the antidote to negative stigmas and negating bias. Moreover, "empathy also is demonstrated by the attitude that reluctance to give up a problem behavior is expected; otherwise, change would have occurred already" (Lewis, 2014, p. 92). In MacLeod's dissertation research (2015), the author highlighted current views of empathy as noted in the work of Lam, Kolomitro, and Alamparambil (2011), which involve three different types of empathy: cognitive (seeing the client's perspective), affective (taking on the emotional experiences of the client by experiencing more of the client's feelings), and behavioral (being able to describe and communicate from the perspective of the client). MacLeod noted that studies show that positive attitudes by counselor trainees matter.

Questions remain, however, as to how effectively therapist or counselor preparation programs can teach, train, and enhance empathy skills (MacLeod, 2015), especially if counselors have deep-seated negative associations regarding addiction, such as those based in moral models that espouse individuals suffering from addiction are basically morally deficient, lack good character, and are weak-willed (Lewis, 2014).

Box 6.4: Exercise for Identifying Stigma Challenges

Conveying Understanding to Alcohol and Other Drug Abusing Clients

Facing Our Stigmas

It is an important professional consideration for counselors to address challenges they may face as substance abuse and addictions counseling services are provided. Consider the following:

Substance Abuse Counseling Issue	Internal Awareness/Stigma That Might Interfere With Conveying Understanding and Unconditional Positive Regard Stigma	Intentional Counselor Actions to Address
	Example:	
Client charged with third DWI while license revoked.	*Discomfort with client*—Why is he or she still out on our roads driving impaired again?	Share feelings of discomfort in supervision
Mother sent by DSS for child neglect due to methamphetamine abuse.	_____ _____	_____
20-year-old sent by university office for possession of marijuana.	_____ _____	_____
13-year-old sent by his pediatrician for binge drinking at the bus stop.	_____ _____	_____
72-year-old grandmother sent by a church counselor after a fall at church, reports of smelling alcohol, and admitting she drinks "only to help me sleep".	_____ _____	_____

List other examples and ways to address stigma for you as a counselor working with individuals abusing substances. _____
_____

SOURCE: Adapted from Parsons & Xhang, 2014. p. 105.

The following is one excerpt that demonstrates the therapeutic power of empathy, as cited in Kirschenbaum's work on the life of Carl Rogers, from a tension-filled, multiday professional training that Rogers led in South Africa in the early 1980s when apartheid ruled the country, beginning with comments from one of the black African group members: "I feel out in the cold. I don't get to know people. They don't get to know me. I would like to be myself here and let you know how I feel" (2009, p. 502). The following concise reflection from Rogers illustrates empathy: "It must be quite an isolated feeling to feel that much of a barrier" (2009, p. 502). Increasing progress was made in the session leading to breakthroughs in the connections with the group of the person quoted above. Later, due to such progress in this same training, Rogers (as cited in Kirschenbaum) adds, "one of the rarest experiences in the life of any one of us is to be deeply heard and understood and not judged . . . when there are the moments in which I unconditionally accept you as a person . . . that's a very healing, very releasing experience" (2009, p. 505). Practicing brief reflections that convey empathy is critically important in the screening process for optimal outcomes.

Box 6.5: Exercise to Practice Reflecting With Empathy

Practice reflections while exercising empathy to try and imagine how life might feel *if* you were experiencing feelings or experiences your client might be.

Trying to allow oneself to more fully empathize with individuals, putting aside preconceived ideas about drug addiction or distractions, such as biases or judgments about addictive disorders, is the greatest goal of the professional addiction counselor. MacLeod (2015) further emphasized the need to conduct substantial research to better understand how best to prepare counselors, especially substance abuse counselors, in skills pertaining to empathy. The use of reflection of content, feelings, or meaning can be important skills in efforts toward enhancing empathy and understanding.

Box 6.6: Exercise to Practice Active Listening and Reflections

First, begin a practice session with a partner acting as a client who has been abusing alcohol and other drugs while you practice the role of a counselor.

Begin the practice session with intentional focus on *using counseling reflection skills only—you can use reflection of content, feeling, or meaning.* Use at least 8–12 reflections without any questions, if at all possible. (These practice sessions may also be very good to videotape, review, and discuss with your instructor or class.)

For example, notice these reflections are at the *beginning of an assessment* session and the counselor does *not* use questions to begin.

Reflection 1. I'm hearing you talk about concerns about drinking and other drug use.

Reflection 2. It sounds like you have a lot on your mind about whether drugs or drinking are causing problems.

Reflection 3. I sense you have a lot to say about concerns with drinking and using other drugs.

Reflection 4. You sound like you really want someone to understand what is going on with you, with your using and drinking.

Reflection 5. You're angry about how much you are using when you don't want to do that anymore.

Your own reflections: _____

_____

_____

Further, it cannot be emphasized enough that a closed-question approach, especially about highly stigmatized issues such as drinking or drug use, is much more likely to create greater defensiveness and denial. As you practiced and learned in foundational counseling skills coursework, closed questions are those questions that result in yes or no limited responses and are to be avoided (Miller & Rollnick, 1991). There are many reasons for this that are beyond the scope of this chapter, but be very aware of any yes/no questions and steer clear of those on a consistent basis. If at all possible, work on converting closed questions into open questions to facilitate greater understanding and trust-building for the best outcome of the session. The addiction counselor needs to pay close attention, especially in the early part of the sessions, to eliminate closed questions when possible.

Imagine meeting a client for the first time, opening the session with the question, which we highly discourage, "Do you drink alcohol?" If your client says no and does not elaborate, your brief screening about the client's alcohol use and any further alcohol screening questions would be very difficult to then introduce. It is often a barrier in effective alcohol or other drug screening to initially inquire whether the person drinks or uses drugs as the client might also be further resistant and present the counselor with comments such as "Why are you asking me about cutting down my alcohol use when I just told you I don't drink?" and "Why are you asking me any of these questions about drugs—are you calling me a liar?" You can see how seemingly common questions can disrupt and derail the important assessment that needs to occur. Rather, it is recommended to introduce a screening session as a brief exploration to better understand the whole person and begin with a valid screening tool. For example, since approximately 70% of the American population drinks alcohol, it can be therapeutic to gently assume the client may drink alcohol thereby normalizing drinking by beginning with the gentle assumption that the person drinks. When clients do not engage in any alcohol consumption, the counselor will be informed of this information without noticeable defensiveness on the part of the client.

Box 6.7: Exercise With and Without Closed Questions

First, begin a practice session with a partner acting as a pretend alcohol-abusing client while you practice the role as a counselor.

Begin the practice session with at least 8–12 closed questions. Consider the following:

Question 1. Do you drink alcohol?

Question 2. Do you have problems with drinking alcohol?

Question 3. Do you drink to excess?

Question 4. Are you ever worried that you drink too much?

Question 5. Do you want to stop drinking?

Questions 6–12. Create your own closed questions and ask your partner, who is acting as a client.

Next, review and discuss with your partner the *experience of asking closed questions*.

What type of climate or feelings do closed questions seem to create in the session?

In you as a counselor?

In your partner playing the role of a client?

Discuss your insights with this practice session.

Now, with your partner, **change the questions** you used into more *open questions*. For example, Question 1 might change to a more open question such as "Since so many individuals drink on occasion in our culture, how often in the past year did you find that you drank beer, wine, or liquor such as in a mixed drink?" Or, "How would you describe your current pattern of drinking?"

Then, *discuss your insights into the importance of open questions for benefiting the client and your counseling.*

In summary, it is critical to help set the tone for the first session with an emphasis on listening first and screening questions later in the session so as to optimize the client's experience of being cared about and understood. Too often negative experiences in a first session can delay a person from returning to any counselor in the future.

Assessment of Use Patterns

Effective Screening in Current Practice

The professional counselor can view assessment along a spectrum ranging from screening using brief screening tools that could involve 2–5 minutes to the more complex multidimensional intensive evaluation that could involve information gathering over 1–3 days. First, screening will be examined in the chapter followed by an overview of more extensive evaluation. Primarily, many counselors, whether specializing in addiction care or not, are able to conduct screening with clients and as such, will be the major focus of this chapter. While screening may not be useful in diagnosing substance use disorders, results from screening may assist both counselor and client to identify if there is a need for an addiction specialist to conduct a more thorough evaluation. Screening can provide some indication, for example, of whether patterns of use fall in the risky range of use versus a substance use disorder. There is a growing body of literature providing evidence-based practice (EBP) of the utility of brief screening tools to better identify patterns of substance use. For the substance use field, these brief screening tools are central to working with individuals in the broader spectrum of risky use. As a reminder, the addiction and substance use field focused so much on either end of the spectrum of prevention of use or intensive treatment of severe substance use disorders that little attention was given to the risky user. Most screening tools exclusively addressed either detection of the presence of addiction or the absence of addiction. Currently, reliable and evidence-based screening tools that can be conducted quickly provide essential therapeutic counseling tools to help identify risky use. Early detection of any health concern, such as risky drinking, is a critical and important step toward addressing unhealthy patterns. Of substantial importance, early screening as a standard of care in every counseling setting can also prevent addiction, reduce negative substance-related consequences, and offer exploration of healthier alternatives as a routine part of counseling. Next, it is important to consider keys to successful screening as a part of the overall assessment picture.

First, increased attention has prompted the field to enhance motivation, for example, avoid the temptation of having the client fill out a screening tool while waiting in the lobby. Increasingly, research demonstrates that the building of the therapeutic relationship with the client is very important, especially at the first session, thus "establishing a personal working relationship and provides a motivational basis on which to ask the client to complete assessment" (Miller & Rollnick, 1991, p. 90). Miller and Rollnick (1991) emphasized the importance of using "evaluation results as part of motivational counseling" (p. 89). Meeting with the client and beginning with a focus on building the professional relationship is critical to successful screening.

The area of evidence-based screening that has received growing attention is due to the reported 38 million binge drinkers in the United States (binge drinking refers to consuming more than five standard drinks for men or more than four standard drinks for women during any one drinking occasion). Alcohol Screening accompanied by a Brief Intervention and, if indicated, Referral to Treatment (SBIRT) is encouraged in settings ranging from your primary care physician's office, the workplace, schools, colleges, or hospitals, to name a few. For a definition of risky alcohol use, first consider individuals who, according to the National Institute on Alcohol Abuse and Alcoholism (NIAAA), "for healthy adults in general, drinking more than the single-day or weekly amounts . . . is considered 'at-risk' or 'heavy' drinking"

(2016, p. 4). Risk advisories specific to alcohol use include daily and weekly amounts: *for men, no more than four standard alcoholic beverages on any one day and no more than 14 standard drinks total per week; for women, no more than three standard alcoholic beverages on any one day and no more than seven standard drinks total per week* (NIAAA, 2016). In reviewing standard drink amounts, one standard drink equals either a 12-ounce can of beer, 8 ounces of malt liquor, 5 ounces of wine, or a shot (1.5 ounces) of 80-proof liquor, such as whiskey (NIAAA, 2016). Moreover, risky users are ruled out from a diagnosis of severe substance use disorder or addiction when the client does not meet *DSM-5* criteria for a diagnosis of a severe substance use disorder or addiction. Historically, risky users receive few clinical services, yet evidence increasingly shows important clinical interventions for risky use can successfully foster healthier changes leading to reduction in the onset of addictive disease, improved health, and reductions in the use of healthcare for complications from risky use. SBIRT is often conducted in a wide range of settings, such as hospital trauma centers, schools and universities, workplaces, primary care doctor's offices, or counseling agencies (Centers for Disease Control and Prevention [CDC], 2014).

Box 6.8: Veronica Getz, Perspective From Administration on Screening and Brief Counseling Interventions With Hospital Patients

Prompt: Why provide SBIRT to trauma patients? Or Why support SBIRT? SBIRT stands for Screening, Brief Intervention, and Referral to Treatment—an evidence-based counseling method to treat substance abuse and alcohol addiction in patients.

As an administrator, one of my biggest responsibilities is ensuring that our care team has the resources needed to provide the safest and highest quality of care for our patients. For trauma and burn patients, this care team includes the front-line EMS responders, emergency department staff, operating room and anesthesia teams, ICU and floor nurses, physical and occupational therapists, pharmacists, surgeons, social workers, professional counselors, and a host of other care providers. Every single member of this team is vitally important to our patients' immediate acute care, but it is our counseling providers who have the paramount accountability in ensuring patients' long-term psychosocial health.

The Substance Abuse and Addiction Counseling program at Wake Forest Baptist Medical Center (WFBMC) arose from the list of requirements to become an accredited Level I Trauma Center. Our comprehensive counseling team has evolved into much more than what is mandated from a standards book, and it is my privilege to support counselors who have such a profound impact on patients and their families. The current team consists of faculty, PhD graduate assistants, PhD and master's interns, a Trauma Survivors Network counselor, and a dedicated SBIRT staff. We invest in their professional development to ensure their continued learning of the most updated methods of treatment, as well as present their findings and discoveries on the national and international stage to allow an even greater impact on patient outcomes. A clinical, research, and educational environment has been fostered, and our patients and their families are the biggest benefactors.

Not only is SBIRT the right thing to do, but it has a positive impact on margin for our medical center. Alcohol-related crashes result in more individuals receiving hospitalized care. Trauma patients who test positive for alcohol at admission have greater injuries, leading to the possibility of increased adverse events, longer length of stay, higher mortality and increased readmissions. SBIRT directly impacts our ability to decrease readmissions by creating a teachable moment with the patient regarding their traumatic event and hopefully using it as a catalyst toward positive change in their lives.

We recognize and respect that substance abuse and alcohol addiction may have led to the traumatic event that brought someone to our trauma center. Our patients deserve to be holistically treated, or those same risky behaviors that initially landed them here can lead to unnecessary repeat visits. Ignoring substance abuse and alcohol addiction in a trauma patient is like putting a bandage on an untreated bullet wound.

We have made great strides over the past few years in growing our counseling team to support the requirements of being a Level 1 Adult Trauma, Level 1 Pediatric Trauma, and Adult and Pediatric Burn Centers. That growth must continue until all of our patients who need SBIRT and counseling services are able to receive the care they deserve.

SOURCE: Veronica Getz. Veronica Acut Getz, MHA, is the administrator for both the Department of Surgery and the Acute Care Surgery Trauma Service Line at Wake Forest Baptist Medical Center.

Extensive research studies suggest SBIRT is an effective tool to help prevent addictive and harmful misuse of alcohol. The SBIRT model is based on one session beginning with the selection of a screening tool. SBIRT has demonstrated benefit in helping people improve their overall health by reducing alcohol-related injury, health complications, subsequent alcohol-related driving arrests, and improved posttraumatic stress disorder response, to name a few beneficial outcomes (Gentilello et al., 1999; Love & Zatzick, 2014; McCambridge & Kypri, 2011; NIDA, 2015a; Zatzick et al., 2014). Key screening tools used in SBIRT will be examined next.

Evidence-Based Practices

Brief Screening Tools

One of the first brief alcohol screening tools, the CAGE Questionnaire, was developed in the early 1980s by Dr. John Ewing at the Center for Alcohol Studies in North Carolina to ask four key questions about alcohol related to (1) previous attempts to reduce drinking, (2) emotional responses about annoyance when drinking patterns are questioned or discussed and (3) guilt or remorse when thinking about drinking events or patterns, and lastly, (4) any incidence of drinking upon awakening; the acronym stands for: C = Cut Down, A = Annoyed, G = Guilt, and E = Eye Opener (Ewing, 1984).

In its original development, the CAGE Questionnaire was specifically designed to eliminate *any* preliminary questions about quantity or frequency of alcohol use; for example, "Do you drink alcohol?" or "How much do you drink?" Those types of questions are strongly discouraged (Ewing, 1984) as amount and frequency can trigger greater defensiveness. Dr. Ewing demonstrated the simple and brief four-item questionnaire could yield important valid and sensitive information about alcohol misuse and risk while also decreasing defensiveness from the person being questioned. It has been shown in national and international research to be an effective screening tool (Steinweg & Worth, 1993). When there are *two or more positive responses on the CAGE*, it is recommended that the client, at a minimum, be considered for a brief counseling intervention as outlined and discussed in Chapter 8 of this text. From primary care physicians to counselors in a variety of settings, the CAGE Questionnaire continues to be used as an important brief screening tool. Those four areas are important in the screening of alcohol use. The only questions that need to be presented to the client are the four CAGE questions in this first stage of screening for alcohol use.

Box 6.9: CAGE

1. Have you ever felt you should **Cut down** on your drinking?

2. Have people **Annoyed** you by criticizing your drinking?

3. Have you ever felt bad or **Guilty** about your drinking?

4. Have you had an **Eye opener** first thing in the morning to steady nerves or get rid of a hangover?

SOURCE: Ewing, J. A. (1984). Detecting alcoholism, the CAGE questionnaire. *Journal of the American Medical Association, 252,* 1905–1907.

As one can see with the way these questions were designed, open questions were not the format selected; for counselors, however, it is highly recommended to consider using this screening tool with consideration for more open-ended formats. For example, how could the first CAGE question be changed to be more open-ended? Consider wording such as "How often have you felt you should cut down on your drinking?" Or, a more open-ended example might be similar to "How has it been for you when you felt, if you did, that you should cut down on your drinking?" or "You may have experienced feelings that you should cut down on your drinking; talk more about that." Another example might be "What happened when you felt you should cut down on your drinking?" Again, the normalizing and subtle assumption that an experience of cutting down on one's drinking can be experienced by drinkers may help the client begin to talk about issues that have been more hidden.

Box 6.10: Exercise for CAGE Screening Practice

Find a partner to practice both types of questions. First, ask questions from the CAGE Questionnaire as you see them in their original form (found in the preceding box above), all closed questions. Note how difficult the screening might go if the client limits their responses to just yes or no. Now, try to change these questions into a more open-ended format, such as "How often have you felt the need to CUT DOWN on your drinking?" Or, alternatively, eliminate the question format and use more of an opening such as "Tell me about times when you've felt the need to CUT DOWN on your drinking."

You can see in this brief practice that the person is more likely to respond with more than a yes or no response when presented with an open-ended question or opening statement while still maintaining the key elements of the CAGE screen: CUT DOWN, ANNOYED, GUILT, AND EYE OPENER. This response is very helpful to aid better understanding and getting to know your client as they work with you in professional counseling. As a reminder, it is always important to check with the manual or guidelines for use of screening and assessment tools to determine if wording changes are allowed.

For the most complete list of screening tools and how to best use them, please consider the chart (see Table 6.1) on the National Institute on Drug Abuse (NIDA) website that displays a variety of the screening tools including the CAGE Questionnaire (2015a).

Of the many short screening tools for alcohol use, perhaps the most studied in many countries around the world and found to be highly effective for screening alcohol use patterns is the Alcohol Use Disorder Identification Test (AUDIT), as developed by Babor, Higgins-Biddle, Saunders, and Monteiro (2001) as a part of an initiative led by the World Health Organization (WHO). WHO is an organization involved in many health concerns worldwide. In the 1980s alcohol problems were consistently problematic in many countries, and efforts began to identify effective strategies to address alcohol misuse; alcohol screening and brief interventions are among the recommended strategies globally to help prevent further negative health consequences (WHO, 2010). The AUDIT was developed and tested in many languages and countries, and it was found to be highly effective and sensitive in detecting risky alcohol use as well as hazardous alcohol misuse (Babor et al., 2001). It consists of 10 questions, is available in either self-report or interview versions, normally takes 5 minutes to administer and 1–2 minutes to score. It can also be used throughout the world at no cost to administer when being used for clinical purposes. A number of settings prefer the AUDIT and range from college counseling centers, outpatient clinics, or work settings to hospital trauma centers. The AUDIT manual provides excellent guidelines for counselors opting to administer the AUDIT and clearly understand the scoring guidelines for use of this screening tool (Babor et al., 2001).

Table 6.1 NIDA Evidence-Based Screening Tools

Choose evidence-based screening tools and resource materials

The table below includes examples of trusted screening tools that are easy to use and available at no charge.

Screening Tool	Substance type		Patient age		How tool is administered	
	Alcohol	Drugs	Adults	Adolescents	Self-administered	Clinician-administered
Prescreen						
NIDA Drug Use Screening Tool: Quick Screen	X	X	X	See APA Adapted NM ASSIST tools	See APA Adapted NM ASSIST tools	X
CRAFFT (Part A) 🗗	X	X		X	X	X
Alcohol Use Disorders Identification Test-C (🗎 AUDIT-C (PDF, 41KB))	X		X		X	X
🗎 Opioid Risk Tool (PDF, 168KB)		X	X		X	
Full Screens						
NIDA Drug Use Screening Tool	X	X	X			X
Alcohol Use Disorders Identification Test (🗎 AUDIT (PDF, 233KB))	X		X			X
🗎 CAGE-AID (PDF, 30KB)	X	X	X			X
🗎 CAGE (PDF, 14KB) 🗗	X		X			X
Drug Abuse Screen Test (🗎 DAST-10 (PDF, 168KB))		X	X		X	X
CRAFFT 🗗	X	X		X	X	X
🗎 DAST-20: Adolescent version (PDF 1.2MB) 🗗		X		X	X	X

SOURCE: NIDA, 2015. Retrieved from https://www.drugabuse.gov/nidamed-medical-health-professionals/tool-resources -your-practice/screening-assessment-drug-testing-resources/chart-evidence-based-screening-tools-adults.

Table 6.2 The Alcohol Use Disorders Identification Test: Interview Version

The Alcohol Use Disorders Identification Test: Interview Version

Read questions as written. Record answers carefully. Begin the AUDIT by saying, "Now I am going to ask you some questions about your use of alcoholic beverages during this past year." Explain what is meant by "alcoholic beverages" by using local examples of beer, wine, vodka, etc. Code answers in terms of "standard drinks." Place the correct answer number in the box at the right.

1. How often do you have a drink containing alcohol?

   (0) Never [Skip to Questions 9–10]
   (1) Monthly or less
   (2) 2 to 4 times a month
   (3) 2 to 3 times a week
   (4) 4 or more times a week

6. How often during the last year have you needed a first drink in the morning to get yourself going after a heavy drinking session?

   (0) Never
   (1) Less than monthly
   (2) Monthly
   (3) Weekly
   (4) Daily or almost daily

2. How many drinks containing alcohol do you have on a typical day when you are drinking?

   (0) 1 or 2
   (1) 3 or 4
   (2) 5 or 6
   (3) 7, 8, or 9
   (4) 10 or more

7. How often during the last year have you had a feeling of guilt or remorse after drinking?

   (0) Never
   (1) Less than monthly
   (2) Monthly
   (3) Weekly
   (4) Daily or almost daily

3. How often do you have six or more drinks on one occasion?

   (0) Never
   (1) Less than monthly
   (2) Monthly
   (3) Weekly
   (4) Daily or almost daily

   Skip to Questions 9 and 10 if Total Score for Questions 2 and 3 = 0

8. How often during the last year have you been unable to remember what happened the night before because you had been drinking?

   (0) Never
   (1) Less than monthly
   (2) Monthly
   (3) Weekly
   (4) Daily or almost daily

4. How often during the last year have you found that you were not able to stop drinking once you had started?

   (0) Never
   (1) Less than monthly
   (2) Monthly
   (3) Weekly
   (4) Daily or almost daily

9. Have you or someone else been injured as a result of your drinking?

   (0) No
   (2) Yes, but not in the last year
   (4) Yes, during the last year

(Continued)

Table 6.2 (Continued)

5. How often during the last year have you failed to do what was normally expected from you because of drinking? (0) Never (1) Less than monthly (2) Monthly (3) Weekly (4) Daily or almost daily	10. Has a relative or friend or a doctor or another health worker been concerned about your drinking or suggested you cut down? (0) No (2) Yes, but not in the last year (4) Yes, during the last year

Record total of specific items here

If total is greater than recommended cut-off, consult User's Manual.

SOURCE: Reprinted from *The Alcohol Use Disorders Identification Test: Guidelines for Use in Primary Care*, T.F. Barbor, J.C. Higgins-Biddle, J.B. Saunders, and M.G. Monteiro, World Health Organization Department of Mental Health and Substance Dependence (2011). Retrieved from: http://www.talkingalcohol.com/files/pdfs/WHO_audit.pdf. Accessed April 10, 2017.

Available for clinical use without permission from the World Health Organization. This AUDIT version reflects U.S. drinking measures to count five standard drinks in Question 3 (Babor et al., 2001).

Box 6.11: AUDIT Podcast Script: Elizabeth White

Hello, and welcome to the Testing Today podcast where we talk about and investigate various assessment tools. I am your host, Liz White, MA, TSN coordinator.

The topic of today, Sunday, June 21, is the Alcohol Use Disorders Identification Test, otherwise known as the AUDIT.

Our exploration of this assessment tool will begin with what it is and how it is currently being used. We will then investigate its psychometric properties and discuss some of its strengths and weaknesses. Finally, we will close out the discussion with multicultural, legal, and ethical considerations of using the AUDIT.

Ready to get started? Let's dive in!

The AUDIT, again, stands for Alcohol Use Disorders Identification Test and it does just that. It is a test that identifies risky alcohol use. Specifically, it is used to identify those individuals who could be diagnosed with alcohol use disorder according to the DSM-5 or ICD-10 criteria.

The AUDIT is comprised of 10 questions with five possible options for answers; each option is worth 0–4 points.

The AUDIT has a couple of alternative versions with a reduced number of questions; the most popular and psychometrically sound version is the AUDIT-C, with C standing for "consumption." It only includes the first three questions of the full AUDIT, which are shown in the AUDIT Interview version in your text.

Since the highest point total for each question is 4, the highest possible score is a 40. The generally accepted score indicating hazardous or harmful alcohol use is anything above an 8. However, recent research suggests that the score indicating risk may need to vary depending on population, but I will go into that a bit later.

The AUDIT is used in various settings all over the world, including, but not limited to, primary care physicians' offices, emergency rooms, jails, EAP offices, veterans' and military affairs, and by many mental health providers. It can be used with clients from the age of 18 all the way to 75. And it can be administered via clinical interview or self-report.

The time has come! Let's talk psychometrics!

The AUDIT has been shown in several studies to have high internal consistency and high reliability in test–retest scenarios. As I mentioned before, several research studies have been conducted to determine what the cut-off scores for at-risk alcohol use should be with various populations. These cut-off scores are determined by measuring the sensitivity, which means it correctly identifies at-risk individuals as at risk, and specificity, or correctly not identifying those not at risk.

On the standard AUDIT with the general population, a cut-off score of 8 tends to produce a sensitivity of .82 and a specificity of .78. Just as an example, say we lower the cut-off score to 6. Our sensitivity goes up to .91. Yay! But the specificity drops to .60. Boo! Researchers are able to determine the most effective cut-off score by finding the one with the highest sensitivity *and* specificity.

In a 2012 study on college students by DeMartini and Carey, they found not just population-specific, but also gender-specific cut-off scores. They recommend a cut-off score of 7 for college-aged males due to a sensitivity of .8 and specificity of .88, and they recommend a cut-off score of 5 for college-aged females, which produced both a sensitivity and specificity rate of .82.

A 2010 study of the AUDIT and the elderly population produced similar recommendations. When utilizing the general population cut-off of 8, the sensitivity was .48. However, when lowering it to 5 for both men and women, the sensitivity and specificity skyrocketed over .85.

What's that? You're ready to talk strengths?

The AUDIT is a strong tool in many areas. Several studies have shown that alcohol use disorders often go undiagnosed and underreported, particularly for non-middle-aged individuals and women. With some basic shifting of cut-off scores depending on the population, the AUDIT is successful in starting the conversation about harmful alcohol use and planting a seed of change for all.

In the 2012 study by DeMartini and Carey, researchers found the AUDIT particularly helpful for identifying hazardous alcohol use among college students who experience the psychosocial implications of abuse without dependence symptoms.

The AUDIT has been shown to be consistently valid and reliable with an r of .86, giving clinicians greater confidence in using it with their clients.

In a 2013 study by Rubinsky et al., the AUDIT was shown to provide early identification of at-risk patients, which led to timely intervention and preoperative abstinence from alcohol. This dramatically reduced postoperative risks including fewer days in the ICU and less time spent in the hospital overall.

Though physicians in the Reinholdz, Fornazar, Bendtsen, and Spak 2013 study claim that the AUDIT questions do not flow well with their typical consultation routine, results indicate that the identification of alcohol use disorder increased when patients completed the AUDIT prior to or during the consultation with their physicians.

Despite all of the strengths, the AUDIT does have its limitations. The greatest of which is that it relies on self-report. Clients must be honest and willing to disclose the characteristics of their alcohol use. If they lie or omit the truth, they may not get the help or intervention they need. One might argue

(Continued)

(Continued)

that by simply asking the questions, the clinician is able to introduce the idea of alcohol misuse or abuse and the client can ponder it and seek help when they feel ready.

Another weakness it seems is the effectiveness of the AUDIT as an Internet-based tool. One 2014 study by Kypri et al. indicated that online administration of the AUDIT is not successful in reducing overall risk in college-aged students. Yet another study, not exclusively focused on college students, claimed that their e-screening of the AUDIT led to decreased alcohol consumption at 3- and 6-month follow-ups.

We're getting near the end of our time together, so, let's look at some multicultural, legal, and ethical considerations of the AUDIT.

In Kypri and colleague's 2014 study conducted in New Zealand, researchers suggested that the difference in amount of alcohol consumption between Maori students and non-Maori students may be a cultural one. Maori students have a stronger group identity than the non-Maori students, leading them to be more receptive and conforming to social norms.

At this point, clinicians must tap into their cultural competencies as they administer the standard form of the AUDIT and consider cultural implications as they arise.

As with any assessment or clinical interview, confidentiality with the AUDIT is important. It is valuable for the accuracy of the results that clients be able to trust the ethical behavior of the clinician and believe that their responses will remain confidential. This is of particular relevance for those who are prohibited from consuming alcohol by law due to being underage or by religious practice. They must be assured that their responses will not get them in trouble or put them in danger.

And that's all the time we have for today. I hope I piqued your interest in the AUDIT and you learned a bit about this fascinating assessment tool. Be sure to listen next week when we will continue our series on substance abuse assessments. I'm your host, Liz White. Thanks for listening.

Elizabeth Bost White, MA, LPCA, LCASA, earned her master's degree in clinical mental health counseling from Wake Forest University and her undergraduate degree also from Wake Forest University in psychology and German. Liz served as the counseling intern for the Burn Unit at Wake Forest Baptist Medical Center. She is currently the Trauma Survivors Network coordinator/counselor at Wake Forest Baptist Medical Trauma Center in North Carolina.

References

Aalto, M., Alho, H., Halme, J. T., & Seppä, K. (2011). The Alcohol Use Disorders Identification Test (AUDIT) and its derivatives in screening for heavy drinking among the elderly. *International Journal of Geriatric Psychiatry, 26*(9), 881–885. doi:10.1002/gps.2498

Babor, T. F., Higgins-Biddle, J. C., Saunders, J. B., & Monteiro, M. G. (2001). *The Alcohol Use Disorders Identification Test: Guidelines for use in primary care.* World Health Organization Department of Mental Health and Substance Dependence. Retrieved from http://www.talkingalcohol.com/files/pdfs/WHO_audit.pdf

DeMartini, K. S., & Carey, K. B. (2012). Optimizing the use of the AUDIT for alcohol screening in college students. *Psychological Assessment, 24*(4), 954–963. doi:10.1037/a0028519

Kypri, K., Vater, T., Bowe, S. J., Saunders, J. B., Cunningham, J. A., Horton, N. J., & McCambridge, J. (2014). Web-based alcohol screening and brief intervention for university students: A randomized trial. *JAMA: Journal of the American Medical Association, 311*(12), 1218–1224. doi:10.1001/jama.2014.2138

Reinholdz, H., Fornazar, R., Bendtsen, P., & Spak, F. (2013). Comparison of systematic versus targeted screening for detection of risky drinking in primary care. *Alcohol and Alcoholism, 48*(2), 172–179. doi:10.1093/alcalc/ags137–

Rubinsky, A. D., Bishop, M. J., Maynard, C., Henderson, W. G., Hawn, M. T., Harris, A. S., . . . Bradley, K. A. (2013). Postoperative risks associated with alcohol screening depend on documented drinking at the time of surgery. *Drug and Alcohol Dependence, 132*(3), 521–527. doi:10.1016/j.drugalcdep.2013.03.022

Sinadinovic, K., Wennberg, P., & Berman, A. H. (2014). Internet-based screening and brief intervention for illicit drug users: A randomized controlled trial with 12-month follow-up. *Journal of Studies on Alcohol and Drugs, 75*(2), 313–318.

Williams, E. C., Rubinsky, A. D., Lapham, G. T., Chavez, L. J., Rittmueller, S. E., Hawkins, E. J., . . . Bradley, K. A. (2014). Prevalence of clinically recognized alcohol and other substance use disorders among VA outpatients with unhealthy alcohol use identified by routine alcohol screening. *Drug and Alcohol Dependence,* 13595–103. doi:10.1016/j.drugalcdep.2013.11.016

A shortened version of AUDIT ("AUDIT-C") uses three questions about alcohol consumption from the 10 questions that comprise the AUDIT (Bradley et al., 2007). Research studies, including substantial research with veterans, validated the AUDIT-C as an effective and brief screening tool for heavy/hazardous drinking in both men and women in a variety of settings (Bradley et al., 2007; U.S. Department of Veteran Affairs, 2014). AUDIT question 3 ("How often in the last year have you had 5 or more drinks on one occasion?") has even been shown to be a single effective screening question. This question screens for past-year risky drinking and/or active alcohol abuse or dependence in both male and female, and it is used extensively with veterans, for example (U.S. Veteran Affairs, 2014). One unique study in an emergency department also found that a single question—"In a typical week, how many days to you get drunk?"—was another optimal way to screen for college students who were at higher risk of injury, such as falls or accidents under the influence of alcohol (O'Brien, McCoy, Rhodes, Wagoner, & Wolfson, 2008).

Additional screening is important for individuals affected by risky use of drugs other than alcohol. As you learned in earlier chapters, increases in the misuse of marijuana and prescription drugs are challenging our nation, with special concern for youth. A brief screening tool that addresses alcohol and other drug use specifically designed for youth under age 21 is recommended by the American Academy of Pediatrics' Committee on Substance Abuse. It was developed to be a quick screening tool, has six questions to help identify if risky use is occurring, and is available to use in counseling settings at no cost to the counselor (CeASAR, 2015). The abbreviation CRAFFT stands for behaviors such as riding in a Car being driven by someone impaired, using drugs or drinking to Relax, using or drinking Alone, Forgetfulness after drinking or using, problems with Friends or Family due to drinking or using, and lastly, getting into Trouble because of using or drinking. Research findings note that a CRAFFT score of 2 or more was a valid indicator of substance abuse problems (Knight, Sherritt, Shrier, Harris, & Chang, 2002).

As noted in Chapter 5, our country faces additional concerns about non-medical prescription drug use (NMPD). Screening for NMPD use can involve brief screens. One particular study noted higher risks of other drug misuse by those involved in NMPD use (Benotsch, Koester, Luckman, Martin, & Cejka, 2011) with higher rates of risky use of alcohol, marijuana, ecstasy, cocaine, methamphetamine, and other stimulants by those who engaged in NMPD use. The National Institute on Drug Abuse (NIDA) brief screens as adapted from WHO are one of the options available to counselors and include an online version that is easy to administer, with aids for feedback to highlight during the brief counseling intervention following the screen (NIDA, 2015b). The online screening tool, the NIDA-Modified (NM) ASSIST tool, helps the client and counselor score the screen for risky NMPD, other drug, and alcohol use. The online screen can be found at www.drugabuse.gov/nmassist and offers guidance for services that may be beneficial to the client, with different recommendations for those scoring in the low, moderate, and severe high-risk ranges. Other categories of drug use, such as hallucinogens, heroin, marijuana, stimulants like cocaine or methamphetamine, and other designer drugs, pose increased risks, and screening for use of all mood-altering substances can help the counselor identify best steps to help the client. It also remains a challenge to develop a brief screen that is also comprehensive for all possible drugs of abuse; the NM-ASSIST is a newer tool that was created to address this challenge.

Previous work stressed concepts related to assessment of substance use disorders, namely, readiness to change. Researchers began to focus on ways to measure and assess a person's stage of change and openness to exploring change. The following sample description shows a key measure used to work with clients on assessing potential readiness to change.

Box 6.12: Stages of Change Readiness and Treatment Eagerness Scale (SOCRATES)

Purpose: Designed to assess client motivation to change drinking- or drug-related behavior. Consists of five scales: precontemplation, contemplation, determination, action, and maintenance. Separate versions are available for alcohol and illicit drug use.

Clinical utility: The SOCRATES can assist clinicians with necessary information about client motivation for change, an important predictor of treatment compliance and outcome, and aid in treatment planning.

Groups with whom this instrument has been used: Adults

Norms: N/A

Format: 40 items; paper-and-pencil

Administration time:	5 minutes
Computer scoring?	No

Administrator training and qualifications: No training required

Fee for use:	No

SOURCE: Center for Substance Abuse Treatment, 1999. Available from: Center for Substance Abuse Treatment. (1999). *Enhancing motivation for change in substance abuse treatment.* Treatment Improvement Protocol (TIP) Series 35. DHHS Publication No. (SMA) 99–3354. Rockville, MD: Substance Abuse and Mental Health Services Administration.

In summary, a variety of screening tools are available to addiction counseling specialists, are available at no charge, are brief and easily scored, can be administered by interview or self-report, and provide valid tools to help clients and counselors learn more about the patterns of the client's use of mood-altering substances. Counselors are then able to begin a brief intervention immediately upon feedback given about the screening results.

Extensive Assessment Tools

Specialists evaluating addiction symptomology may conduct much more extensive assessments. Intensive addiction treatment programs often conduct such assessments under the guidance of a licensed or certified addiction specialist, depending on state professional practice board regulations. While there are a number of assessment tools ranging from structured interviews to online assessment, the clinician's interaction and evaluation of the client's responses are an important part of the evaluation process. In general, reviewing assessment tool validity and reliability with data regarding sensitivity and specificity are important in the selection of assessment tools as explained in the AUDIT podcast in Box 6.11, earlier in this section. At times, regulatory bodies specify which assessment tools may be selected, for example, in cases involving a driving while impaired (DWI) citation, and certain approved assessment tools can only be used as specified by the state's regulating authority. Assessments may also include a urine drug screen, breathalyzer, or more extensive testing in addition to psychological assessment tools. There are a variety of assessment tools, often involving varying costs, that can be purchased, with software versions that produce an automated report; Substance Abuse Subtle Screening Inventory (SASSI-3) in its recent revision (SASSI Institute, 2016), and the Substance Abuse Screener for American Sign Language (SAS-ASL) are some examples (Guthman, Lazowski, Moore, Heineman, & Embree, 2012). The NEEDS Assessment tool is another validated instrument and is an approved tool for DWI evaluations in Georgia, for instance; the assessment tool takes 26 minutes on average to complete, with 130 questions at a fifth-grade reading level, designed for adults with a comprehensive focus on substance abuse, life stressors, psychological attitudes, emotions, legal issues, educational and vocational background, test-taking attitudes, and pertinent criteria for determining level of care recommendations (ADE Incorporated, 2015). At times, it assists in the assessment process to determine much more extensive information, and the structured interview is often used. One type of structured interview is examined next.

More in-depth structured interviewing assessment tools are found, for example, in the Addiction Severity Index (ASI), 5th edition (Treatment Research Institute [TSI], 2014), often cited as one of the leading assessment tools in the United States for determining the extent of addiction. Due to the extensive questions and information gathered in either the online version or published version, the ASI ranges from specific patterns of use of any mood-altering substances to legal, psychiatric, social, family, medical, and other difficulties; the interview is designed to be conducted in a very specific manner. Training manuals and training resources are necessary to be able to administer the ASI. As with any assessment tool, studying and reviewing the training manual is required before use of the evaluation instrument. Other similar assessment tools with substantial evidence of their effectiveness include

Composite International Diagnostic Interview (CIDI);

Structured Clinical Interview for DSM-IV (SCID);

Alcohol Use Disorders and Associated Disabilities Interview Schedule (AUDADIS);

Psychiatric Research Interview for Substance and Mental Disorders (PRISM); and

Semi-Structured Assessment for Drug Dependence and Alcoholism (SSADDA).

Most extensive evaluations need to be conducted by a certified or licensed addiction counselor specialist as specified by the test publisher.

Finally, the work of assessment is continually changing and improved tools advance the care we can provide to clients suffering with substance or process-related use disorders and risky use complications. It is important to examine examples of how assessment is conducted in a variety of settings as we review in this next section.

Effective Assessment in Current Practice

In current practice it is important to consider trends in the United States. The National Institute for Alcohol Abuse and Alcoholism (NIAAA) believes that about 28% of adults, approximately 69 million adults, fit the definition of risky drinkers, which places these drinkers at greater risk for alcoholism, liver complications, and other problems (2016). Further, more than half of all current drinkers who are categorized as risky drinkers are also risky users of tobacco or other mood-altering drugs, and are at increased risk for developing addiction (CASAColumbia, 2012). The combined percentage of risky users of addictive substances including tobacco, alcohol, prescription medications, and illegal drugs is estimated to be nearly one-third of the U.S. population aged 12 and older, at approximately 80.4 million individuals (CASAColumbia, 2012). Examples of risky use include the college student engaging in binge drinking on some weekends or the person prescribed pain medication who then takes more than prescribed in a risky, non-prescribed manner. Of the 28% of drinkers who are at risk, for instance, all have greater likelihood to develop an alcohol use disorder. The 2012 seminal study by CASAColumbia, *Addiction Medicine: Closing the Gap Between Science and Practice*, highlighted the urgent need to address untreated addiction conditions in medicine. Their findings show alarming annual trends in the treatment of other health conditions less prevalent than addiction, for example, 25.8 million people have diabetes, with $43.8 billion spent for their medical care; $86.6 billion is spent on cancer treatment for 19.4 million cancer patients; $107 billion is spent for cardiac conditions affecting 27 million individuals, yet estimates show far more individuals—40.3 million people—are addicted and yet only $28 billion is spent for addiction treatment. It is also clear that the burden of untreated addiction and risky use contributes to the disease burden in diabetes, cancer, and heart conditions. Increasingly, the addiction counselor is also working in health care settings due to this unmet need to address the critical needs in health care settings such as hospitals and primary care physician offices. The ability of the counselor to conduct various assessments in the recognition of substance use complications is gaining in importance and can result in expanding career opportunities as well as helping individuals who otherwise might go unserved and untreated for substance-related or process-related addictive disorders and risky use that is increasingly seen as a major gap in assessment needs.

Box 6.13: Screening: Olivia Currin, a Counselor's Perspective

When picking my practicum site, I investigated many different options but never thought about the trauma center until I received the e-mail with the application for the Wake Forest Baptist Medical Center (WFBMC) Trauma Center. I read the description of the expectations for the practicum/internship experience and became very intrigued. I remember thinking that I had no idea that counselors had this presence in hospitals. One reason I was drawn to counseling for graduate work was the versatility in settings. I remember getting the e-mail offering me the practicum position with the Trauma Center Screening Brief Intervention Referral to Treatment (SBIRT) team; I was excited and very unsure of what to expect from this opportunity. Once starting my practicum, I quickly realized the importance of counselors as part of the trauma team. Across the country at least 50% of trauma patients are admitted with positive toxicology of either alcohol or drugs. At other trauma centers across the country, many patients will not have the opportunity to speak with a counselor but at WFBMC there is a unique opportunity to receive SBIRT from a counselor or counselor intern. I would like to share my reflections on my experience at WFBMC as part of Dr. Laura Veach's counseling team.

(Continued)

(Continued)

The hospital environment alone is unique, and then when you throw the idea of counseling into the mix—there are many moving pieces. I have found that I enjoy the fast pace and "keep you on your toes" environment. There is no way to truly explain this counseling experience, but on some days it is very similar to a carnival fun house of not knowing what to expect around every corner. Instead of greeting my client in a waiting room and bringing them back to my office, I am entering into their private hospital room. It begins with a routine of checking the chart to make sure I have the right room for the patient, using hand sanitizer before knocking on the patient's door, and being open to what I am going to learn on the other side of the door. The patient could greet you in a friendly or irritated way—this response could be heightened when you introduce yourself with additional irritation or, conversely, a sense of relief. You have entered the person's temporary bedroom with the added vulnerability of them being in a hospital gown and experiencing substantial pain due to their trauma. There are so many pieces of the puzzle to put together; I am challenged to be very empathetic and attuned to the individual to ensure the success of my support that I am there to offer. Support is the first priority, but there is the opportunity to conduct screening and brief intervention surrounding the individual's alcohol or drug use when appropriate. I have been amazed with the willingness and readiness of the individual to engage in change talk. The ability to use the AUDIT and the CAGE Questionnaire to conduct the screening can open many different doors for each patient. I appreciate the vulnerability that patients are willing to experience, as well as the trust they show me when discussing such personal and emotional topics.

The opportunity that I have had to be part of the counseling team at WFBMC has provided me with experiences and skills that will follow me into all of my future counseling experiences. This counseling experience is truly humbling and gives you multifaceted respect for people. And the learning has been so amazing that I accepted an offer for a full-time counselor position here.

SOURCE: Olivia Currin. Olivia Currin, MA, LPCA, LCASA, is a substance abuse counselor at Wake Forest Baptist Medical Trauma Center and a recent graduate with her master's counseling degree from Wake Forest University.

Various settings can be key for screening individuals for risky use patterns. Next we will examine a few examples of screening in select settings. In health care settings, for example, the American College of Surgeons (ACS) Committee on Trauma initiated a policy in 2006, the first health care mandated requirement in the nation pertaining to alcohol assessment, namely alcohol screening and intervention (Zatzick et al., 2014). The new policy required protocols be met to maintain hospital accreditation as a Level I Trauma Center; alcohol screening and brief counseling interventions in all Level I Trauma Centers became the standard of care as a result of this new accreditation standard. Level I Trauma Centers can use the "teachable moment" generated by alcohol-related traumatic injury as a gateway to effective prevention of future alcohol abuse, alcoholism and alcohol-related reinjury, and hospital readmissions.

Box 6.14: SBIRT Perspectives From a Trauma Surgeon, Dr. Preston Miller

As a trauma surgeon at a busy Level I Trauma Center, I have found having behavioral health professionals providing SBIRT services to our patients to be very valuable. It has long been recognized that risky drinking plays a role in up to 50% of traumatic injuries seen at trauma centers in the United States. During my initial training, many years ago, the general concept was that our job as surgeons was to identify and fix injuries when possible, and the behavioral health problems would be dealt with another day. It has become clear in the intervening years that treating concomitant behavioral health issues such as substance abuse in concert with injury treatment is important and effective. SBIRT in the acute setting has been shown to decrease trauma recidivism and lead to durable changes in drinking behavior in many patients. New data are emerging that suggest that this is even applicable in the severe or dependent alcoholic. Given the data demonstrating efficacy of such programs, the American College of Surgeons (ACS) now requires an SBIRT program as one of the pieces necessary for ACS certification as a Level I Trauma Center. Since the SBIRT program inception at our institution, we have also seen data documenting durable changes in risky drinking associated with intervention.

My belief is that integration of trained counselors providing SBIRT services into our multidisciplinary trauma team has additional benefits. The daily screening that goes on for patients at risk provides important information about substance abuse and other problems that may be of vital importance to the overall care of patients. Other behavioral health issues such as traumatic stress, depression, and anxiety may be identified and strategies set in place to begin dealing with them. Recognizing and treating such problems early will allow for more effective recovery from the physical and mental wounds of the injury as time progresses. SBIRT integration into trauma services is the beginning of a more comprehensive recognition of the role of behavioral health management in recovery from traumatic injury.

SOURCE: Preston Miller. Preston Miller, MD, is a trauma surgeon and professor with more than 25 years in a Level I Trauma Center.

Coauthor's Note: The trauma center noted in several features in this chapter admits over 3,000 individuals each year for traumatic injuries and burns from motor vehicle crashes, gunshot wounds, falls, suicide attempts, assaults, motorcycle accidents, recreational vehicle accidents (e.g., ATV, dirt bikes, jet skis), and accidental or intentional fires. Hospital trauma centers often have the highest concentration of substance use–related admissions. Our Level I Trauma Center began alcohol screening and brief intervention services in 2006 and has devoted specialized addiction counselor services to this important area of care, successfully intervening with individuals addicted as well as those at substantial risk for addiction. For the past decade, our counseling team has provided SBIRT in the hospital trauma unit, the burn unit, the pediatric trauma unit, and beginning this year, on two medical units in the general hospital setting. We have successfully provided training to more than 50 counseling students at the master's and doctoral levels. In addition, we have conducted seven research studies in this time period.

Another example of important screening and brief intervention involves young women of childbearing age. Researchers have conducted novel studies at various sites to combine alcohol screening and brief intervention with birth control interventions (Velasquez et al., 2010). Findings suggest EBP for screening young women to enhance their choices to change drinking behaviors, lessen risks of fetal alcohol–exposed pregnancies, and improve their knowledge about safer choices regarding pregnancy. One model program, designed for work with Alaskan and American Indian women, is based in extensive evidence through the CHOICES model that has repeatedly shown reductions in alcohol-exposed pregnancies in women from diverse backgrounds and is outlined in detail through the No Fetal Alcohol Syndrome (NOFAS) website (NOFAS, 2014).

For young clients, special considerations are important and differ from individuals considered adults, usually minors under age 18. In addition to alcohol, any use of mood-altering substances, such as marijuana, by youth is deemed risky as that use is illegal. Many addiction specialists agree that screening adolescents for substance use is critically important (Knight, Roberts, Gabrielli, & Van Hook, 2016; Parrish & Daetwyler, 2013; Sterling, Kline-Simon, Wibbelsman, Wong, & Weisner, 2012; Winters & Kaminer, 2008). Screening should include objective testing if possible, such as urine drug screens (UDS) or other chemical testing procedures, self-report by the young person and caregivers when possible, and the use of a valid screening instrument. It is important to highlight the need for skilled screening and intervention due to challenges when medical professionals are often lacking time and training resources to conduct effective screening and interventions. For example, an important study examining data in the Kaiser Permanente managed care system by Sterling and colleagues (2012) found that pediatricians often miss major opportunities to screen for substance use issues and only 5% of the more than 400 pediatric physicians in the study used evidence-based screening tools with significant differences between higher self-reported MD screening as compared with actual screening documentation in the medical record. The top three major obstacles to screening as identified in the study included (1) 80% noted problems because physicians indicated too much time was involved in screening, (2) 32% noted that confidentiality regulations were an obstacle to screening, and (3) 30% indicated that physicians often expected youth's expected dishonesty when screened (Sterling et al., 2012). It is clear for many medical professionals (physicians, nurses, medical social workers) that counselors skilled in screening and intervention services can be an important team member working in medical settings too. Increasingly, substance abuse counselors are working within primary care physician offices and other medical settings.

In addition, confidentiality and legal circumstances need to be clarified to the adolescent and caregiver. Challenges increase when the counselor is determining how to best maintain the confidentiality for the youth yet balance caregivers' needs for involvement in the screening and assessment process (Kerwin et al., 2015). Special consideration is needed to check pertinent state laws that also outline the youth's right to privacy and confidentiality pertaining to screening, assessment, or recommendations for treatment (Kerwin et al., 2015; Winters & Kaminer, 2008). There is therapeutic value when the young client develops trust and rapport with the counselor and can explore effective ways to communicate with parents and loved ones about substance-related concerns and treatment needs. Extensive knowledge, supervision, and practice is often involved in assessment settings working with youth. In addition, there can be rare events that bring about a conflict between legal confidentiality guidelines and ethical dilemmas. For example, legally in some states, a parent may be entitled to be notified when a minor is seeking treatment for a substance use disorder. However, the counselor may have an ethical dilemma to contact the parent who has been sanctioned in the past for abuse of that young client, especially in cases where the parent has introduced the drugs of abuse to their child and, in fact, actively engages in alcohol and other drug use with the young client. The counselor is best served by seeking supervisory and professional consultation to determine the course of actions to best care for the young client.

In summary, based on knowledge gained by working with risky drinkers and users in a variety of settings, such as schools, workplaces, hospital trauma centers, medical units, primary care physician offices, and colleges and universities, it is critical that assessment with screening tools for risky use become a standard part of the intake process by all counselors since the number of individuals who may become addicted can be substantially reduced if screening occurs before the onset of an alcohol use disorder, for example. Lastly, it is important to keep in mind that the spectrum of assessment ranges from brief screening to more extensive evaluation. For the most part, in current practice, effective and evidence-based screening can take place in any counseling setting whereas extensive evaluation more often occurs in a substance-related treatment setting. Next, we highlight the continued practice of skills pertaining to the evidence-based tools used in assessment and include one such case illustration using the evidence-based AUDIT.

Skills in Action

Box 6.15: Case Illustration of Screening Practice

You have just conducted an AUDIT screening with a 32-year-old single male who came into the community college counseling center expressing concerns about his drinking beer. He has just scored a 14 on the AUDIT screening tool, and you need to provide his results to him. The following is a case example of providing information about the screening only. The brief counseling intervention will be illustrated in the next chapter. Imagine your top three considerations as you provide these screening findings. Reflect on the key considerations and how you would want to provide those screening findings to a new client. Discuss in class any barriers or opportunities you believe are important in the brief screening case illustrated in Box 6.16.

Box 6.16: Screening

Counselor:	The AUDIT is conducted all over the world; it is to help individuals explore how their drinking might be affecting their health and health risks. The scores range between 0 and 40. For men, scores between 0 and 7 are considered the lowest risk. Scores between 8 and 15 show increased risk and indicate hazardous drinking. Scores above 16 are considered severe risk and would best be further explored with an addiction specialist. I'm wondering if you would like to talk about your scores and if you might have an idea of where your score might be?
Client:	Oh, maybe an 8?
Counselor:	From adding up your answers, it shows a score of 14 . . .
Client:	That's not sounding good. I thought it would be in the low-risk range.
Counselor:	You're concerned about this news and may be wondering about your health risks looking at this new information.
Client:	Yeah, that's more to think about and try to figure out what that means.

Experiential Skills Learning Activity

It is often suggested that enhancing empathy, an important skill for screening and assessing, can be achieved through an experiential learning task focused on abstaining from something that the individual would consider challenging to stop, such as snacking on chocolate, sugary candies, or posting and checking social media, for a prescribed amount of time. The experiential activity is then designed so that counseling trainees can begin to develop increased sensitivity through personal experiences of abstaining, craving, slipping, and change in behaviors. With guidance from the faculty, the student can then reflect deeply on the process of change, the internal messages that often arise about succeeding or failing, aspects of shame, and rejecting or seeking help from others. As in addictions counseling, the important work of processing feelings, thoughts, and behaviors while abstaining is critical to maximize empathy awareness. In addition, as with addictions counseling, it is emphasized that participation in the abstention exercise is voluntary. A different option can be provided for those electing an alternative choice.

More research will help identify effective ways to enhance empathy for counseling work with individuals with substance use disorders and risky use. Additional creative techniques can be used, and research into efficacy of such techniques will benefit both the counseling field and our clients (Warren, Hof, McGriff, & Morris, 2012). Assessment has expanded over the recent decades and it is hoped that with greater ability and tools to screen, assess, and evaluate substance use or addictive process disorders, life-enhancing changes and growth can be potentiated.

RESOURCES FOR FURTHER LEARNING

Assessment—Addiction Severity Index (ASI)

http://www.tresearch.org/wp-content/uploads/2012/09/ASI_Clinical_Training.pdf

CAGE Screening Tool

http://www.med.unc.edu/alcohol/

Drug-Related Screening Resources

https://www.drugabuse.gov/nidamed-medical-health-professionals/tool-resources-your-practice/screening-assessment-drug-testing-resources/chart-evidence-based-screening-tools-adults

Fetal Alcohol Prevention

http://nofas.org

Reviewing Alcohol Screening Issues

http://www.alcoholscreening.org/Home.aspx

Reducing Alcohol Problems

http://www.cdc.gov/vitalsigns/alcohol.html

Screening Tool—CRAFFT

http://www.ceasar.org

Screening Tool, Other Drugs—ASSIST

http://www.drugabuse.gov/nmassist/

World Health Organization—Alcohol Screening

http://www.who.int/substance_abuse/en/

REFERENCES

ADE Incorporated. (2015). *NEEDS Assessment*. Clarkston, MI: ADE Incorporated. Retrieved from http://www.adeincorp.com/documents/NEEDS_Ref_Guide.pdf

American Psychiatric Association (APA). (2013). *Diagnostic and statistical manual of mental disorders* (5th ed.). Arlington, VA: American Psychiatric Publishing.

Babor, T. F., Higgins-Biddle, J. C., Saunders, J. B., & Monteiro, M. G. (2001). *The Alcohol Use Disorders Identification Test: Guidelines for use in primary care* (2nd ed.). Published by the Department of Mental Health and Substance Dependence, World Health Organization. Retrieved from http://whqlibdoc.who.int/hq/2001/WHO_ MSD_MSB_01.6a.pdf

Benotsch, E. G., Koester, S., Luckman, D., Martin, A. M., & Cejka, A. (2011). Non-medical use of prescription drugs and sexual risk behavior in young adults. *Journal of Addictive Behaviors, 36*, 152–155.

Bradley, K. A., DeBenedetti, A. F., Volk, R. J., Williams, E. C., Frank, D., & Kivlahan, D. R. (2007). AUDIT-C as a brief screen for alcohol misuse in primary care. *Alcoholism: Clinical and Experimental Research, 31,* 1208–1217. doi:10.1111/j.1530-0277.2007.00403.x

CASAColumbia. (2012). *Addiction medicine: Closing the gap between science and practice.* Retrieved from http://www.centeronaddiction.org/addiction-research/reports/addiction-medicine

Center for Adolescent Substance Abuse Research (CeASAR). (2015). *CRAFFT tool.* Retrieved from http://www.ceasar.org/CRAFFT/index.php

Center for Substance Abuse Treatment (CSAT). (1999). *Enhancing motivation for change in substance abuse treatment.* Treatment Improvement Protocol (TIP) Series 35. DHHS Publication No. (SMA) 99-3354. Rockville, MD: Substance Abuse and Mental Health Services Administration. Retrieved from http://www.ncbi.nlm.nih.gov/books/NBK64117/

Center for Substance Abuse Treatment (CSAT). (2000). *Integrating substance abuse treatment and vocational services.* (Treatment Improvement Protocol [TIP] Series, No. 38.) Figure 7-3: Sample Consent Form. Rockville (MD): Substance Abuse and Mental Health Services Administration (US). Available from http://www.ncbi.nlm.nih.gov/books/NBK64273/

Centers for Disease Control and Prevention [CDC]. (2014). *Vital signs: Alcohol screening and counseling.* Retrieved from http://www.cdc.gov/vitalsigns/alcohol-screening-counseling/

Council for Accreditation of Counseling & Related Educational Programs (CACREP). (2016). *2016 CACREP Standards.* Retrieved from http://www.cacrep.org/for-programs/2016-cacrep-standards/

Ewing, J. A. (1984). Detecting alcoholism: The CAGE Questionnaire. *Journal of American Medical Association, 252,* 1905–1907.

Gentilello, L., Rivara, F., Donovan, D., Jurkovich, G. J., Daranciang, E., Dunn, C. W., . . . Ries, R. R. (1999). Alcohol interventions in a trauma center as a means of reducing the risk of injury recurrence. *Annals of Surgery, 230,* 473–483.

Guthman, D., Lazowski, L. E., Moore, D., Heineman, A. W., & Embree, J. (2012). Validation of the substance abuse screener in American sign language. *Rehabilitation Psychology, 57,* 140–148. doi:10.1037/a0028605

Kerwin, M. L. E., Kirby, K. C., Speziali, D., Duggan, M. Melitz, C. Versek, B., & McNamara, A. (2015). What can parents do? A review of state laws regarding decision making for adolescent drug abuse and mental health treatment. *Journal of Child and Adolescent Substance Abuse, 24,* 166–176. Retrieved from https://www.ncbi.nlm.nih.gov/pmc/articles/PMC4393016/

Keyes, K. M., Hatzenbuehler, M. L., McLaughlin, K. A., Link, B., Olfson, M., Grant, B. F., & Hasin, D. (2010). Stigma and treatment for alcohol disorders in the United States. *American Journal of Epidemiology, 172,* 1364–1372. doi:10.1093/aje/kwq304

Kirschenbaum, H. (2009). *The life and work of Carl Rogers.* Alexandria, VA: American Counseling Association.

Knight, J. R., Roberts, T., Gabrielli, J., & Van Hook, S. (2016). *Adolescent alcohol and substance use and abuse.* Retrieved from https://brightfutures.aap.org/Bright%20Futures%20Documents/Screening/pdf

Knight, J. R., Sherritt, L., Shrier, L. A., Harris, S., & Chang, G. (2002). Validity of the CRAFFT Substance Abuse Screening Test among clinic patients. *Archives of Pediatric & Adolescent Medicine, 156,* 607–614. doi:10.1001/archpedi.156.6.607

Kunkel, T. (2012). *Future trends in state courts 2012: Substance abuse and confidentiality: 42 CFR Part 2.* Retrieved from http://www.ncsc.org/sitecore/content/microsites/future-trends-2012/home/Privacy-and-Technology/Substance-Abuse.aspx

Lam, T. C. M., Kolomitro, K., & Alamparambil, F. C. (2011). Empathy training: Methods, evaluation practices, and validity. *Journal of Multidisciplinary Evaluation, 7*(16), 162–200. Retrieved from http://journals.sfu.ca/jmde/index.php/jmde_1/article/view/314/327

Lewis, T. F. (2014). *Substance abuse and addiction treatment: Practical application of counseling theory.* Upper Saddle River, NJ: Pearson Education.

Lloyd, C. (2013). The stigmatization of problem drug users: A narrative literature review. *Drugs: Education, Prevention and Policy, 20,* 85–95. doi:10.3109/09687637.2012.743506

Love, J., & Zatzick, D. (2014). Screening and intervention for comorbid substance disorders, PTSD, depression, and suicide: A trauma center survey. *Psychiatric Services, 65*(7), 918–923. doi:10.1176/appi.ps.201300399

MacLeod, B. P. (2015). *The effects of an experiential learning activity on counselor trainees' empathy and attitudes towards substance abuse.* (Unpublished doctoral dissertation). University of North Carolina at Charlotte, Charlotte, NC.

McCambridge, J., & Kypri, K. (2011). Can simply answering research questions change behaviour? Systematic review and meta analyses of brief alcohol intervention trials. *PLoS One, 6*(10), e23748. doi:10.1371/journal.pone.0023748. Epub October 5, 2011.

Miller, W. R. (2014). Celebrating Carl Rogers: Motivational interviewing and the person-centered approach. *Motivational Interviewing: Training, Research, Implementation, Practice, 1*(3), 4–6. doi:10.5195/mitrip.2014.54

Miller, W. R., & Rollnick, S. (1991). *Motivational interviewing: Preparing people to change addictive behavior.* New York, NY: Guilford.

Miller, W. R., & Rollnick, S. (2012). *Motivational interviewing: Helping people change* (3rd ed.). New York, NY: Guilford.

National Institute on Alcohol Abuse and Alcoholism (NIAAA). (2016). *Rethinking drinking.* NIH Publication No. 15-3770, Revised May 2016.

National Institute on Drug Abuse (NIDA). (2015a). *Evidence-based screening tools for adults.* Retrieved from https://www.drugabuse.gov/nidamed-medical-health-professionals/tool-resources-your-practice/screening-assessment-drug-testing-resources/chart-evidence-based-screening-tools-adults

National Institute on Drug Abuse (NIDA). (2015b). *NIDA-modified ASSIST.* http://www.drugabuse.gov/nmassist/

National Organization on Fetal Alcohol Syndrome (NOFAS). (2014, August). *Implementing CHOICES in clinical settings that serve American Indian and Alaska Native women of childbearing age.* Retrieved from http://www.nofas.org/wp-content/uploads/2014/08/Implementing-CHOICES-in-Clinical-Settings-that-Serve-American-Indian-and-Alaska-Native-Women-of-Childbearing-Age.pdf

O'Brien, M. C., McCoy, T. P., Rhodes, S. D., Wagoner, A., & Wolfson, M. (2008). Caffeinated cocktails: Energy drink consumption, high-risk drinking, and alcohol- related consequences among college students. *Journal of Academic Emergency Medicine, 15*, 453–460.

Parrish, S., & Daetwyler, C. J. (2013). Substance use disorders in adolescents: Screening and engagement in primary care settings. Retrieved from https://webcampus.drexelmed.edu/nida/module_2/default_FrameSet.htm

Parsons, R. D., & Zhang, N. (2014). *Becoming a skilled counselor.* Thousand Oaks, CA: Sage.

Remley, T. P., & Herlihy, B. (2007). *Ethical, legal, and professional issues in counseling* (Updated 2nd ed.). Upper Saddle River, NJ: Pearson Education.

Rogers, C. R. (1957). The necessary and sufficient conditions of therapeutic personality change. *Journal of Consulting Psychology, 21*, 95–103.

SASSI Institute. (2016). *SASSI Online.* Retrieved from https://www.sassi.com/products/web-based/

Steinweg, D. L., & Worth, H. (1993). Alcoholism: The keys to the CAGE. *The American Journal of Medicine, 94*, 520–523.

Sterling, S., Kline-Simon, A. H., Wibbelsman, C., Wong, A., & Weisner, C. (2012). Screening for adolescent alcohol and drug use in pediatric health-care settings: Predictors and implications for practice and policy. *Addiction Science and Clinical Practice, 7*(13). Retrieved from http://www.ascpjournal.org/content/7/1/13

Treatment Research Institute (TSI). (2014). *Assessment and evaluation resource center.* Retrieved from http://www.tresearch.org/tools/download-asi-instruments-manuals/

U.S. Department of Veteran Affairs. (2014). *Alcohol: Frequently asked questions.* Retrieved from http://www.queri.research.va.gov/tools/alcohol-misuse/alcohol-faqs.cfm

Velasquez, M. M., Ingersoll, K. S., Sobell, M. B., Floyd, R. L., Sobell, L. C., & von Sternberg, K. (2010). A dual-focus motivational intervention to reduce the risk of alcohol-exposed pregnancy. *Cognitive and Behavioral Practice, 17*(2), 203–12.

Walker, R., Logan, T. K., Clark, J. J., & Leukefeld, C. (2005). Informed consent to undergo treatment for substance abuse: A recommended approach. *Journal of Substance Abuse Treatment, 29*, 241–251.

Warren, J. A., Hof, K. R., McGriff, D., & Morris, L.-N. B. (2012). Five experiential learning activities in addictions education. *Journal of Creativity in Mental Health, 7*, 273–288. doi:10.1080/15401383.2012.710172

Winters, K. C., & Kaminer, Y. (2008). Screening and assessing adolescent substance use disorders in clinical populations. *Journal of American Academy of Child and Adolescent Psychiatry, 47,* 740–744.

World Health Organization (WHO). (2010). *Global strategy to reduce the harmful use of alcohol* Retrieved from http://www.who.int/substance_abuse/alcstratenglishfinal.pdf

Young, M. E. (2012). *The art of helping: Building blocks and techniques* (5th ed.). Upper Saddle River, NJ: Pearson Education.

Zatzick, D., Donovan, D. M., Jurkovich, G., Gentilello, L., Dunn, C., Russo, J., . . . Rivera, F. P. (2014). Disseminating alcohol screening and brief intervention at trauma centers: A policy relevant cluster randomized effectiveness trial. *Addiction, 109,* 754–765. doi:10.1111/add.12492

7

Diagnosis of Substance-Related and Addictive Disorders

LEARNING OBJECTIVES

Upon completion of reading this chapter and completing the suggested activities, the learner will

- identify the specific criteria for diagnosing a substance use disorder (SUD);
- list the key specifiers for indicating the severity of the SUD;
- discuss the 10 drug classifications for diagnostic classification;
- describe at least two models of diagnosing SUD;
- use the appropriate numeric codes to record a diagnosis; and
- describe the importance of exploring risky use if diagnostic criteria are not met.

Knowledge

Understanding Diagnosis

Much has been written about diagnosing an individual; the power of a diagnosis can be both beneficial and detrimental. Examples exist of individuals suffering because businesses, such as life insurance companies, have reportedly rejected coverage of individuals with an addiction diagnosis. Thomas Szaz wrote years ago about the potential for negative problems and complications when a culture becomes focused on diagnosing and labeling (1960). It is important that the beginning counselor have an awareness of the power of diagnosis, especially as it pertains to substance use disorders; once diagnosed with an opiate use disorder, for example, it may follow that individual for their lifetime.

Conversely, a formal diagnosis for individuals can also bring important awareness to a condition that is serious, requires specialized care and planning, and is lifelong. Some clients report great relief when a diagnosis is made; it can be validation that there is something that has happened to me, it is not a moral failing nor a shameful disease, the condition has a name, and most importantly, research and knowledge exists that provides further information about the condition and effective treatment for this brain disease. In addition, the diagnosis can substantiate further the medical nature of the diagnosis of addiction, in other words, a brain disorder. For many clients, this may provide an alternative understanding that tackles myths and negative stigma. For example, the moral model is more apt to label addiction as a lack of moral character and willpower. A medical diagnosis involving a brain disorder can challenge stigma and help the client understand that their behavior is not a personal reflection of their moral character as much as it is a hijacked brain (Schomerus et al., 2010). Others may refer to their diagnosis as more of a justification of aberrant, addictive behavior patterns and point to the diagnosis as the reason they cannot be held accountable for their behaviors. With substance use disorders, it can also be an important opportunity for the counselor to clarify to the client and loved ones that while the diagnosis may be lifelong, the way the condition is treated has everything to do with how crippling the diagnosis will be experienced and perceived. In the addiction treatment field, it has been commonly pointed out that while there is no cure for a diagnosis involving addiction, it is 100% treatable, thus addictive behaviors and continued loss of control can improve with optimal treatment response.

Finally, because of the stigma and power of a diagnosis, the licensed addiction counselor making a diagnosis, as our profession trains us to do, need always maintain a careful and caring approach to diagnosing, gather as much pertinent information as possible, and be thorough with examining all pertinent criteria related to diagnosing. Sadly, it has been this licensed clinical addiction specialist's observation that for far too many clients, specialized help for addiction occurs when the person is suffering in the late stages of the disease. At that point and with such advanced symptoms that are classically described, others have duly noted that even a 3-year-old child can make the diagnosis at that point. For example, in alcoholism, late-stage symptoms can include pronounced hand tremors, ruddy complexion, spider veins pronounced in the facial area, distended abdomen due to liver failure and ascites, and a malnourished state due to poor nutritional intake when drinking alcohol upon awakening throughout most days. For any counseling professional, it is critically important to carefully assess and diagnose symptoms earlier in the downward spiral of addiction. The use of screening and assessment tools on a routine basis for any client seeking counseling becomes an important way for earlier and more careful diagnosing to occur. Moreover, it is equally important to provide information to the client if the criteria are not met for a diagnosable substance use disorder yielding no diagnosis, yet, risky use patterns are noted and need to be highlighted when risky use is evident.

In this chapter an overview of diagnosing models will be reviewed; it is also expected that all professional counselors will have received extensive training in diagnosing methods of mental disorders. This chapter, therefore, will focus exclusively on substance use and pertinent addictive process (behavior) disorder diagnoses based on an expected understanding of professional methods of diagnosing mental disorders. First, we can examine an overview of current models in the addiction field when diagnosing a substance use disorder with special focus on major diagnostic influences in the United States.

Overview of Current Diagnosis Models

As noted in earlier chapters, diagnosis pertaining to addictive disorders is currently most influenced by the *Diagnostic and Statistical Manual of Mental Disorders* (5th ed.; *DSM-5*), often seen as the primary diagnostic manual for all psychiatric diagnoses (APA, 2013). Since the early 1980s, the *DSM* offered terminology and a comprehensive model for diagnosing mental disorders. The *DSM* has become the most prominent approach to diagnosis in the United States. It has been revised continually since the 1980s to reflect better understanding through careful research and examination of substance use disorders. Currently, addictive use disorders are included in the *DSM-5* in the chapter titled "Substance-Related and Addictive Disorders." The *DSM* was first published in 1952 and, as will be presented in this chapter, it has undergone several revisions with major changes in the most recent 2013 revision, *DSM-5*. Other models of diagnosing are also briefly examined in this chapter, including global models and newer research-based diagnostic models.

National Institute of Mental Health Research Domain Criteria

An important newer approach to conceptualizing diagnoses has emerged from the National Institute of Mental Health (NIMH). The Research Domain Criteria (RDoC) exists to provide a new construct for studying and classifying mental disorders (NIMH, 2015). Research findings from studies ranging from genes to individual reports have been synthesized and organized within a matrix (NIMH, 2015). Important biological, genetic, and behavioral information is continually being analyzed to better classify mental disorders. Studies, such as a recent study examining bipolar and schizophrenia disorders, noted significant improvements in classifying disorders utilizing more of the biological and genetic information in addition to behavioral symptoms and observations. Clementz and colleagues (2015) noted that certain biomarkers, for example, were better able to distinguish different cases with psychosis histories in superior ways as compared to using descriptive classifications alone, such as those in the *DSM-5*. It is hoped that future research will provide clinicians with improved diagnostics that involve biomarkers, such as blood tests, in addition to clinical observations. The counseling speciality in addictive disorders could benefit enormously if reliable biomarkers were available; old-timers in the past have jokingly remarked, "I wish addicts and alcoholics would just break out in purple spots, then we could all clearly see when addiction was underway." With the critical research being conducted and analyzed in the RDoC, there is hope that physical blood or other lab tests would provide clearer answers before the progression of addiction is so far advanced that it is imminently life threatening. Progress continues to be made in this area of diagnostics, yet much more remains to be studied (NIMH, 2015). Another area of focus within diagnostic models involves the global community. Mental disorders, including substance use disorders, are not unique to the United States; consequently, it behooves us to be able to communicate globally in shared models of diagnosing and diagnostic classification systems so that we are all better able to be "singing out of the same hymnbook," in essence. The following section looks at a model used internationally that is very important in understanding diagnosing models.

International Classification and Diagnosis

The global issues pertaining to substance-related health problems also continue to be important for the field of addiction counseling. One of the leading global organizations involved in major health issues of all types is the World Health Organization (WHO). Scientific leaders in WHO spend considerable resources to research and attend to health issues and crises, such as the Ebola virus crisis. In addition, WHO produces an official coding system called the International Classification of Diseases (ICD). The most recent ICD version adopted in the United States in 2015 is the 10th version, also called ICD-10 (Optum, 2016). Increasingly, the *DSM-5* committees found it important to align *DSM* codes with the international coding system of the ICD in order to help the two diagnostic classification systems represent similar health conditions and disorders by using a uniform coding system and language. Consequently, the *DSM-5* is closely organized to reflect the previous ICD-9, the current ICD-10 and the upcoming ICD-11 coding system (APA, 2013). These steps taken for *DSM-5* are also seen in the changes of diagnostic areas; the previous *DSM* Global Assessment of Functioning (GAF) Scale used in the defunct multiaxial diagnosing model in Axis V, for example, has been completely replaced by the WHO Disability Assessment Schedule (WHODAS) in order to be more unified in our clinical coding and clinical diagnostic work within the global community as we diagnose individuals suffering from substance use disorders and the resultant impact from the disabling disorder. In order for billing and reimbursement of counseling provided to individuals, the ICD-10 codes are prominent in a uniform coding system. Thus, the international coding system and diagnosing classifications are integral to all professional counseling provided to clients. With the recent ICD-10 codes, a much larger number of possible codes that are more specific to the condition being treated are now available. The ICD-10 codes are required to be used in accordance with the *DSM-5*, the most well-known diagnostic model in the United States when diagnosing substance use disorders, as will be presented in the next section.

DSM-5 and New Updates

Historical Changes

Efforts to update the substance use disorder section in the fifth edition of the *DSM* resulted in major changes with the 2013 publication. Important newer concepts of a substance use disorder include a greater emphasis on the "underlying change in brain circuits" (APA, 2013, p. 483). The revised definition that is important to highlight further specifies that a substance use disorder involves "a problematic pattern of use leading to clinically significant impairment or distress" (APA, 2013, p. 490) involving *two or more* of the 11 diagnostic criteria that have occurred *within a 12-month time period*. The *DSM-5* provides a much more complete diagnostic spectrum of substance use disorders than earlier editions because it is now providing a new continuum of severity instead of the previous dichotomous classifications. Previous versions of the *DSM* included diagnoses, if criteria were met, that were limited to either substance abuse or substance dependence (APA, 2013). The older diagnosis model of substance abuse was removed in this recent revision and is no longer included in the common language within the *DSM-5*. To clarify, the *DSM-5* no longer endorses use of diagnoses such as "abuse." Further, the term "dependence" is used only to indicate biological or physiological dependence with certain prescribed medications that is not to be confused with the pattern of a diagnosable substance use disorder. At times, professionals have contributed to confusion by misunderstanding physiological dependence. The *DSM-5* aids in clarification since physiological dependence alone should not be confused with a diagnosable addictive disorder. Moreover, as we will see when examining criteria, an individual does not have to experience physical dependence to meet criteria for a diagnosable substance use disorder. The case illustration with Marissa (see Box 7.1) is provided as one example of differing terms between addictive disorders and physical dependence.

Box 7.1: Case Illustration of Physical Dependence

A woman, Marissa, was prescribed an anti-anxiety medication on a short-term basis by her primary care physician due to complicated bereavement related to the recent loss of her spouse. Over the course of one month of use of the medication she and her physician determined she would no longer be prescribed the medication. When she suddenly stopped the medication, Xanax (the commercial product name) or as it is known by its generic name, alprazolam, she experienced physical symptoms of withdrawal related to the rapid discontinuance of the drug. Because her body had developed a physical dependence on the medication, she experienced physical symptoms of mild withdrawal. Yet she has no other patterns of symptoms that meet criteria for a substance use disorder. Would she be diagnosed with a Xanax use disorder? Based on the limited physical dependence she experienced and no *DSM-5* criteria being met, a diagnosis of addictive or Xanax use disorder would be incorrect and inappropriate.

Next, other terms have been carefully analyzed for inclusion in the newly revised *DSM-5*. Many specialists have worked decades attempting to clarify appropriate terms regarding disorders related to substances. Due to an abundance of terms related to substance use disorders, such as addiction, chemical dependence, or substance abuse, the *DSM-5* considered how to best clarify the diagnostic spectrum related to clinically significant problematic use. Terminology of "addiction" is not utilized in the new revision, rather, "addictive disorders" is used and "the more neutral term *substance use disorder* is used to describe the wide range of the disorder, from a mild form to a severe state of chronically relapsing, compulsive drug-taking" (APA, 2013, p. 485). The new terminology is reflected in the title heading of the section, "Substance-Related and Addictive Disorders," and further, substance use disorders or substance-induced disorders are the main classifications. Now, classification is more reflective of the full spectrum of substance-related disorders and utilizes a severity specifier to indicate how the substance use disorder is distinguished as mild, moderate, or severe. Moreover, for the first time a gambling disorder, long considered a process addictive disorder by specialists, has been included in this chapter and is removed from its previous classification as an impulse-related disorder. Other changes include criteria that were specifically examining legal problems associated with substance use were excluded from this revision, a clear distinction between medically dependent symptoms is differentiated from addictive symptoms, a new criterion was added related to cravings and urges to use, withdrawal from cannabis (marijuana) was added for the first time as another symptom within the cannabis use disorder, caffeine withdrawal was also newly added but there is no caffeine use disorder in this edition either, the previous polysubstance dependence diagnosis has been eliminated, and tobacco use disorder is also included within this *DSM-5* section on substance-related disorders (APA, 2013). Importantly, criteria are found throughout the *DSM-5* for substance-induced mental conditions and additional sections examine criteria for various substance intoxication and withdrawal. The major groups of drugs remain and 10 groups are divided as follows: alcohol; caffeine; cannabis; hallucinogens; inhalants; opioids; sedatives, hypnotics, and anxiolytics; stimulants; tobacco; and other drugs.

An additional aid for the diagnosing counselor involves groupings of how criteria can be clustered. The 11 diagnostic criteria referenced in the *DSM-5* (APA, 2013) are arranged in four clusters that can be clinically useful as follows: first, impaired control (symptoms 1–4), social areas of concern (symptoms 5–7), risky use (symptoms 8–9), and last, physical symptoms (10–11). To underscore its importance, at no time is there a requirement for a physical symptom, such as withdrawal, to be present in order for a substance use disorder to be diagnosed. Again, only two of the 11 criteria must be present for the individual to be considered to have a SUD; it is not specified that the criteria come from any one grouping or cluster. The next beneficial aid in the *DSM-5* model pertains to specifying if the disorder is mild, moderate, or severe.

For the severity specifier, mild, two or three symptom criteria must be met; for moderate use disorder, four or five criteria must be met; for the severe specifier to be used, six or more of the criteria would be met; and if only one or no criterion is met, there is no diagnosis (APA, 2013) yet the clinician may carefully consider if risky use is present and provide feedback to the client about risks of continued use.

Box 7.2: Exercise 7.1: Practice Opportunity—Drug Classifications

Table 7.1 Drug Class Examples

To refresh your memory about the various classes of drugs, in the box below list at least three types of specific substances in each class of drugs as demonstrated with the first drug, alcohol, as shown.

Drug	Examples of three types of substances
1. Alcohol	beer, wine, vodka
2. Caffeine	
3. Cannabis	
4. Hallucinogens	
5. Inhalants	
6. Opioids	
7. Sedatives, Hypnotics, and Anxiolytics	
8. Stimulants	
9. Tobacco	
10. Other Drugs (steroids, nitrous oxide, certain herbs such as kava, or new designer or counterfeit drugs with unknown adulterants)	

Just as importantly, it is often valuable to examine what is *not* included in the criteria for diagnosing a SUD. At no time does the *DSM-5* indicate that certain criteria must be present in any one cluster, rather it is if *two or more criteria are present*. The counselor may also note that there are no quantitative or frequency amounts specified in order to meet diagnostic criteria. To illustrate further, a threshold amount of cocaine or a threshold frequency of cocaine use is not a part of any of the diagnostic criteria— there is no one established amount or frequency that signifies a diagnosable SUD; rather, the emphasis centers around what clinically significant impairment or distress occurs when the individual is using, craving, or withdrawing from the substance(s). An additional example with alcohol, for instance, means that the counselor could not make a diagnosis based on a person who drinks 40 beers per drinking episode—that amount alone does not meet any of the criteria of a SUD. Those new to the diagnosing of a SUD often mistakenly believe that there is some established threshold amount or frequency that must surely mean the person has an addictive disorder. It is clear in the *DSM-5* that a certain amount or a certain frequency of using are not part of the criteria for diagnosing a SUD. Other factors to consider in diagnosing pertain to documentation of the diagnosis.

When writing out or recording the diagnosis, it is important that the actual drug of concern is named in the diagnosis instead of the more generic class of drugs. For example, instead of writing "stimulant use disorder," the particular drug, such as cocaine, would be listed in the diagnosis as follows: Cocaine use disorder. As counselors have specific coursework on using the *DSM-5*, the addiction counselor is also expected to record numeric codes that accompany the substance-related diagnosis. Beginning in early October 2015 the only numeric codes to be used are the ICD-10 codes; the ICD-10 *F codes are in parentheses* in each use disorder section (Gintner, 2014; Optum, 2016). It is important to remember that the new ICD-10 codes have numerical codes representing many conditions including mental conditions. For instance, Gintner (2014) highlights an example of one code being able to represent alcohol use disorder whereas a different code can represent a complication such as alcohol-induced psychosis. Examples of recording substance use disorders with ICD-10 codes, diagnosis, and criteria symptom groupings are provided in Tables 7.2, 7.3, and 7.4, below.

An additional option for diagnosing SUD includes the specifier, moderate use when 4–5 symptoms within the *DSM-5* criteria are present. Table 7.3 depicts an individual who meets the criteria for a substance use disorder and the moderate specifier would be applied.

Lastly, in Table 7.4, the criteria for a severe use disorder are met as shown in the illustration. Notice the areas pertaining to impaired control that are more clearly involved in this example of a severe SUD.

Importantly, for the SUD diagnosis, it is important to specify if the disorder is either in early remission (3 months to 12 months without any of the diagnosing criteria being present, except for the criteria involving craving) or sustained remission (12 months or longer since the diagnosing criteria have not been evident except for criteria

Table 7.2 Case Example: Mild Use: 2–3 Symptoms, Mild Alcohol Use Disorder, (F10.10)

SYMPTOM	Substance	Grouping
CRITERIA 6: Overdoing drinking at the past four annual company parties leading to a supervisory referral to the company employee assistance program due to inappropriate language to several coworkers at the last party.	Alcohol	Social Impairment: Continued use despite recurring alcohol-related interpersonal problems.
CRITERIA 9: Continuing to drink alcohol on a regular basis while seeing a therapist for depressed mood.	Alcohol	Risky Use: Continued use of a known depressant despite complications with depressed mood.

Table 7.3 Case Example: Moderate Use: 4–5 Symptoms, Moderate Alprazolam Disorder, (F13.20)

SYMPTOM	Substance	Grouping
Criteria 4: Noted cravings for Xanax, especially in the mornings.	Xanax (Alprazolam)	Cravings: Increased compelling urges to use Xanax despite thinking that taking more Xanax is concerning.
Criteria 6: Overdosing incidents at the home leading to increasing arguments with spouse about Xanax overuse.	Xanax (Alprazolam)	Social Impairment: Continued use despite recurring Xanax-related interpersonal problems.
Criteria 9: Continuing to take Xanax on a regular basis after the treating psychiatrist discontinued the prescription when any anxiety disorder was ruled out.	Xanax (Alprazolam)	Risky Use: Continued use of a known anti-anxiety medication despite ruling out anxiety mood disorder.
Criteria 10: Secretly taking more Xanax in increasing amounts to experience euphoria.	Xanax (Alprazolam)	Tolerance: The need for markedly increased Xanax pills to be able to experience the desired effect of the Xanax.

SOURCE: APA, 2013, p. 485.

of craving). In addition, if the person is in a setting where the substance is restricted from use, it should also be specified in the diagnosis as "in a controlled environment" or if the individual is "on maintenance therapy" this should be added to the diagnosis (APA, 2013, p. 484). An additional added diagnosis relates to a process disorder, gambling, and will be reviewed in the next section.

In the newest section of the chapter on addictive disorders in the *DSM-5*, it is important to examine the newly included *gambling disorder* criteria and diagnosis as they differ from the criteria for a substance use disorder. Previous diagnostic manuals included gambling, but not in the addictive process section; instead gambling disorder had been in a section for Impulse-Control Disorders. This change in *DSM-5* to include gambling as an addictive disorder is a profound development for addiction counselors working with individuals who struggle with a behavior or process that is viewed as addictive. First, note that the definition of a use disorder is similar in defining a gambling disorder (GD) as one that involves a recurring and persisting pattern of gambling behavior that has resulted in clinically important and significant problems over a

Table 7.4 Case Example: Severe Use: Six or More Symptoms, Severe Alprazolam Use Disorder, (F13.20)

SYMPTOM	Substance	Grouping
Criteria 9: Continuing to take Xanax on a regular basis after the treating psychiatrist discontinued the prescription when any anxiety disorder was ruled out.	Xanax (Alprazolam)	Risky Use: Continued use of a known anti-anxiety medication despite ruling out anxiety mood disorder.
Criteria 6: Overdosing incidents at the home leading to increasing arguments with spouse about Xanax overuse.	Xanax (Alprazolam)	Social Impairment: Continued use despite recurring Xanax-related interpersonal problems.
Criteria 10: Secretly taking more Xanax in increasing amounts to experience euphoria.	Xanax (Alprazolam)	Tolerance: The need for markedly increased Xanax pills to be able to experience the desired effect of the Xanax.
Criteria 4: Noted cravings for Xanax, especially in the mornings.	Xanax (Alprazolam)	Cravings: Increased compelling urges to use Xanax despite thinking that taking more Xanax is concerning.
Criteria 4: More MDs seen for Xanax.		Cravings: See above.
Criteria 11: Withdrawal		Cravings: Xanax to relieve tremors.

SOURCE: APA, 2013, p. 510.

12-month time period (APA, 2013). Rennert and colleagues (2014) examined a number of individuals receiving treatment for substance use disorders to examine the prevalence of GD with the new *DSM-5* criteria. Findings indicated that the criteria now used in the *DSM-5* have increased sensitivity in detecting GD in addition to further need for more advanced studies regarding diagnosing GD (Rennert et al., 2014). It is an important step to review the differences in the criteria used in diagnosing GD.

As an important model of diagnosis, the *DSM-5* has distinct criteria for diagnosing GD. The criteria needed to establish a diagnosis of a gambling disorder involves the presence of at least *four of eight criteria*. Those eight criteria include similarities as seen in a substance use disorder but specifically involve (1) gambling tolerance (needing more money and increased betting to obtain the expected euphoria defined as tolerance issues); (2) negative moods when attempting to cut down or quit gambling (loss of control issues); (3) repeated attempts to stop or limit gambling activities and money spent (loss of control issues); (4) mental preoccupation and obsessing about gambling and ways to increase funds in order to gamble; (5) seeking gambling as mood elevator for euphoric relief when distressed; (6) increased gambling activity after losses in attempts to regain gambling losses; (7) relationship losses due to gambling; and (8) increasing reliance on others for increasing amounts of money. A final important distinction for the GD is a reminder that any of the criteria described above that are present must not be better explained by a manic episode. In other words, to differentiate a gambling disorder from mania and a manic event is very important. If the symptoms are better explained by a manic event, the GD criteria would not be used and a gambling disorder would not be diagnosed. As seen in the substance use disorder criteria, it is also important to distinguish on the spectrum if the GD is mild (4–5 symptoms); moderate (6–7 symptoms); or severe (8 criteria are met). Additional specifiers are needed if the gambling disorder is episodic (several months between problematic and distressing gambling symptoms) or persistent (continuous problematic and distressing gambling symptoms over years). If the individual diagnosed previously with GD and has had at least 3 months but less than 12 months of recovery, specify the GD is "in early remission" (APA, 2013). If the recovery period exceeds 12 months, then specify "in sustained remission" as per the *DSM-5*. The diagnosis of a gambling disorder is the only addictive process categorized in the *DSM-5*.

Other process addictions that involve much discussion, debate, and disagreement about inclusion in the *DSM* include food addictive disorders, sexual addictive disorders, workaholism, compulsive spending/buying, and Internet gaming or technology addictive disorder (Acosta, Lainas, & Veach, 2013; Ahmed, Guillem, & Vandaele, 2013; Chamberlain & Zhang, 2009; Stoeber, Davis, & Townley, 2013). Diagnosing in these areas is often self-initiated since many resources are available through the Internet and 12-step groups that try to answer key questions about these disorders. It is expected that controversy will remain and extensive research opportunities exist to help us understand better the full extent of process addictive disorders.

Lastly, cultural differences are important for the counselor to consider in all diagnoses, especially substance-related and addictive disorders. What one culture may view as a spiritual connection with deceased loved ones, another culture may view as the symptoms of delusion. Much criticism has been voiced over the cultural insensitivity seen in the diagnostic process. For example, the *DSM-5* GD section notes higher rates of GD among African Americans than European Americans and Hispanic Americans with no mention of Asian American individuals (APA, 2013), yet much has been written regarding the Asian American community and particularly concerning vulnerability of problem gambling and gambling disorders (Fong & Tsuang, 2007; Raylu & Oie, 2004). Gender considerations are also important cultural considerations in the diagnosing process; in the *DSM-5* Sedative, Hypnotic, or Anxiolytic Use Disorder Section under the heading pertaining to culture-related diagnostic issues (each section has a subsection on culture-related issues), the only entry briefly notes "females may be at higher risk than males for prescription drug misuse of sedative, hypnotic, or anxiolytic substances" (APA, 2013, p. 554). Yet, the Centers for Disease

Control and Prevention (CDC) noted in 2010 data that benzodiazepines (drugs such as Xanax, Valium, or Ativan often prescribed for anxiety symptom management) were the primary reason, out of all prescription drugs, for emergency room visits by women, exceeding even opiate pain-relieving drugs (CDC, 2013). The statistical report also determined alarming trends involving women: since 2007 more women's deaths were due to drug overdoses than deaths attributed to motor vehicle crashes; women were four times more likely to die from drug overdoses than homicide; and moreover, the data covering 1999 through 2010 showed the rate of overdose deaths for women was nearly twice that for men (CDC, 2013). It is critical that addiction counselors continue to explore cultural considerations as diagnoses are determined (Sun, 2009). Often that will involve information beyond that found in the *DSM-5*.

In summary, the counselor now has more tools for making an accurate diagnosis with *DSM-5* criteria, and it is also equally important to explore helpful techniques to begin to work with the client when a diagnosis has been made. The next section will examine the importance of providing the diagnosis to the client and next steps for planning how to best provide care to the individual with a substance use disorder.

Evidence-Based Practices

Along with the importance of an accurate diagnosis when a substance use disorder is present, it is also helpful to understand how to best convey a diagnosis to the client. There is no one way to best provide a diagnosis to a client, but there are important considerations and the new counselor will be working with a clinical supervisor as various experience is gained when providing a diagnosis. One is reminded that the counselor will be conveying this diagnosis to an individual who is experiencing many reactions to hearing a professional, perhaps for the first time, say that a substance use disorder diagnosis has been made. Therapeutically, the confirmation of a diagnosis can be a very pivotal moment in the helping relationship. If the counselor conveys judgmentalism or harshness, the client is more likely to reject the diagnosis and treatment recommendations. When the counselor conveys warmth and unconditional positive regard, the client may be more able to process the various reactions when a diagnosis is made. The counselor is encouraged to focus on empathy with delivering a diagnosis. Imagine, briefly, how you might experience a professional counselor sitting with you to inform you that you meet the criteria for a mental brain disorder that currently has no cure, requires lifelong management, and includes substantial behavior changes. The diagnosis of a substance use disorder is serious, often complicated by myths and misunderstandings, shame, guilt, and anger. Given the complicated reactions to SUD, diagnoses should be conveyed with compassion and hope (Miller, 2015). In addition, the more the counselor can provide factual information to the client, the better the outcome may be. The dialogue that follows in Box 7.3 is a demonstration of a client just learning of the diagnosis of a severe cannabis use disorder.

Box 7.3: Case Study: Providing the Diagnosis

Counselor:	Based on the assessment results and our time together exploring your substance use, the results indicate a positive finding in terms of a marijuana use disorder. Hearing me say that may bring up different feelings and thoughts—it may be helpful to begin to share what's going through your mind now.
Counselor:	[Allows Silence]
Client:	I guess it's not a surprise, but I was hoping I wasn't that bad off. And then, again, I don't know; I didn't think anyone could really get addicted to marijuana.
Counselor:	Lots of mixed feelings are going on with you now—it's hard to take it all in. That seems to be something I see regularly . . . at first there are many mixed feelings, thoughts, and questions.
Client:	Yeah, I just don't want to have to deal with this. . . . I don't see how I can quit, but I don't see how I can keep smoking up all my extra money—it sucks.
Counselor:	You're feeling torn—like you're stuck in between how it's been and what you want to do as you've gotten serious about getting clean.
Client (tearful):	That's it—so torn. So hard.

Box 7.4: Exercise 7.2: Practice Session

Imagine how you would feel as a counselor providing a diagnosis to a client. What would you most want the client to know? How would you say it? Take a few moments and reflect on important insights you notice that can help you when you begin to provide a SUD diagnosis to clients. In addition, practice several case practice sessions and experiment with specific words you might use to provide a SUD diagnosis.

For evidence-based practice, it is important for the counselor to be able to consult the *DSM-5* to provide additional knowledge that may also be informative and based in data that can address questions your client may ask. For an individual facing a tobacco use disorder that is classified as severe, it may be helpful to review information in the prevalence section within the *DSM-5* section pertaining to a tobacco use disorder. As an example, it may be helpful to convey to the client that many individuals with a tobacco use disorder began smoking as an adolescent, most went on to smoke daily, and 22% of adults in the United States are former smokers (APA, 2013) as a way to instill hope and convey universality. By providing evidence-based knowledge, the client may be able to have a better understanding of the many facets of the particular SUD.

Importance of Diagnosis for Effective Treatment Planning

It will come as no surprise that a working diagnosis is often tied to effective treatment planning. In order to know how to best help clients, it can be beneficial to know what key criteria within a diagnosis are being met. The care plan is better individualized with specific information regarding each criterion. The strength of the *DSM-5* system provides a common language for describing behaviors and patterns in each criteria that must be met in order for a diagnosis to be made.

Box 7.5: Diagnosing of Substance Use Disorders With *DSM-5*

DSM-5 National Epidemiologic Survey on Alcohol and Related Conditions-III (NESARC-III) RESULTS

An important survey of over 35,000 individuals in the United States was conducted by the National Institute of Alcohol Abuse and Alcoholism (NIAAA). For the fourth time since 1998, results of this survey are of major importance for understanding the prevalence of alcohol use disorders and related comorbid conditions. This particular survey, National Epidemiologic Survey on Alcohol and Related Conditions-III (NESARC-III), utilized the newly revised diagnostic criteria of the *DSM-5* when conducting face-to-face interviews of the representative adult sample (18 years of age and older). The extensive evaluation tool, the Alcohol Use Disorder and Associated Disabilities Interview Schedule (AUDADIS-5), was the instrument used in the surveys along with saliva samples for genetic research; important genetic findings are anticipated in 2017 (NIAAA, 2016). Certain prevalence findings, as analyzed by Grant and colleagues (2015), are highlighted with timely and important knowledge addiction counselors need when diagnosing alcohol use disorders. The interviews were conducted between 2012 and 2013 and provide the most recent look into how the *DSM-5* diagnostic criteria—using mild, moderate, and severe specifiers along a spectrum of alcohol use—inform specialists working in the addictive disorders field.

First, the findings underscore a substantial prevalence of alcohol use disorders with a notable lifetime prevalence of 29.1% for diagnosable alcohol use disorders, which computes to nearly three in 10 adults having an alcohol use disorder during one's lifetime. Next, the related problems with alcohol use disorders are also substantial in conjunction with depressive, bipolar I, antisocial, and borderline personality disorders. Anxiety-related disorders were also seen as a co-occurring disorder at a moderate rate. Moreover, treatment for individuals suffering from alcohol use disorders occurs in less than 20% of those meeting *DSM-5* criteria. Of particular concern, white (32.6%) and Native American (43.4%) men have increased incidence in their lifetime of an alcohol use disorder (Grant et al., 2015). In addition, those adults who have never married also have increased rates of alcohol use disorders (35.5%) during their lifetime. Overall, the research findings indicate that more individuals and loved ones are affected by alcohol use disorders in light of the revised *DSM-5* spectrum for diagnosing alcohol use disorders. Other substances were also studied by Grant and colleagues in an additional report (2016).

When analyzing results for the patterns related to drug use other than alcohol, Grant and colleagues (2016) noted nearly one in 10 adults in the United States met criteria for a drug use disorder (DUD) (9.9%). Drugs specifically included marijuana/cannabis, amphetamines/stimulants, designer/club drugs such as Molly, cocaine, hallucinogens, opioids including heroin and non-heroin opioids, sedative/antianxiety drugs, and inhalants. As with alcohol use patterns, DUD was seen more often in men, white and Native American adults. In the analysis, Grant and colleagues saw important overlap with DUD and depressive, dysthymia, bipolar I, PTSD, and personality disorders (borderline, antisocial, and schizotypal). A slightly greater number of adults with DUD, nearly one-fourth, were found to have received treatment for DUD during their lifetime, yet only 13.5% were seen as having received DUD treatment within the year.

In conclusion, the greater prevalence of substance use disorders, as seen when utilizing the *DSM-5* criteria, provides important knowledge and urgency as counselors are faced with the challenge of accurately diagnosing substance use disorders. Both analyses by Grant and colleagues (2015, 2016) underscore the need for all clients to be evaluated for substance use disorders, particularly those seeking help for depressive disorders, bipolar I, PTSD, anxiety, and personality disorders, especially in light of the unacceptably low numbers of individuals receiving treatment for substance use disorders who may also be diagnosed with any of the aforementioned disorders. It is believed that with proper and accurate substance use disorder diagnoses, especially at earlier stages of severity, more individuals can benefit from improved care for substance use disorders. In addition, as Grant and colleagues conclude, "study results also reinforce the urgency of destigmatizing DUD and educating the public, clinicians, and policy makers about its treatments" (2016, p. 46).

These applicable criteria can then be included in treatment planning to better inform the client of specific indicators of the disorder, show how the criteria apply to each individual, and create a unified plan to address each pertinent criterion. For example, the American Society of Addiction Medicine (ASAM), founded in 1954 just as alcoholism was being recognized by the American Medical Association as a disease, is a leading organization that has produced guidelines for counselors and addiction medicine doctors to use in guiding treatment decisions. The guideline, edited by Dr. David Mee-Lee (2014), also has a software edition, and is titled *The ASAM Criteria: Treatment Criteria for Addictive, Substance-Related, and Co-Occurring Conditions.* It is a valuable resource for the licensed addiction counselor in critical diagnostic and treatment planning for any individual with substance-related use disorders. The information provided by ASAM notes that in a recent survey, 43 of the 50 U.S. states are required to use a standard set of criteria for patient care and approximately two-thirds of these states require the use of *The ASAM Criteria* (ASAM, 2014).

The criteria can be used to help plan care and consider the best level of care; in other words, will the client benefit from traditional outpatient counseling sessions once or twice per month or a residential level of care? Considerations for the licensed addiction counselor can be helpful when deciding what type of plan is needed for this client. For instance, if a client is assessed and does *not* meet the two or more criteria needed for a diagnosis of a substance use disorder, Mee-Lee guides the counselor to consider the early intervention level of treatment such as SBIRT services in the client's treatment plan. If diagnostic criteria are met for a substance use disorder, Mee-Lee recommends extensive consideration of six important dimensions regarding the client's care. If one looks at the whole person as affected by addiction, there are six dimensions that are particularly important to examine: withdrawal or intoxication concerns, medical conditions, emotional and psychological issues, receptivity to making changes regarding the substance use disorder, relapse or continuing with use, and lastly, the client's recovery environment. These six key areas are useful for treatment planning all throughout the client's care and serve as a unifying structure for counseling teams and addiction medical professionals to use a common language in communicating about care and in communicating with the client about the major areas of their care plans. Extensive training, software, and resources are available for further use in the treatment and care planning criteria at the ASAM website: www .asamcriteria.org.

Accurate Diagnosis

Missed Diagnosis

The new *DSM-5* committees went to great lengths over many years to make diagnosing of substance use disorders more accurate. However, it is also clear that there can be symptoms of a substance use disorder that also mirror symptoms in other mental disorders. For example, an individual struggling with a severe cocaine use disorder will have some symptoms that match criteria for bipolar disorder, such as symptoms seen in a hypomanic episode. Such symptoms include periods of time involving at least four consecutive days with abnormally elevated or irritable mood with abnormally high levels of activity. As you can imagine, an individual showing repeated use of cocaine might also have similar symptoms of the high energy and euphoric mood during cocaine binging followed by irritable mood and agitated high energy in the pursuit of additional cocaine. For clinicians with little training in diagnosing substance use disorders and an absence of a substance-focused evaluation, the diagnosis of the cocaine use disorder may be missed. The clinical recommendations, then, may be exclusively focused on treating a bipolar disorder condition, thereby missing important clinical care. The individual may have both bipolar disorder and cocaine use disorder, considered a co-occurring disorder or comorbidity; however, without careful evaluation it may be very challenging for the clinician to make an accurate diagnosis. The *DSM-5* points out that in over half of individuals with a bipolar disorder there is also a co-occurring substance use disorder, especially alcohol use disorders (APA, 2013). Consequently, the diagnostic process should include consideration of sections within the mental disorders that examine differential diagnoses, substance-induced disorders, and licensed addiction counselors are often tasked with carefully evaluating clients who have been diagnosed with other mental disorders but have never been evaluated for substance use patterns.

Dual Diagnoses and Comorbidities As noted in the preceding section, co-occurring mental disorders are prominent in individuals diagnosed with substance use disorders. Terminology such as dual diagnosis and comorbidity are often used interchangeably to signify the individual has a diagnosis involving a substance use disorder in addition to another mental disorder. It is important for the diagnosing addiction counselor to review additional mental disorders, for example, the schizophrenia spectrum and other psychotic disorders since a large number of individuals are noted to have substance use disorders in addition to schizoaffective disorders and substance-induced psychotic disorders. An example is given for an individual who is experiencing delusions related to his severe cocaine use disorder; *DSM-5* directs the clinician to record both the cocaine-induced psychotic disorder with onset during intoxication *and* the severe cocaine use disorder coding (APA, 2013, p. 112). Other examples include panic disorders where intoxication by stimulants or withdrawal from depressants "can precipitate a panic attack" (APA, 2013, p. 213). Lastly, a major depressive disorder is also associated frequently with substance-related disorders and alcohol (Grant et al., 2015), a central nervous system depressant, which is an important substance to evaluate when symptoms of depression are present or lack of progress is a concern in treatment for depression. The action of the depressant—alcohol—can interfere with medications, and alcohol is often discouraged while treatment for depression is underway as it can further depress one's mood.

In summary, many improvements are now available to the counselor working with individuals as the client may strive to understand what is happening when struggling with substance use concerns. A knowledgeable counselor can provide expertise with continued professional development and experience in accurate diagnosing of substance-related or addictive disorders as noted in the *DSM-5*. Much work has been done to also provide a global bridging to the ICD classification of disorders. Currently the ICD-10 is in use but the newly revised ICD-11 will be released in the future, which will more closely align to the detail found in the DSM classifications (Gintner, 2014).

Skills in Action

Consider these case illustrations from the previous section of this chapter and refer to the *DSM-5* section on Substance-Related and Addictive Disorders. Generate new symptoms for each of the following cases.

What would other possible clinical grouping clusters, such as loss of control, and symptoms include? Generate at least two other clusters with specific related symptoms that meet the *DSM-5* criteria as shown in Table 7.5 and 7.6 below.

Table 7.5	Exercise 7.3, Moderate Use: 4–5 Symptoms, Alprazolam Use Disorder, Moderate, (F13.20)

SYMPTOM	Substance	Grouping
Criteria 9: Continuing to take Xanax on a regular basis after the treating psychiatrist discontinued the prescription when any anxiety disorder was ruled out.	Xanax (Alprazolam)	Risky Use: Continued use of a known anti-anxiety medication despite ruling out anxiety mood disorder.

(Continued)

Table 7.5 (Continued)

Criteria 6: Overdosing incidents at the home leading to increasing arguments with spouse about Xanax overuse.	Xanax (Alprazolam)	Social Impairment: Continued use despite recurring Xanax-related interpersonal problems.
Criteria 10: Secretly taking more Xanax in increasing amounts to experience euphoria.	Xanax (Alprazolam)	Tolerance: The need for markedly increased Xanax pills to be able to experience the desired effect of the Xanax.
Criteria 4: Noted cravings for Xanax, especially in the mornings.	Xanax (Alprazolam)	Cravings: Increased compelling urges to use Xanax despite thinking that taking more Xanax is concerning.
ANOTHER Criteria EXAMPLE:		ANOTHER GROUPING EXAMPLE:

Box 7.6: Exercise 7.4: Severe Use: Six or More Symptoms, Cannabis Intoxication, With Perceptual Disturbances (With Cannabis Use Disorder, Severe, F12.222)

Note: *When a cannabis intoxication disorder is also present with a cannabis use disorder, as in the following case with daily use and the client, Bill, is heavily impaired when he arrives for the session, the DSM-5 instructs the clinician to avoid using both the disorder coding and the intoxication coding, rather, use ONLY the intoxication coding as seen above, which also notes the comorbid severe cannabis use disorder.*

Table 7.6 DSM-5 DIAGNOSIS: Cannabis Intoxication, With Perceptual Disturbances (With Cannabis Use Disorder, Severe)

SYMPTOM	Substance	Grouping
Criteria 9: Continuing to smoke marijuana on a regular basis despite episodes of paranoia heightened by use of cannabis and smokes just before entering the session with the counselor.	Cannabis (Marijuana)	Risky Use: Continued use of marijuana despite exacerbation of paranoia episodes; not able to abstain while knowing the clinically significant difficulties arising from use.
Criteria 6: Smoking at home with increased frequency leading to increasing arguments with spouse about marijuana use.		Social Impairment: Continued use despite recurring cannabis-related interpersonal problems.

SYMPTOM	Substance	Grouping
Criteria 10: Buying and smoking marijuana in increasing amounts to experience any euphoria with increased recognition that increasing amounts are not producing the expected euphoria.		Tolerance: The need for markedly increased cannabis to be able to try to experience the desired effect of the cannabis.
Criteria 4: Noted cravings for marijuana leading to repeated daily use while promising self and family abstinence.		Cravings: Increased compelling urges to use cannabis despite making promises to stop.
Criteria 2: Promised family three times within the past 6 months to completely abstain from marijuana; unable to abstain for 24 hours.		Impaired control: Unsuccessful efforts to control use.
Criteria 3: Increasing time away from home and workplace in order to make more frequent purchases of marijuana.		Impaired control: Leaving work without notice and coming home very late several days each week to make additional purchases of cannabis.
ANOTHER Criteria EXAMPLE:		ANOTHER GROUPING EXAMPLE:
ANOTHER Criteria EXAMPLE:		ANOTHER GROUPING EXAMPLE:

Box 7.7: Exercise 7.5: Practice in Diagnosing

1. In small groups, discuss at least three benefits and three challenges of providing a diagnosis of a SUD to a client. Reflect on how you will address the challenges to diagnosing as discussed. What are the top five considerations you will want to remember?

2. Generate an example of three different types of a substance use disorder. Describe symptoms that would meet the criteria for mild use, one that does not meet criteria yet is considered risky use, and a third case that meets the criteria for a severe substance use disorder. If in a small group of learners, compare and contrast your case with others and determine similarities and differences in symptoms. Why do you think that a severe SUD is markedly different from a mild SUD? List at least three considerations that will help you understand the difference between a mild SUD and a more severe SUD.

RESOURCES FOR FURTHER LEARNING

American Society of Addiction Medicine

http://www.asamcriteria.org

Addiction and Diagnosis Training Resources and Webinars

http://www.nattc.org

American Psychiatric Association

http://www.apa.org

National Council on Problem Gambling

http://www.ncpgambling.org

Sex Addicts Anonymous

https://saa-recovery.org

REFERENCES

Acosta, K. M., Lainas, H., & Veach, L. J. (2013). An emerging trend: Becoming aware of technology addiction. *NC Perspectives, 8*, 5–11.

Ahmed, S. H., Guillem, K., & Vandaele, Y. (2013). Sugar addiction: Pushing the drug–sugar analogy to the limit. *Current Opinion in Clinical Nutrition and Metabolic Care, 16*, 434–439.

American Psychiatric Association (APA). (2013). *Diagnostic and statistical manual of mental disorders* (5th ed.). Washington, DC: Author.

American Society of Addiction Medicine (ASAM). (2014). *Frequently asked questions.* Retrieved from http://www.asamcriteria.org

Centers for Disease Control and Prevention (CDC). (2013, July). Vital signs: Overdoses of prescription opioid pain relievers and other drugs among women – United States, 1999-2010. *Morbidity and Mortality Weekly Report, 62*. Retrieved from http://cache.boston.com/bonzai-fba/Original_PDF/2013/07/02/Vital_Signs_Drug_Overdoses_Women_dated_July_2_2013_eBook__1372790347_8716.pdf

Chamberlain, C. M., & Zhang, N. (2009). Workaholism: Health and self-acceptance. *Journal of Counseling and Development, 87*, 159–169.

Clementz, B. A., Sweeney, J. A., Hamm, J. P., Ivleva, E. I., Ethridge, L. E., Pearlson, G. D., . . . Tamminga, C. A. (2015). Identification of distinct psychosis biotypes using brain-based biomarkers. *The American Journal of Psychiatry*, Advance online publication retrieved from http://www.ncbi.nlm.nih.gov/pubmed/?term=Identification+of+Distinct+Psychosis+Biotypes+Using+Brain-Based+Biomarkers; http://dx.doi.org/10.1176/appi.ajp.2015.14091200

Fong, T. W., & Tsuang, J. (2007, November). Asian-Americans, addictions and barriers to treatment. *Psychiatry*, 51–58.

Gintner, G. G. (2014, February). *New ICD-10 codes: Here's what CMHCs need to know about the new ICD-10 codes.* Retrieved from http://www.amhca.org/?page=Advocate20140201

Grant, B. F., Goldstein, R. B., Saha, T. D., Chou, S. P., Jung, J., . . . Hasin, D. S. (2015). Epidemiology of DSM-5 alcohol use disorder: Results from the National Epidemiologic Survey on Alcohol and Related Conditions III. *Journal of the American Medical Association Psychiatry, 72*, 757–766. doi:10.1001/jamapsychiatry.2015.0584

Grant, B. F., Saha, T. D., Ruan, W. J., Goldstein, R. B., Chou, S. P., . . . Hasin, D. S. (2016). Epidemiology of DSM-5 alcohol use disorder: Results from the National Epidemiologic Survey on Alcohol and Related Conditions III. *Journal of the American Medical Association Psychiatry, 73,* 39–47. doi:10.1001/jamapsychiatry.2015.2132

Mee-Lee, D. (2014). *What's new in DSM-5 and the new ASAM criteria?: Implications in an era of healthcare reform.* Retrieved from Addiction Technology Transfer Center Network [ATTC] website: http://www.attcnetwork .org/find/news/attcnews/epubs/addmsg/ATTCmessengerMarch2014articleDSM5_ASAM.pdf

Miller, G. A. (2015). *Learning the language of addiction counseling* (4th ed.). Hoboken, NJ: Wiley & Sons.

National Institute of Alcohol Abuse and Alcoholism (NIAAA). (2016). National Epidemiologic Survey on Alcohol Use and Related Conditions-III. Retrieved from http://www.niaaa.nih.gov/research/nesarc-iii

National Institute of Mental Health (NIMH). (2015). *Biomarkers outperform symptoms in parsing psychosis subgroups.* Retrieved from https://www.nimh.nih.gov/news/science-news/2015/biomarkers-outperform -symptoms-in-parsing-psychosis-subgroups.shtml

Optum. (2016). *ICD-10 transition: You asked, we answered.* Retrieved from https://www.providerexpress.com/ content/dam/ope-provexpr/us/pdfs/adminResourcesMain/dsm5_icd10/icd10QA.pdf

Raylu, N., & Oei, T. P. (2004). Role of culture in gambling and problem gambling. *Clinical Psychology Review, 23,* 1087–1114.

Rennert, L., Denis, C., Peer, K., Lynch, K. G., Gelernter, J., & Kranzler, H. R. (2014). DSM-5 gambling disorder: Prevalence and characteristics in a substance use disorder sample. *Experimental and Clinical Pharmacology Journal, 22,* 50–56. doi:10.1037/a0034518

Schomerus, G., Lucht, M., Holzinger, A., Matschinger, H., Carta, M. G., & Angermeyer, M. C. (2010). The stigma of alcohol dependence compared with other mental disorders: A review of population studies. *Alcohol and Alcoholism, 46,* 105–112.

Stoeber, J., Davis, C. R., & Townley, J. (2013). Perfectionism and workaholism in employees: The role of work motivation. *Personality and Individual Differences, 55,* 733–738.

Sun, A.-P. (2009). *Helping substance-abusing women of vulnerable populations: Effective treatment principles and strategies.* New York, NY: Columbia Press.

Szasz, T. S. (1960). The myth of mental illness. *American Psychologist, 15,* 113–118.

Brief Counseling Interventions ❖

LEARNING OBJECTIVES

Upon completion of reading this chapter and participating in the guided exercises, the learner will be able to

- understand the need for brief interventions in the addictions counseling field;
- distinguish between multiple brief intervention approaches and identify clinical settings they are utilized in; and
- begin practicing skills of brief intervention models under supervision of an advanced counselor.

In Chapter 6 we discussed the assessment process for addictions, and in Chapter 7 we discussed the diagnostic process and recent changes to the standard diagnostic manual emphasizing the spectrum of addiction disorders. This current chapter examines the growing field of brief counseling interventions, which may be used at different points along the addiction spectrum. Historically, these have been found to occur between assessment and diagnosis following a short screening tool. We are encouraged that these interventions have been found to be applicable for individuals along the full range of the spectrum, not only the diagnostic portion of the arc.

In this chapter, we will begin with discussing the history of brief interventions, and discuss the need for this type of approach for working with clients. Specific models such as the FRAMES model (Miller & Sanchez, 1993), the Brief Negotiated Interview (D'Onofrio, Pantalon, Degutis, Fiellin, & O'Connor, 2005), and a client-centered subjective model developed by Dr. Laura Veach will be introduced. The use of this approach in a variety of settings (e.g., medical settings, school settings, and judicial settings) will be discussed, and a case study will demonstrate the utility of brief interventions.

History of Brief Interventions

The first empirical investigation examining the utility of brief intervention for addiction has been credited to Griffith Edwards and his colleagues for a study conducted in 1977. The study team enrolled 100 males addicted to alcohol and randomized the participants into a traditional treatment group or a single-session treatment group, following a 3-hour assessment session (Edwards et al., 1977). They completed follow-up interviews with 94% of the participants, and discovered that there were no significant differences in outcomes between the two groups, suggesting that brief one-session treatment was just as meaningful as the longer intensive treatment common of the time. In further support for the findings of the original Edwards et al. study, the participants were followed up with 12 years later, and again, there was no difference found in outcomes between the two treatments (Heather, 2004). The foundation for providing brief interventions was laid.

Since the Edwards et al. (1977) study there have been numerous studies examining the use of brief interventions for risky use of alcohol and other drugs. In fact, conducting a Google Scholar search for the words "brief interventions" provided over 2.2 million hits of scholarly works (e.g., books, peer-reviewed articles). Wilk, Jensen, and Havighurst (1997) conducted the first meta-analysis of brief interventions among heavy alcohol drinkers, marking this heavy use by binge activity but not dependence. The meta-analysis included studies conducted in both health care settings (e.g., primary care, emergency departments) and substance abuse treatment centers. After identifying 12 studies that fit inclusion criteria, the authors found that heavy drinkers who received an intervention were more than 2 times as likely to moderate their drinking, as compared with those individuals who did not receive the intervention.

Since the Edwards et al. study, brief interventions have expanded into numerous settings, including health care, university, school settings, and mental health service providers.

The Substance Abuse and Mental Health Services Administration (SAMHSA) has provided millions of dollars in funding to examine the benefits of brief interventions, and more specifically the program titled Screening, Brief Intervention and Referral to Treatment (SBIRT). Within SBIRT, brief interventions are a core component, providing care to individuals identified as at risk via the initial screening—in danger of developing addiction, or suffering other negative consequences from alcohol and/or drug use (e.g., death, injury, sexually transmitted diseases).

Box 8.1: SBIRT

"Screening, Brief Intervention, and Referral to Treatment (SBIRT) is an evidence-based practice used to identify, reduce, and prevent problematic use, abuse, and dependence on alcohol and illicit drugs. The SBIRT model was incited by an Institute of Medicine recommendation that called for community-based screening for health risk behaviors, including substance use." (Substance Abuse and Mental Health Services Administration, n.d., para. 1).

A 10-year review of SBIRT-funded research was conducted by SAMHSA in 2012, with results suggesting the model, and specifically brief interventions, to be highly effective at reducing risk for individuals. From over 425 settings, the research conducted intakes with approximately 1.5 million individuals, and completed 6-month follow-ups with 21,035 people. Of these follow-ups, the rate of abstinence increased to 41.1% at follow-up from 16.1% who identified abstinence at intake. In addition to substance-related outcomes, rates of employment, and stable housing increased at follow-up, and there was a decrease in criminal justice activity for the participants. Mental health outcomes indicated decreases in depression rates (47.3% at intake vs. 37.3% at follow-up), anxiety (46.7% at intake vs. 40.5% at follow-up), reported hallucinations (8.3% at intake vs. 5.6% at follow-up), and in reported suicide attempts (4.5% vs. 1.5%). In addition, risky behaviors, such as unprotected sex with an HIV-infected partner or unprotected sex with an intravenous (IV) drug user, were also found to decrease at follow-up. Overall, the research supporting the SBIRT model, and specifically brief interventions, has a wide breadth of positive outcomes any professional counselor would be excited to see in his or her client population.

Need and Evolution of the Brief Intervention Model

The need for brief intervention models has risen out of the recognition of the power of early interventions as well as the need to identify the treatment gap in our country. The Early Intervention Foundation defines early intervention as "taking action as soon as possible to tackle problems for children and families before they become more difficult to reverse" (n.d., para. 1). The problem that becomes difficult to reverse, as it is relevant to our discussion, is that of addiction. The treatment gap refers to the identified need for addiction treatment among members of our society, but a lack of individuals receiving treatment. For instance, in 2014, there were 22.5 million Americans aged 12 or older who were recognized as needing treatment for a substance use disorder, either alcohol or illicit drugs (SAMHSA, 2015). Of these 22.5 million people, only 4.1 million received some form of treatment, and only 2.6 million received treatment at a specialty addiction treatment facility (SAMHSA, 2015). This means that over 70% of individuals needing treatment for a substance use disorder did not receive treatment during 2014. The individuals that make up the 70% represent the essence of the treatment gap phenomenon.

Brief interventions assist with early intervention efforts, and these initiatives help address the growing treatment gap by meeting people where they are, which is often not in the treatment facilities as shown by the statistics above. These individuals are often easily identified through other avenues, such as the two to be discussed further in this chapter, the medical setting and the university setting. Additional settings such as the criminal justice field and employment settings will be examined in further detail in Chapter 11. It is important to keep in mind that any setting in which a professional counselor finds himself or herself working would be a good setting for brief intervention implementation, given appropriate approval through administrative routes.

Definition of Brief Intervention

There are many different definitions for what constitutes a brief intervention (BI). Many models emphasize the adherence to principles of motivational interviewing (MI) developed initially by Miller in 1983, and refined by Miller and Rollnick in 1991. MI is a client-centered counseling style in which the client is encouraged to consider how they may overcome their ambivalence about change (Miller & Rollnick, 2002). What we feel crucially important to emphasize about the MI approach is that at the heart of the model is adherence to Rogers's (1957) core conditions of counseling. According to Miller and Rollnick (2002), "It is love, and profound respect that are the music in motivational interviewing, without which the words are empty" (p. 13).

Box 8.2: Motivational Interviewing and Empathy

"It is love, and profound respect that are the music in motivational interviewing, without which the words are empty" (Miller & Rollnick, 2002, p. 13).

MI is not something you do *to* a client, but something you use to *engage with* a client, a small difference in words but a vast distinction in actions. MI is included in the National Registry for Evidence-based Programs and Practices (NREPP), and is cited in over 27 other interventions included in the registry. Not only can MI form the basis for a singular session (i.e., brief intervention), but it may also be used as part of an ongoing relationship with clients.

Our definition of a BI follows: a BI capitalizes on a teachable moment in which an individual has been identified as being at risk for personal, medical, employment, and/or familial problems related to his or her substance use and is provided the opportunity for an individualized discussion about reducing his or her risk. The following section provides reviews of three models of brief interventions. It is important to note that in addition to brief intervention, some literature cites brief treatment. The primary difference between brief intervention and brief treatment involves treatment requiring more time, however there is no specific difference agreed upon in the literature.

FRAMES

In 1993, Miller and Sanchez developed the FRAMES model, which was identified after reviewing interventions and identifying the most effective components. FRAMES is an acronym for feedback, responsibility, advice, menu, empathy, and self-efficacy. Feedback involves the provider discussing the individual's personal risk factor or impairment level due to alcohol consumption levels. The second element is that of responsibility; that it is the individual's personal responsibility for change, building that individual's sense of personal control in relation to making a change. Advice involves an explicit message to the individual, either written or verbal, that a change is necessary. The menu component involves making available a variety of suggested change activities the individual may consider, while remembering that the responsibility is up to the individual to decide what would be most appropriate for him or her. Empathy is a crucial element included within the FRAMES model; an attitude of warmth, reflective and understanding, is key to establish empathy within the brief intervention. Lastly within the FRAMES model is the enhancement of individual self-efficacy, building the notion that change is possible. The FRAMES model as proposed by Miller and Sanchez offers a blueprint of six elements that have been found to produce change following brief interventions.

The FRAMES model is used in the evidence-based programs Drinker's Check-Up and College Drinker's Check-Up (SAMHSA, 2014d, 2014c). The programs are computer-based intervention programs with the main aims of reducing users' alcohol use and consequences from use. Both programs have been reviewed by NREPP and are included in the registry.

Brief Negotiated Interview (BNI)

The BNI was developed by D'Onofrio et al. in 2005, and was targeted for use by personnel in emergency departments. The BNI has four critical components: "(1) Raise the subject of alcohol consumption, (2) provide feedback on the patient's drinking levels and effects, (3) enhance motivation to reduce drinking, and (4) negotiate and advise a plan of action" (D'Onofrio et al., 2005, p. 3). The overarching goals of the BNI are to reduce an individual's alcohol use and also reduce his or her instances of driving under the influence. In 2013, the BNI was reviewed and included in NREPP.

Client-Centered Subjective Model

Dr. Laura Veach developed this alternative model in 2006, choosing to avoid focusing on an individual's consumption rates and patterns, and instead focusing on the client's reported reasons for alcohol use. Adherence to this model includes avoiding discussion of the numbers associated with an individual's drinking and even avoiding the discussion of safe drinking limits suggested by NIAAA, common practices in both of the above-referenced models. Instead, the counselor elicits the client's subjective experience of drinking by using reflective listening techniques. The focus of this intervention is on the reasons behind one's alcohol use, and consideration of alternative ways of achieving the desired outcomes reported by the client. This intervention was tested in a Robert Wood Johnson randomized clinical trial with hospitalized trauma patients. Patients were randomized to one of two intervention arms, the traditional quantity–frequency type of discussion, or the innovative client-centered subjective counseling model. The results of the *Teachable Moment* study (O'Brien, Reboussin, Veach, & Miller, 2012) indicated that there were no differences between the treatment arms at follow-up, providing an initial evidence base for this alternative intervention model.

The three above-referenced brief intervention models are a small representation of what exists in the literature. Overall, all brief intervention models emphasize respect for the individuals we are interacting with. It is crucially important for all individuals involved with this type of work to do a thorough self-inventory of biases as these will emerge and interfere with client care if not identified and challenged.

Evidence-Based Practices in Clinical Settings

The treatment gap in our society indicates that approximately 70% of individuals needing addiction-related treatment are not receiving such care (SAMHSA, 2015). Although these individuals are not receiving specialized addiction treatment, it is also unlikely that they are living in isolation, completely off the grid. Two settings in which we are likely to interact with these individuals are medical settings and university settings. As mentioned earlier, other common areas for interaction will be explored in Chapter 11.

Medical Settings

Alcohol in particular takes a devastating toll on our nation's health care system. Williams et al. (2010) determined that approximately 25% of all patients admitted to general hospitals have alcohol use disorders, or were injured due to risky drinking. This corresponds to an earlier estimate that 24% to 31% of emergency department patients are there due to alcohol misuse (D'Onofrio & Degutis, 2004/2005). Further estimates suggest that approximately 15% to 20% of patients within primary care have alcohol use disorders (McQuade, Levy, Yanek, Davis, & Liepman, 2000). And the most significant population, by prevalence rate, is the trauma population, with upward of 50% of patients being hospitalized as a result of injuries incurred as a result of the patient's or another individual's alcohol consumption (American College of Surgeons [ACS] Committee on Trauma, 2003).

Primary Care

Primary care specialists are the generalists of the medical field. Most of us typically use primary care physicians as an entry point into the medical community, whether as a last stop due to cold and flu symptoms, or in order to facilitate a referral with another medical specialist (e.g., oncologist, podiatrist, ob-gyn). Primary care has been identified as an opportune setting for implementation of SBIRT services (Moyer, 2013). Structured literature reviews and meta-analyses support the implementation of these practices in primary care (Williams et al., 2011). Reduction in illicit drug use, reduction in alcohol use, and also reduced days of alcohol intoxication are some of the positive outcomes associated with providing such services in primary care (Gryczynski et al., 2011). SAMHSA has recognized the importance of providing such services in primary care settings and has developed a medical residency training program specializing in SBIRT

(Agerwala & McCance-Katz, 2012). There has been some difficulty in implementation due to lack of substance use disorder knowledge, lack of time issues, and other logistic issues (Agerwala & McCance-Katz, 2012). The positive outcomes associated with providing these services in primary care, along with the trouble of some medical practitioners to fully engage with the model, provide strong support for professional counselors to be involved in these activities.

Emergency Medicine

The emergency department setting sees a large number of patients seeking care for substance-related issues each year (D'Onofrio & Degutis, 2010). Patients may be seeking medical care due to an injury incurred while intoxicated, which will be further explored in the trauma care section below, or they may be seeking care for another illness related to substance use (e.g., pancreatitis, withdrawal symptoms). Patients that are risky users of substances may also be seeking care for an illness that primarily is not due to his or her alcohol or drug use; this highlights the opportunity to interact with individuals that are not actively seeking treatment in addiction centers, yet are interacting with our health care system. One of the most well-known full-scale implementation efforts of brief interventions in the emergency department setting is known as Project ASSERT. Project ASSERT was initiated in the mid-1990s, and found large changes in participants' alcohol use, frequency of drinking six or more drinks in one settings, and satisfaction with the program at follow-up (Bernstein, Bernstein, & Levenson, 1997). Project ASSERT has had success with implementation following the initial settings (e.g., D'Onofrio & Degutis, 2010) and is now identified as an evidence-based program listed in the NREPP.

Trauma Care

As indicated above, many patients seek health care for injuries incurred while intoxicated. In fact, according to the American College of Surgeons Committee on Trauma (2006) approximately 50% of all trauma patients have alcohol in their systems at the time of injury. The startling numbers have led Desy, Howard, Perhats, and Li (2010) to declare that alcohol is the "single greatest contributor to injury in the United States" (p. 538). It is not difficult to understand the need for providing brief interventions within the trauma setting, particularly following the research support examined below.

The results of the first randomized control trial of alcohol interventions in a Level I Trauma Center were reported by Gentilello et al. (1999). The purpose of the study was to identify whether providing a brief intervention to trauma patients would limit recurrent traumatic injuries and subsequent visits to the trauma center. The total sample size was 762, with both intervention and control groups (366 and 396 participants, respectively). The researchers reported a 47% reduction in new injuries that would have involved a subsequent visit to the trauma center in the intervention group, and a 48% reduction in inpatient hospital admissions for the intervention group, both results significantly different from the control group. The results also suggested a reduction in alcohol consumption in both groups. The reported reduction was significantly greater for the intervention group (21.8 standard drink per week reduction) in comparison to the control group (6.7 standard drink per week reduction). Although both groups reduced their alcohol consumption level, the control group's reduction diminished over time, while the intervention group maintained reduction in alcohol consumption at follow-up. The results of the study by Gentilello and his colleagues not only provided significant hope for intervening with the trauma population but also a strong empirical foundation from which other research could be conducted.

In 2006, the American College of Surgeons (ACS) mandated the screening and brief intervention mechanisms be implemented nationwide in order for trauma centers to uphold Level I and Level II accreditation (Gentilello, 2007). According to the ACS Committee on Trauma (2006),

> alcohol is such a significant associated factor and contributor to injury that it is vital that trauma centers have a mechanism to identify patients who are problem drinkers. Such mechanism is essential in Level I and II trauma centers. In addition, Level I centers must have the capability to provide an intervention for patients identified as problem drinkers. (p. 116)

Trauma care represents a unique opportunity for professional counselors to be involved in the immediate aftermath of an alcohol-related injury. Both of the authors of this text have provided care to patients in trauma settings and recognize the powerful moments such injuries provide to helping patients rethink their alcohol and other drug use.

School Settings

There may be no other opportune setting to intervene early with adolescents' alcohol and drug use as there is in the school setting. There is a drop-out crisis in our country, with over 1 million students dropping out each year (Balfanz, Bridgeland, Bruce, & Fox, 2012). Although the literature related to school drop-out patterns identifies school engagement, suspensions, and even familial responsibilities as primary drop-out reasons (Doll, Eslami, & Walters, 2013), we are positive substance use and abuse may be an underlying reason for these drop-outs. For example, the reason for lack of school engagement may be due to the fact that an individual is smoking marijuana before coming to school in the morning. Or a reason for suspension might be that the student had substances on the campus. Because of a recognized role substances play in the lives of adolescents and harms associated with use, there have been screening and brief counseling intervention efforts implemented across the country with beneficial outcomes reported.

Mitchell et al. (2012) conducted a study with adolescents aged 14–17 in 13 different school-based clinics in New Mexico. Students were screened using the CRAFFT screening tool (see Chapter 6 for a review) in the health clinic and, if screened positive, were referred to the behavioral health counselor (masters level) on site at the school. Results from the study found significant reduction in drug use and a significant reduction in days drinking to intoxication. In addition, the researchers found a reduction in reported days drinking alcohol, although this was a non-significant reduction. These results are important to consider the wide impact that providing screening and brief services to students can have, all while being implemented within the school setting. It would behoove all school systems to embrace a mode of brief intervention delivery, to target the most at-risk students, and encourage success not only in their current lives, but also in their futures.

College and University Settings

According to the National Institute for Alcohol Abuse and Alcoholism (NIAAA; 2015), approximately 80% of college students report alcohol use. In addition, approximately 22.3% of full-time college students aged 18–22 reported illicit drug use in 2013 (SAMHSA, 2014a). A surprising number of college students are engaging in risky substance use, which leads to adverse effects such as slipping grades, relational difficulties, and also to severe consequences such as death.

It is no surprise to many that university settings have recognized the value of providing brief interventions for students identified as partaking in risky substance use. The three main routes for an individual to become identified as someone who could benefit from a brief intervention are through university judicial programs, student health centers, and/or mental health counseling centers. We will offer an example of each of the different entrance points through case studies.

Case Study 8.1: Entry Point 1, Judicial Program

Selma is a 19-year-old white woman, attending a local state school. Selma is a sophomore although because of advanced placement credits from high school is taking upper-level courses with juniors and seniors. Most of Selma's friends are older, and many have recently reached the legal drinking age. Selma has maintained great grades throughout her two years at the university and has been active in many different campus organizations. One Friday night, Selma and her friends were having a small get-together in the university apartments. There was a knock on the door, and the campus police officers were responding to a noise complaint from a neighbor. Once the campus police officers saw the alcohol they requested to see all individual's identifications, and Selma of course was identified as being underage. She received a citation and a referral to the judiciary committee of the school. Selma attended her judicial hearing and was mandated to community service hours and was required to attend a meeting with the university's addiction counselor. During their initial meeting, Selma was provided a questionnaire to complete, and her counselor discussed the results of the survey and they discussed Selma's drinking.

Now consider that you were Selma's counselor as you answer the following questions.

1. What are some reasons Selma might want to consider cutting back on her drinking?

2. What are some reasons Selma might have for not wanting to cut back on her drinking?

3. What information would you want to help Selma understand about her drinking?

4. Is there anything else you would want to talk with Selma about?

Case Study 8.2: Entry Point 2, Student Health Center

James is a 22-year-old Asian American male who is coming to the student health center because of cold symptoms. When James arrives at the center he is invited to check in for his appointment using a computer system. James has to enter his personal information and then is asked a series of questions. One of the questions asks James about his alcohol use and his medication use. James enters that he has approximately three beers on the weekends, and also takes Adderall. After James completes the check-in process he is invited into the exam room. Dr. Ortiz enters the exam room and continues to conduct a full evaluation of James, attending to his symptoms of common cold. James is primarily concerned because the cold symptoms have lasted for over a month. Dr. Ortiz discusses appropriate over-the-counter medications James may find relief from, and he also asks about his Adderall use because it is not documented in his chart. James reports that he gets the medication from his roommate; it helps his focus as he is studying for the LSAT for law school, and he assures Dr. Ortiz it is not like he is "popping the pills like crazy, only about a couple a week." Dr. Ortiz is concerned about James's use of non-prescribed medication as well as his combination of alcohol. Dr. Ortiz discusses his concerns with James and provides a referral to the campus addiction counselor who has an office right down the hall from Dr. Ortiz. James must stop by the office to schedule an appointment before leaving.

Now consider that you were James's counselor as you answer the following questions.

1. How would you begin the session with James?

2. What information do you feel you need to know but were not provided with above, and where would you get that information?

3. What do you think James is feeling about having to come see you?

4. What concerns you about James's situation?

Case Study 8.3: Entry Point 3, University Counseling Center

Lily is a 20-year-old biracial woman, in her third year of college. Lily recently transferred to a college closer to home as her father was diagnosed with Alzheimer's. Lily has been attending the university counseling center for three sessions. Lily initially began attending due to issues with her family. Due to her father's illness, Lily has had a lot of responsibility placed on her, and although she is happy to help, she reports feeling angry that she is not able to enjoy college "like all of my other friends." Lily discusses with her counselor that the only time she is able to be free from the stress of her family is on the weekends when she goes out with her friends. Lily and her friends have a local restaurant they go to and are friends with the bartenders, who will serve them although they are underage. The counselor asks about Lily's alcohol consumption rates and Lily reports drinking upward of seven or eight cocktails and a few shots on most Friday nights.

Now consider you are Lily's counselor as you answer the following questions.

1. Are you concerned with Lily's alcohol use report? If so, what is concerning?

2. How would you tell Lily you are concerned?

3. It might be helpful to talk to Lily about what she gets out of drinking; how would you broach that with her?

4. What information would you feel Lily needs to know about her alcohol use?

The stories of Selma, James, and Lily are common situations happening daily on college campuses throughout our country. Fortunately, there is support for intervening with students following situations similar to the above-referenced case studies.

Reduction in alcohol consumption and a reduction in alcohol-related consequences following a brief intervention primarily focused on alcohol use are two such positive outcomes of intervening with college students (Martens et al., 2007). The overall positive findings of providing brief interventions have led to the development of evidence-based programs (EBPs) for use with college students. Two of these EBPs will be examined further, and both are listed in the NREPP.

Brief Alcohol Screening and Intervention for College Students (BASICS)

As mentioned above, the BASICS program is included in the NREPP, which speaks to the strength of the research supporting the program. According to SAMHSA (2014b), BASICS has been approved for use among college students, aged 18–25, and research has included appropriate racial and ethnic diversity for wide implementation. The intervention model includes two 1-hour interview sessions, as well as an online assessment survey. Students attend the first session, which is an information gathering session, particularly concerned with identifying alcohol consumption patterns and the student's beliefs about drinking. The student is then provided information about taking the online survey before the next session, and instructed to monitor his or her drinking between the sessions. During the second session, the student receives personalized feedback about his or her drinking and what risks are involved with that drinking. The counselor is also making sure to attend to the rapport with the student, and embraces the core conditions of Carl Rogers's (1957) framework of empathy, unconditional positive regard, and genuineness throughout the sessions.

College Drinker's Check-Up (CDCU)

The CDCU is a computer-based brief motivational interview designed to reduce alcohol use by men and women aged 18–25 who engage in heavy episodic drinking (aka, binge drinking) (SAMHSA, 2014c). The CDCU uses the FRAMES (Miller & Sanchez, 1993) model of brief interventions, and is uniquely tailored to the individual's responses. Participants in clinical trials have been found to have fewer drinks per week, a lower number of drinks in heavy episodic drinking periods, and a lower estimated blood alcohol level during heavy drinking periods as compared with control groups (SAMHSA, 2014c).

Skills in Action

Case Studies

Below you will find two case studies of the use of brief counseling interventions in settings commonly employing professional counselors. The first is an examination of the use of BIs in a school setting, and the second in a medical trauma unit. We are hopeful the two different settings, and cases, will encourage you to consider how and when you will be able to implement these useful interventions in whichever setting you practice in your clinical future.

Case Study 8.4: Tommy, High School Student

Tommy, a 15-year-old high school sophomore, has been referred to the school counselor's office. Tommy's teacher overheard Tommy discussing his previous weekend with some friends in geometry class. Tommy reportedly was talking about how his older brother (a junior in the same high school) was able to get some beers and they had a little party. The school counselor knows Tommy very well, as he is an excellent student, being placed in honors courses since he began at the school two years ago. Tommy has just one older brother, and his mother is a single mother after Tommy's other parent passed away approximately 2 years ago. The school counselor was surprised to receive the referral but eager to talk to Tommy.

School Counselor (SC): What brings you in today, Tommy?

Tommy (T): Mrs. Johnson said I had to come talk to you; didn't she call you?

SC: Yes, she did, but I want to hear from you what brings you in.

T: Ugh, this is so stupid; I don't even need to be here. Just because someone thinks they overheard something, it is no one's business here what I do outside of school!

SC: You're frustrated and in your opinion this is being blown out of proportion.

T: Yes! I mean, OK, so my brother and I had some beers this weekend, it is not like we are the only ones in this school to ever drink . . . gosh, if you all even knew what went on!

SC: In comparison with what others are doing, your drinking feels very minor.

T: Yes!

SC: I hear that this is frustrating for you, and I also want to be able to talk to you some more about drinking. Would it be OK if I ask you some questions?

T: I mean, are you just trying to get me in more trouble?

SC: No, what I want to do is help you think about the decisions you are making, and maybe give you more information about alcohol and what risks it has. I want to get a better picture of what your risk might be so I have a better understanding of you. Does that sound OK?

T: Sure, whatever

[SC continues to administer the CRAFFT screening tool (overview in Chapter 6). The screening results are then given to Tommy.]

SC: Tommy, thank you for going through those questions with me. What was that like for you?

Figure 8.1   Tommy's CRAFFT Results

C	Have you ever ridden in a car driven by someone (including yourself) who was "high" or had been using alcohol or drugs? _____
R	Do you ever use alcohol or drugs to relax, feel better about yourself, or fit in? __X__
A	Do you ever use alcohol or drugs while you are by yourself, alone? _____
F	Do you ever forget things you did while using alcohol or drugs? __X__
F	Do your family or friends ever tell you that you should cut down on your drinking or drug use? _____
T	Have you ever gotten in trouble while you were using alcohol or drugs? _____
	Total 2/6

SOURCE: Knight, J. R., Sherritt, L., Shrier, L. A., Harris, S. K., & Chang, G. (2002). Validity of the CRAFFT substance abuse screening test among adolescent clinic patients. *Archives of Pediatrics & Adolescent Medicine*, *156*(6), 607–614.

T: Umm, fine.

SC: OK, well the results this screening tool help me understand where you are in terms of risk, either none, little, medium, or high risk. Before I tell you the results, where do you think you fall in terms of your risk?

T: Umm, probably like none. I mean I have drank but it is not often, and it's not like I'm getting wasted.

SC: For you, based upon your use history and the amount you are drinking, you feel as though it is not of any risk to you.

T: Right.

SC: I hear you, and based upon these results, you are at some risk, but it is little. That is higher than no risk, however. What do you think about that?

T: Well, isn't that your job? To tell me it is risky?

SC: You're worried that I have ulterior motives with this screen. And maybe you are right, but only because I am worried about you. I have seen the negative side effects of alcohol use, starting out as very little risk and elevating very quickly into high risk, and I worry about that being your pathway.

T: But, you know me; you know that is not what is going to happen to me!

SC: Don't you think everyone thinks that it will never happen to them?

T: Hmm, I guess I didn't think of that, but really, I won't let it.

SC: Well, how about we talk some about your drinking.

T: What about it?

SC: Well, tell me some about what drinking does for you?

T: I don't really know, I mean I haven't thought of that.

SC: That makes sense, but thinking back on it now, what do you think?

T: It is just fun! My brother and I just have so much fun, laughing, doing stupid dances we don't normally do; it's like we are little kids again, just having fun.

SC: Alcohol helps you have fun; lets you cut loose.

T: I guess so; like I said, just cut loose.

SC: That makes sense; a lot of people drink alcohol for that reason. I wonder, when you don't have alcohol, what other ways you cut loose?

T: I guess there are a lot of ways. Just being with my brother, we normally just mess around like goofs anyway, or like with my friends after soccer practice, we just are crazy.

SC: You are able to enjoy the same benefits like being able to cut loose, without having to have alcohol.

T: Yeah, like I said, I don't have a problem.

SC: Right, and that's true right now. In the future though, that could be more difficult for you. The more people use alcohol to cut loose, the more that becomes their go-to way to relax. This all has to do with our brains.

T: What do you mean?

SC: Our brains are still developing well into your mid-20s. That is another whole 10 years, and even after that they have the ability to change, and be altered. But what they are really working on now, is forming neuropathways. These are shortcuts for our brain to remember for the future. If your brain finds that it can cut loose after using alcohol quicker than in other situations, it might wire a pathway that makes that the first choice when you are feeling stressed and need to relax.

T: Whoa, really? That sounds weird.

SC: Yeah! It is exciting because we're learning more about the brain all of the time.

T: Yeah, I mean I would never want to be one of those bums, just drinking all of the time.

SC: Do you know anyone like that in your life?

T: My uncle. I mean, he is able to work and do a good job, but immediately when he walks in the door in the evening, he walks right to the fridge and grabs a beer, and then it's all downhill from there. Every holiday he gets bombed throughout the day.

SC: Although you love your uncle, you can recognize that his drinking is interfering in his ability to be present with you all during important holidays.

T: Yeah, I would never want to be like that. Last year he couldn't even play in our flag football game on Turkey Day because he was too tipsy.

SC: I wonder when your uncle started drinking, and how early he learned to relax by drinking.

T: Probably pretty young; I mean, that was way back when he could just walk in and buy a pack of beer for himself and no one questioned it.

SC: For you, getting beer is more difficult.

T: Yeah, I mean, I haven't even ever bought it, it's been my brother, but it has been difficult for him.

SC: There is a lot to be concerned with, money, getting in trouble . . .

T: Yeah, that'd be the worst; my mom would kill me.

SC: That sounds like another reason your drinking is risky.

T: Umm, I guess so; my mom has been through a lot, and so have we, but I would hate to disappoint her.

SC: You really care about her, and making sure your relationship is solid.

T: Absolutely, she's the only parent I have left.

SC: I'm wondering, after this conversation we've had, do you think your drinking is more risky than you initially thought?

T: Umm, I guess a little, again, not like I have a major problem, but if you mean risk then yeah, I can see that.

SC: Are you willing to make some changes with your drinking?

T: Well, yeah, I hate feeling guilty and lying to my mom whenever I drank the night before. I get this feeling in the pit of my stomach that I just hate.

SC: It sounds like that feeling is almost even enough for you to not drink again.

T: Yeah, it is horrible, but of course I always forget about that when I start drinking.

SC: What is one way you think you could remind yourself about that feeling, to help you not drink?

T: Hmm, umm, I don't know. . . . I've never even talked about it or thought about it before.

SC: This is the first time you're really aware of the power of that feeling.

T: Yeah.

SC: Maybe, just us talking about it might be enough.

T: Hmm . . .

SC: And if it isn't, you can always come back and talk again.

T: OK, wow, I can't believe I just talked to you about this.

SC: You're surprised how much you were able to talk to me.

T: Yeah.

SC: That makes sense, especially since I think you thought you were going to get into trouble first thing. But what I heard from you, Tommy, is that your drinking isn't a huge part of your life, but that it does have some negative effects for you, and also some risk. And I also heard that you are concerned about that, and are willing to make some changes, and cut down on your drinking, or even stop completely. Would you agree?

T: Absolutely, that nails it.

SC: Well, thank you for talking to me; and remember, my door is always open, ok?

T: 'K.

SC: Alright, well here is a pass to get back to class.

Case Study 8.5: Jasmine, Medical Trauma Patient

Jasmine, a 43-year-old African American woman, has been admitted to the local Level I Trauma Center. Jasmine's reason for hospitalization was listed as pedestrian-struck, indicating she had been struck by a motor vehicle. Further investigation into the medical report indicates that Jasmine had reportedly been outside a local restaurant and she was arguing with another individual when she stepped off the curb of the sidewalk right into the street. At the same time, a car was passing by at a high rate of speed and struck Jasmine in the right leg. Jasmine had to be air lifted to the trauma center. Upon being admitted, Jasmine's blood alcohol level (BAL) was taken as well as her urine drug screen. The results of the tests showed Jasmine's BAL was 0.30, and she tested negative on her urine drug screen. Jasmine was taken immediately to surgery for injuries to her leg and also her pelvis. It is four days later that the counselor is able to meet with Jasmine.

Counselor approaches client's hospital room, and knocks.

C (Counselor):	Good afternoon, Jasmine; is it ok if I come in?
J (Jasmine):	Sure, come on in; everyone else just barges in here!
C:	Yes, you are probably pretty used to people making your room theirs by now.
J:	You have no idea . . .
C:	Well, thank you for allowing me to come in. My name is Eli, and I am a counselor here at the trauma center. Have you ever talked with a counselor before?
J:	You mean like a guidance counselor? Ha, maybe way back when I was in high school.
C:	Yes, well counselors do work in a variety of different places, and I work here. Before we get started I wanted to let you know that what we talk about stays between us, unless I'm concerned for a few different reasons. Those would be if you are contemplating suicide or homicide; if I become aware of any abuse toward children, the elderly, or individuals that are unable to care for themselves; or if I am subpoenaed. I also might have to talk to the medical team if there is something I am concerned with about your medical care. Does this all sound OK to you?
J:	Wait, you mean besides those things, you won't go run your mouth to my nurse?
C:	That is correct.
J:	Hmm, sounds great; everyone is so nosey around here!

C:	It sounds like people have really been interested in getting to know you.
J:	Yes, but it's not just me, I have learned about all of the drama going on between all of the staff here—some people just like to hear themselves talk!
C:	It sounds like you have just fit in perfectly around here; people feel really comfortable talking to you.
J:	Yeah, I've always been told I'm a good listener. I guess that's what happens when you have five younger siblings.
C:	That sounds like a lot of responsibility.
J:	Oh, you have no idea. So, what are you here for?
C:	I am here because I go around and talk with all the patients here about their injury. Do you mind telling me about the night you were brought here?
J:	Well, from what I remember, because it is all a little fuzzy, I was arguing with my boo, and walked out of the restaurant and boom! Here I am.
C:	You remember being out and getting into an argument then waking up here. You mentioned your memory is a little fuzzy.
J:	Yeah, I think they gave me a lot of drugs in the helicopter and then I had surgery. Whew!
C:	Your body has gone through a lot in the past few days, more than usual. Have you ever been injured before?
J:	Not like this! I mean, the worst I have ever been hurt is a broken wrist, and that was back in high school when I played basketball.
C:	So this experience sounds like it is completely new to you!
J:	And I never want to go through this again.
C:	We want to help avoid that too. Another part of what I do with patients here is talk to them about their alcohol use. I know you said your memory was fuzzy that night, and I was wondering if we could talk about your drinking the other night?
J:	You got me! Yeah, I had a few glasses of wine, I mean, it wasn't much, but yes, I was drinking.
C:	Could I go ahead and ask you some questions about your drinking?
J:	Sure, shoot . . .

[The counselor proceeds to conduct the AUDIT screening tool (reviewed in Chapter 6) with Jasmine.]

C: Thanks for going through all of those questions with me, Jasmine. Have you ever been asked any questions like that before?

J: Nope, first time for that.

C: OK, well, let me explain these questions. All of these questions give me a number anywhere from zero, which is someone who doesn't drink alcohol, to a 40, which is someone who would be answering "every day" to most of those questions I asked you. This then is like a scale of risk, from 0–40. Where do you think your score is, considering risk associated with your drinking?

J: Umm, risk? What do you mean?

C: Well, some of those questions asked about risk, about injury, about missing out on responsibilities, or not being able to stop drinking once you started.

J: Hmm . . . umm, I'd say probably like a 9.

C: And what led you to say 9 and not 10.

J: 10 just feels like a bigger deal, and I'm not that bad. But I do see there is some risk when I drink, like we talked about when I wish I could have taken back what I said to my friend after New Year's last year. I really regret that and don't think it would have happened if I wasn't so drunk.

C: For you, you recognize that your drinking does suggest some risk, but that you feel comfortable it has not gotten out of hand.

J: Yes.

C: This tool also has cut-off scores for us to use, and I'm curious what your reaction is if I told you that a score of 4 or more for a woman your age is when we start to become concerned.

J: 4? Is that a joke? I feel like that would be so easy to get!

C: It sounds silly to you that the number is so low.

J: Yes! I mean, come on!

C: Well, that is true that the number is low, and part of that is we have learned that alcohol has a lot more risk than we used to think. But in terms of your number, you weren't too far away from your actual score, which was a 13.

J: Dang, I'm over 10!

C: You are over 10.

J: Are you sure you calculated that right?

C: You're concerned I added the numbers wrong. It sounds like this is hard to believe that your number would be that high.

J: Yes, like I said, I know there is a little risk, but a 13?

C: I wonder what a 13 looks like to you.

J: Well, a 13 is someone who is always getting in arguments with her family, is never going to work, or doesn't even have a job.

C: And that is very different from you.

J: Yes, I always go to work!

C: You are proud of your work ethic.

J: Of course I am.

C: I wonder about the other part of your 13 definition though, the arguments part.

J: Well, OK, that I might be able to see a bit.

C: During the screening, you told me that you regretted getting into a fight with your best friend last New Year's. And earlier you mentioned getting into a fight with your boo right before you ended up on your way here.

J: I know I have a loud mouth, and when I drink it is like my filter is turned off!

C: That sounds like something you don't like about your drinking.

J: Absolutely not! I would never say half of the stuff I say when I am drinking but it just comes out, and then you can't get those words back.

C: Jasmine, this makes complete sense. Did you know that the first thing alcohol does in our brains is lower our inhibitions. This means that we end up doing things we normally wouldn't do when we are sober. That sounds just like what you are describing.

J: Yes! Ugh, I really hate that.

C: That is something you dislike about your drinking; is there anything else you dislike about drinking alcohol?

J: Well, the hangovers—who likes those?

C: True, normally that is a big disadvantage to drinking. How often do you have a hangover?

J: Well, like a "can't-get-out-of-bed-or-move" one is like only once a month, but I do get headaches pretty regularly.

C: And what happens during those hangovers?

J: I just lay there and think about how I shouldn't have had as much as I did, and how much I hate feeling like that.

C: Regret is a common feeling on those days for you.

J: Yes!

C: Jasmine, I wonder if you have ever thought of cutting down on your drinking?

J: You mean stopping drinking? What would I do with my time?

C: Stopping all together sounds unreasonable for you. What about just cutting back?

J: Oh, umm, well yeah, of course I can do that. I guess I've just never tried to before; I didn't have a reason.

C: And now, you'll have a reason?

J: Well, for one, I don't think I'll be going out much with a broken hip! And I am guessing I'll be on some heavy medicine when I leave and I never drink while taking prescription medicine.

C: That is an important rule for you.

J: Yes, I have heard nightmare stories about people blacking out and not even knowing what happens to them, and I do not want that to be me.

C: You're very clear about that rule.

J: Absolutely!

C: In the coming few weeks it sounds like your drinking is going to change as a result of this accident, but I'm wondering if you see how your drinking contributed to you ending up here.

J: Well, if we just follow the series of events, if I wasn't drinking so much I wouldn't have started that argument, which means I wouldn't have gone outside to get away from him and then boom, no broken hip!

C: Now you recognize that your drinking may have helped get you in here. I only ask because before on that questionnaire, you said you hadn't ever been hurt as a result of your drinking.

J: Hmm, well I guess I didn't think of it like I did now since we've been talking, like about the arguments and stuff.

C: So being able to talk with me helped you see this situation a little differently.

J: Yes, and ugh, if only I could have just kept my mouth shut!

C: And in the future, if you monitor your drinking more carefully you may find your mouth stays shut more easily.

J: True, that is a plus!

C: On a scale from 1 to 10, with 1 representing not committed and 10 representing a full commitment, how committed are you to making a change with your drinking?

J: I'd say probably a 7.

C: Wow, a 7! What made you say 7 and not a 6?

J: I mean I'm not a 10, no way, but I see the need, and can definitely see myself making some changes, and 6 in school would be 60%, which is failing!

C: It is important for you to pass, just like it is important to stick to your no drinking while on medication rule.

J: Yes, exactly.

C: Well, Jasmine, just one last question. You've talked about being committed to making a change, and you are clear about that, but I'm wondering what that change will actually look like for you.

J: Hmm, umm, I guess I just see myself only having one or two glasses of wine, instead of the three or four I usually have.

C: You can envision sticking to one or two glasses. What would make you not stick to that?

J: Well, the bartender always just pours up my glass! That would make this tricky.

C: I wonder if you could talk to the bartender before you begin drinking, and explain your two-glass rule. What would that be like?

J: Yeah, I mean, I know all of the bartenders there! I don't think that'd be a problem at all, and it works out better for them not having to give away free booze.

C: It sounds like all of what we talked about is possible for you, and you are committed to living a healthier life.

J: Yes, I mean, I'm no spring chicken anymore, and I want this to be the last trip to the hospital for a *long* time!

C: Well, Jasmine, thank you for taking the time to talk to me. I hope our paths don't cross like this again.

J: Me too—thank you though! Have a good day.

Experiential Skills Learning Activity

Choose one of the five case studies presented throughout this chapter to practice a brief intervention with a role-play client. Pair up with a classmate and have one role-play the counselor and the other role-play either Selma's, James's, Lily's, Tommy's, or Jasmine's case. After the role-play, discuss with one another the experience. As the counselor, reflect on what you wish you would have said, what you wish you would have known to tell the client, and what you would do differently next time. All of these questions are important for reflection to help you feel more confident in your abilities in the future. As the client, reflect on your overall feeling during the exercise. Did you feel respected and invited to be a part of the process? If not, share with your partner what may have helped you feel that way.

This chapter covered an introduction to brief interventions. We discussed the historical origins of the interventions, and discussed common models of brief interventions.

In addition, we discussed the evidence base of brief interventions in the medical setting as well as university setting and provided case studies for review. Chapter 9 will expand our discussion attending to brief interventions in the legal and employer settings.

RESOURCES FOR FURTHER LEARNING

Books and Book Chapters

American College of Surgeons Committee on Trauma. (2006). *Resources for the optimal care of the injured patient.* Chicago, IL: Author.

Heather, N. (1995). Brief intervention strategies. In R. K. Hester & W. R. Miller (Eds.), *Handbook of alcoholism treatment approaches: Effective alternatives* (2nd ed., p. 105–122). Boston, MA: Allyn & Bacon.

Heather, N. (2004). Brief interventions. In N. Heather & T. Stockwell (Eds.), *The essential handbook of treatment and prevention of alcohol problems* (pp. 117–138). Hoboken, NJ: John Wiley & Sons.

Miller, W. R., & Rollnick, S. (2013). *Motivational interviewing: Helping people change* (3rd ed.). New York, NY: Guilford.

Article

Gentilello, L. M., Rivara, F. P., Donovan, D. M., Jurkovich, G. J., Daranciang, E., . . . Ries, R. R. (1999). Alcohol interventions in a trauma center as a means of reducing the risk of injury recurrence. *Annals of Surgery, 230*(4), 473–480.

Websites

SAMHSA SBIRT Resources

http://www.integration.samhsa.gov/resource/sbirt-resource-page

Brief Intervention Training Videos, Boston University School of Public Health

http://www.bu.edu/bniart/sbirt-in-health-care/sbirt-educational-materials/sbirt-videos/

International Network on Brief Interventions for Alcohol & Other Drugs (INEBRIA)

http://inebria.net/

Rethinking Drinking: Alcohol and Your Health, National Institute on Alcohol Abuse and Alcoholism

http://rethinkingdrinking.niaaa.nih.gov

REFERENCES

Agerwala, S. M., & McCance-Katz, E. F. (2012). Integrating screening, brief intervention, and referral to treatment (SBIRT) into clinical practice settings: A brief review. *Journal of Psychoactive Drugs, 44*(4), 307–317.

American College of Surgeons Committee on Trauma. (2003). *Alcohol and injury* [PowerPoint slides]. Retrieved from http://www.facs.org/trauma/alcslide.html

American College of Surgeons Committee on Trauma. (2006). *Resources for the optimal care of the injured patient.* Chicago, IL: Author.

Balfanz, R., Bridgeland, J. M., Bruce, M., & Fox, J. H. (2012). *Building a grad nation: Progress and challenge in ending the high school dropout epidemic.* Retrieved from http://files.eric.ed.gov/fulltext/ED530320.pdf

Bernstein, E., Bernstein, J., & Levenson, S. (1997). Project ASSERT: An ED-based intervention to increase access to primary care, preventive services, and the substance abuse treatment system. *Annals of Emergency Medicine, 30*(2), 181–189. doi:10.1016/S0196-0644(97)70140-9

Desy, P. M., Howard, P. K., Perhats, C., & Li, S. (2010). Alcohol screening, brief intervention, and referral to treatment conducted by emergency nurses: An impact evaluation. *Journal of Emergency Nursing, 36*(6), 538–545. doi:10.1016/j.jen.2009.09.011

Doll, J. J., Eslami, Z., & Walters, L. (2013). Understanding why students drop out of high school, according to their own reports: Are they pushed or pulled, or do they fall out? A comparative analysis of seven nationally representative studies. *SAGE Open, 3*(4), 1–15. doi:10.1177/2158244013503834

D'Onofrio, G., & Degutis, L. C. (2004/2005). Screening and brief intervention in the emergency department. *Alcohol Research & Health, 28*(2), 63–72.

D'Onofrio, G., & Degutis, L. C. (2010). Integrating project ASSERT: A screening, intervention, and referral to treatment program for unhealthy alcohol and drug use into an urban emergency department. *Academic Emergency Medicine, 17*, 903–911. doi:10.1111/j.1553-2712.2010.00824.x

D'Onofrio, G., Pantalon, M. V., Degutis, L. C., Fiellin, D. A., & O'Connor, P. G. (2005). Development and implementation of an emergency practitioner-performed brief intervention for hazardous and harmful drinkers in the emergency department. *Academy of Emergency Medicine, 12*(3), 249–256.

Early Intervention Foundation. (n.d.). *What is early intervention?* Retrieved from http://www.eif.org.uk/what-is-early-intervention/

Edwards, G., Orford, J., Egert, S., Guthrie, S., Hawker, A., Hensman, C., . . . Taylor, C. (1977). Alcoholism: A controlled trial of "treatment" and "advice." *Journal of Studies on Alcohol, 38*(5), 1004–1031. doi:10.15288/jsa.1977.38.1004

Gentilello, L.M. (2007). Alcohol and injury: American college of surgeons committee on trauma requirements for trauma center intervention. *The Journal of Trauma Injury, Infection, and Critical Care, 62*, S44–S45. doi:10.1097/TA.0b013e3180654678

Gentilello, L. M., Rivara, F. P., Donovan, D. M., Jurkovich, G. J., Daranciang, E., . . . Ries, R. R. (1999). Alcohol interventions in a trauma center as a means of reducing the risk of injury recurrence. *Annals of Surgery, 230*(4), 473–480.

Gryczynski, J., Mitchell, S. G., Peterson, T. R., Gonzalez, A., Moseley, A., & Schwartz, R. P. (2011). The relationship between services delivered and substance use outcomes in New Mexico's screening, brief intervention, referral and treatment (SBIRT) initiative. *Drug and Alcohol Dependence, 118*(2–3), 152–157.

Heather, N. (2004). Brief interventions. In N. Heather & T. Stockwell (Eds.), *The essential handbook of treatment and prevention of alcohol problems* (pp. 117–138). Hoboken, NJ: John Wiley & Sons.

Knight, J. R., Sherritt, L., Shrier, L. A., Harris, S. K., & Chang, G. (2002). Validity of the CRAFFT substance abuse screening test among adolescent clinic patients. *Archives of Pediatrics & Adolescent Medicine, 156*(6), 607–614.

Martens, M. P., Cimini, M. D., Barr, A. R., Rivero, E. M., Vellis, P. A., Desemone, G. A., & Horner, K. J. (2007). Implementing a screening and brief intervention for high-risk drinking in university-based health and mental health care settings: Reductions in alcohol use and correlates of success. *Addictive Behaviors, 32*(11), 2563–2572. doi:10.1016/j.addbeh.2007.05.005

McQuade, W. H., Levy, S. M., Yanek, L. R., Davis, S. W., & Liepman, M. R. (2000). Detecting symptoms of alcohol abuse in primary care settings. *Archives of Family Medicine, 9*, 814–821.

Miller, W. R. (1983). Motivational interviewing with problem drinkers. *Behavioural Psychotherapy, 1*, 147–172.

Miller, W. R., & Rollnick, S. (1991). *Motivational interviewing: Preparing people to change addictive behavior.* New York, NY: Guilford.

Miller, W. R., & Rollnick, S. (2002). *Motivational interviewing: Preparing people to change* (2nd ed.). New York, NY: Guilford.

Miller, W. R., & Sanchez, V. C. (1993). Motivating young adults for treatment and lifestyle change. In G. L. Howard (Eds.), *Issues in Alcohol Use and Misuse by Young Adults* (p. 55–82). Notre Dame, IN: University of Notre Dame Press.

Mitchell, S. G., Gryczynski, J., Gonzales, A., Moseley, A., Peterson, T., O'Grady, K. E., & Schwartz, R. P. (2012). Screening, brief intervention, and referral to treatment (SBIRT) for substance use in a school-based program: Services and outcomes. *The American Journal on Addictions, 21*, S5–S13. doi:10.1111/j.1521-0391.2012.00299.x

Moyer, V. A. (2013). Screening and behavioral counseling interventions in primary care to reduce alcohol misuse: US Preventive Services Task Force recommendation statement. *Annals of Internal Medicine, 159*(3), 210–218.

National Institute for Alcohol Abuse and Alcoholism (NIAAA). (2015). *College drinking.* Retrieved from http://www.niaaa.nih.gov/alcohol-health/special-populations-co-occurring-disorders/college-drinking

O'Brien, M. C., Reboussin, B., Veach, L. J., & Miller, P. R. (2012). *Robert Wood Johnson Grant # 65032: The Teachable Moment Study* [Unpublished research report].

Rogers, C. R. (1957). The necessary and sufficient conditions of psychotherapeutic change. *Journal of Consulting Psychology, 21*, 95–103.

Substance Abuse and Mental Health Services Administration (SAMHSA). (n.d.). *SBIRT resource page.* Retrieved from http://www.integration.samhsa.gov/resource/sbirt-resource-page

Substance Abuse and Mental Health Services Administration (SAMHSA). (2012). *State of SBIRT 2003–2012: Review and discussion of SAMHSA funded SBIRT initiatives* [PDF file].

Substance Abuse and Mental Health Services Administration (SAMHSA). (2014a). *Results from the 2013 national survey on drug use and health: Summary of national findings.* Retrieved from http://www.samhsa.gov/data/sites/default/files/NSDUHresultsPDFWHTML2013/ Web/NSDUHresults2013.pdf

Substance Abuse and Mental Health Services Administration (SAMHSA). (2014b). *Brief alcohol screening and intervention for college students (BASICS).* Retrieved from http://www.nrepp.samhsa.gov/ViewIntervention .aspx?id=124

Substance Abuse and Mental Health Services Administration SAMHSA. (2014c). *College drinker's check-up.* Retrieved from http://nrepp.samhsa.gov/ViewIntervention.aspx?id=230

Substance Abuse and Mental Health Services Administration (SAMHSA). (2014d). *Drinker's check-up.* Retrieved from http://nrepp.samhsa.gov/ViewIntervention.aspx?id=14

Substance Abuse and Mental Health Services Administration (SAMHSA). (2015). *Receipt of services for behavioral health problems: Results from the 2014 national survey on drug use and health.* Retrieved from http://www .samhsa.gov/data/sites/default/files/NSDUH-DR-FRR3-2014/NSDUH-DR-FRR3-2014/NSDUH-DR-FRR3 -2014.pdf

Wilk, A. I., Jensen, N. M., & Havighurst, T. C. (1997). Meta-analysis of randomized control trials addressing brief interventions in heavy alcohol drinkers. *Journal of General Internal Medicine, 12*, 274–283.

Williams, E. C., Johnson, M. L., Lapham, G. T., Caldeiro, R. M., Chew, L., Fletcher, G. S., . . . Bradley, K. A. (2011). Strategies to implement alcohol screening and brief intervention in primary care settings: A structured literature review. *Psychology of Addictive Behaviors, 28*(2), 206–214.

Williams, E. C., Palfai, T., Cheng, D. M., Samet, J. H., Bradley, K. A., Koepsell, T. D., Saitz, R. (2010). Physical health and drinking among medical inpatients with unhealthy alcohol use: A prospective study. *Alcoholism: Clinical and Experimental Research, 34*(7), 1257–1265. doi:10.1111/j.1530- 0277.2010.01203.x

Intensive Family Interventions ❖

LEARNING OBJECTIVES

Upon completion of reading this chapter and participating in the guided exercises, the learner will be able to

- identify the instances when a family intervention is appropriate;
- list the different approaches to family interventions;
- discuss the appropriateness of using anecdotal evidence to guide decisions;
- describe at least two models of family intervention; and
- apply the steps of family intervention work to a clinical case.

Risky use of substances does lead to concern for those close to the individual, and for many by the time addiction is activated (remember the spectrum) there have been numerous events elevating that concern. As a counselor, the below quotes are a few examples of what you may hear from concerned family members in your role as a professional counselor. Indeed, many of you, even before your career decision to become a counselor, have either heard these words or maybe even spoken them yourself.

"I'm just not sure what to do anymore. My partner, John, he is just drinking so much. I feel like I have tried everything. He just doesn't listen to me anymore, and it seems like he just doesn't care."—Jamie, 35 years old

"Jasmine is just out of control! You should see her; every night after work she goes out for "happy hour" with some friends for work—every night! And it's not just for one or two drinks, she comes home bombed! I am afraid to go to sleep thinking I'm going to get a call from the police or a hospital."—Tyler, 27 years old

"Quantel is not doing well. I have been getting calls from the school that he has been skipping, and this is not just a once in a while thing, but at least once a week. I've had it up to here (raises hand above head). He doesn't respect me, he steals my money, and I recently found the liquor bottles in our house had all been replaced with water! I'm not sure when he drank it, but this is getting ridiculous. He's only 14 years old!"— Maria, 40 years old

Knowledge

What comes to your mind when you hear the word *intervention*? It would surprise us if there were not either a thought or visual picture of the current A&E channel television reality show *Intervention*. This television show has been on the air since 2005 (A&E Networks, 2015), and due to the success of the show, other shows (e.g., VH1's *Celebrity Rehab* and *Sober House*) focusing on addiction topics have emerged (Kosovski & Smith, 2011). At the center of the story is an individual (or individuals) and his or her struggle with addiction, as well as family members struggling with their relationship with the addicted individual. Key stakeholders (family members and other supportive individuals that have a vested interest in the well-being of the addict) seek the help of a professional to intervene. On one hand the show has increased the dialogue concerning addiction, although Kosovski and Smith (2011) are concerned about the image being televised.

"Ironically, although this show [*Intervention*] attempts to normalize addiction for lay audiences and promote recovery efforts, the presentation of extreme cases may prevent some viewers from personally identifying with the show's subjects or mobilizing to get their loved ones help." (Kosovski & Smith, 2011, p. 852)

These concerns are related to the limited view of addiction depicted on the show (i.e., extreme cases), the ethical nature of informed consent for services, and the exclusive use of private inpatient treatment facilities, typically out of reach for the majority of those needing treatment. In our opinion, these concerns are valid and in addition the show is missing a thorough understanding of the professional counselor's efforts, beyond showing up to the intervention and transporting the individual to treatment. An unclear picture of the role professional counselors have in this process has emerged, and we hope to provide clarity here.

Historical Perspective

In order to fully understand the role of a professional counselor, it is important for us to examine the history of interventions. Without doubt, interventions have been around for as long as individuals have struggled with risky use of substances and behaviors and someone has been affected enough to say something. For the formal intervention process, Vernon Johnson formed the Johnson Institute in 1966, for the purpose of educating society about chemical dependency (Hazelden Betty Ford Foundation, 2016b). This work sprang from Johnson's work as a minister, and from working with his congregation members to help those living with addiction (Jay & Jay, 2008). In addition to an educational mission, the Johnson Institute developed an approach to working with chemically dependent individuals, the early intervention (Kinney & Leaton, 1983). The thinking of the time used to be that the individual needed to reach his or her rock bottom; however, the new approach attempted to show that caring family members and friends could step in and intervene earlier in the addictive cycle. The belief was that this would create a crisis for the individual, and that recovery was possible through this entry point. In 1978, the wife of United States' President Gerald Ford, Betty, received one of these interventions (Clark, 2012).

In her memoir, Betty Ford describes being the recipient of two interventions. Following the first intervention, which was conducted by the Ford family housekeeper, her personal secretary, one of Betty's children, and a medical physician, she states,

> It was brave of them, but I wasn't in the mood to admire them for their courage; I was completely turned off. I got very mad, and was so upset that, after everyone left, I called a friend and complained about the terrible invasion of my privacy. (Ford, 1978, p. 281)

Those concerned about Ford's future did not allow her reaction to stop them, and within approximately one week, a second intervention was conducted. This time, the intervention included all of her immediate family (husband and children) as well as medical professionals from the Navy. The intervention team had previously met with the doctor, who served as head of the Navy's Alcohol and Drug Rehabilitation Service, to discuss how to proceed and what each family member would say.

Following the second intervention Ford reflects, "All of them hurt me. I collapsed into tears. But I still had enough sense to realize they hadn't come around just to make me cry; they were there because they loved me and wanted to help me" (Ford, 1978, p. 282). Ford went on to check into the Navy's treatment program, and after receiving treatment, went on to be an advocate for passionate care for those living with addiction. In 1982, the Betty Ford Center was opened in Rancho Mirage, California, and the organization has since gone on to form a partnership with the Hazelden organization—now named the Hazelden Betty Ford Foundation (Hazelden Betty Ford Foundation, 2016a).

It is difficult to trace back the historical roots of interventions. We do know that the Johnson Institute's model appears to represent the historical beginnings of the professional intervention process now recognized and practiced today. Different intervention models will be examined in the following section.

Evidence-Based Practices (EBP)

In Chapter 2 we discussed EBP and have examined different practices throughout the preceding chapters. It is now time to introduce a new term, *anecdotal evidence*. Anecdotes are defined as "a usually short narrative of an interesting, amusing, or biographical incident" (Anecdote, 2015, para. 2). The last part of this definition, *biographical incident*, is relevant to our discussion here. Anecdotal evidence in reference to our discussion concerning addiction treatment refers to individuals' own unique stories of how they have entered into recovery, or family members' stories about the process of helping a family member. Basically, anecdotes are stories about things that have worked on the individual level. These anecdotes provide information to clinicians, which can have a profound influence on decision-making activities (Enkin & Jadad, 1998). In an examination concerning implementation of evidence-based practice guidelines conducted by Lomas, Enkin, Anderson, Hannah, Vayda, and Singer in 1991 (as cited by Enkin & Jadad, 1998), health care workers relied more on peer recommendations based on experiences than the formal guidelines, which highlights the powerful role of anecdotal information.

Anecdotal evidence is crucially important to understand in addiction interventions. Intervention efforts have grown out of a recognized need and desire for family members to intervene in crucial moments. There are a variety of methods established that we will examine below, however it is important to note that rigorous scientific examination of these interventions is limited (Copello, Velleman, & Templeton, 2005). What is prevalent is the anecdotal information from family members following the process, and those that were the recipients of the intervention. Enkin and Jadad (1998) state, "If no formal evidence can be found, anecdotal information provides the best and only information on which to base our understanding and decisions" (p. 965). We also believe anecdotal information provides important directives when there is limited information regarding intervention effectiveness and efficacy.

The formal intervention procedures to be outlined below are limited in rigorous scientific examination. However, due to the anecdotal evidence found in client reports and from our colleagues and supervisors, we have decided to include these. In addition, these have been accepted as appropriate methods within the professional treatment community.

Johnson Institute Model

As highlighted above, Vernon Johnson began working with family members initially during his time as a minister. This led him to develop the Johnson Institute in 1966. The book *Intervention: A Step-by-Step Guide for Families and Friends of Chemically Dependent Persons* was written by Johnson in 1986, and as the title states, is a how-to guide for conducting an intervention. The first part of the book contains psychoeducational material to educate family members and friends about addiction. Johnson believed, and it has been shown, that it is crucial for individuals to learn about addiction, specifically the brain mechanisms at play. This can help family members understand that it is a brain disease and not a moral failing on the part of their family member. The second part of the book examines the actual act of intervening. The first phase of this is to assemble a team, and the second phase involves gathering information for the intervention. This information is lists of specific instances where the individual's addiction has specifically caused concern for the team member. The next phase involves examining possible treatment options. It is important to note here that this book is written for the family members and concerned friends, not necessarily addiction counselors. Therefore, it is possible family members and friends may be conducting this intervention without the assistance of a professional counselor. However, it is our hope that the more counselors who are educated and trained in intervention techniques, the more availability families have in reaching out. With that being said, examining treatment options would be an important activity for the professional counselor to do, considering their advanced knowledge with treatment programs and options. Following the identification of treatment options, and the compiled information from the team members, the intervention is conducted with the individual and is done by surprise.

Lonneck, Garrett, and Banks (1996) compared the Johnson Institute intervention model with four other models used to refer individuals to treatment. The other models were coerced, non-coerced, and two variations on interventions (i.e., unrehearsed and unsupervised). The results of the study show that the Johnson Institute intervention outperformed the other referral sources, as individuals who had undergone an intervention based in the Johnson model were more likely to enter treatment. They were also more likely to complete treatment, along with those in the coerced group. These findings were important considering to this date there has been limited examination of these family intervention models in general.

Love First Model

The Love First model was developed by Jeff and Debra Jay in 2000. As the name of the model suggests, the key component and distinguishing feature of this model is the focus on love or compassion. Similar to the Johnson Institute model, the Love First model does not require that a professional counselor (identified as the "interventionist" from here on) be involved in the intervention process, as the book written by Jay and Jay (2008) includes instructions to intervene for any group of people concerned about someone else's use/behaviors. The following description will be written from the perspective of using an interventionist.

According to the Love First model, once a concern about a family member or friend is raised, contact is made with a professional interventionist who has been trained according to the model (see end of chapter for training information). The interventionist then plans an initial meeting with the concerned group. This group is targeted to be no more than eight people, and it is important that this includes those closest to the individual. After the initial meeting, the interventionist has specific duties, and the group has duties. Of utmost importance throughout this process is that the group is able to keep the plan from the individual so it is conducted with an element of surprise.

Following hearing from the group about their respective concerns, the members are instructed to go home and write two letters. The first letter (i.e., the love letter) is written to the individual and discusses the history of the relationship between the letter writer and the individual struggling with addiction, his or her specific concerns about the use/behavior, and cites some specific examples of when harm was caused to the individual and their relationship. At the end of the letter, the concerned member asks the addicted individual to seek the treatment that has been identified by the interventionist. Treatment may involve any level of treatment (e.g., support group attendance, individual counseling, group therapy, outpatient program, or inpatient program). The second letter is the "bottom line" letter. This is composed of the things the concerned group member will no longer do that may be seen as enabling/supporting the addiction. These are often difficult for family members and friends to commit to, and the interventionist is a great resource to process this with. The interventionist can challenge the group members to consider hypothetical situations and develop their own techniques for managing and sticking to their bottom lines. After all group members have written their letters, which may have been reviewed and edited by the interventionist, a dress rehearsal is planned. This is a designated time in which the group will practice reading their letters and also make decisions on the order for reading the letters. According to Jay and Jay (2008), the love letters are read first, and if the individual agrees to go to treatment following the first letter, no more are read. This can be thought of as a path of least resistance. In the event the individual does not agree by the end of the love letters, the bottom-line letters are read. If the group gets to the end of the bottom-line letters and the individual does not agree to treatment, the group now has to initiate their bottom lines and it is important for them to hold each other accountable. If the individual does agree to treatment and that is an inpatient facility, the letters are sent to the treatment program to be included as part of his or her admission file. The idea is that if the person decides to leave treatment, they could use the letters to remind the person why they did choose treatment initially.

ARISE Intervention Model

The ARISE Intervention model was originally developed for the times that a concerned individual contacts a treatment program for help with someone that is abusing substances (Garrett, Landau-Stanton, Stanton, Stellato-Kabat, & Stellato-Kabat, 1997). The founders of the model (Garrett et al., 1997) describe it as

> a three stage, graduated continuum of intervention designed to utilize the concern of the chemically dependent person's family and friends toward maximizing both engagement and, hopefully, retention in chemical dependency treatment. Each stage involves an increased commitment of therapeutic and familial/network resources, compared to the stage which precedes it. (Prochaska & Di Clemente, 1986, as cited in Garrett et al., 1997, p. 238)

The three stages of the model are (a) telephone coaching, (b) mobilizing the network, and (c) the ARISE Intervention. The telephone coaching process involves a series of

12 steps for the call receiver to discuss with the concerned individual. This step involves gathering information relevant to the chemically dependent person's use and history, and toward the end involves encouraging the caller to speak with the user about coming in for an evaluation appointment. Regardless of whether the individual agrees to come in for the evaluation, the identified network will come to the appointment. Garrett et al. (1997) note that sometimes more than one phone call is needed, but it is not common to need more than two.

The evaluation appointment is scheduled during the first phone call (Garrett et al., 1997) and the appointment involves the network of concerned individuals who show up. If the person of concern does show up, the evaluation is conducted, and the beginning focus is on engaging that individual in treatment. The second part involves uniting the network of concerned individuals. These individuals will be required to meet with the chemically dependent person biweekly or once per month, which is all outlined in the form of a contract. Regardless of if the dependent person engages in treatment or in the group meetings, the network group still meets and then decides whether stage three is required. Stage three as outlined by Garrett et al. (1997) is the ARISE Intervention, which is described as a less confrontational Johnson intervention. Garrett and colleagues clearly delineated the steps of the ARISE Intervention model in a 2008 publication.

The model has received wide recognition as one of the only evidence-based programs for interventions. The ARISE Intervention model was examined in a National Institute on Drug Abuse–funded study and the results were reported in 2004. The study examined whether someone struggling with a substance use disorder would seek treatment following a phone call to the program by a concerned family member or friend (Landau et al., 2004). The authors reported that 83% of their study participants engaged in treatment or self-help programs following the phone call. Treatment was varied and included detoxification, inpatient/residential, intensive outpatient, outpatient, and aftercare. Of specific importance to the intervention program was that of the clients who engaged in treatment, 70% of those only required the use of the lowest level of effort by the intervention program (Landau et al., 2004). In addition, the results highlighted how rapid the success of the program can be, with 50% of those who did engage in treatment or self-help to have done that within one week of the initial phone call (Landau et al., 2004). Having the evidence to back up the intervention program has solidified the ARISE Intervention model's place in intervention services.

Family Support

The discussion thus far has been concerned with how families may intervene with a member who is experiencing distress from their addiction. It is important to acknowledge that beyond the focus on the individual living with addiction, family members of that individual also need support. This support may come in the form of counseling, and/or through support groups.

Box 9.1: The Intervention Experience Through the Eyes of the Interventionist

Contrary to the impressions on TV and in movies, intervention is an experience that impacts every member of the team, not just the "interventionee." In my work as an interventionist, I welcome family members and friends who are at their wits' end and desperate for someone to knock some sense into their loved one because all their own efforts to date have failed. The three elements I bring to the equation are hope, direction, and support.

On arrival, the family's goal is for me to help them get their loved one to say "yes" to treatment. But *my* goal is to help everyone in the room learn what it will take for the family as a whole to experience the promises of recovery. That begins with helping the intervention team feel safe to hope again. They need to hear that I believe that we can structure an intervention that will help their loved one agree to treatment; that treatment will be successful; that sustainable, long-term recovery can be a reality; and that I can help them. Because I believe, they can begin to believe and thus rekindle their hope.

Once the family can hope, they become very open to learning how to prepare, what messages to convey, and what to expect. While many counselors are trained to be non-directive and to follow the leading of the client, interventionists must be directive, explicit, and willing to take charge. Intervention teams are grateful for this and willingly follow our lead when we do so respectfully and with explanation.

One of the most beautiful parts of the experience for me is helping intervention team members remember the good times. Many times, their anger and frustration is so all-consuming that they have forgotten all the wonderful things about this person they love so much. Sometimes they are so angry and hurt that they have actually tried to stop loving because it hurt too much. As I insist that they tap into memories and their love, their anger often simmers down and the most beautiful stories emerge! They allow themselves to feel their love and to feel vulnerable again. This is essential to the success of the intervention, but it is also one of my favorite parts.

In the preparation process, I listen, I teach, I edit, and I soothe. Intervention preparation is a very unnerving experience for family members, and I spend a great deal of time and energy answering questions, encouraging and supporting members of the intervention team. I instruct the family how to initiate the admission with the treatment center because I cannot ethically do so. I evaluate safety concerns—for the intervention team, the interventionee, and for myself. Once admission has been approved, I plan travel, direct the packing process, and develop estimates for my time and expenses for the intervention and transport process. I also sometimes complete special tasks like securing a phone card or spending money for use by the individual once they are admitted to treatment or the purchase of an inexpensive cell phone in the event that phone service is disconnected as a bottom line if the individual elects *not* to go to treatment. I am strategizing and trying to think of a contingency for every possible scenario, which is, of course, impossible.

As the intervention meeting begins, I find that I am always nervous. No matter how many times I facilitate an intervention, my heart is always pounding in the first few seconds. I have worked with individuals who practically said "yes, I'll go to treatment" before the process even began, and I have had one or two who literally ran immediately out of the room and fled the scene before the first word could be spoken! That is always every family's fear, by the way. Interestingly, even those who immediately ran away were admitted to treatment and have made great progress in recovery. Some people experience the show of love and encouragement in the spirit in which it is intended, while others feel threatened and angry. But once the shock of the first few seconds is over, I am able to settle down and assume my role. Despite my best efforts the night before, it is never possible to anticipate all the twists and turns. So my abilities to stay calm, stay compassionate and patient, and exercise clinical judgment under pressure are needed every single time.

As the interventionist, I have a powerful role to play in the room. I always sit on the floor to minimize any perception of threat, and I am careful to model the utmost respect and kindness. I know that I have prepared the team well, and I have made sure to strategically position those who command the most respect from the individual. So there is no need for me to demonstrate my power. The team is the one that has the real power—the power of love. As letters are read and tears are shed, the individual is moved emotionally. Those emotions may not be stronger than the voice of their addiction screaming loudly in their minds though. So firm, immediate bottom lines may be needed to help boost their willingness to move from the contemplative to preparation stage of change.

If the intervention process does not yield a positive outcome within about 2 hours, it could be a long day or even a long few days before the individual is able to commit to admission. If so, my role as interventionist continues as I support the team, encourage them to hold firm to their bottom lines, answer the interventionee's questions, and plan for a later admission. Good planning, a well-prepared team, patience, flexibility, sound clinical judgment, and excellent counseling skills are needed in every intervention.

My counseling skills and quick-thinking skills are needed all the way to the admission too. After we have departed from the team and are in route to the treatment center, I shift between allowing reflective, respectful periods of silence to answering questions about treatment and recovery to small talk (to offer some distraction and relief from the intensity of the experience) to offering comfort, encouragement, and reassurance that treatment and recovery will bring relief.

Although I certainly keep the team informed until the admission is certain and complete, I also stay engaged with the family and the team after admission. They too need to begin to examine their own issues and the changes that will be needed for *their* recovery to begin and for them to best support their newly recovering loved one. When the family joins with the client in the treatment and recovery process, the prognosis for long-term, sustainable recovery is improved dramatically. But make no mistake, the family, the team, *and* the interventionist will all need a few days to rest and recover from the intensity of the experience. Then the *real* work begins.

SOURCE: Ginny Miles. Ginny Mills, MAEd, LPC-S, LCAS, CSI, is the founder and clinical director of Full Life Counseling and Recovery, with offices in Winston–Salem and Raleigh, North Carolina. Ginny is a licensed professional counselor–supervisor, a licensed clinical addiction specialist, and a certified clinical supervisor–intern. She is a graduate of Wake Forest University (MAEd and BA) and has served on the North Carolina Substance Abuse Professional Practice Board.

Family Counseling Models

While an in-depth discussion of family counseling is beyond the scope of this textbook, it is important to note some landmark theories and concepts relevant to working with addicted families. Salvador Minuchin (1974) developed structural family therapy. Minuchin's model is based on understanding the structure of families, all in relation to the ideal hierarchical structure he hypothesizes. According to Minuchin, families are composed of three subsystems: the spousal system, the parental system, and the sibling system. Each system is separated by boundaries, yet when these boundaries are either too rigid or nonexistent, problems occur. When the boundaries are nonexistent, families become enmeshed, and when boundaries are too rigid families can become disengaged. The work conducted by Minuchin, and those working from a structural family therapy model, would involve joining with the family, understanding the current family structure, and then working to restructure the systems with functional/appropriate boundaries.

Murray Bowen is the developer of natural systems theory, also known as the Bowenian approach (Becvar & Becvar, 2013). Bowen's work involves the construction and examination of genograms, a visual representation of a family's structure over time (consider it a professional family tree). Once the counselor and client complete the genogram, composed of at least three generations, the genogram is examined. Much of Bowen's work centers on how individuals relate to one another, and these relationships are visible through the genogram construction. A foundational concept is that of differentiation of self, represented by a spectrum of zero to 100 (Kerr & Bowen, 1988). The lower quartile, according to Kerr and Bowen (1988), represents individuals who have a hard time distinguishing thoughts from feelings, and who have little recognition of their own existence and are instead influenced by those they are in contact with. This is a stark contrast from the upper quartile, represented by individuals who have a deep understanding of their own experiences, and someone who "is able to balance thinking and feeling: capable of strong emotion and spontaneity but also possessing the self-restraint that comes with the ability to resist the pull of emotionality" (Nichols, 2014, p. 71).

Another concept observed through the genogram is that of a triangle, the "smallest stable relationship unit" (Kerr & Bowen, 1988, p. 134). Triangles form when there is a disruption in a relationship between two people, and one of those individuals seeks a third person to diffuse the anxiety caused from the disruption (Kerr & Bowen, 1988). For example, a mother of a son who was recently arrested with a driving while intoxicated charge gets into a verbal argument with him about his drinking. The mother believes he is brushing off the incident and is concerned he needs treatment. After the son storms off, frustrated with his mother, she turns to her partner for support. The partner has then become "triangulated" in this instance—the mother is looking to release some of the anxiety that has built up as well as seek the support of another individual. This pattern can play out over and over with different family members, and with different issues. In addition, individuals with a lower level of differentiation tend to become triangulated easier than those that are more differentiated.

In addition to having knowledge of Salvador Minuchin's and Murray Bowen's work, a counselor working with families might find it helpful to have knowledge related to codependency and family roles in addiction. Thombs (2006) defines codependency as "an unhealthy pattern of relating to others" (p. 207), in which an individual in a close relationship to someone living with addiction themselves loses "all sense of 'self' or identity and [becomes] emotionally dependent on the addict" (p. 208). This term is used in the field of addiction when working with families to help explain the experiences they are having, however this does not come without controversy. The concept has been the subject of critique through the years (Anderson, 1994), although it is still being investigated through empirical research (Marks, Blore, Hine, & Dear, 2012). Marks et al. (2012) developed an instrument to measure codependency and found high correlation of the codependency scale with measures of mental health (i.e., depression, anxiety, stress) among survey responders. In addition, the scale was found to identify members of a Codependence Anonymous group from the general population (Marks et al., 2012). Counselors working with family members need to have familiarity with this term as families may be exposed to it through popular-psychology means (e.g., self-help books, television shows).

Family members may also present to counseling having had exposure to the idea of "family roles," from the works of Claudia Black (1981) and Susan Wegscheider-Cruse (1985). According to Alford (1998), children living in families with one or more parents in active addiction tend to take on specific roles in order to emotionally survive in their chaotic families. The roles identified by Wegscheider-Cruse are the hero, the scapegoat, the lost child, and the mascot, with each title exemplifying the characteristics of the role. Although these family roles have little research support (Alford, 1998), understanding the language is important for counselors who will come in contact with family members.

Family Support Groups

While some family members may seek the assistance of a counselor for themselves or as a group, there are many who will seek out mutual support groups run by peers, not professionals. The most widely known groups are Al-Anon/Alateen and Adult Children of Alcoholics/Dysfunctional Families (ACOA). According to Al-Anon Family Groups (2015), the first family support groups started to form in 1939, followed by the official founding of Al-Anon in 1951. It was just six years later that the peer teen support group, Alateen, was founded in 1957. The program is based in the 12 Steps and has worldwide membership. Members are able to attend meetings in person, by telephone, and online. Interested individuals can call the headquarters to locate a meeting (1-888-4AL-ANON/1-888-425-2666) or by visiting the website at www.al-anon.org.

The other organization, Adult Children of Alcoholics (ACOA) World Service Organization, is an organization for individuals who were raised in an addicted household, and it is also based on an adaptation of the 12 Steps (ACOA World Service Organization, 2017). One important distinct contribution from the ACOA organization is the Laundry List—a list of 14 traits members of ACOA may have in common. Meetings are also held in person, via telephone, or online and can be found using the search option on the main ACOA website (meetings.adultchildren.org/meetings). As a professional counselor, you will find it helpful to have the phone numbers and websites of these programs easily accessible when talking with family members.

Skills in Action

The following section will allow you to apply the concepts you have learned about in this chapter. First, we will present a case illustration in which you will be able to see a counselor work through an intervention process with a family. Please keep in mind that the intervention models detailed in this chapter are much lengthier than those in Chapter 8. Therefore, some information has been condensed to provide an overview of the process. Second, you will be presented with a case and will be prompted to consider how you would proceed with the given information.

Case Study 9.1: Planning and Executing a Family Intervention for Alicia

Virat is a professional counselor working in private practice. He holds dual licensure as a Chemical Dependency Counselor and a Licensed Professional Counselor. Virat specializes in working with addicted families and has a large referral base from families he has worked with in the past. One Tuesday afternoon, Virat receives the following phone call:

Virat:	Good afternoon, this is Virat; how may I help you?
Phone Call:	Umm, I'm ok. Well, I'm not really; I'm worried about my daughter-in-law. She really needs help.
Virat:	Is she in immediate harm? Is she suicidal or homicidal?
Phone Call:	No, no, I don't think so, but she's an addict, and it's all just too much.
Virat:	You are very concerned about your family member. And I'm sorry, but I didn't get your name.
Phone Call:	Oh gosh, I'm sorry! I am a wreck. My name is John.
Virat:	Hi, John, I'm glad you called. Would you be able to come in for an appointment this week?
John:	Umm . . . yes, are you available tomorrow?
Virat:	Yes, how would one o'clock be?
John:	Great. Thank you.
Virat:	OK, I will see you at 1 o'clock tomorrow afternoon. Goodbye.
John:	Bye.

At this point there is not much for Virat to do besides gather information; his red flags are raised that an intervention may be necessary. From his work he has learned that when family members are able to reach out to a professional counselor, they are really struggling. Often, professional counselors are the last resort, and Virat knows this all too well in his work. Because of this, he knows that he will speak with John tomorrow, and in their meeting he will focus on gaining a clear picture of the situation with his daughter-in-law, and also mainly focus on gaining information about other concerned family members and friends.

John arrives at Virat's office, and the following dialogue follows after John signs all necessary paperwork (i.e., informed consent, privacy practice notice).

Virat: Welcome, John. Go ahead and start where you feel comfortable.

John: Oh boy, I don't even know where to begin.

Virat: How about you start by telling me about you and your family.

John: Hmm, OK. My name is John, obviously, and I am 57 years old. I have twin sons, Michael and Daniel, who are 33 years old, and my partner passed away 10 years ago.

Virat: I'm sorry to hear that.

John: Thank you; it was lung cancer and very, very sudden.

Virat: That is never easy.

John: A year before she passed, Daniel married Alicia, his high school sweetheart. I keep hoping for grandchildren, but that hasn't happened yet, which I guess is a good thing for right now.

Virat: And Michael, is he in a relationship?

John: No, he is the bachelor of the two, vowed off of relationships years ago.

Virat: Every family has their own George Clooney!

John: Yes, Michael is ours, and Daniel is our rom-com man.

Virat: It is Alicia that you are concerned for, correct?

John: Yes, I just found out that she has been doing cocaine. I mean, cocaine! I'm not saying I've never seen the stuff, or even tried it, but that was 30 years ago. Things were different.

Virat: I'm wondering if you could tell me more about your concerns about her use.

John: Sure. So, Alicia is a lawyer, working her way up to partner in a big firm here in town. She went to the state college for law school and just became laser focused on making partner once she graduated. Apparently she is a really great at what she does, but what do I know? I am a high school science teacher; I really have no clue what she does all day every day, or why it is so hard.

Virat: You have a hard time understanding your daughter-in-law's professional life.

John: Yes, but it's not just me. Dan doesn't get it either. He says that he just nods and smiles when she talks about work, but just really doesn't get it.

Virat: And tell me more about Dan.

John: Oh, Danny Boy—he is the sweetheart of the two. He is a veterinarian's assistant. It was his dream to become a vet, but he just couldn't get the grades he needed to get into vet school. But he didn't want to just abandon his dream so he found some way to do what he loves.

Virat: He found his passion in life, and it sounds like almost everyone in your family has too.

John: Yes, that is true, we all love our jobs. I mean there is the nonsense every now and again like with any job, but overall, we're all happy. But Alicia, she has more pressure than any of us.

Virat: You can understand the amount of stress she is constantly under.

John: Yes, I get that. What I don't understand is how she is able to go on coke binges, liquor lunches, and happy hours every day and still wake up and get to work!

Virat and John continue to talk about John's family, and more specifically Alicia's family and her use patterns. Virat is becoming increasingly concerned about Alicia's use and her history. He learns that in the past three years, she has been arrested twice for drinking and driving, although both charges were dropped. John is unsure if that is because of her connections or because she was able to fight a good case, but regardless, she does not have any criminal record. Alicia comes from an upper-middle-class family, both parents still alive, and is an only child. Virat learns that Alicia has often spent more time with Daniel's family, as there has always been some tension between her and her parents, primarily her mother. John is unsure about the tension, which he reports is odd because he often enjoys lunch with her parents at the country club they all belong to. During these lunches they never mention concerns, and speak highly of Alicia. Throughout the rest of the session, John details Alicia's use, at least what he knows of it. Virat is concerned about all of this, and asks John what he knows about family interventions.

John: Like the TV show? I mean, I don't know if she's that bad.

Virat: Well, that TV show has done some good for helping people understand addiction and what an intervention may look like, but it is also not accurate for everything. From what I'm hearing from you, an intervention may be a good idea—at least something for us to consider.

John: Hmm, wow, I mean I know I came here because I heard you were good at working with families in our situation, and I guess I knew that was a possibility, but now that you've said that, it's hard to imagine.

Virat: I wonder if me saying that has confirmed something you have thought about for a while, and in a sense, has made it more real.

John: (pauses for a long moment) . . . hmm, well, you may just be right. But where do we even start?

Virat: You are concerned there is so much to do, and that is why I am here. What I would like you to do is to talk to Dan about your concerns. Also, begin thinking about who you feel are the important people in Alicia's life. You mentioned there is some tension between her parents, but your suspicions are that is mainly between her and her mother correct?

John: Umm, yeah.

Virat: Well, something I know about this process is that it is very important to consider who we involve in this process. Although I do not know her mother, their relationship does have me concerned, and I may advise not to engage her in this process as of right now. But her dad does seem to have a good relationship with her. How about you go ahead and talk to Dan about all of this. I'd like to meet you as soon as possible after you have identified a team of people all concerned about Alicia's life. Would you be able to call and schedule that once you speak to Dan and get a good idea of who to involve?

John: Yeah, Dan is coming over tonight for dinner because she has to work late, so it is perfect timing.

Over dinner that night, John starts talking to Dan about the session this afternoon. Dan appears distraught, and agrees that they need to do something. When John discusses that they need to put together a team, the following list emerges: John, Dan, Michael (Dan's twin brother), Patrick (Alicia's father), Rosa (Alicia's cousin), and Estefania (Alicia's best friend). Dan confirmed that Alicia and her mother have a strenuous relationship. Her mother is highly critical of her, was disappointed at her choice to go to law school, and always pressures her about when she will have children. John calls Virat the next day to let him know how the conversation with Dan went, and upon receiving the news, he was instructed to find out when everyone would be able to come in for a group appointment, and to call back and schedule that. John decided to ask Dan for help with contacting each person and having a conversation about what was going on. All of the identified individuals agreed they are concerned about Alicia and were willing to come in for an appointment.

Upon meeting the team for the first time, Virat introduces himself and explains his role with the forth-coming process. He also asks each member of the team to introduce themselves, explain their relationship with Alicia, and discuss their concern for Alicia. He then describes the process for the intervention, explaining he follows the Love First model (Jay & Jay, 2008). He explained the purpose of the two types of letters, and encouraged individuals to begin writing as soon as possible. He also asked that they send the letters to him so he can provide suggestions. The team agrees to meet in two weeks for a dry run, in which they will decide the order of the letters. In addition, Virat asks each member to think of reasons that Alicia will say no to seeking treatment the day of the intervention. Based upon Alicia's substance use history and limited experience seeking treatment (attended AA groups after one arrest before the charges were dropped), it is possible she will be able to get accepted into an intensive outpatient treatment facility. Virat asks Dan to find out about medical insurance for treatment coverage. The team dismisses, each person tasked with his and her own responsibilities. Dan becomes the lead contact person for Virat, due to his relationship with Alicia. All individuals are asked to remain quiet about what is going on, as in the model the intervention is typically a surprise event.

Dan gets back to Virat the next day with the insurance information, and Virat immediately starts looking into treatment facilities. Fortunately, he has strong relationships with treatment providers in the area and has identified three facilities that are open to accepting Alicia, if she agrees. Virat contacts Dan and discusses the treatment options, and asks him to make a decision for the main one, as well as the backup. In the meantime, Virat has received the love letters from everyone, and the bottom-line letters from everyone but Patrick (Alicia's father). He has provided feedback about the letters and has reached out to Patrick about his bottom-line letter. Patrick describes his concern for Alicia, and also his guilt for not doing enough to prevent this. Virat explains the process again, that the bottom-line letters will not be used unless needed, and this does seem to reassure Patrick; he sent his letter the next day.

Two weeks have passed, and each team member has written their letters and they are all meeting with Virat to have a dry run of the intervention. First, the team discusses who they feel should go first, agreeing on Dan and Patrick, followed by Estefania, Michael, Rosa, and John. Each team member takes their time reading their love letters, and then the bottom-line letters are read. They all agree they are doing the right thing, and Estefania takes responsibility for getting Alicia to the intervention site. They have agreed to do it at Rosa's house, as the girls have a weekly wine and TV night each Wednesday. Tomorrow they will all meet there.

The Intervention

Virat, Michael, Daniel, Patrick, John, and Rosa are all patiently awaiting Estefania and Alicia. They are solemn and quiet, and Michael can't stop pacing. "What if she hates us forever? What if she doesn't want to go?" are just a few of the concerns heard from the group. Estefania's car pulls into the driveway, and the group is aware the time has come. The team is assembled in the living room, which is positioned to the right of front entrance, and Alicia recognizes everyone immediately.

Alicia:	Hey, everyone! Umm, what are you all doing here? This is ladies' night.
Virat:	Hi, Alicia. My name is Virat, and we are all here because we are concerned. Would you mind taking a seat? (The empty chair is positioned between her father and husband.)
Alicia:	Umm, this is not what I think it is, is it?
Virat:	Help me understand what you think is going on.

Alicia: This cannot be an intervention; no way.

Virat: Well, you are correct, this is an intervention. Your family and friends are very concerned, and we ask that you take the time to listen to them.

Alicia: Wow, no way; this is ridiculous.

Virat: It seems impossible that this is happening right now. Would you listen to each person talk to you?

Alicia: I mean, whatever, fine; I will listen to you, but wow, I can't believe this!

Virat: We only ask that you listen.

Alicia: Fine, go ahead.

Alicia's father Patrick begins by reading his love letter. He describes her childhood and their shared passion of tennis. He speaks of extravagant vacations, and everyday evenings spent at home. He discusses his concern, the times she has hurt him, and asks her to consider going to treatment tomorrow. Alicia is crying, and remains silent. Daniel begins, and again asks her to seek treatment tomorrow. She remains silent, until after the fourth reader, Michael. Michael says, "Alicia, it breaks my heart to see you like this. I hurt for you and for all of us. Please, say you'll try it out." Alicia finally speaks, "I can't believe all of this; how did I get here? I will try, but I'm not making any promises." After agreeing to attend the intensive outpatient treatment program, the group continues to have a conversation with Alicia. Throughout the discussion she has many concerns about why she actually cannot go. For example:

Alicia: But, I have to work; what am I supposed to do?

Virat: According to federal law, your employer has to hold your position for you while you are in treatment, no questions asked.

Alicia: Rosa, I told you that I would watch your dog when you go on vacation next week. How am I supposed to do that if I'm in treatment all day?

Rosa: I have already asked my sister to watch the dog.

Alicia: Treatment programs are expensive; how are we going to make it work?

Dan: I've already talked to our insurance company, and they will be paying 80% of the costs. The remaining is not a concern for us financially; I've already budgeted it in.

The team was able to handle the concerns posed by Alicia because they did their background homework. Upon ending, Alicia asks if she is allowed to stay at home with Dan tonight. Virat explains that she will be able to be home with him every night, due to the nature of the program. If she finds that it would help to be more isolated, they can revisit the treatment program to ensure they have the right match. Alicia appears relieved, and exhausted. She says she just wants to sleep, and then start working on making everyone proud again.

The next morning, Virat meets Alicia and Dan at the treatment facility. He is able to introduce her to the intake coordinator and explain the process to Dan. After Alicia is checked in, Dan and Virat walk back to the parking lot. Virat discusses the importance of Dan also being in counseling during this process, and maybe considering joining an Al-Anon support group. Dan appears reluctant, and so Virat describes the meeting, and suggests that some of the team members go together to experience it for the first time. Dan agrees something like that might be helpful, and agrees to seek out a meeting. Virat then reminds Dan that he is available throughout the process, and asks him to schedule a follow-up appointment, once Alicia is discharged from treatment. Dan agrees, and the two part ways.

Experiential Skills Learning Activity

Samuel, "Sam," is a 48-year-old Latino American male living in Southeastern Louisiana. Sam has been employed as an auto-mechanic, working on large-scale machinery (e.g., tractor trailers, buses). Sam has been married to Renee (a 46-year-old African American woman) for the past 15 years, and they have one child, Justin (7-year-old biracial male). Renee has called your office because she is concerned about Sam's use of the prescription pain medicine oxycodone. She says his prescription is ending quicker than it should, and she is concerned he has been buying extra in between his prescriptions. Sam was in a car accident 14 months ago; he was rear-ended while at a red light and fractured a few vertebrae in his back. He has struggled with back pain ever since. You meet Renee when she comes to your office, looking for answers on what she should do. She is becoming increasingly concerned with leaving their son alone with Sam, as last week she came home to find Justin alone, unsupervised in the kitchen attempting to cook dinner. Sam was asleep on the couch, and Renee was unable to wake him. He eventually woke up, but it was after Renee was in hysterics, and right before she called an ambulance. Sam said he was "just tired" from a long day at work, but when Renee went back into the kitchen she found a bag of pills in his coat pocket, and a few empty beers in the garbage. "That was it, I'm scared. I don't know what to do anymore."

- As the counselor contacted by Renee, please describe what other information you may want from Renee about Sam's use:

  _____

  _____

  _____

  _____

  _____

- Based upon the information you have in the case above, and the further information you gather, do you believe an intervention is warranted for Sam? Provide a rationale:

  _____

  _____

  _____

  _____

  _____

- If you do believe an intervention is warranted, whom would you want to involve in the process?

  _____

  _____

  _____

  _____

  _____

- Choosing an intervention model covered in this chapter, detail your steps for working with Renee, Sam, and the other individuals you chose to involve. Once you have developed a plan, discuss with a partner:

  _____

  _____

  _____

  _____

  _____

Conclusion

Interventions have most likely been around as long as someone was concerned with another's use of substances and risky behavior. The chapter began with some historical information about interventions, introduced the term *anecdotal evidence*, and discussed intervention models such as the Love First, the Johnson Institute model, and the ARISE Intervention. The chapter has concluded with an example intervention dialogue between concerned family members and someone struggling with an addiction. It is the hope that the reader of this chapter has begun to consider how intricate and complex of a process providing interventions can be, and if interested in becoming an interventionist, will seek training of a model.

RESOURCES FOR FURTHER LEARNING

Websites

ARISE Intervention Model Training Information

http://www.arise-network.com/training-events/

Love First Intervention Model

http://lovefirst.net

Contact Number: 1-800-220-4400

Specific information about Love First Training: http://lovefirst.net/training-2/

Books and Articles

Jay, J., & Jay, D. (2008). *Love first: A family's guide to intervention.* Center City, MN: Hazelden.

Johnson, V. E. (1986). *Intervention: A step-by-step guide for families and friends of chemically dependent persons.* Center City, MN: Hazelden.

Garrett, J., Landau, J., Shea, R., Stanton, M. D., Baciewicz, G., & Brinkman-Sull, D. (2008). The ARISE intervention: Using family and network links to engage addicted persons in treatment. *Journal of Substance Abuse Treatment, 15*(4), 333–343.

Garrett, J., Landau-Stanton, J., Stanton, D., Stellato-Kabat, J., & Stellato-Kabat, D. (1997). ARISE: A method for engaging reluctant alcohol- and drug-dependent individuals in treatment. Albany-Rochester Interventional Sequence for Engagement. *Journal of Substance Abuse Treatment, 14*(3), 235–248.

Landau, J., & Garrett, J. (2006). *Invitational intervention: A step-by-step guide for clinicians helping families engage resistant substance abusers in treatment.* North Charleston, SC: BookSurge.

McGoldrick, M., & Gerson, R. (2008). *Genograms: Assessment and intervention* (3rd ed.). New York, NY: W. W. Norton & Company.

REFERENCES

A&E Networks. (2015). *Intervention videos: Season 1.* Retrieved from http://www.aetv.com/shows/intervention/video/season-1

Adult Children of Alcoholics (ACOA) World Service Organization. (2017). *FAQ.* Retrieved from http://www.adultchildren.org/faq#where

Al-Anon Family Groups. (2015). *History.* Retrieved from http://al-anon.org/al-anon-history

Anecdote. (2015). In *Merriam-Webster.com.* Retrieved from http://www.merriam-webster.com/dictionary/anecdote

Anderson, S. C. (1994). A critical analysis of the concept of codependency. *Social Work, 39*(6), 677–685.

Alford, K. M. (1998). Family roles, alcoholism, and family dysfunction. *Journal of Mental Health Counseling, 20*(3), 250–260.

Becvar, D. S., & Becvar, R. J. (2013). *Family therapy: A systemic integration* (8th ed.). Upper Saddle River, NJ: Pearson.

Black, C. (1981). *It will never happen to me: Children of alcoholics as youngsters, adolescents, adults.* New York, NY: Ballantine Books.

Clark, C. D. (2012). Tough love: A brief cultural history of the addiction intervention. *History of Psychology, 15*(3), 233–246. doi:10.1037/a0025649

Copello, A. G., Velleman, R. D. B., & Templeton, L. J. (2005). Family interventions in the treatment of alcohol and drug problems. *Drug and Alcohol Review, 24,* 369–385. doi:10.1080/09595230500302356

Enkin, M. W., & Jadad, A. R. (1998). Using anecdotal information in evidence-based health care: Heresy or necessity? *Annals of Oncology, 9,* 963–966.

Ford, B. (1978). *The times of my life.* New York, NY: Harper & Row.

Garrett, J., Landau, J., Shea, R., Stanton, MD., Baciewicz, G., & Brinkman-Sull, D. (2008). The ARISE intervention: Using family and network links to engage addicted persons in treatment. *Journal of Substance Abuse Treatment, 15*(4), 333–343.

Garrett, J., Landau-Stanton, J., Stanton, D., Stellato-Kabat, J., & Stellato-Kabat, D. (1997). ARISE: A method for engaging reluctant alcohol- and drug-dependent individuals in treatment. Albany-Rochester Interventional Sequence for Engagement. *Journal of Substance Abuse Treatment, 14*(3), 235–48.

Hazelden Betty Ford Foundation. (2016a). *It's official: Hazelden, Betty Ford Center have merged.* Retrieved from http://www.hazelden.org/web/public/hazelden-betty-ford-press-release.page

Hazelden Betty Ford Foundation. (2016b). *Johnson institute transfers key programs and products to Hazelden.* Retrieved from https://www.hazelden.org/web/public/johnson_institute_09.page

Jay, J., & Jay, D. (2008). *Love first: A family's guide to intervention* (2nd ed.). Center City, MN: Hazelden.

Johnson, V. E. (1986). *Intervention: A step-by-step guide for families and friends of chemically dependent persons.* Center City, MN: Hazelden.

Kerr, M. E., & Bowen, M. (1988). *Family evaluation: An approach based on Bowen theory.* New York, NY: W. W. Norton.

Kinney, J., & Leaton, G. (1983). *Loosening the grip: A handbook of alcohol information.* St. Louis, MO: The C.V. Mosby Company.

Kosovski, J. R., & Smith, D. C. (2011). Everybody hurts: Addiction, drama, and the family in the reality television show *Intervention. Substance Use & Misuse, 46,* 852-858.

Landau, J., Stanton, M. D., Brinkman-Sull, D., Ikle, D., McCormick, D., Garrett, J., . . . Wamboldt, F. (2004). Outcomes with the ARISE approach to engaging reluctant drug- and alcohol-dependent individuals in treatment. *The American Journal of Drug and Alcohol Abuse, 30,* 711–748. doi:10.1081/ADA-200037533

Loneck, B., Garrett, J. A., & Banks, S. M. (1996). A comparison of the Johnson Intervention with four other methods of referral to outpatient treatment. *American Journal of Drug and Alcohol Abuse, 22*(2), 233–246.

Marks, A. D. G., Blore, R. L., Hine, D. W., & Dear, G. E. (2012). Development and validation of a revised measure of codependency. *Australian Journal of Psychology, 64,* 119–127. doi:10.1111/j.1742-9536.2011.00034.x

Minuchin, S. (1974). *Families and family therapy.* Cambridge, MA: Harvard University Press.

Nichols, M. P. (2014). *The essentials of family therapy* (6th ed.). Boston, MA: Pearson.

Prochaska, J. O., & Di Clemente, C. C. (1986). Toward a comprehensive model of change. In W.R. Miller & N. Heather (Eds.), *Treating addictive behaviors: Processes of change.* New York, NY: Plenum.

Thombs, D. L. (2006). *Introduction to addictive behaviors* (3rd ed.). New York, NY: Guilford.

Wegscheider-Cruse, S. (1985). *Choice making: For codependents, children and spirituality seekers.* Pompano Beach, FL: Health Communications.

10

Societal Systems Impacted by the Addiction Spectrum: Legal, Workplace, and Medical Settings ❖

LEARNING OBJECTIVES

Upon completion of reading this chapter and participating in the guided exercises, the learner will be able to

- articulate the impact substance and behavioral use disorders have on systems in our society;
- identify evidence-based programs to implement within the three distinct settings discussed; and
- consider systemic variables when working with clients in either legal, medical, or employer settings.

This chapter focuses on three systems in our society that are greatly affected by the addiction spectrum. It may be no surprise to some of you that the legal and medical settings are included in this chapter, given the news stories we are exposed to daily. However, the workplace setting may be more of a surprise, and we will explore these issues now.

Knowledge

Workplace Settings and the Impact of the Addiction Spectrum

"Donna, you don't look so great today," says Donna's manager, Karen. "Yeah, I'm just feeling a little under the weather; maybe I picked up that bug that's been going around the kids' school," replies Donna. "OK, well, take care of yourself; let me know if you need to go home early," says Karen. "Thanks, I think I might head home now," says Donna.

In the above dialogue, Karen mentions concern for her employee Donna, who appears to be under the weather. Karen notes after the conversation that this is the third time this month she has spoken to Donna about her not looking well, and wonders if more is going on than a stomach bug.

Workplace settings in the United States are affected by the addiction spectrum. There is a difference, however, in how the workplace setting is affected depending on the employee's own unique situation. For example, from the above conversation we may identify Karen, a 47-year-old woman who consumes approximately 10–15 glasses of wine per week but does not drink every day or have many adverse consequences related to her drinking, more toward the risky use zone of the spectrum graphic as seen in Figure 10.1.

However, Bill is a 32-year-old male and employed at the same workplace as Donna. Bill was recently in a car accident while on duty driving the company delivery vehicle. For some time, Bill has been abusing prescription pain medication, which was

Figure 10.1   Karen's Individualized Spectrum

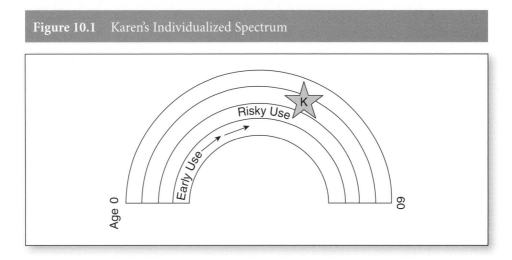

in his system at the time of the accident, and it was also discovered that he had alcohol in his system (a blood alcohol level of .113) at the time of the accident. Bill's placement on the addiction spectrum, as seen in Figure 10.2, differs from Donna.

Not only are employers affected by increased absenteeism when employers are unable to attend work, but they are also affected by presenteeism. Presenteeism is when employees are physically present at the workplace but not able to function up to their normal abilities due to a hangover or maybe sleepiness from using substances on the night before (B.I.G. Initiative, 2011). Other issues related to addiction in employment settings include increased workers' compensation claims related to substance misuse on the job, higher turnover rates, and increased health care expenses for employers and employees (B.I.G. Initiative, 2011).

There are employment settings that have been found to have a higher correlation of addiction-related issues, although no industry is exempt from being affected. For example, employees in the food service industry (e.g., bartenders, servers) and the construction industry have been found to have higher rates of alcohol use disorders than the general public (Gold, Byars, & Frost-Pineda, 2004). However, it may surprise many of you that approximately 10% to 20% of medical physicians may develop a substance use disorder during their careers (Berge, Seppala, & Schipper, 2009). There are formal professional treatment programs for some professional disciplines such as pilots, medical doctors, nurses, and lawyers. These programs are regulated by the professional discipline and are aimed at helping an individual who has had their license to practice removed or restricted due to an identified substance use disorder. These programs involve active participation in treatment, and they often include monitoring of the individual through formalized mechanisms.

It is crucially important that all counselors working with any individual who is currently employed, or will be employed in the future, understand the issues surrounding addiction and the workplace, including understanding the legal rights of employers and

Figure 10.2 Bill's Individualized Spectrum

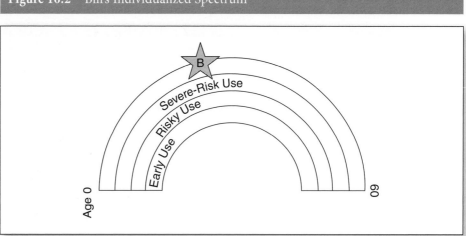

employees. The Substance Abuse and Mental Health Services Administration (SAMHSA) publishes a comprehensive brochure titled "Know Your Rights: Are You in Recovery from Alcohol or Drug Problem?" In short, it is important to know that an individual who is in recovery from a substance use disorder can qualify as an individual with a disability under the following legislation: The Americans with Disabilities Act, The Rehabilitation Act of 1973, The Fair Housing Act, and the Workforce Investment Act. Protections include that an individual would be protected from discrimination by these laws. It is illegal for employers to refuse to hire, fire, or discriminate based upon their disability (SAMHSA, 2004). For instance, prior to employment, employers are not allowed to inquire about whether an individual has a disability, or about their abuse or addiction to drugs or alcohol; however, it is legal for employers to ask about use of substances and if an applicant can perform the job requirements (SAMHSA, 2004). It is really important for employers and employees alike to understand the Family and Medical Leave Act (FMLA), which provides provisions for substance use disorder treatment. Under this act, employers must allow employees up to 12 weeks of unpaid leave to seek treatment without punishing them for this absence (SAMHSA, 2004). It is important for employees to note that they are not eligible for FMLA until they have worked for the employer for at least 12 months, and worked a minimum of 1,250 hours in that previous 12 months (SAMHSA, 2004). All professional counselors should review the SAMHSA brochure, in order to understand all of the nuances regarding discrimination protections for employees who may need to seek treatment.

Legal System and the Impact of the Addiction Spectrum

> "Hey, it's me, Kevin. I need you to come pick me up, just please don't ask me any questions. I had a bad night; I'm OK, but I got punched in the face by a bouncer. Anyways, one thing led to another and I need you to pick me up down at county jail. Please . . . don't freak out, I just need you to come."

In the second quote, we hear from Kevin, who is calling his partner to pick him up after spending the night in the county jail. Kevin was at a local bar with some friends when someone started harassing him. Kevin became angry and attempted to punch the other person when the bouncer got involved. Kevin was quite aggressive, and the bouncer (while defending himself) punched Kevin. The bouncer was able to then take Kevin outside where the police were waiting for him. After arresting him for drunk and disorderly conduct, they performed a search in which they found a small baggie of marijuana in his pocket.

More than half (52%) of the United States federal prison population consists of individuals serving sentences for drug-related offenses, primarily drug trafficking (Adams, Samuels, & Taxy, 2015). This percentage is increasing, with the number of drug offenders in federal prisons growing over 60% from the late 1990s to 2012 (Adams et al., 2015). The Bureau of Justice Statistics (as cited in Travis, Western, & Redburn, 2014) estimated that approximately 68% of individuals currently held in jails and prisons meet the criteria for a substance use disorder, with the majority being for alcohol and other drugs simultaneously. These statistics were based upon the past DSM-IV-TR (American Psychiatric Association [APA], 2000) diagnostic framework of substance abuse or substance dependence classification system. In addition to multiple substances involved in addictive processes, many inmates have co-occurring disorders (i.e., mental illness and addiction), which complicates screening, assessment, and treatment (Travis et al., 2014).

While there are plenty of individuals currently serving time with addiction treatment needs, unfortunately, there is a lack of availability of treatment programs to provide services to those in need (Travis et al., 2014). This lack of availability results in less than 15% of those needing treatment having the access (Travis et al., 2014). The most common type of help available in the criminal justice system is self-help groups, individual and group counseling, cognitive therapies, and therapeutic communities (Dietch, Carleton, Koutsenok, & Marsolais, 2002). There is a noted lack of evidence-based treatments being implemented in these settings (Dietch et al., 2002; Travis et al., 2014). Reasons for this lack of implementation vary, however, some may be due to budget concerns, lack of available personnel to provide treatment, and lack of space (Dietch et al., 2002).

Medical Settings and the Impact of the Addiction Spectrum

> "Hi, John, my name is Dr. Warren Francis and I am a surgeon here. I'm not sure if you remember much from last night, but you were brought to our trauma center after being involved in a car accident. This happened around 10 o'clock, and you were rushed immediately to surgery. We are confident you will not need more surgery, but you will be here for a little while recovering."

In this third quote, Dr. Francis is speaking to John, who was in a car accident. What we come to learn is John was driving under the influence of alcohol and marijuana. He had a blood alcohol level of .187 and suffered a minor concussion along with a broken leg. John had been over at a friend's house watching a basketball game and was heading home when the accident happened.

The effects of the spectrum of addiction cause a significant burden to our health care system in the United States. The health care system is composed of a variety of different specialties, for example, emergency departments, trauma centers, primary care physician offices, pediatrician offices, and the many specialty care providers (e.g., ear nose and throat surgeons, obstetricians, podiatrists). Each system faces challenges related to the addition spectrum and are particularly burdened by alcohol related concerns:

- General hospital setting: Approximately 25% of all patients admitted to general hospitals have alcohol use disorders (Williams et al., 2010).
- Emergency department setting: Estimates suggest between 24% and 31% of emergency department patients have alcohol-related disorders (D'Onofrio & Degutis, 2004/2005).

- Primary care setting: Estimates suggest that approximately 15% to 20% of patients have alcohol use disorders (McQuade, Levy, Yanek, Davis, & Liepman, 2000).
- Trauma setting: Upward of 50% of patients are hospitalized as a result of injuries due to the patient's or another individual's alcohol consumption (American College of Surgeons, 2003).

Evidence-Based Practices

This section will review research related to each of the settings examined within this chapter. The programs chosen for review in these sections are due to their recognition among professionals and/or their inclusion with SAMHSA's National Registry of Evidence-based Programs and Practices (NREPP; as discussed in Chapter 2). The programs included here for each setting are by no means exhaustive but are a sampling of evidence-based programs available for each setting.

Box 10.1: Search Tip for Finding Programs Related to Criminal Justice Programs

National Registry of Evidence-based Programs and Practices Search Tip! To find programs related to criminal justice programs, use the advanced search options and include special populations such as "justice-involved youth" and/or "justice-involved adults." In addition, you may search under setting for "court" and/or "correctional facility."

Legal Settings

The research that examines addiction treatment within the criminal justice population are mainly concerned with two main outcome variables: (1) incidences of re-offending following release (also known as recidivism) and (2) relapse of substance use. Mitchell, Wilson, and MacKenzie (2012) conducted a meta-analysis evaluating 74 research studies of treatment within the criminal justice system worldwide, with the majority being based in the United States. These studies involved a variety of treatment modalities: therapeutic community models, boot camp style treatment, counseling (including self-help groups, education programs, and cognitive and life skills programs), and narcotic maintenance programs. Therapeutic communities were found to have the most consistent results, including reductions in both recidivism and relapse (Mitchell et al., 2012). Programs based upon the boot camp model were found to not have any reduced impact on either recidivism or substance use patterns. These authors further discuss the importance of these findings for policymakers so that they may make informed decisions when considering program implementation.

Drug Courts

Drug-court programs aim to assist the individual involved in a drug-related offense in lieu of incarceration in a jail or prison setting; for this reason, these are also known as diversion programs. These began in Miami-Dade County, Florida, in 1989, and have since spread across the nation (Belenko, 2002). Belenko (2002) describes the drug-court system:

> In contrast [to the criminal court system], drug courts typically set aside the determination of guilt or imposition of a sentence and, by addressing the offender's substance abuse and related problems, seeks to reduce the probability of relapse and new criminal behaviors. The offenders are provided the clinical and social services that are considered necessary to address their specific problems. (p. 302)

Drug courts make referrals to treatment programs. Using either one specific treatment program for drug-court clients in the local area or following an assessment of the client's substance use disorder, the staff will make a referral to a treatment program specific for the client's needed level of care (Belenko, 2002). Regardless of the program, within the drug-court format there are generally three treatment stages (Belenko, 2002). The first stage involves assessment, treatment planning, and orientation to the program; the second involves the main treatment phase; and the third stage focuses on relapse prevention along with aftercare planning. All three phases last a few months each, totaling one year (Belenko, 2002). Throughout the entire drug-court program, the court is involved in monitoring via frequent in-person visits with the judge as well as urinalysis tests.

Research findings suggest that drug courts have had positive effects on reducing an individual's substance use and reducing future criminal behavior (Mitchell, Wilson, Eggers, & MacKenzie, 2012). In addition, these courts reduce the demand on the criminal court system. Drug courts are divided into adult and youth programs; the following program is specifically designed for offending juveniles.

Reclaiming Futures

The Reclaiming Futures Program is a six-step community-organizing initiative sponsored by the Robert Wood Johnson Foundation, and targets substance-using individuals in the juvenile court system (Butts, Roman, & Gitlow, 2009). The leading assumption of the program is "that positive outcomes for youth are best achieved when service delivery systems are well managed and coordinated, and when they provide young people with comprehensive, evidence-based substance abuse treatments along with other interventions and supports" (Butts & Roman, 2007, p.2). The six steps of the model are (1) initial screening, (2) initial assessment, (3) service coordination, (4) initiation, (5) engagement, and (6) transition (Reclaiming Futures, 2016) (See the Resources for Further Learning section of this chapter for the website that describes this model in detail.) Initial program evaluations of 10 sites across the United States focused on systemic change in administration, collaboration, and quality of services provided and found significant changes in all but one area (i.e., partner involvement) as a result of program implementation (Butts & Roman, 2007).

In addition to the 10-site evaluation, four specific programs were evaluated for youth outcomes located in New Hampshire, Illinois, California, and Washington. Each of the programs provided unique summary outcomes based upon differences in program implementation specific for the location. Overall, there were positive outcomes reported for the youth across all programs including youth receiving more screening and assessment of potential substance use issues, and more participation in treatment programs (Butts et al., 2009). The researchers were unable to measure recidivism rates across sites due to data collection issues; however, the California location found that youth involved in the Reclaiming Futures program had lower rates of recidivism than youth not involved in the program (Butts et al., 2009). More research concerning program implementation and associated youth outcomes is encouraged by the researchers.

Mississippi Alcohol Safety Education Program (MASEP)

This program is listed in SAMHSA's NREPP program. According to the NREPP (2015), this program began in the late 1970s and is offered to first-time offenders following arrests for driving under the influence (DUI). The MASEP curriculum includes training on topics such as problem-solving and critical-thinking skills, and is delivered in a variety of modalities including but not limited to group discussions, lectures, homework, and in-class exercises (NREPP, 2015). Program participants meet once per week for 3-hour sessions over a 4-week time period. Robertson, Gardner, Xu, and Costello (2009) evaluated the effectiveness of the MASEP program on DUI recidivism for a 3-year period and found support for the program. These authors analyzed data from an 8-year period, with over 30,000 MASEP program participants. The results of the Robertson et al. study highlight that there was a statistically significant DUI recidivism reduction over the 3-year period. The authors highlight there were demographic differences among the groups, with women being least likely to have a future DUI offense, and ethnic minorities (in comparison to whites) being less likely to recidivate during the follow-up time period.

In-Prison Programs

As mentioned above, the previous programs serve as jail-diversion programs, however there are initiatives for treatment within the criminal justice system. The following two programs are listed in SAMHSA's NREPP registry.

Correctional Therapeutic Community (CTC) for Substance Abusers

The CTC program is designed for four specific outcomes among offenders who have multiple arrests for drug offenses and chronic substance abuse. The intended outcomes are to reduce re-arrest, increase abstinence from drugs, reduce relapse, and increase post-release employment (NREPP, 2013). The program lasts for 6 months and is intended for those that are approaching prison release. According to the NREPP (2013), the CTC is an in-prison residential treatment intervention and consists of five phases of treatment. Phases 1, 2, and 3 occur during the first 3 months of the program, and include assessment, evaluation, orientation, and active involvement in the program (i.e., morning meetings, personal reflections, and counseling). The last phases of the program occur in the second 3-month time frame and focus on planning for prison release. Included during this time are employment preparation (e.g., mock interviews, resume preparation, seminars on job seeking), aftercare planning, and financial planning through opening a bank account and developing a budget (NREPP, 2013).

Results from program evaluation suggest that CTC program participants are less likely than control group participants to be re-arrested after 4.5 years and more likely to be abstinent from illicit drug use after 4.5 years; for those who did relapse, they had a longer time abstinent to first relapse than those in the control group, and were significantly more likely to have gained and maintained employment following release (NREPP, 2013). These findings are encouraging for the use of the therapeutic community model within the criminal justice system.

Forever Free

The Forever Free program is specifically intended for incarcerated females ages 26–55 that struggle with drug use (NREPP, 2006). The program is 4–6 months in length and includes a variety of services, including individual counseling, educational seminars (e.g., self-esteem, anger management, posttraumatic stress disorder, parenting), 12-step programs, parole planning, and urine testing (NREPP, 2006). Program participants are involved in treatment 5 days per week for 4 hours per day, totaling 20 hours per week. Following 1 year after release from incarceration, program participants were found to report less drug use within the past 30 days, as well as the past year in comparison to control group participants (NREPP, 2006). In addition, program participants were found to be less likely to be returned to prison after a parole violation, less likely to be arrested in the year after release, and had a higher percentage of employment in comparison with control groups (65.3% vs. 44.7%, respectively) (NREPP, 2006). All of the significant findings for Forever Free program participants led to the inclusion of the program within the NREPP database.

Box 10.2: Search Tip for Finding Employer Programs

National Registry of Evidence-based Programs and Practices Search Tip! To find programs related to employer programs, use the advanced search options and search for "workplace."

Workplace Settings

In order to reduce absenteeism and presenteeism concerns, many employers are implementing programs to assist employees with substance use issues. Many of these programs are initiated through the employee assistance programs (EAPs) offered by employers. Although EAP programs can provide a wide range of services, the ultimate goal is to increase productivity and healthy functioning in the workplace (International Employee Assistance Professionals Association, 2017). Services may include consultation, screening for behavioral health concerns, consultation for financial issues, and counseling for many presenting concerns, addiction being one. The structure of EAPs is different depending in the employer; some have an on-site office for employees (mostly large institutions), and others relying on a telephone-based system along with contracting out to local service providers (e.g., a counselor in the employer's community will provide services for the EAP). Professional counselors may interact with EAPs in a variety of different ways, such as by being employed as an EAP counselor, by helping a client navigate their EAP system, or by using the EAP services for their own needs.

A recent initiative has been to train EAP counselors to provide SBIRT services. The SBIRT program includes screening, brief interventions, and referrals to treatment (when needed) and was described in Chapter 8, Brief Counseling Interventions, and an example of an EAP intervention session is included in the skills section of this chapter. For these reasons we will not go into detail within this chapter but encourage readers to review Chapter 8. In addition to our writing on brief counseling interventions, the Brief Intervention Group (B.I.G.) Initiative published a learner's guide specifically for employee assistance personnel to learn about SBIRT and implementation in programs. Information about the guide can be found at the end of this chapter. Next, two workplace programs, which are included in NREPP's database, will be discussed.

Healthy Workplace

The Healthy Workplace program was first included in the NREPP database in 2008. The program is a compilation of five intervention programs intended for users in the risky-use zone of the addiction spectrum and is delivered in a small-group educational format (NREPP, 2008a). The programs are intended to reduce unsafe drinking and drug use, increase the motivation for reducing alcohol use, and increase healthy lifestyles of employees.

Findings from research examining the Healthy Workplace program found participants reported significantly less frequent alcohol consumption in comparison to control participants, had higher motivation to cut back on the amount of alcohol they consumed, and a great reduction in substance use other than alcohol (NREPP, 2008a). In addition to the reductions in substance use, findings also support an increase in helpful behaviors such as healthy eating and weight management (NREPP, 2008a). The program combines substance abuse prevention and early intervention within a health promotion framework, hoping to reduce the stigma of substance abuse (NREPP, 2008a).

Wellness Outreach at Work

In a similar nature to the Healthy Workplace program (NREPP, 2008a), the Wellness Outreach at Work (NREPP, 2008b) is a program focused on overall health, and infuses substance use (alcohol and tobacco) within the general health framework. According to the NREPP (2008b) description, if a workplace setting chooses to implement this program, all employees (who voluntarily choose to) receive a 20-minute health screening, and receive immediate personalized, one-on-one coaching for health concerns. In addition, education and counseling related to alcohol use, tobacco use, and weight control are provided. Following the immediate feedback, employees participate in four sessions throughout a 1-year period, which are individualized to the employee and corresponding concerns (NREPP, 2008b).

Research findings of the Wellness Outreach at Work program found participants reduced alcohol consumption, both for those who received ongoing follow-up counseling and for those who only received one brief counseling session following the screening (NREPP, 2008b). Program participants were also found to have higher rates of smoking cessation, and involvement in workplace programs for smoking cessation, as well as improved health outcomes such as greater weight loss and better controlled blood pressure (NREPP, 2008b). Considering the impact substance use can have on an employee's functioning at work (covered previously), the findings of the Wellness Outreach at Work program are encouragi ng for all workplace settings to consider implementation.

Medical Settings

As identified earlier in this chapter, many medical settings provide services to individuals falling at all different areas on the addiction spectrum. One of the most widespread programs used in a variety of medical settings is SBIRT. Findings of SBIRT research in medical settings were described in Chapter 8, and we encourage you to review those now. Medication assisted treatment programs will be discussed here.

Medication-Assisted Treatment

Medication-assisted treatment (MAT) is the use of medications to prevent future relapse and harms associated with substance use. In recent years, there has been a surge in opioid overdoses across our country, with prescription opioids being involved in 16,651 overdose deaths and heroin being involved in 3,036 overdose deaths (Volkow, Frieden, Hyde, & Cha, 2014). According to Volkow and colleagues (2014), the three medications used (although underutilized considering the potential target population) in MAT for opioid addiction are methadone, buprenorphine, and naltrexone. Each of these medications has been found to have successful outcomes such as reducing an overdose risk, increasing a user's involvement in treatment, and even reducing criminal involvement (Volkow et al., 2014). The underutilization is due to a variety of factors, such as lack of available prescribers and misconceptions about the use of MAT (Volkow et al., 2014). There is a large debate within the addiction treatment profession about prescribing medication to treat substance addiction, particularly among those that favor the abstinence-only model. Readers are encouraged to review some further readings on both sides of the debate to truly become informed.

MAT has been embraced in a variety of settings, including the criminal justice system. The following is a reflection from a professional counselor working in the criminal justice system about her experience with evidence-based programs, and MAT specifically.

Box 10.3: Evidence-Based Practice in Mandated Treatment Programs: One Counselor and Supervisor's Perspective

Mandated treatment for drug offenders often has a negative connotation. After four years of working within this setting, including clients from jail diversion programs, drug court, and graduates of in-house jail and prison treatment programs, despite the negative associations of the population, I can still say I believe in the ability of clients to succeed. Optimism is often hard to maintain when there is a seemingly revolving door of clients coming in and out of treatment. Yet there are individuals that while mandated to treatment chose to see it as an opportunity to change. The majority of the clients I have seen come with a lifetime history within the judicial system. Some have spent more times in active addiction and in jails or prisons than they can recall out of it. But sometimes these are the clients that get the most out of treatment. The goal of treatment for these clients is more than recovery from substance use—it is the opportunity for rehabilitation and reentry into society. Some return to school, finish a GED, learn to read, get their first legal job, and go on to lead a productive life in society. Mandated treatment can be an opportunity within the terms of probation.

The ability to offer evidence-based practice (EBP) within the mandated setting is not challenging due to the population but because of systemic issues. The implementation of an EBP is complicated when viewed within an agency or other system as the system is generally set within its ways, or each member of the system operates from a different perspective. To integrate a unified treatment method throughout this organization can be challenging. Additionally, there are state or contractual requirements to fulfill. Some EBP stakeholders may set requirements that treatment includes certain treatment formats or topics, such as addressing criminal thinking, encouraging the use of their own treatment modalities, and employability skills. Also, the court system, including problem-solving courts such as drug courts and jail diversion programs, remain active in the treatment by requiring updates on the client or the offender in probationary terms. It is these extraneous forces that can further complicate a seamless implementation of an EBP.

In my experience I have seen the implementation and acceptance of one specific EBP increase in recent years, and that is medical-assisted treatment (MAT). Much of this acceptance and growth is due to the attention on opiate use and heroin overdoses that has touched many through public personas and for me, personally, through clients I've treated in the past. The pharmaceutical naltrexone, which is manufactured by Alkermes, Inc. under the name of Vivitrol (Naltrexone for extended-release injectable suspension), was approved by the Food and Drug Administration (FDA) as a pharmaceutical option for alcohol use disorder clients in 2006, and use with opiates was approved by the FDA in 2010. Naltrexone is a once-monthly injection that blocks the brain's receptors that usually correspond with the effects of alcohol and opiates; it is an opioid antagonist that does not stimulate the dopamine reward system. The injection lasts 28–30 days, and the client must be active in weekly therapy. The most common side-effects I've heard involve site injection reactions and headaches. If a client on naltrexone drinks or uses an opiate, the injection prevents the "high" a client would normally experience. The pharmaceutical company literature presents this as a protective factor, and it does make sense; supervised medical attention is required to break through the block if medically necessary. "What's the point in continuing to drink or use opiates

(Continued)

(Continued)

if there is no momentary pleasure?" is something I've heard from some clients who are invested in their recovery, that as soon as they relapse, they regret reactivating the addiction, a cycle of use, and that the momentary high was not worth it. Yet, with opiates it is a vicious beast that requires continuous deposits to prevent withdrawal; in active addiction, using opiates is easier than withdrawing from opiates.

In my time in mandated treatment for substance use disorders, I've seen an increase in the availability of funding from the federal and state levels and correction department for this MAT pharmaceutical. The ability to offer it comes with requirements, from the funders, and to maintain the fidelity or best practice protocols. The agency I've worked for is fortunate to have a primary health care clinic that enables both our outpatient and residential programs to offer this monthly injection to clients. If a program does not have a health clinic component or working relationship with one, then it is difficult to implement this EBP. In order to be eligible for this and continue with the program, clients must be screened, lab tested, have their injection sites examined for reactions, obtain a written prescription for the injection, and have timely monthly injections. All of this must be in coordination with counseling services on a weekly basis for 1 hour with a treatment goal related to the naltrexone component.

In addition to the resources needed to implement this EBP, recruiting clients to participate offers its own unique challenges. Some clients have told me that when the rumors start going around and they hear about a new drug that completely "messes you up," they can't wait to try it. Yet with a dramatic sense of irony, when I tell clients about a medication that can potentially help them with withdrawals, recover and maintain the recovery, but not offer any highs, they are skeptical and focus on the potential side effects and the size of needle required. In residential treatment, rumors and gossip spread fast. Once I had a client who had a site injection reaction; it was temporary, and not a risk to the client, but this temporary site injection reaction quickly became the story of a client who now required reconstructive plastic surgery because of the reaction!

There are certainly challenges to implementing EBPs, specifically within the mandated treatment field. Yet the increase in attention toward substance use disorders, such as the surge in opiate use and overdose, has increased the availability of EBP treatment modalities such as MAT. Some states, including Florida where I gained most of my experience, have authorized doctors to prescribe naloxone to at-risk opiate users; naloxone is an opioid antidote. The equivalent of naloxone for an opiate user is an EpiPen to an individual with a peanut allergy—it can save their life. With this shift in the public perception and acceptance of the EBP, MAT will hopefully carry over to all aspects of substance use disorders.

SOURCE: Gemma Philage. Gemma Philage, MS, LMHC, LMFT, is completing her PhD at Barry University (Miami, Florida) and is employed as a private contractor for the U.S. government. She is a licensed mental health counselor and licensed marriage and family therapist. She previously served as a clinical supervisor for an inpatient addiction treatment center in Miami, where she provided clinical services and supervised clinical work.

Skills In Action

Box 10.4: Case Illustration of Anjolie, Employee Assistance Program Client

Anjolie, a 45-year-old single woman, is referred to the employee assistance program (EAP) of a large accounting firm following a string of absences. Particularly of concern according to the referral is that the absences came with no advanced notice, and were during the company's busiest season. Due to her absence, Anjolie had to complete five sessions with the EAP counselor. The following is the transcript from Anjolie's first session:

Counselor (Michael):	Welcome to counseling, Anjolie; my name is Michael, and I will be working with you for the next few sessions. Tell me about other times you've been in counseling.
Client (Anjolie):	Umm, I haven't. Well, does my school counselor count? Haha, that was years ago, though!
Michael:	Well, yes, school counselors are trained just as mental health and addiction counselors are trained! So, although you laughed, it was a good exposure. (Michael continues to review agency's documents pertaining to informed consent.) Do you have any questions before you sign?
Anjolie:	Well, you said that everything we talk about stays between us, but what happens since Mr. Jimenez said I had to come here?
Michael:	You're concerned that because you are mandated to come, that I will have to report information to Mr. Jimenez.
Anjolie:	Well, since you put it like that, yes!
Michael:	I understand, and let me explain that. Although you were mandated to come here by your employer, I am only allowed to disclose your attendance to them. So, that will be happening, but beyond that I will not be reporting anything to them, like anything related to what we talk about.
Anjolie:	Oh, OK. (Client signs documents.)
Michael:	Right as I said that, your shoulders looked like they relaxed.
Anjolie:	Wow, very observant! Yes, I mean I just hate being in trouble, and I'm pretty much an open slate to everyone who asks, so I wouldn't want to get myself in trouble.
Michael:	I'm curious what would get you in trouble.
Anjolie:	Oh, god, almost everything in my life! Ha, I mean, I'm joking; I'm a pretty boring person, just me and my cat . . .

(Continued)

(Continued)

(Counselor and client go on to build therapeutic rapport. The client appears to relax and the counselor attempts to learn more about the client, including history, cultural identity, and education. Three times during the discussion the client has eluded to risky alcohol use, as well as marijuana use occasionally. The counselor feels as though a transition into a screening and brief counseling intervention is warranted, and begins that below.)

Michael:	Anjolie, thank you for sharing all of that information with me about your family and history. I noticed a few times you mentioned drinking alcohol and also smoking marijuana, and I was wondering if I could ask you a few more questions about that.
Anjolie:	Sure, like I said, I'm an open book.
	(Counselor conducts the AUDIT [Review Chapter 6] to assess for alcohol risk. The counselor does not do a specific screening for marijuana, as her use alone is risky. The client's AUDIT results will be discussed below.)
Michael:	Thank you for going through those questions with me, Anjolie; what was that experience like?
Anjolie:	Umm, I guess some were difficult to answer, as I've never thought of that. You know, like when you asked me about feeling guilty; sure I've felt that, but I haven't known that I've felt that per se.
Michael:	The experience was somewhat difficult for you, just because you hadn't necessarily been conscious of these feelings or thoughts before.
Anjolie:	Right!
Michael:	Well, I appreciate that, and that is similar to how other people feel. These questions give me a score from anywhere from zero to 40. A score of zero indicates that someone doesn't have any risk, most likely because they do not drink alcohol, and a score of 40 is someone who is answering "every day" for almost all of those questions; you might know someone like that in your life.
Anjolie:	Yes, like I said when you asked some of those, my dad just couldn't stop ever!
Michael:	Right. Anjolie, when you think about your own risk, where would you score yourself thinking about zero meaning no risk and 40 being severely at risk?
Anjolie:	Hmm . . . umm, maybe like a 10. I mean I'm nowhere near the 40, but I realize there is some risk.
Michael:	I hear that you feel confident you are more toward the lesser side of risk than the higher side. I wonder if you feel you are so different from your father.
Anjolie:	Yes! He was obviously a 40, probably a 50 even though that isn't a real number here.
Michael:	For you, what are some of the risks that made you score yourself a 10?

Anjolie:	The guilty feelings for one. I told you that story about yelling at my ex on my birthday because I thought he forgot to get my favorite birthday cake, and it exploded into this huge thing, only for me to find out that there was a cake, it was just at the surprise party he planned for later in the night. Ugh, I felt like such a jerk.
Michael:	As you told that story, and again now, it looks like you feel those guilty feelings in your gut again.
Anjolie:	Yes! (Client grabs stomach.) It sucked, sucked so much!
Michael:	That is one example of risk, particularly for your emotions. What is another reason for your rating of 10?
Anjolie:	I know that I drink a lot. I mean, I live alone, I come home from work, and I pop open a bottle or drink what was left over from the night before. It's my routine; I know I should go to the gym, but I settle in to the bottle, microwave my dinner, and watch some *Jeopardy!*
Michael:	You recognize your patterns and that drinking wine is your go-to way to relax after a long day.
Anjolie:	Absolutely!
Michael:	It sounds like you acknowledge there is risk associated with your drinking, and I'm concerned that you are not sure about the severity of your drinking. You indicated your score might be around a 10, but you actually scored a 23. (Client's eyebrows arch up.) You look surprised by that number.
Anjolie:	Yeah, crap, that is closer to 40 than I thought; ughhh, no, that can't be!
Michael:	This doesn't feel right for what you know about yourself.
Anjolie:	Yeah, like I said, I am nowhere near my father!
Michael:	This is surprising and somewhat frustrating because you try hard to not follow in his footsteps.
Anjolie:	Yes, and I am not him.
Michael:	Would you like to know why your score is a 23?
Anjolie:	Yes, please enlighten me!
Michael:	The number one reason your score is elevated has to do with the amount and frequency that you drink. You indicated you drink two or three glasses of wine every day. That means you drink about 15 glasses of wine per week. Have you ever heard of the safe drinking guidelines?
Anjolie:	Safe drinking? No . . .

(Continued)

(Continued)

Michael:	Well, there are these researchers out there, and they identified there are limits to what men and women should drink to prevent further risk from alcohol. They are different for women and men, just based upon our body chemistry differences.
Anjolie:	OK.
Michael:	For a woman your age, the limits are to have no more than three drinks in one day, and no more than seven drinks in one week.
Anjolie:	*Seven*? Oh boy . . .
Michael:	That number sounds very low to you.
Anjolie:	Yeah, I mean, you just calculated it—what did you say I was drinking per week?
Michael:	You reported three and sometimes five glasses of wine per night, and that is every night, maybe with one night off per week. If we averaged to four glasses per night times six nights, that is 24 glasses per week, more than three times the recommended limit.
Anjolie:	Whoa, wait, you said three to five glasses; I said I have a little less than a bottle or finish a bottle . . .
Michael:	Do you know how much wine is considered a standard drink? That would be the equivalent of one beer, or one shot of liquor.
Anjolie:	Umm, I mean, one glass of wine!
Michael:	Yes, and we all know how much a glass of wine can vary, right? Have you ever seen that "wine glass," which is really just a glass covering for a bottle? That alone tells us how varied it is. However, the standard drink of wine is the equivalent of 5 ounces of wine, which means in a regular bottle of wine, there are five glasses.
Anjolie:	Whoa, if my friends knew this . . .
Michael:	That is very surprising for you.
Anjolie:	Yes, I mean, we go through so many bottles some nights! Whew.
Michael:	It sounds like this piece of information is really challenging what you thought you knew.
Anjolie:	Yeah, I mean, that is a huge difference. And again, you said I'm drinking three-plus times the amount I should be. That is not good.
Michael:	I'm wondering if you would be willing to talk about some ways you could cut down on your drinking.
Anjolie:	Yes, please, I'm getting a little scared now.
Michael:	You're feeling scared.
Anjolie:	Yes, I am no spring chicken! Gosh, I do not want to be like my dad, ahh. Not good.

Michael:	I am wondering about your alcohol use, and about the reason you were referred to me. Your employer said you have been missing a lot of work lately.
Anjolie:	You caught me! I have been sick, just unable to get out of bed some days.
Michael:	And this is the busy season for you and the company. I wonder how stressed you have been lately.
Anjolie:	Haha, is that even a question? I mean, imagine being the only woman and it is tax season, we work 15- to18-hour days, go home to sleep, and go back to work. I just can't do it.
Michael:	Anjolie, when you say that you are too sick to go to work, are you working off a hangover?
Anjolie:	Umm, sometimes, but I have also been really sick, like bronchitis.
Michael:	Well, that makes sense. When we drink alcohol above the recommended limits, we put our immune system at risk. It is not able to do its job like it normally does.
Anjolie:	I didn't realize that.
Michael:	Yes, and when we continue to drink while we are sick it takes us much longer to heal.
Anjolie:	Well, no wonder I've had this cough for over a month now!
Michael:	This new information is resonating with you and providing some reasons for what you have been feeling lately.
Anjolie:	Yes! Oh boy, I've really gotten myself into trouble, haven't I?
Michael:	Well, the good news is that we are talking about this now. And it sounds like you are willing to change your drinking. What does change look like to you?
Anjolie:	Well, what did you say is the number of glasses I can have in one day?
Michael:	The recommended limit is no more than three in one day, but no more than seven in one week.
Anjolie:	So, I could still have a glass of wine after work every day, but only one. And probably smaller than I normally pour.
Michael:	That is correct; on a scale from 1 to 10, with 1 being not committed and 10 being overly committed this is something you will do, how committed are you to making this change?
Anjolie:	Honestly, probably a six. I want to do it, but I know myself.
Michael:	What might make your score a 7?
Anjolie:	A 7? Whenever I make a change, I like to see change to know it is working. I guess that means time.
Michael:	Having time to see the benefits will make you commit to this change even more so.

(Continued)

(Continued)

Anjolie: Yes.

Michael: That makes sense. And you may begin to see changes even quicker than you think. Now, on one of the questions you denied ever having to have a drink first thing in the morning, but you did say sometimes your hangovers are strong enough to make you miss work. Do you ever find yourself having the shakes or any such feelings like that?

Anjolie: No, my dad used to do that I guess. He used to have to have the "hair of the dog" first thing to help him out of bed, but I've never done that. I never even drink before 7 p.m.

Michael: OK, I'm just concerned about withdrawal based upon how often you have been drinking, and sometimes even little amounts combined with drinking frequently can cause someone to be at risk for alcohol withdrawal, especially if there is a family history of alcohol withdrawal complications. If, while you are cutting down you notice yourself feeling odd, and that your hands are shaking, please go to the closest emergency room. Does that sound like a plan?

Anjolie: Yeah, I mean I don't think we have to worry about that, but I will keep that in mind.

Michael: Also, Anjolie, I know we focused today on your alcohol drinking, but I was wondering if we may be able to explore your marijuana use next time we meet. It doesn't have to be the entire session, but if we could just talk some.

Anjolie: Sure, we'll just flip to that chapter in my open book.

(Counselor and client close for the day. Counselor summarizes the entire session as well as the commitment to change from the client.)

Experiential Skills Learning Activity

In groups of two you will conduct a role-play counseling session. One person will serve as the counselor, the other as the client. As a team you will decide which setting the counselor is seeing the client in for the first time (i.e., workplace, legal, or medical) and you will work together to come up with the *presenting problem* (i.e., the story of why the client is coming for counseling). Conduct a 20-minute role-play counseling session, and switch so each partner is able to serve as the counselor once. Following the role-play, discuss the following questions:

- How comfortable did you feel as the counselor/client in this scenario? What would have made you more or less comfortable?
- What further information did you wish you had as the counselor? How might you go about gaining this information?
- How would the conversation have changed if you encountered this client in one of the other two settings discussed in this chapter?

Modifications for the Experiential Skills Learning Activity

Depending on time availability, you may consider doing a shorter (10 minutes) or longer (30 minutes) role-play activity. In addition, you may consider using groups of three, with the additional person acting as an observer and timekeeper. This would also allow for more feedback beyond the reflections of personal experiences in the roles of counselor/client.

RESOURCES FOR FURTHER LEARNING

Training Manual

B.I.G. Initiative. (2011). *The employee assistance professional's guide to screening, brief intervention and treatment.* Chicago, IL: Author.

http://bigsbirteducation.webs.com/eaplearnersguide.htm

Cost: $25

Websites

Forever Free Program

https://www.crimesolutions.gov/ProgramDetails.aspx?ID=40

Reclaiming Futures Model

http://reclaimingfutures.org/model/model-how-it-works

The Brief Intervention Group—Employee Assistance Program Focus

http://bigsbirteducation.webs.com/thebiginitiative.htm

International Employee Assistance Professionals Association

http://www.eapassn.org/

Webinars and Online Courses

EAP, SBIRT, and DOT-Covered Employees

Presented by Dr. Tamara Cagney and Laura Lacey Dasher, LCSW, SAP, SAE
http://bigsbirteducation.webs.com/dotsapemployees.htm

Employees and Their Family Members

Presented by Sis Wenger
http://bigsbirteducation.webs.com/familymembers.htm

The EAP and Behavioral Health Professional's Guide to Screening, Brief Intervention and Treatment (SBIRT) Online Course (6 hours, free)

Hosted by the Employee Assistance Professionals Association (EAPA)

http://bigsbirteducation.webs.com/onlinecourse.htm

Further Reading

Center for Substance Abuse Treatment. (2005). *Medication-assisted treatment for opioid addiction in opioid treatment programs. Treatment Improvement Protocol (TIP) Series 43.* (DHHS Publication No. SMA 12-4214). Washington, DC: Substance Abuse and Mental Health Services Administration.

McPherson, T. L., Goplerud, E., Derr, D., Mickenberg, J., & Courtemanche, S. (2010). Telephonic screening and brief intervention for alcohol misuse among workers contacting the employee assistance program: A feasibility study. *Drug and Alcohol Review, 29,* 641–646.

Substance Abuse and Mental Health Services Administration (SAMHSA). (2004). *Know your rights: Are you in recovery from alcohol or drug problems?* [SAMHSA Publication PHD1091]. Retrieved from http://store.samhsa.gov/product/Are-You-in-Recovery-from-Alcohol-or-Drug-Problems-Know-Your-Rights/PHD1091

REFERENCES

Adams, W., Samuels, J., & Taxy, S. (2015). *Drug offenders in federal prisons: Estimates of characteristics based on linked data* (Bureau of Justice Statistics Report #NCJ 248648). Retrieved from http://www.bjs.gov/content/pub/pdf/dofp12_sum.pdf

American College of Surgeons Committee on Trauma. (2003). *Alcohol and injury* [PowerPoint slides]. Retrieved from http://www.facs.org/trauma/alcslide.html

American Psychiatric Association. (2000). *Diagnostic and statistical manual of mental disorders* (4th ed., text rev.). Washington, DC: Author.

Belenko, S. (2002). Drug courts. In C. G. Leukefeld, F. Tims, and D. Farabee (Eds.), *Treatment of drug offenders: Policies and issues* (pp. 301–318). Washington, DC: Springer.

Berge, K. H., Seppala, M. D., & Schipper, A. M. (2009). Chemical dependency and the physician. *Mayo Clinic Proceedings, 84*(7), 625–631.

B.I.G. Initiative. (2011). *The employee assistance professional's guide to screening, brief intervention and treatment.* Chicago, IL: Author.

Butts, J. A., & Roman, J. (2007). *Changing systems: Outcomes from the Robert Wood Johnson Foundation reclaiming futures initiative on juvenile justice and substance abuse.* Retrieved from http://reclaimingfutures.org/members/sites/default/files/main_documents/changing_systems2007.pdf

Butts, J. A., Roman, J. K., & Gitlow, E. (Eds.). (2009). *Organizing for outcomes: Measuring the effects of reclaiming futures in four communities.* Retrieved from http://reclaimingfutures.org/members/sites/default/files/main_documents/organizing_for_outcomes_2009.pdf

Dietch, D. A., Carleton, S., Koutsenok, I. B., & Marsolais, K. (2002). Therapeutic community treatment in prisons. In C. G. Leukefeld, F. Tims, & D. Farabee (Eds.), *Treatment of drug offenders: Policies and issues* (pp. 127–137). New York, NY: Springer.

D'Onofrio, G., & Degutis, L. C. (2004/2005). Screening and brief intervention in the emergency department. *Alcohol Research & Health, 28*(2), 63–72.

Gold, M. S., Byars, J. A., & Frost-Pineda, K. (2004). Occupational exposure and addictions for physicians: Case studies and theoretical implications. *Psychiatric Clinics of North America, 27,* 745–753.

International Employee Assistance Professionals Association. (2017). *Definitions of an employee assistance program (EAP) and EAP core technology.* Retrieved from http://www.eapassn.org/About/About-Employee-Assistance/EAP-Definitions-and-Core-Technology

McQuade, W. H., Levy, S. M., Yanek, L. R., Davis, S. W., & Liepman, M. R. (2000). Detecting symptoms of alcohol abuse in primary care settings. *Archives of Family Medicine, 9,* 814–821.

Mitchell, O., Wilson, D. B., Eggers, A., & MacKenzie, D. L. (2012). Assessing the effectiveness of drug courts on recidivism: A meta-analysis review of traditional and non-traditional drug courts. *Journal of Criminal Justice, 40,* 60–71. doi:10.1016/j.jcrimjus.2011.11.009

Mitchell, O., Wilson, D. B., & MacKenzie, D. L. (2012). The effectiveness of incarceration-based drug treatment on criminal behavior: A systematic review. *Campbell Systematic Reviews, 18.* doi:10.4073/csr.2012.18

National Registry of Evidence-based Programs and Practices (NREPP). (2006). *Forever free.* Retrieved from http://legacy.nreppadmin.net/ViewIntervention.aspx?id=118

National Registry of Evidence-based Programs and Practices (NREPP). (2008a). *Healthy workplace.* Retrieved from http://legacy.nreppadmin.net/ViewIntervention.aspx?id=148

National Registry of Evidence-based Programs and Practices (NREPP). (2008b). *Wellness outreach at work.* Retrieved from http://legacy.nreppadmin.net/ViewIntervention.aspx?id=56

National Registry of Evidence-based Programs and Practices (NREPP). (2013). *Correctional therapeutic community for substance abusers.* Retrieved from http://legacy.nreppadmin.net/ViewIntervention.aspx?id=338

National Registry of Evidence-based Programs and Practices (NREPP). (2015). *Mississippi alcohol safety education program (MASEP).* Retrieved from http://nrepp.samhsa.gov/ProgramProfile.aspx?id=21#hide4

Reclaiming Futures. (2016). *How the model works.* Retrieved from http://reclaimingfutures.org/model/model-how-it-works

Robertson, A. A., Gardner, S., Xu, X., & Costello, H. (2009). The impact of remedial intervention on 3-year recidivism among first-time DUI offenders in Mississippi. *Accident Analysis and Prevention, 41,* 1080–1086. doi:10.1016/j.aap.2009.06.008

Substance Abuse and Mental Health Services Administration (SAMHSA). (2004). *Know your rights: Are you in recovery from alcohol or drug problems?* [SAMHSA Publication PHD1091]. Retrieved from http://store.samhsa.gov/product/Are-You-in-Recovery-from-Alcohol-or-Drug-Problems-Know-Your-Rights/PHD1091

Substance Abuse and Mental Health Services Administration (SAMHSA). (2015). *Forever free.* Retrieved from http://legacy.nreppadmin.net/ViewIntervention.aspx?id=118

Travis, J., Western, B., & Redburn, F. S. (Eds.). (2014). *The growth of incarceration in the United States: Exploring causes and consequences.* Washington, DC: National Academies Press.

Volkow, N. D., Frieden, T. R., Hyde, P. S., & Cha, S. S. (2014). Medication-assisted therapies: Tackling the opioid-overdoes epidemic. *The New England Journal of Medicine, 370*(22), 2063–2066.

Williams, E. C., Palfai, T., Cheng, D. M., Samet, J. H., Bradley, K. A., Koepsell, T. D., . . . Saitz, R. (2010). Physical health and drinking among medical inpatients with unhealthy alcohol use: A prospective study. *Alcoholism: Clinical and Experimental Research, 34*(7), 1257–1265. doi:10.1111/j.1530-0277.2010.01203.x

11

Intensive
Addictions
Counseling

❖

LEARNING OBJECTIVES

Upon completion of this chapter, the learner will be able to

- describe at least three main evidence-based counseling approaches used in intensive addictions counseling settings;
- list at least one neurobiological aspect important for understanding the treatment of a substance use disorder; and
- cite three levels of care for intensive treatment of process addictions.

Knowledge

Addictions counseling has undergone major changes in the last 25 years, especially within the intensive levels of care, such as residential addiction treatment, inpatient hospital addiction treatment, partial hospitalization, and intensive outpatient programs (IOP) for addictive disorders. While entire books have been written to describe intensive addictions counseling approaches and models, it is beyond the scope of this chapter to be all-inclusive of the lengthy history of intensive counseling. Rather, a focused overview of key areas of new evidence in addictions treatment settings will be the focal point in this chapter. An examination of important developments for the addiction counselor will contain information such as evidence-based approaches within various modalities and key populations, such as women's issues related to addictive disorders and intensive treatment as identified in a valuable resource revised in 2015 by the Center for Substance Abuse Treatment (CSAT). Key neurobiological considerations will also be reviewed in relation to main classifications of drug classes, including alcohol. A review of intensive treatment considerations, though limited due to a paucity of evidence-based research and intensive treatment outcome data, regarding process addictions such as gambling, Internet, gaming, sex, and food addictive disorders will be included within the chapter also. This chapter will focus on the leading evidence-based intensive treatment approaches currently used in the United States.

Gone are the days when the primary intensive approach to counseling an individual with an addictive disorder meant inhumane treatments such as isolation of alcoholics on deserted islands, exposing alcoholics to a toxic dose of paraldehyde causing near-death episodes that would be negatively associated with drinking, or Towns' tonics containing hallucinogenic belladonna (Travis, 2009). Subsequently, uninformed approaches relied heavily on psychoanalytic approaches to uncover what psychological distress was causing addictive-type personalities and addicted behaviors as seen in the 1920s with "the proto-psychologists known as 'alienists' [who] had played an important role in the development of the American Association for the Cure of Inebriates" (Travis, 2009, p. 27). Much effort went into analyzing childhood events or social influences that "caused" addiction to address what Karl Abraham described as the "unresolved oral fixations, and that liquor was their unhealthy substitute for mature heterosexual relationships" (Travis, 2009, p. 27). Many individuals suffering from addictive disorders learned how to review past traumas and events to discern how those brought about the addictive behaviors. At times, clients have been prompted to gain cognitive insights into their lives so as to better figure out how to resolve past hurts, losses, abuses, and negative patterns with expectations that once those cognitive insights occurred the addictive behaviors would cease. Since very little neurobiological evidence existed regarding addiction as a brain disease, addicts could spend years in therapy gaining insights that did nothing to treat what came to be known as a primary disease, not caused by psychological events, rather caused by the brain's response to activation of the brain's reward pathways and disruption in the normal processing of mood-altering chemicals bathing the brain. Advancing a medical understanding of addiction began in the 1940s and 1950s, leading to the current stance that "addiction cannot be cured but can be brought into remission through a program of treatment, abstinence from all psychoactive substances, and supported recovery" (Smith, 2012, p. 1). Supported recovery often includes intensive addiction counseling where clients best gain insights into behaviors that enhance healing and coping with the chronic brain disease of a severe substance use disorder or other related addictive disorder. For the most complete look at select theories commonly used in addiction treatment, see also the text by Lewis (2014). Regardless of the theory used in an intensive treatment setting, the structure of the treatment approach can have similar features that will be briefly reviewed next.

The accompanying graphic (see Figure 11.1) highlights how intensive addiction counseling can be comprehensive and include various settings and services. The American Society of Addiction Medicine (ASAM) offers one of the most comprehensive

Figure 11.1 Components of Comprehensive Drug Abuse Treatment

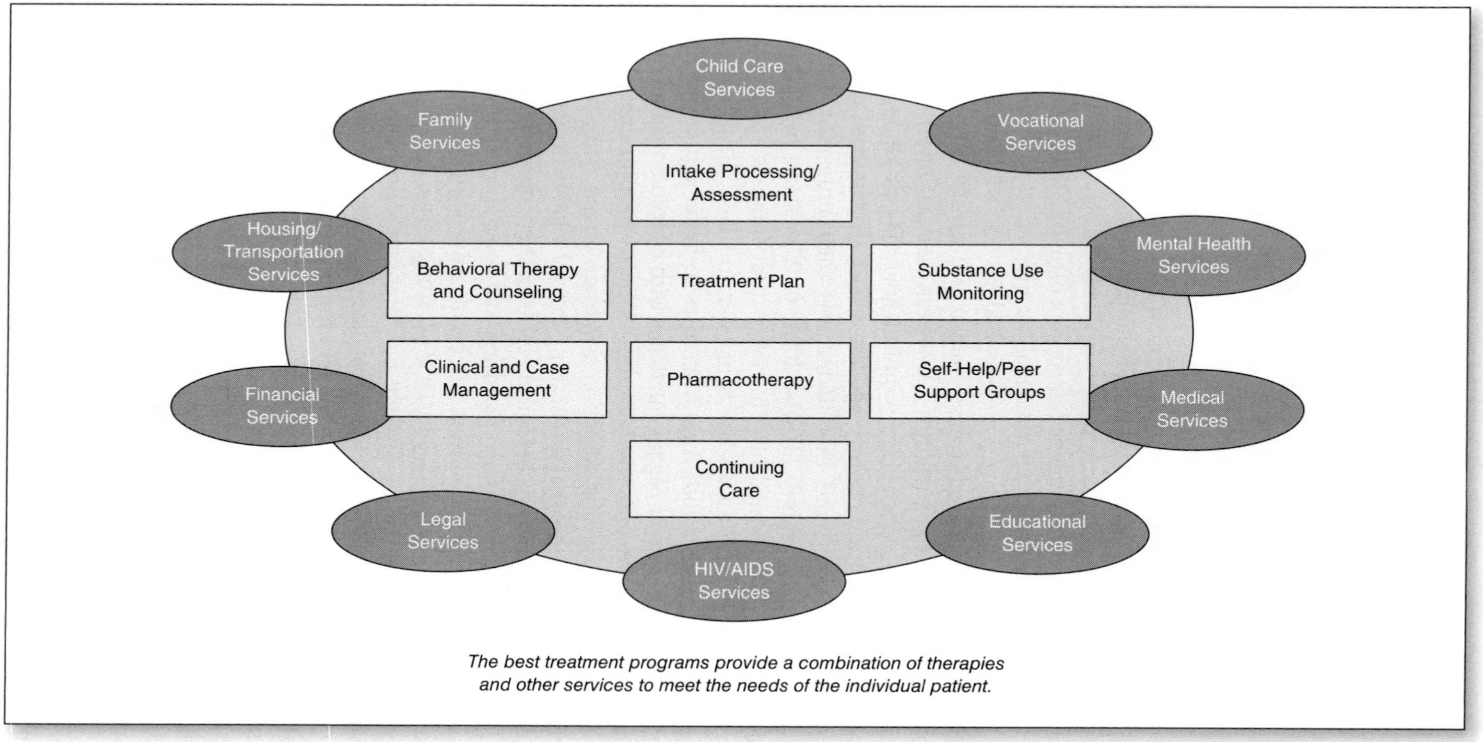
Child Care Services
Family Services
Vocational Services
Intake Processing/ Assessment
Housing/ Transportation Services
Behavioral Therapy and Counseling
Treatment Plan
Substance Use Monitoring
Mental Health Services
Financial Services
Clinical and Case Management
Pharmacotherapy
Self-Help/Peer Support Groups
Medical Services
Continuing Care
Legal Services
Educational Services
HIV/AIDS Services
The best treatment programs provide a combination of therapies and other services to meet the needs of the individual patient.

SOURCE: National Institute on Drug Abuse (NIDA). (2012). *Principles of drug addiction treatment.* (3rd ed.), p. 8. Retrieved from https://www.drugabuse.gov/sites/default/files/podat_1.pdf.

statements about addiction recovery: "Recovery from addiction is best achieved through a combination of self-management, mutual support, and professional care provided by trained and certified professionals" (ASAM, 2016).

Even in the recent decades, gone are the vast majority of clients spending 28 days in an inpatient addiction treatment facility. Beginning in the early 1990s, U.S. managed care changes in reimbursement began to demand evidence for reasons a person in a residential treatment program needed to have exactly 28 days of intensive addictions treatment (Veach, Remley, Kippers, & Sorg, 2000). Moreover, questions centered around how it was possible that 28 days was a standard for almost everyone. What was so magical about 28 days, about an intensive residential stay, and how did that one approach fit a wide range of use disorders, from cocaine to opioid to marijuana to alcohol to multiple substance use disorders? And why were so many residential programs using one primary model, the Minnesota model, based on a multidisciplinary approach? All these questions began to stimulate more research and outcome studies. The Yale Plan Clinics, outpatient alcoholism treatment, had actually begun in the 1940s to serve as an alternative to costly residential treatment (Travis, 2009). First, the Minnesota model of treatment needed careful examination since it was the primary intensive treatment model in the United States.

To better understand the leading model of intensive addiction counseling treatment, a brief overview of the Minnesota model will be provided. The Minnesota model was designed based on clinical work that began in the 1950s at Hazelden (Spicer, 1993), a residential treatment approach that started literally in Hazel's Den in Minnesota. Before the 1950s, as you learned in Chapter 1, most addiction treatment focused on harsh approaches that were not yielding sustained sobriety in many individuals. Harsh treatment approaches, for example, drew from the rapidly developing theories connected to behavioral modifications. Aversion therapy was a new approach that involved administration of drugs causing vomiting after drinking alcohol or mild shocks delivered to the individual consuming alcohol (Kinney & Leaton, 1987). With new theories being created about caring for individuals and behavior changes combined with remarkable stories of sustained recovery through Alcoholics Anonymous self-help groups, new approaches to intensive treatment were begun.

The Minnesota model is a prominent approach to caring for individuals struggling with addictive disorders. Dan Anderson, a prominent leader and psychologist, was credited as the architect of the Minnesota model (Spicer, 1993). He was former director of Hazelden, a pioneer in residential addiction treatment in Minnesota. He was likely influenced by major psychological theories in development in the 1940s that heavily influenced many aspects of therapy and counseling throughout the United States. In particular, more counseling and psychology theories were receiving much attention, having been introduced at several of the leading universities at the time. In addition, small-group modalities were being encouraged during the 1950s and 1960s due to findings that outcomes were improved when therapy was conducted in small groups rather than individual sessions. Dan Anderson's graduate studies in clinical psychology in the 1950s at Loyola University in Chicago, Illinois, also coincided with an emphasis on social psychology and group work as pioneered by Kurt Lewin, for example. In addition, the 1960s heralded the beginning of the cognitive theory revolution as Aaron Beck pioneered cognitive theory.

As Anderson began his work as a psychologist at the Wilmar State Hospital in Minnesota, he was assigned to the "inebriates" who were considered by many to be far less desirable to provide services to than those struggling with the harshest mental illnesses, even those that included psychosis (Hazelden, 2016). Anderson's primary contributions centered around a recognition of the need for a multidisciplinary approach with such multicomplex problems he had seen in those struggling with recovery from alcoholism. He pioneered having professionals from counseling, spirituality, psychology, psychiatry, medicine, recreational therapy, and peers from the recovery community of self-help groups such as Alcoholics Anonymous all working together as a team to provide intensive services for the medical, spiritual, emotional, and psychological devastation of an addictive disorder (Hazelden, 2016).

The Minnesota model is a model often used for intensive addiction treatment settings and continues to provide a multidisciplinary model using evidence-based theoretical approaches predominantly through group counseling modalities. Because the Minnesota model is multidisciplinary, various counseling theories are often used with client treatment, especially in the intensive levels of care. Key theoretical interventions, supported by research (CSAT, 2015; Lewis, 2014; Miller, 2015) that are often used in the Minnesota model include theories and approaches such as TSF (Twelve-Step Facilitation); cognitive behavioral therapy (CBT); behavioral, person-centered, motivational interviewing (MI), family systems, Adlerian, Gestalt, existential, feminist-relational theory, strength-based, solution-focused, reality therapy, Moreno's theory using psychodrama, and Frankl's logotheory. While it is important to consider applications of various theories to treating addictive disorders and increasing research studies comparing different treatment approaches, Miller (2015) aptly notes that research supports key findings showing that addiction counselors "may not need to be as concerned with the type of treatment the client receives for the addiction as much as that it be delivered by competent addiction professionals." (p. 106). This chapter will highlight select approaches used in the intensive addiction treatment setting.

Evidence-Based Practice

TSF: Twelve-Step Facilitation Model

With funding from the National Institute on Alcohol Abuse and Alcoholism (NIAAA), a trail-blazing new research study was launched, Project MATCH (Babor, Miller, DiClemente, & Longabaugh, 1999; Project MATCH Research Group, 1993, 1997a, 1997b, 1998a, 1998b, 1998c, 1998d). It was the largest research study of its kind designed to match different therapies to addicted client needs. This major undertaking involved over 1,500 client participants where one of three different treatment approaches (intervention arms) were used with the participants. One of those three approaches involved the newly developed motivational enhancement therapy (MET) for a total of four sessions during a 12-week period, another was CBT for 12 sessions over 12 weeks, and the third was also conducted weekly for 12 weeks, titled Twelve-Step Facilitation (TSF). TSF consisted of an approach that emphasized 12-step recovery supports in addition to professional counseling. The emphasis on 12-step groups is tied to the history of the Minnesota model. Alcoholics Anonymous (AA) was the first of the 12-step groups and recently marked its 80th year in 2015. AA has reached well over 69 countries, consists of over 2 million members globally, and expected 61,000 convention attendees at its 2015 convention (AA, 2016a). It is described as a grass-roots movement, revolutionary, and at times confusing in many ways by providing nonprofessional recovery tools in that one member helps another without any hierarchical structure (there is no president of AA, for example). In one of its key 12 guiding principles, note that AA is not affiliated with any treatment center or paid professional approach (Travis, 2009). Many other 12-step groups exist for addictive processes ranging from narcotics (Narcotics Anonymous), cocaine (Cocaine Anonymous), gambling (Gamblers Anonymous), and eating (Overeaters Anonymous) to Al-Anon for those struggling with a loved one's alcohol addiction. Often 12-step groups can best be described with a primary focus on mutual help and an emphasis on joining in a recovering community (Travis, 2009). The TSF approach working with AA, for example, can best be described from an excerpt for the training manual for counselors providing TSF in the original study:

> This [TSF] therapy is grounded in the concept of alcoholism as a spiritual and medical disease. The content of this intervention is consistent with the 12 Steps of Alcoholics Anonymous (AA), with primary emphasis given to Steps 1 through 5. In addition to abstinence from alcohol, a major goal of the treatment is to foster the patient's commitment to participation in AA. During the course of the program's 12 sessions, patients are actively encouraged to attend AA meetings and to maintain journals of their AA attendance and participation. Therapy sessions are highly structured, following a similar format each week that includes symptoms inquiry, review and reinforcement for AA participation, introduction and explication of the week's theme, and setting goals for AA participation for the next week. Material introduced during treatment sessions is complemented by reading assignments from AA literature. (Nowinski, Baker, & Carroll, 1999, p. x)

All sessions in the study were provided in an individual modality with participants who were identified with alcohol use disorders. Of note, the findings did not indicate that matching to one approach over the other had any benefits per se but findings did show all three treatment approaches had beneficial effects on lowering drinking levels and improving life-enhancing outcomes. Moreover, the benefits were seen to remain over a 3-year follow-up period. What makes this so important for evidence-based models is the role of TSF. First, the TSF approach was designed to be able to be compared to the other two models with as much similarity as possible. Conversely, in most counseling that encourages 12-step support, the clients are heavily involved in group counseling modes, yet the TSF was delivered only in the 12 individual counseling sessions and evidence still revealed positive client outcomes.

Box 11.1 Twelve-Step Facilitation Therapy Manual

Stages of Acceptance

Step 1 of Alcoholics Anonymous reads as follows:

WE ADMITTED WE WERE POWERLESS OVER ALCOHOL—THAT OUR LIVES HAD BECOME UNMANAGEABLE

Step 1 is, in fact, a complex statement. Its essence is the acceptance of personal limitation, in this case, one involving the loss of control over drinking. Although some individuals apparently achieve this acceptance via a single leap of faith, it is also possible to think of acceptance as a process involving a series of stages:

- Stage 1: "I have a problem with alcohol."
- Stage 2: "Alcohol (drinking) is gradually making my life more difficult and is causing problems for me."
- Stage 3: "I have lost my ability to effectively control (limit) my use of alcohol, and the only alternative that makes sense is to give it up."

When discussing Step 1, it may be helpful to keep these stages of acceptance in mind and to work with patients toward the end of helping them achieve acceptance in stages.

To begin, facilitate a discussion of Step 1, reading it aloud and then talking about it, making sure to cover the following points:

- "What does this statement mean to you? What is your initial reaction to it? Does it make you mad at all?"
- "How do you relate to the concept of powerlessness? What kinds of things are you powerless over? Can you understand how some people can be powerless over alcohol?"
- "At this point, do you believe that you can still control your use of alcohol? On what basis do you believe this?"
- "In what ways has your life become unmanageable?" Using a chalkboard or flipchart, list ways in which the patient's life has become increasingly unmanageable.

Say to the patient something like the following:

> "Step 1 represents a statement of personal limitation. Accepting powerlessness over alcohol is much like having to accept any other personal limitation or handicap. Some people who have a hard time relating to Step 1 as it is written relate to it better if it is framed in terms of limitation. I would like you to think of times in your life when you were confronted by a limitation of some sort. It could be physical, intellectual, economic, or whatever. Whatever it was, it stood between you and something you wanted. What was it?"

Anger, anxiety, and depression are typical reactions to limitation. Acceptance of alcoholism, like acceptance of any limitation, is a grief process. Denial has a place in this process, as do anger and sadness. One stage of grief is "bargaining." As it applies to Step 1, bargaining is alcoholics' secret belief that they can "safely" drink; in other words, that they can control their drinking.

Explore this idea of bargaining, which is part of our natural defense against accepting loss and limitation. In this case, the loss is the loss of control over alcohol use, and the limitation is the fact that the patient can no longer safely drink.

Describe and explain the following forms of denial:

- Refusing to face facts: Refusing to do a serious alcohol history, refusing to acknowledge negative consequences of use, rejecting clear evidence of tolerance, and refusing to go to AA meetings.
- Minimizing the facts: Understating negative consequences, tolerance, and so forth.

Topic 2: Step 1—Acceptance

Twelve-Step Facilitation Therapy Manual, pp. 39–40

Alcoholics Anonymous

- Avoiding: Sleeping a lot, becoming socially isolated, or becoming compulsive (addictive) in some other way, such as work or eating.
- Exaggerating others' use in an effort to "normalize" one's own use.
- Blaming someone/something else for alcohol use (a bad marriage, family conflicts, feeling depressed, etc.), as opposed to accepting the fact that cravings for alcohol are responsible for use.
- Bargaining: Trying to limit or control either the amount or type of alcohol used or when it is used.
- Rationalizing: Making up "good" reasons (usually ones that will get sympathy) for drinking.

Work with patients to list some of the ways in which they are denying their powerlessness and the limitation of alcoholism.

The therapist should now provide a brief summary of AA: It is a peer-help movement (a fellowship) that was started by a physician and a stockbroker who had tried their best to control their alcohol use over many years, only to conclude defeat. If it would be helpful, read the following excerpt:

> Most of us have been unwilling to admit we were real alcoholics. No person likes to think he is bodily and mentally different from his fellows. Therefore, it is not surprising that our drinking careers have been characterized by countless vain attempts to prove we could drink like other people. The idea that somehow, someday he will control and enjoy his

(Continued)

(Continued)

drinking is the great obsession of every abnormal drinker. The persistent illusion is astonishing. Many pursue it into the gates of insanity or death. ("Alcoholics Anonymous," p. 30)

Explain that the fellowship of AA was founded on this simple idea: Some people, for some reason, simply could not stop their use of alcohol by relying on individual willpower alone; instead, they had to come to terms with the need to abstain from alcohol altogether and to seek support from others in making whatever changes were necessary to do so.

Explain that AA is based on the following key ideas:

- There is no cure for alcoholism; no treatment will enable an alcoholic to drink safely.
- Abstinence—staying sober One Day at a Time—is the only viable option for alcoholics.

Recovery Tasks – Meetings

Reading

- Self-reliance is not enough, and the support of peers with the same problem is vital to sustained recovery.

Finally, the therapist should review the main goals of AA to make sure that the patient clearly understands the following:

- The goal of AA is to avoid that first drink.
- AA asks its members not to think about forever, but rather to focus on each day of sobriety.
- AA is not looking for perfection. Slips are less important than what one does about them. Progress is more important than perfection.

SOURCE: Nowinski, J., Baker, S., & Carroll, K. (1999). *A clinical research guide for therapists treating individuals with alcohol abuse and dependence.* National Institute on Alcohol Abuse and Alcoholism [NIAAA] Project MATCH Monograph Series, Volume 1. (NIH Publication No. 94-3722) National Institutes of Health, NIAAA. Rockville, MD: NIAAA.

Various additional TSF approach findings highlighted multiple benefits of AA attendance and engagement: at a 16-year follow-up, 70% of participants regularly attending AA at least 27 weeks out of the year were abstinent at the 16-year mark thereby supporting a "dose response" theory of the more AA, the better the projected outcome toward recovery, which was also noted in Project MATCH findings (Babor & Del Boca, 2003; Kaskutas, 2009); approximately half attending AA/12-step meetings were remaining abstinent at 1-, 5- and 8-year marks compared with only 20% showing abstinence if not attending AA/12-step meetings (Kaskutas, 2009); TSF participants showed higher rates of abstinence related to other drugs of abuse as well (Babor & Del Boca, 2003); and, participants of Project MATCH who reported AA involvement were more inclined to achieve sustained abstinence regardless of either of the three treatment approaches they had been assigned (Kaskutas, 2009). Specifically, Kaskutas noted when looking at TSF, CBT, and MET comparisons in the research, "In the Project MATCH outpatient arm, rates of alcohol abstinence were significantly higher for those treated in TSF at 1 year and 3 years" (2009, p. 5). Finally, additional analyses used sophisticated statistical tools to address research challenges about AA attendance and noted evidence of causality with beneficial recovery progress seen as AA attendance increased, especially in those Project MATCH participants in the outpatient treatment level (Magura, Cleland, & Tonigan, 2013). It is particularly noteworthy that Magura and colleagues highlighted "clinicians are justified in recommending AA to their patients as an effective tool of recovery" (2013, p. 384). Resources that remain key to the addiction counselor utilizing a TSF approach include workbooks such as *A Gentle Path through the Twelve Steps, Revised Edition*, that provide innovative strategies for helping clients develop a family tree of addiction, for example, or skills at developing self-affirmations while making recovery-oriented changes with work on each of the 12 steps (Carnes, 1993). Thus, TSF is seen as an important evidence-based intensive addictions treatment approach. It is important to avoid confusing support such as Alcoholics Anonymous with TSF, as the 12-step groups themselves are not to be considered professional therapy. The professional work is conducted by TSF-trained counselors.

Box 11.2: ONE PERSON'S ACCOUNT OF RECOVERY FROM CANNABIS USE DISORDER

Micro-Encapsulated Calcification of the Human Psyche: My Odyssey With Marijuana

Reefer, hooch, bang, smoke, ill, chronic, "bo," red, skunk, sensimilia, gold, boat—by any other name I did them all and they were and are all the same, at least as it relates to the impact it has had on my life, the people, places, things, situations, playmates, and playgrounds—all of which have been impacted on and by my decision to engage in this grand, episodic experience.

I am finally grateful today for the prolonged and episodic journey this substance took me on, for I would not be here today had it not placed me on this trajectory combined later with those important, sometimes daily, choices of recovery. I wish to submit and prove to you that the use of marijuana uninterrupted leads to a disease model that is intractable but curable. It is a disease to the extent that my choices and decisions for an extended amount of years into my life were solely predicated, first, on my ability to acquire, and then use this substance. It impacted my feelings and sensibility to the extent that I could neither feel normal nor operate wholesomely without this substance within my metabolism. The great fortune of this experience is that I am the 1 in 99 who "catches a miracle" and am healed without having to entertain the classic recovery system. I do not advise or recommend this for anyone viewing this.

I am a proponent of the disease model because my life was unmanageable; I could not proficiently conduct the affairs of my life (family, home, career, hopes, dreams, and aspirations) while

(Continued)

(Continued)

actively romancing this substance. The cunning and baffling component of my use was that I felt I was operating normally because, from the psycho and pharmacological aspects of a disease, I was in what I classify as a state of eroding calcification. This supports the science that says that use of this substance creates an antigen that corrodes the brain, endorphins that control the pleasure centers in our brains, which creates the same metaphoric state as does the corrosion of the terminals of a battery. This clogs the natural electronic mechanisms that control our ability to live in the real here and now.

Looking back, in retrospect, this substance's utility lay in the fact that it created a prophylactic cocoon that, while permeable, covered my intellect and emotions resultantly, granting me the sensation that all was fine since I was maintaining the semblance of functionality, which it did. But moreover, what it did was to stifle my self-actualization and reaching my full God-given potential. I was mired into a prolonged period of mediocrity that became my new aspiration and my new norm.

In short order, after September 4, 1988, I made a conscious and moral decision to simply not touch this substance again. I still loved and craved it, but I simply did not touch. Resultantly since that time, I, for a period of time, attended Narcotics Anonymous; counseled others who shared this disease; completed my degree in education; completed 29 years in education; assisted in founding a charter school; became a trainer on diversity, leadership, and athletics; became an athletic administrator and an award-winning coach—winning two state football championships in the process; and having countless scholars and athletes to refer to me as "Dad" and "Coach." I am the father of five children and six grandchildren, and retiree from the state educational system.

SOURCE: HB Harris. Respectfully submitted by Cheikh we Sizwe (aka HBH—hotep ase heri).

Cognitive Behavior Therapy (CBT)

As Lewis (2014) notes, cognitive and behavior theories combined to become a major approach known as cognitive behavioral therapy (CBT) for intensive treatment settings and will be examined next as a brief overview is provided.

First, it is important to review the contributions of the CBT model for addictive disorders as first developed by Beck, Wright, Newman, and Liese (1993). A major emphasis in the application of CBT counseling those individuals with addictive disorders involves a person's cognitive beliefs (distorted thinking) accompanied by the person's response (extreme feelings, negative moods, and cravings for mood-altering drugs or behaviors) that result in actions (use of drugs/behaviors or alternative coping to sustain recovery) (Lewis, 2014). See Table 11.1.

Greater emphasis by the CBT counselor is placed on helping the client to become clearer on key cognitive beliefs that interfere with recovery or perpetuate harmful use or behavior. Challenges to automatic thoughts, such as "I cannot get clean" or "I do not know how to stop drinking, I am helpless" are a major part of the counselor's intensive work with the client diagnosed with an addictive use disorder. Other examples of cognitive distortions that wreak havoc in the person striving toward recovery from

Table 11.1	Cognitive Behavioral Theory: Client and Counselor Perspectives	

CBT Key Highlights	Client With Substance Use Disorder or Related Addictive Disorder, such as Gambling Disorder	Counselor's Observations
Cognitive Beliefs	Self beliefs: "There is something really wrong with me to drink like that, but somehow I should be able to figure out how to quit when the time comes . . . maybe tomorrow?" "I am not even sure I should even try to change since something is really bad wrong with me." "Maybe I'm one of those people that isn't supposed to recover." "I should resign myself to just being like this—no use trying to change."	*Distorted thinking* like: "I cannot get sober" "I will never get better" "Other people might be able to do this changing to recover but I am not one of them" "I give up" "I don't really need counseling or any help; I have faith that change will happen if it's God's will"
Response – Emotional	Range of emotions can include generalized anxiety, deep sadness, loneliness, self-pity, rage, confusion, feeling torn, feeling defeated, depressed, hurt, guilt, shame, or grief.	A *range of affect* displayed, such as tearful affect, resignation, flat affect, angry affect, avoidance of eye contact, sad affect, labile affect, bereaved, or confused affect. *Defense mechanisms exhibited to counselor* may be adaptive or maladaptive and include: Blaming, splitting, projection, isolation, minimizing, justifying, denial, or rationalizing (Miller, 2015).
Actions	Continued or return to substance use or addictive processes/behaviors; refusal of healthy alternative behaviors *or* conversely, increased counseling sessions, increased attendance at recovery support meetings, and adding other health-enhancing actions.	Cancellation of counseling sessions or not showing up for scheduled sessions; leaving intensive addiction treatment setting against medical advice (AMA); attending sessions under the influence; discontinuing recovery support activities/meetings *or* conversely, increased requests for intensifying counseling, transfer to higher level of care, increased recovery meeting attendance with increased sharing about cravings, self-beliefs, and addictive behaviors.

addictive disorders include rigid thinking, such as polarizing all-or-nothing thoughts. For example, "I will never recover, it is impossible," "I will never drink again," or "no one really cares about me at all"—these comments often keep the recovering person stuck in what the 12-step groups often refer to as "stinking thinking," and CBT provides evidence-based strategies to help manage cognitive distortions in more productive ways.

First, in a CBT-addictive counseling (CBT-AC) approach, Lewis (2014) stresses the importance of setting the counseling session agenda each time in working with the client. The importance of the agenda is underscored when working with addiction issues and clients when "discussions too often steer in directions where not much is accomplished" (Lewis, 2014, p. 124). Emotions are also explored that are connected to automatic thinking. One can see how depressed or anxious moods can interfere with thinking about using drugs or behaviors to escape such moods. Interventions by the counselor then, such as a mood check, are included in each counseling session (Lewis, 2014). Thought-stopping techniques geared toward an understanding of the addictive cycle are critical in CBT-AC, and clients learn new ways to change negative thinking by using CBT-AC. Often this includes a daily thought record to help the client become more aware of distorted thinking resulting in harmful behaviors, like skipping meetings with an addiction counselor or going out for just an hour of gambling, drinking, or using other harmful substances when trying to achieve sobriety. As Miller (2015) noted, the same negative patterns can be reversed using CBT-AC as applied to a recovery process of hopeful thinking, healthy emotional response, followed by actions that support recovery.

In addition, important evidence-based screening tools can aid the counselor in quickly and regularly assessing the emotional responses and emotional status while using the CBT-AC approach and include the Beck Depression Inventory-II (BDI-II; Beck, Steer, & Brown, 1996), the Beck Anxiety Inventory (BAI; Beck, 1993), or the Symptom Checklist 90, for example. These assessment tools can provide further screening information as the client is working toward goals of recovery. Further, homework assignments to incorporate new thinking patterns and self-statements oriented toward recovery, for example, are added ways to help clients using the CBT-AC approach.

In summary, many intensive addiction programs incorporate a number of the previously described elements of CBT-AC as part of the treatment approach. This CBT-AC approach is considered a prominent evidence-based and effective therapeutic approach in the intensive treatment of addictive disorders.

Relational Model

With the heightened recognition that women, too, are severely affected by addictive disorders, research that was advanced in the 1970s by Carol Gilligan and Jean Baker Miller established the important relational model as a preferred theory for counseling women. Cultural considerations pertaining uniquely to women remain an additional contribution of the model and became part of its identity, thus named relational-cultural theory

(CSAT, 2015). The importance of women's unique ways of being in the world stressed the importance of community and connection with others as critical for well-being rather than a counseling focus on "self" primarily (CSAT, 2015). Knapp (2004) wrote about women's unique struggles with appetites and addictive processes as "a much broader constellation of hungers and longings and needs . . . experienced with particular intensity and in particularly painful ways by women—to partake of the world, to feel a sense of abundance and possibility about life" (p. 2). In the intensive addiction treatment setting, then, it is important for women to also acquire and practice tools to foster healthy connections with other women, to address the loss of the relationship with the predominant drug or behavior relative to the addictive process, and to therapeutically share hidden shame in order to further break long-standing codes of silence that prevent important connections with others (CSAT, 2015). Another tool, Women for Sobriety (WFS), provides additional mutual help resources toward recovery that sets itself apart from 12-step groups and has grown slowly since the 1970s (Travis, 2009). Various addictive processes, such as eating disorders, can also involve specialized training and a multidisciplinary team with nutritional specialists, for example. In summary, the use of the relational-cultural model is an important one to consider for intensive treatment when working with women and recovery goals.

Motivational Interviewing (MI)

The first text on MI was published in 1991, *Motivational Interviewing: Preparing People for Change*, and is now in its third edition in 2013. The authors outlined an approach, the MI model (Miller & Rollnick, 2013), and it is now commonly adapted by many treatment clinicians throughout a variety of settings such as health care, correctional settings, and social work (Walters, Cornett, & Vader, 2012). Miller was able to utilize person-centered theory as developed by Carl Rogers (Miller, 2014) and apply it with a keen understanding of the addictive struggles with motivation, ambivalence, denial, and distortion to develop the effective MI model (Miller, 2015). MI continues its evolution toward training others in vital elements of client change talk, also found in solution-focused brief approaches, along with the importance of reflecting empathy. In addition, the MI model has often been associated with the transtheoretical model (TTM), yet Miller and Rollnick assert that "MI is not meant to be a comprehensive theory of change, and the popular TTM stages of change are not an essential part of MI" (2013, p. 35). Rather, TTM stages of change, as shown in Figure 11.2, can be complementary.

Efforts continue to specify exact training methods to achieve maximum use of MI, such as in hospital trauma centers (Darnell, Dunn, Atkins, Ingraham, & Zatzick, 2016). Many tools exist to help supervisors ensure MI is being utilized; counseling tapes are reviewed and scored with an important supervisory tool, the Motivational Interviewing Treatment Integrity system, otherwise known as the MITI (Darnell et al., 2016; Walters et al., 2012), as more research studies continue to try to isolate the keys to how MI best works in order for training in this model to be more consistent. Roadblocks to MI are noted in Figure 11.3.

Figure 11.2 Readiness to Change: Examples

Readiness to Change

Key concepts – Stages of Change

Example

Open Solution-Oriented Question: How willing are you to change what you do about getting drunk?

1. **Maintenance** = Very willing, I made significant changes and have not gotten drunk for <u>MORE than 6 months</u>.

2. **Action** = Willing, I made significant changes and have not gotten drunk in <u>LESS than 6 months AND I entered this intensive treatment program</u>.

3. **Preparation** = Somewhat, I intend to make changes in the <u>next 30 days</u> *and make a written plan to enter intensive treatment.*

4. **Contemplation** = Not yet, but I intend to in the <u>next 6 months</u>.

5. **Precontemplation** = Not at all now, and I do NOT intend to in the <u>next 6 months</u>.

✓ **Assess** readiness to change = MOTIVATION continuously
✓ **Avoid** treating clients as if in Action Stage
✓ **Set** realistic goals
✓ **Help** change <u>process</u> match the <u>stage</u> of change
✓ **Remember**, change is rarely linear and consider cultural impacts.

SOURCE: DiClemente, Doyle, & Donovan, 2009.

Figure 11.3 Roadblocks to MI

Counselor: *Whoa*

- Frequent questions, especially closed questions
- Bias toward one side or the other
- Being the EXPERT
- Jargon and labels
- Close-minded to complex individual issues
- BLAME Game—watch those "you" statements

SOURCE: Motivational Interviewing Tips as adapted by Veach, from Miller & Rollnick, 2013, pp. 39–47.

One acronym, OARS, has been used to highlight key elements of MI as depicted in the list in Box 11.3.

Box 11.3: Aids to Foster MI

Counselor: GO

OARS+

GO

- **O**pen?
- **A**ffirming client
- **R**eflection skills are very important
- **S**ummaries: Brief and overall
- **+** Help client identify change talk (acknowledge, validate, recognize, underscore, scaling, pros, cons, prompt, "what if . . .?," exceptions, future pace)

SOURCE: Motivational Interviewing Tips as adapted by Veach, from Miller & Rollnick, 2013, pp. 62–73.

While MI efficacy is well known from the Project MATCH MET study findings in the mid-1990s (Project MATCH Research Group, 1998d), increasing attention has centered on the utility and sustainability of strict adherence to MI in the field due to the extensive costs involved to provide necessary training, extensive supervision taping review with specific MI feedback, and treatment fidelity (McCambridge, 2013). Important findings note the challenges of proficiency in foundational skills of MI involving effective open questions and complex reflections that require consistent clinical supervision and review of taped sessions (Darnell et al., 2016). However, for those trained and credentialed in MI, it is an important evidence-based counseling approach with prominent benefits for intensive addiction treatment settings.

Brain Stimulation Approaches

In other developments, particularly important in the intensive addictions counseling settings, addiction medicine and the brain are gaining in utilization. Pioneers in the neurobiological science of addiction and recovery have added substantially to how we understand and treat addiction. The addiction counselor of today is best served by understanding his or her role in a multidisciplinary team, especially in terms of how he or she can communicate effectively in the language of the physician specializing in addiction medicine regarding brain stimulation methods that can be used with clients. Briefly consider, for example, how key studies are now examining neuroadaptations of the PFC (prefrontal cortex), the executive decision-making area in the brain. More emphasis is being focused on brain dysregulation issues causing major problems in the brain's inhibitory pathways (how the brain applies the brakes on drug use). Feil and colleagues (2010) emphasized new intensive treatments that involve brain stimulation techniques targeting the PFC as an important tool to help reduce cravings and relapse. Other novel approaches involve invasive brain stimulation, such as DBS (deep brain stimulus), which requires surgical implantation of a device in the brain that can be programmed remotely. DBS has been shown to help with movement disorders such as Parkinson's disease, for example. Also, noninvasive brain stimulation (NIBS) techniques involve electrodes sending electrical signaling through the scalp (Martinez & Trifilieff, 2015). These newer promising methods are transcranial electrical and magnetic stimulations (tES and TMS). Both methods are presenting new additional ways to add to addiction treatment by primarily giving new brain information about brain circuitry and improved ways to view different brain regions, especially related to cravings, triggers to use, inhibitory pathways, and frontal cortex damage by addictive processes (Martinez & Trifilieff, 2015). When addiction counselors continue to seek professional education and training about brain stimulation techniques, the counselor can advocate on the client's behalf for these additional approaches to treat addiction. The counselor is also equipped with knowledge that can help answer the client's questions when they see news reports that are increasingly focusing on brain stimulation addiction approaches.

Other Considerations for Intensive Counseling of Individuals with Addictive Disorders

Alcohol and Other Addictive Substances

Considerable research indicates that the addiction counselor needs to consider the amount of brain damage done by years of addictive patterns. Using sophisticated brain imaging equipment such as MRI, PET, and SPECT scanning, brain changes are found in the prefrontal cortex area, the orbito-frontal cortex, and the anterior cingulate areas—all are involved in frontal lobe executive decision making and thinking and can be especially vulnerable to the effects of alcohol, a powerful neurotoxic drug (Feil et al., 2010). For alcohol, other uses of brain stimulation were reported to reduce cravings in a transcranial direct current stimulation (tDCS) study (Broggio et al. as cited in Feil et al., 2010). Therefore, intensive treatment is increasingly taking into consideration ways to help treat the damaged brain of someone with a moderate to severe alcohol use disorder. Feil and colleagues write, "Preliminary neuropsychological studies revealed an association between impaired cognitive inhibitory control and alcohol dependence" (2010, p. 263). Further, "in heavy drinkers, behavioral inhibitory deficits were related to an increased risk of developing alcohol dependence" (p. 263), thus educating those working with clients struggling with alcohol use disorders that their particular brain structure may have made them more susceptible to an alcohol use disorder. Imagine how clients would respond to intensive group counseling sessions where the group topic centered around knowledge that the client had physical vulnerabilities to addiction that had nothing to do with their willpower, moral compass, religious orientation, or psyche. What do you think a client would experience if you could explain to them that the way that their brain is structured may have had a significant impact on their susceptibility to the addictive disorder(s) they face? More brain studies have identified other preexisting structural changes including reduced DLPFC (dorsolateral pre-frontal cortex) brain volume matter, decreased DLPFC electrical activity (often associated with increased impulsive behavior), and lower electrical activity in the orbitofrontal cortex (OFC) and the anterior cingulate cortex (ACC), to name only a few of the findings from brain research in the past decade (Feil et al., 2010). While the counselor does not need to teach sophisticated brain anatomy to clients, it can be useful to help clients understand there are identified areas of the brain that research has discovered are very important in the development of addictive disorders. For example, the ACC can be described as a unique bridge in the brain between cognitive functioning and emotions (Stevens, Hurley, & Taber, 2011).

Tobacco

In the review of intensive treatment for tobacco addiction, much of the focus, interestingly, for a highly addictive drug has included less intensive approaches. As is emphasized in research (Feil et al., 2010), tobacco use disorders involve chronic use and frequent relapse as many work to recover. Nicotine craving can begin within minutes of the last cigarette, with increasing cravings that are sustained for hours. Much of the current approach with tobacco cessation includes education; medication, such as nicotine patches where the person can slowly withdraw from the main addicting agent, nicotine; and limited coaching from a health professional. Unlike many other addictive drug treatment approaches, tobacco and nicotine do not usually involve intensive treatment approaches and most of the emphasis has been focused on abstinence as the

Box 11.4: Learning Activity

Consider how you would describe the research findings about preexisting structural differences in the brain that might predispose someone to a severe alcohol use disorder.

Would you use any photos from the Internet? Or draw diagrams? Or look for a YouTube video? Or search SAMHSA for materials?

What obstacles might you encounter in trying to explain this information to your client?

As an activity, find a peer student and prepare a 15-minute explanation of brain basics and addictive disorders.

At the conclusion of your presentation to your peer, provide the student peer with a questionnaire or short test that evaluates what learning the student peer was able to attain from your presentation. List at least three new ideas you could add or change in your presentation to make the presentation clearer to your clients.

primary recovery goal. Findings show how difficult recovery can be since even small amounts of nicotine have an observable effect on the brain and has been shown to improve memory, executive functioning, attention, and more important frontal lobe functions (Feil et al., 2010). When ceasing nicotine use, brain studies show effects that the brain is operating less efficiently, such as reduced frontal lobe and executive functioning. Newer treatment approaches find benefits from brain stimulation studies showing they "transiently reduce cigarette craving and cigarette consumption" (Feil et al., 2010, p. 270), especially when targeting brain stimulation to the frontal lobe regions of the brain.

Heroin

Often, a person diagnosed with a moderate to severe heroin use disorder will be referred to intensive addiction treatment. Heroin is considered the most abused of the opiate classification of drugs (Feil et al., 2010). Frequently, however, the first attempts at recovery do not often occur in a residential setting. Most current intensive treatment approaches involve medication-assisted therapy (MAT) approaches (NIDA, 2015). Contrary to popular media, heroin withdrawal is not considered a life-threatening condition and therefore does not require hospitalization for withdrawal. Heroin is an opiate and depressant, therefore, when withdrawal occurs, it is a highly distressing experience that clients often describe as the worst experience of their lives. They may report they feel like they are dying due to intense flu-like symptoms, for example, yet, medically the withdrawal is not seen as a medical emergency. Thus, the withdrawal issues are critically important to manage in the early days of the intensive addiction setting to enhance treatment retention. Brain studies also suggest deterioration specific to opiate use can damage the disinhibition functions resulting in greater risk-taking and poorer decision making such as leaving treatment early (Feil et al., 2010). Grey matter loss persists even after long-term abstinence according to certain studies (Feil et al., 2010). Medical teams respond quickly to begin the regimen that is necessary for heroin withdrawal management. Without those resources to manage the intense withdrawal, many patients will leave treatment early to avoid the intense distress of opiate withdrawal. Once withdrawal is stabilized by the medical team, especially if being treated with a MAT, harm-reduction approach such as methadone or buprenorphine, counselors will notice the client may be able to participate more fully in group or individual counseling sessions. MAT has been increasingly cited as a primary approach to treat opiate use disorders. Recent research involving long-term follow-up notes that one of the main medications, buprenorphine, is found to reduce opiate cravings while blocking the "high" if other opiates are used, thus discouraging slips and relapses while increasing sustained abstinence from opiates (NIDA, 2015). Data indicated that even after just over three years, those who were abstaining had increased to nearly two-thirds of the study group with less than 10% continuing to meet *DSM-5* criteria for an opiate use disorder. Heroin use disorders are complicated and "consistent with other reports indicating that some users of prescription opioids switch to heroin, 1 in 10 users who had not used heroin before the start of the study reported injecting heroin by month 30" (NIDA, 2015, p. 2). Increasing research into more effective strategies for heroin and other opiate use disorders is needed. Currently, MAT approaches have been shown to improve outcomes in the treatment of heroin addiction.

Cocaine

The stimulant drug cocaine remains a prominent drug of addiction and is often described as "one of the most highly reinforcing drugs available" (Feil et al., 2010, p. 252). In its concentrated and smokeable form, crack cocaine has made recovery difficult to achieve and sustain. As with nicotine and cigarette smoking, the speed of the reinforcement is almost instantaneous. Since smoking can introduce the mood-altering substance in the bloodstream within 4 seconds, it is no wonder that any addictive drug in smokeable form will be extremely difficult in sustaining recovery efforts. Smoking crack cocaine, then, is one of the most problematic since frequent use can quickly lead to a severe cocaine use disorder (CUD). Intravenous, snorting, or other methods of cocaine use remain problematic, with effective CUD-specific treatments elusive (Leeman, Robinson, Waters, & Sofuoglu, 2014). Several research findings point out that individuals with a severe cocaine use disorder have substantial brain damage and "display impaired memory, attention and decision-making" with "dysfunctional inhibitory control of impulsive behaviors" (Feil et al., 2010, p. 256). Cues and cravings for cocaine are being investigated because of the strength of craving that seems to be much more difficult to manage (Leeman et al., 2014). Brain stimulation techniques have shown particularly compelling results, especially with reducing cravings when specific areas of the prefrontal cortex were targeted (Feil et al., 2010). Others highlight problems, as a result of the pronounced brain damage, which may make therapies that are highly focused on cognitive abilities, such as CBT-AC, more difficult and less effective for those in treatment for severe cocaine use disorders (Leeman et al., 2014). The National Registry of Evidence-based Programs and Practices (NREPP) lists one particular evidence-based treatment approach for CUD reviewed in 2007 that involves supportive-expressive psychotherapy (NREPP, 2016). This approach involves time-limited sessions utilizing reflective listening and expressive approaches to help individuals aged 18–55 diagnosed with CUD begin to process their struggles in a more expressive manner.

Further, "unlike tobacco, alcohol or opioid addiction, no effective pharmacological treatments are available for CUD" (Leeman et al., 2014, p. 471), yet promising areas using techniques to modulate brain functioning in attentional bias by moving the focus of attention away from drug use–related cues are yielding new ways to help improve retention in treatment as noted by Leeman and colleagues. Evidence indicates there are limited options specific to improving treatment outcomes for CUD, but it is important to continue to add to our evidence-based knowledge with approaches such as the supportive-expressive psychotherapy as noted. Additional research would contribute to our work with clients to help establish and sustain recovery.

Process Addictions

Intensive treatment is also provided for certain process addictive disorders. As previously noted, the classification of process addictions as an accepted diagnostic category is currently in flux. Adding to the evolving professional views of process addictions as a diagnosable disorder, noted addiction specialists emphasize that neuroscience has shown that "process addictions, including food, sex, shopping and gambling . . . based on an understanding that both psychoactive drugs and certain behaviors that produce a surge of dopamine in the midbrain are the biological substrate for addictive behavior" (Smith, 2012, p. 1). However, a wide variety of treatment approaches exist for individuals with eating disorders, gambling, and sexual disorders, for example, that do not provide counseling from a process addiction perspective. In addition, there are no evidence-based programs listed in NREPP that address food, sex, or Internet addiction at this time. For the focus of this section, intensive counseling that utilizes process addiction approaches will be provided.

Food Addiction

Behaviors or processes that addiction specialists deem as an addictive process remain controversial (Veach, Rogers, Moro, Essic, & McMullen, 2016; Yau, Gottlieb, Krasna, & Potenza, 2014). It is no surprise, then, that intensive treatment for what would be described as food addiction varies widely. Yau and colleagues indicate that very little research has been conducted to study treatment comparisons, but in many intensive treatment settings for food addiction, a combination of CBT, dialectical behavior therapy, family therapy, interpersonal psychotherapy, nutrition counseling, medication-assisted therapies using antidepressant medications, and self-help group encouragement are the primary approaches. A major difference from other substance-related addictive disorders pertains to the initial emphasis on abstinence. While abstaining from nutritional foods is not an option, some treatments focus on abstinence from sugar, often showing brain changes similar to other mood-altering drugs (Yau et al., 2014). Treatment outcomes can use tools such as the *Yale Food Addiction Scale Version 2.0* (Gearhardt, Corbin, & Brownell, 2016) to track progress being made at regular intervals.

The graphic produced by the Office on Women's Health (2012) is one example of important educational information that can be provided to clients in an intensive addiction counseling treatment setting who are struggling with anorexia, one of the eating disorders that addiction specialists often regard as a process addiction. Clients can be educated on different approaches, including the evolving science regarding eating disorders and process addictions, while also learning the various intensive treatment options. Next, a process addiction that has had a substantial amount of clinical focus but is not yet a recognized diagnosis in the *DSM-5* pertains to addictive sexual disorders.

Sex Addiction

For intensive treatment to help clients struggling with addictive disorders related to sexual behaviors or processes, various treatment approaches are available (Veach et al., 2016). More research is needed on the most effective models, but cognitive behavioral therapies (CBT) are often indicated as well as treatment of hypersexual-related emotional regulation with stress management techniques (Murray, Pope, & Willis, 2017). Treatment can include a holistic approach to address impulse control techniques, emotional regulation therapies, abstaining from harmful sexual behaviors and triggers or cues that promote harmful sexual behaviors (compulsive viewing of Internet pornography sites, for example), referral to 12-step support groups, relapse prevention, couples therapies, and addressing other addictive disorders, when present (Murray et al., 2017).

Medications are often included in treatment of sexual addictive disorders, especially antidepressants, and counselors are urged to support communication between the client and the medical prescribing team so clients will make progress (Murray et al., 2017). Additional research is needed in sexual addictive disorders, especially pertaining to vulnerable populations such as youth, women, racial and ethnic groups, older adults, and sex offenders (CSAT, 2015; Murray et al., 2017).

In her seminal text on loved ones living with someone suffering with a sexual addictive disorder, Dr. Jennifer Schneider emphasized the key areas of couples counseling that should also be a part of intensive treatment for a sexual addictive disorder (1988) and include professional counseling with an understanding of sexual addiction; knowledge about 12-step groups such as Sex and Love Addicts Anonymous (slfaaws.org), Sexaholics Anonymous (SA.org), and S-Anon (sanon.org) for family and friends seeking support; and an openness to facing one's own addictive relationship cycle, echoing again that an addictive disorder negatively impacts the health of the family as well as the addict. Couples and family counseling are important areas of continued professional development for the addiction counselor.

Technology Addiction: Internet and Online Gaming

Internet addiction disorder (IAD), as outlined by Weinstein, Feder, Rosenberg, and Dannon, can be described as "excessive or poorly controlled preoccupations, urges, or behaviors regarding Internet use that lead to impairment or distress" (2014, p. 99), yet treatment remains controversial (Young & de Abreu, 2011). However, in China and South Korea, intensive treatment and research focused on IAD, which is also considered a public health crisis, is advancing (Cash, Rae, Steel, & Winkler, 2012). Preliminary evidence in the United States, mostly testing CBT approaches with Internet addiction (Cash et al., 2012; Weinstein et al., 2014) and Internet gaming disorders, yields positive findings. Diagnosis of IAD remains under the section needing further study in the current *DSM-5* (American Psychiatric Association, 2013). Specialists in IAD, similar to approaches with food addictive disorders, do not advocate total abstinence from technology and the Internet (Cash et al., 2012). Of the limited residential programs for IAD, a program in Washington called reSTART offers detoxification from technology for 45 to 90 days in conjunction with multidisciplinary and multitheoretical approaches involving CBT, adventure-based counseling, brain stimulation, mindfulness, animal-assisted therapies, and 12-step work, to highlight a few of the key approaches included in the reSTART intensive treatment model (Cash et al., 2012).

Particular attention to 12-step groups such as On-Line Gamers Anonymous, begun in 2002 with a TSF counseling approach, is a recommended intensive treatment model (Kiraly, Nanygyorgy, Griffiths, & Demetrovics, 2014) and importantly, initial evidence views the TSF approach for IAD as beneficial. Because of increasing evidence suggesting greater problems with attention deficit and impaired executive functioning in frontal lobe areas in the brain, treatment has also included pharmacotherapy to help address the neurological components of IAD (Weinstein et al., 2014). Other studies of medications that might help in treating IAD (Han, Hwang, & Renshaw, 2010) noted that early studies show utility with an atypical antidepressant, bupropion SR, for Internet and gaming addiction patients. Related, but considered a unique process addiction by Griffiths, Kuss, and Demetrovics (2014), is the social networking addiction characterized by substantial impairment in overall functioning with increasing compulsive use of social networking sites while limiting interactions outside of computer access, especially pertaining to face-to-face social activities. Ongoing and new research that yields effective evidence-based approaches is critically needed in these rapidly intensifying addictive process disorders related to the all-encompassing umbrella concept of technology addiction.

In summary, whether intensive treatment is indicated for substance or process addictions, continued research, especially in personalized medical adjunctive therapies and evidence-based counseling approaches, is important to understand best practice. In the following section, we will look further at placement criteria and levels of care that should be considered in the spectrum of care options for individuals struggling with substance or process use disorders.

Intensive Levels of Care and Placement Criteria

As noted in Chapter 7, the American Society of Addiction Medicine (ASAM), produced guidelines for counselors to guide decisions related to levels of care for substance use disorders. The guideline, *The ASAM Criteria: Treatment Criteria for Addictive, Substance-related, and Co-Occurring Conditions* provides options for care ranging from weekly individual outpatient sessions to intensive medical monitoring in a hospital when diagnostic criteria are met for a severe substance use disorder with severe withdrawal complications (2016). Six therapeutic dimensions are considered: physical withdrawal or intoxication concerns, physical medical conditions, emotional/psychological issues, motivation to change, relapse risks, and recovery environment supports or barriers. Depending on how each of the dimensions are impacted by substance use disorder(s), guidance is provided for the corresponding and most appropriate level of care. The American Society of Addiction Medicine (ASAM) criteria includes 4 main levels of care:

Level I – *Outpatient*;

Level II – *Intensive Outpatient Treatment/Partial Hospitalization*;

Level III – *Residential services*; and

Level IV – *Medically managed by a medical team in a hospital unit.*

In this section, we will review the most utilized levels of care with intensive addiction treatment.

Level II: Intensive Outpatient Treatment (IOT) and Partial Hospitalization Programs

Since the early 1990s, IOT and Partial Hospitalization levels of care have served as the primary approach for many individuals, adults and adolescents, diagnosed with a substance use disorder, especially if no prior treatment has been attempted and the level of use disorder is mild or moderate and no medical withdrawal monitoring is required. In 2006, the Center for Substance Abuse Treatment (CSAT) developed a guide for IOP that is available at no cost at www.samhsa.gov as *Treatment Improvement Protocol No. 47* (2006); a Quick Guide is also useful as a quick reference tool and can be electronically downloaded at no cost. The following highlights IOT features:

- 6–30 counseling and session hours per week
- step-up and step-down levels of care that differ in intensity and overall length of stay
- a minimum of three days/evenings per week over the course of three months is highly recommended, followed by outpatient continuing care, usually once per week for approximately 12 weeks
- core services can include, but are not limited to

  o ongoing assessment and individualized treatment planning conducted with the client and at times, family/loved ones;
  o group, individual, and/or family counseling;
  o psychoeducational sessions;
  o introduction to support groups, such as 12-step groups;
  o relapse prevention focus;
  o substance use monitoring with random breathalyzer or urine drug screens conducted; and
  o career counseling or employee assistance program coordination.

- Partial hospitalization services are longer sessions per day and per week, and may also include

  - outpatient detoxification
  - child care

(CSAT, 2006, pp. 4–5)

Level III: Residential Addictions Treatment

Special considerations that are best cared for in a residential setting, Level III care, remain an important option for some individuals with more complicated substance use disorders. Residential settings can be the preferred level of care for those with additional challenges, such as the older client with severe addictive use disorder who also may have deficits in physical areas such as cognitive abilities or mild dementia, often due to alcohol abuse over many years, for example. Other individuals that may benefit from residential care for extended periods of treatment include adolescents, medical professionals such as doctors or nurses, clients with a history of chronic relapsing, and individuals with other mental health issues that are interfering with optimal response to addictive disorder outpatient treatment. There is no set timeframe that works uniformly for all clients; rather, individualized care planning will guide the recommendations for a residential treatment stay.

In conclusion, this chapter provided an overview of a very complex picture regarding intensive treatment for substance use disorders. With the focus of this textbook on the full spectrum, ranging from experimental and risky use to addictive processes, this chapter served to introduce key aspects of intensive treatment and approaches prevalent in the United States. Models of placement, such as the American Society of Addiction Medicine's Patient Placement Critieria-2, are important for counselors to use for determining appropriate levels of care. Continued effective counseling approaches combined with beneficial research discoveries remain important needs for intensive addiction treatment. Other important complications often seen in intensive treatment for use disorders, such as psychiatric conditions, are discussed in the following chapter on cross addictions and comorbidities.

Skills in Action

Case Study 11.1: Alise

Alise is a 34-year-old mother of two children (ages 10 and 13) and recently separated from her partner of 18 years. She has been a full-time high school teacher for 8 years, with frequent complaints about job stress and relationship dissatisfaction.

She is referred to see you as a counselor due to a recent arrest for DWI while she was vacationing at a beach resort. Her main presenting issue is her stated embarrassment and fears about her recent DWI arrest. She reports difficulty coping with the publicity fears due to her work as a public school teacher and her separation from her partner. She is tearful as she talks about how alone she feels and is having difficulty managing her worries. She is also requesting information about taking some pills to help her reduce anxiety. During your assessment Alise also reveals that she has been drinking wine nearly every day, has given up many activities due to her daily drinking, is finding that she has increased the amount of wine she consumes to be able to experience any relaxation, and in the past 3 months she has noticed that she has a noticeable tremor in her hands when she goes for more than a day without drinking. In addition, she talks about the increasing time that she has spent meeting partners online for sexual activities that contributed to her separation from her partner.

You share with Alise your recommendation for intensive counseling for her alcohol use disorder and further evaluation for her sexual behaviors.

Begin to consider what therapeutic approach(es) might be helpful in your work with Alise.

Imagine that you are in your counseling internship as you consider these questions. In the case study above, what other issues might be important to evaluate while Alise is receiving intensive counseling? Make a list of the possible areas to further explore while she is in intensive treatment. Note how many other screenings or assessments might be helpful in your care with her. For example, do you need to explore any child neglect or abuse if her children are at risk? If so, how and when would you involve your clinical internship supervisor?

Further areas of concern: Suicide? Self-harm risks? Prescription drug misuse? Anxiety disorder? Risk of HIV or sexually transmitted diseases?

Go online and identify at least one agency in your area that might provide further services for your client. Gather information about how you would contact each of the agencies if you needed to make a referral. For example, if you deemed your client is at high risk of HIV, where would you refer her for further confidential testing?

Experiential Skills Learning Activity

TSF: Attend at least two *open* 12-step meetings, as explained further in Box 11.5.

First, go online and follow the link for AA for Professionals at the AA.org website. Be sure to study the meaning of *open meeting*.

http://www.aa.org/pages/en_US/information-for-professionals

Research the various publications by clicking on each brochure.

It is also important to become familiar with a variety of different 12-step groups, so another activity can involve looking online for at least three other types of 12-step groups to become familiar with how they are structured.

Box 11.5: Additional Learning About 12-Step Meetings

Attending 12-Step Meetings Learning Activity

All genuine education comes about through experience.

— John Dewey

The 12 Steps - Considerations

- 12-step programs began with Alcoholics Anonymous (AA) in 1935 (Spicer, 1993) as two men began meeting regularly to support their abstinence (Kurtz, 1979).
- Twelve unique steps to recovery were written to help guide others in their attempts to live fully; a life-changing approach, *"not a sobriety program but a living program"* (Kurtz, 1979, p. 238).
- AA 2016 WORLD MEMBERSHIP, 2.1 MILLION (AA, 2016b)
- Other 12-step groups include Narcotics Anonymous (NA), Cocaine Anonymous (CA), Al-Anon (those affected by alcoholics), and Nar-Anon (those affected by addicts).
- Twelve-step groups are often both confusing and misinterpreted. AA, for example, "is easily misunderstood without the context of lived experience and meaning-making of the membership as a whole" (van Wormer & Davis, 2003, p. 378).
- An *open meeting* welcomes anyone who chooses to attend, "generally one recovering person speaks to the group about his or her addiction and recovery story, and nonaddicts can attend and listen" (Miller, 2015, p. 233).
- *Closed meetings*, on the other hand, are strictly for those who desire membership in the related 12-step group.
- At Drexel University College of Medicine in Philadelphia, Pennsylvania, attending an open meeting is required of approximately 300 nursing and medical students annually, with goals of increasing awareness and correcting misconceptions about AA (Alcoholics Anonymous World Services, Inc., 2008).
- The *Twelve Traditions*, developed within 12-step groups, are important to read and review carefully because they enable an outsider to better understand the very different mechanics of 12-step group organization and operation "that challenges dominant cultural expectations regarding hierarchy, power, and models of helping" (van Wormer & Davis, 2003, p. 378). Whereas the 12 steps are a guide for individual recovery, the Twelve Traditions serve as a guide for group structure and unity.
- There is no president of AA or any other 12-step group, "our leaders are but trusted servants, they do not govern" (*Narcotics Anonymous*, 1987, p. 55) and *each group is autonomous* and does not present itself as any formal therapy group or as a professional treatment approach.
- In the 12-step community, *sponsors* are in recovery from their own addiction; they also have a sponsor, and they help guide the new member with the 12 steps. Developing a working relationship with a sponsor is the "heart of . . . recovery from addiction—one addict helping another" (*Narcotics Anonymous*, 1987, p. 53). Sponsors may guide the member in issues

ranging from handling conflict at home or at work, handling success, increasing responsible behavior, and successfully addressing any issue that may impede continued recovery of the member.

From Syllabus: *In conjunction with selected AA volunteers who speak to the class beforehand about attending 12-step meetings,* students are also expected to attend a minimum of *three open* 12-step meetings within a given time frame, normally in a 4- to 6-week period. And then write a *one-page* summary for *each* meeting of what was learned. Other guidelines include:

Please *do not use any names (anonymity is essential), remember to go to* <u>open</u> *meetings only for AA, NA, or CA groups. Speaker meetings are recommended.*

Include feelings about the meeting. Also, describe any feelings, issues, or resistance you experienced before attending the meetings. Did you go alone? Why? Why not? What stood out for you? How will you use this experience in your counseling?

Provocative thinking combined with learning-in-action is evident throughout my course Addictions Counseling. As one example, students are challenged to deepen their empathy with addicted clients. To best accomplish this goal, students are given, in addition to standard assignments and textbook material, provocative reading assignments from qualitative works in the field, assignments to attend at least three open 12-step meetings, weekly journaling, and as an option, a personal abstinence project. Harm reduction models, for example, take on new meaning when students are grappling with their own abstinence from a desired substance, such as chocolates. Empathy with those struggling with cravings indeed is experienced in a much different way as compared, for example, to reading about the concept of craving as depicted in research literature. Students quest independently for their own deeper understanding as to what is effective in treating cravings; in other words, they have a more personal investment in understanding and utilizing effective skills and techniques in addiction counseling issues. For me, one of the most optimal experiences as an educator is to be a part of such contextual learning.

Dr. Laura Veach

SOURCE: Original work by Laura Veach, PhD.

RESOURCES FOR FURTHER LEARNING

Academy for Eating Disorders: http://www.aedweb.org/

Alcoholics Anonymous: http://www.aa.org

Extensive training, software, and resources are available to further use the treatment and care planning criteria at the following:

American Society of Addiction Medicine website: http://www.asamcriteria.org

National Association of Anorexia Nervosa and Associated Disorders: http://www.anad.org/

National Eating Disorders Association: http://www.nationaleatingdisorders.org/

http://www.Foodaddictionsummit.org

Office on Women's Health: http://www.womenshealth.gov

On-Line Gamers Anonymous: http://www.olganon.org/

Sex Addicts Anonymous: http://www.saa-recovery.org/

S-Anon for loved ones affected by Sex Addiction: http://www.sanon.org

Yale Rudd Center: http://www.uconnuddcenter.org

REFERENCES

Alcoholics Anonymous. (2016a). *Alcoholics Anonymous to celebrate its 80th year.* Retrieved from http://www.aa .org/press-releases/en_US/press-releases/alcoholics-anonymous-to-celebrate-its-80th-birthday-at-2015-international-convention-in-atlanta-july-2-5

Alcoholics Anonymous. (2016b). *Estimates of A.A. Groups and Members as of January 1, 2016.* Retrieved from http://www.aa.org/assets/en_US/smf-53_en.pdf

Alcoholics Anonymous World Services, Inc. (2008, Summer). *About AA: A newsletter for professionals.* Retrieved from http://www.aa.org/lang/en/subpage.cfm?page=9

American Psychiatric Association. (2013). *Diagnostic and statistical manual of mental disorders* (5th ed.). Arlington, VA: American Psychiatric Publishing.

American Society of Addiction Medicine (ASAM). (2016). *ASAM definition of addiction.* Retrieved from http://www.asam.org/quality-practice/definition-of-addiction

Babor, T., & Del Boca, F. K. (2003). *Treatment matching in alcoholism.* New York, NY: Cambridge Press.

Babor, T. F., Higgins-Biddle, J. C., Saunders, J. B., & Monteiro, M. G. (2001). *The Alcohol Use Disorders Identification Test: Guidelines for use in primary care* (2nd ed.). Published by the Department of Mental Health and Substance Dependence, World Health Organization. http://whqlibdoc.who.int/hq/2001/WHO_MSD_MSB_01.6a.pdf

Babor, T. F., Miller, W. R., DiClemente, C., & Longabaugh, R. (1999). A study to remember: Response of the project MATCH research group. *Addiction, 94*(1), 66–69.

Beck, A. T. (1993). *Beck Anxiety Inventory.* New York, NY: Pearson.

Beck, A. T., Steer, R. A., & Brown, G. K. (1996). *Beck Depression Inventory II.* New York, NY: Pearson. Retrieved from http://www.pearsonclinical.com/psychology/products/100000159/beck-depression-inventoryii-bdi -ii.html

Beck, A. T., Wright, F. D., Newman, C. F., & Liese, B. S. (1993). *Cognitive therapy of substance abuse.* New York, NY: Guilford.

Carnes, P. (1993). *A gentle path through the Twelve Steps* (Rev. ed.). Center City, MN: Hazelden.

Cash, H., Rae, C. D., Steel, A. H., & Winkler, A. (2012). Internet addiction: A brief summary of research and practice. *Current Psychiatry Reviews, 8,* 292–298.

Center for Substance Abuse Treatment (CSAT). (2006). *Substance abuse: Clinical issues in intensive outpatient treatment.* Treatment Improvement Protocol (TIP) Series No. 47. DHHS Publication No. (SMA) 06-4182. Rockville, MD: Substance Abuse and Mental Health Services Administration.

Center for Substance Abuse Treatment (CSAT). (2015). *Substance abuse treatment: Addressing the specific needs of women.* Treatment Improvement Protocol (TIP) Series, No. 51. HHS Publication No. (SMA) 15-4426. Rockville, MD: Center for Substance Abuse Treatment.

Darnell, D., Dunn, C., Atkins, D., Ingraham, L., & Zatzick, D. (2016). A randomized evaluation of Motivational Interviewing training for mandated implementation of alcohol screening and brief intervention in trauma centers. *Journal of Substance Abuse Treatment, 60,* 36–44.

DiClemente, C. C., Doyle, S. R., & Donovan, D. (2009). Predicting treatment seekers readiness to change their drinking behavior in the COMBINE Study. *Alcoholism, Clinical and Experimental Research, 33*(5), 879–892.

Feil, J., Sheppard, D., Fitzgerald, P. B., Yucel, M., Lubman, D. I., Bradshaw, J. L. (2010). Addiction, compulsive drug seeking, and the role of frontostriatal mechanisms in regulating inhibitory control. *Neuroscience and Biobehavioral Reviews, 35,* 248–275.

Gearhardt, A. N., Corbin, W. R., & Brownell, K. D. (2016). Yale Food Addiction Scale Version 2.0. *Psychology of Addictive Behaviors, 30,* 113–21. doi:10.1037/adb0000136

Griffiths, M. D., Kuss, D. J., & Demetrovics, Z. (2014). Social networking addiction: An overview of preliminary findings. In *Behavioral addictions. Criteria, evidence, and treatment* (pp. 119–141). Boston, MA: Elsevier Science Inc. Academic Press.

Han, D. H., Hwang, J. W., & Renshaw, P. F. (2010). Bupropion sustained release treatment decreases craving for video games and cue-induced brain activity in patients with Internet video game addiction. *Experimental & Clinical Psychopharmacology, 18,* 297–304. doi:10.1037/a0020023

Hazelden. (2016). The Dan Anderson Research Award. Retrieved from http://www.hazeldenbettyford.org/butler-center-for-research/dan-anderson-research-award

Kaskutas, L. A. (2009). Alcoholics Anonymous effectiveness: Faith meets science. *Journal of Addictive Diseases, 28,* 145–157. doi:10.1080/10550880902772464

Kinney, J., & Leaton, G. (1987). *Loosening the grip: A handbook of alcohol information* (3rd ed.). St. Louis, MO: C. V. Mosby Company.

Kiraly, O., Nagygyorgy, K., Griffiths, M. D., & Demetrovics, Z. (2014). Problematic online gaming. In K. P. Rosenberg & L. C. Feder (Eds.), *Behavioral addictions.* Boston, MA: Elsevier Science Inc. Academic Press.

Knapp, C. (2004). *Appetite: Why women want.* Berkeley, CA: CounterPoint Press.

Kurtz, E. (1979). *Not God: A history of Alcoholics Anonymous.* Center City, MN: Hazelden Educational Materials.

Leeman, R. F., Robinson, C. D., Waters, A. J., & Sofuoglu, M. (2014). A critical review of the literature on attentional bias in cocaine use disorder and suggestions for future research. *Experimental and Clinical Psychopharmacology, 22,* 469–483. doi:10.1037/a0037806

Lewis, T. F. (2014). *Substance abuse and addiction treatment: Practical application of counseling theory.* Upper Saddle River, NJ: Pearson Education, Inc.

Magura, S., Cleland, C. M., & Tonigan, J. S. (2013). Evaluating Alcoholics Anonymous's effect on drinking in Project MATCH using cross-lagged regression panel analysis. *Journal of Studies on Alcohol and Drugs, 74,* 378–385.

Martinez, D., & Trifilieff, P. (2015). *Brain stimulation as a potential treatment for addiction.* Retrieved from http://www.asam.org/magazine/read/article/2015/08/14/brain-stimulation-as-a-potential-treatment-for-addiction

McCambridge, J. (2013). Brief intervention content matters. *Drug and Alcohol Review, 32*(4), 339–341. doi:10.1111/dar.12044

Miller, G. A. (2015). *Learning the language of addiction counseling* (4th ed.). Hoboken, NJ: John Wiley & Sons.

Miller, W. R. (2014). Celebrating Carl Rogers: Motivational interviewing and the person-centered approach. *Motivational Interviewing: Training, Research, Implementation, Practice, 3,* 4–6. doi:10.5195/mitrip.2014.54

Miller, W. R., & Rollnick, S. (2013). *Motivational interviewing: Helping people change* (3rd ed.). New York, NY: Guilford.

Murray, C. E., Pope, A. L., & Willis, B. T. (2017). *Sexuality counseling: Theory, research, and practice.* Thousand Oaks, CA: Sage.

Narcotics Anonymous (4th ed.). (1987). Van Nuys, CA: NA World Service Office, Inc.

National Institute on Drug Abuse (NIDA). (2012). *Principles of drug addiction treatment.* (3rd ed). Retrieved from https://www.drugabuse.gov/sites/default/files/podat_1.pdf

National Institute on Drug Abuse (NIDA). (2015). *Long-term follow-up of medication-assisted treatment for addiction to pain relievers yields "cause for optimism."* Retrieved from https://www.drugabuse.gov/news-events/nida-notes/2015/11/long-term-follow-up-medication-assisted-treatment-addiction-to-pain-relievers-yields-cause-optimism

National Registry of Evidence-based Programs and Practices (NREPP). (2016). *Supportive-expressive psychotherapy.* Retrieved from http://legacy.nreppadmin.net/ViewIntervention.aspx?id=80

Nowinski, J., Baker, S., & Carroll, K. (1999). *A clinical research guide for therapists treating individuals with alcohol abuse and dependence.* National Institute on Alcohol Abuse and Alcoholism [NIAAA] Project MATCH Monograph Series, Volume 1. (NIH Publication No. 94-3722) National Institutes of Health, NIAAA. Rockville, MD: NIAAA.

Office on Women's Health. (2012). *Anorexia fact sheet.* Retrieved from https://www.womenshealth.gov/publications/our-publications/fact-sheet/anorexia-nervosa.html

Project MATCH Research Group. (1993). Project MATCH: Rationale and methods for a multisite clinical trial matching patients to alcoholism treatment. (1993). *Alcoholism: Clinical and Experimental Research, 17,* 1130–1145. doi:10.1111/j.1530-0277.1993.tb05219.x

Project MATCH Research Group. (1997a). Project MATCH secondary a priori hypotheses. *Addiction, 92,* 1671–1698. doi:10.1111/j.1360-0443.1997.tb02889.x

Project MATCH Research Group. (1997b). Matching alcoholism treatments to client heterogeneity: Project MATCH posttreatment drinking outcomes. *Journal of Studies on Alcohol, 58,* 7–29.

Project MATCH Research Group. (1998a). Matching alcoholism treatments to client heterogeneity: Treatment main effects and matching effects on drinking during treatment. *Journal of Studies on Alcohol, 59,* 631–639.

Project MATCH Research Group. (1998b). Matching alcoholism treatments to client heterogeneity: Project MATCH three-year drinking outcomes. *Alcoholism: Clinical and Experimental Research, 22,* 1300–1311. doi:10.1097/00000374-199809000-00016

Project MATCH Research Group. (1998c). Matching patients with alcohol disorders to treatments: Clinical implications from project MATCH. *Journal of Mental Health, 7,* 589–602. doi:10.1080/09638239817743

Project MATCH Research Group. (1998d). Therapist effects in three treatments for alcohol problems. (1998). *Psychotherapy Research– 8,* 455–474. doi:10.1093/ptr/8.4.455

Schneider, J. P. (1988). *Back from betrayal: Recovering from his affairs.* Center City, MN: Hazelden Foundation.

Smith, D. E. (2012). Editor's note: The process addictions and the new ASAM definition of addiction. *Journal of Addictive Drugs, 44,* 1–4. doi:10.1080/02791072.2012. 662105

Spicer, J. (1993). *The Minnesota model: The evolution of the multidisciplinary approach to addiction recovery.* Center City, MN: Hazelden Educational Materials.

Stevens, F. L., Hurley, R. A., & Taber, K. H. (2011). Anterior cingulate cortex: Unique role in cognition and emotion. *Journal of Neuropsychiatry and Clinical Neurosciences, 23,* 120–125. Retrieved from http://neuro.psychiatryonline.org/doi/pdf/10.1176/jnp.23.2.jnp121

Travis, T. (2009). *The language of the heart: A cultural history of the recovery movement from Alcoholics Anonymous to Oprah Winfrey.* Chapel Hill: The University of North Carolina Press.

van Wormer, K., & Davis, D. R. (2003). *Addiction treatment: A strengths perspective.* Pacific Grove, CA: Brooks/Cole.

Veach, L. J., Remley, T. P., Kippers, S. M., & Sorg, J. D. (2000). Retention predictors related to intensive outpatient programs for substance use disorders. *American Journal of Drug & Alcohol Abuse, 26,* 417–428.

Veach, L. J., Rogers, J. L., Moro, R. R., Essic, E. J., & McMullen, J. W. (2016). Process addictions. In D. Capuzzi & M.D. Stauffer (Eds.), *Foundations of addictions counseling* (3rd ed., pp. 48–65). New York, NY: Pearson.

Walters, S. T., Cornett, M., & Vader, A. M. (2012). Coding criminal justice interactions with the MITI: Recommendations for research and practice. *Motivational Interviewing: Training, Research, Implementation, Practice, 1*(1), 25–30. doi:10.5195/mitrip.2012.9

Weinstein, A., Feder, L. C., Rosenberg, K. P., & Dannon, P. (2014). Internet addiction disorder: Overview and controversy. In K. P. Rosenberg & L. C. Feder (Eds.), *Behavioral addictions: Criteria, evidence, and treatment.* Boston, MA: Elsevier Science Inc. Academic Press.

Yau, Y. H. C., Gottlieb, C. D., Krasna, L. C., & Potenza, M. N. (2014). Food addiction: Evidence, evaluation, and treatment. In K. P. Rosenberg & L. C. Feder (Eds.), *Behavioral addictions: Criteria, evidence, and treatment.* Boston, MA: Elsevier Science Inc. Academic Press.

Young, K. S., & de Abreu, C. N. (Eds.). (2011). *Internet addiction: A handbook and guide to evaluation and treatment.* Hoboken, NJ: John Wiley & Sons.

12

Cross Addictions and Comorbidities

❖

LEARNING OBJECTIVES

The learner will be able to

- define cross addiction;
- describe at least two evidence-based approaches to use in counseling individuals with cross addiction;
- define comorbidities;
- cite examples of comorbidities, both physical and psychological, as related to substance use or process addictive disorders; and
- provide a description of one evidence-based approach for treating comorbidities and cross addiction.

Knowledge

For many years the concept of the individual in recovery for a substance use disorder was at a heightened risk for becoming addicted to a different or new substance has been emphasized in the addiction field. Important brain changes, according to research studies, show "that long-term drug abuse results in changes in the brain that persist long after a person stops using drugs" (National Institute on Drug Abuse [NIDA], 2012, p. 7). Addiction specialists have cautioned clients that there is a greater susceptibility to triggering a new addictive cycle if other addictive substances are used after establishing recovery. This pattern of developing additional addictive use disorders is referred to as *cross addiction*. For example, an individual might achieve recovery from a severe heroin use disorder and within 6 months begin smoking marijuana with no expectation of problems since "heroin was such a hard drug and the only one causing any problems"—only to learn later that a severe cannabis use disorder had also developed. As the *DSM-5* points out pertaining to clients with a cannabis use disorder, "74% report problematic use of a secondary or tertiary substance: alcohol (40%), cocaine (12%), methamphetamine (6%), and heroin or other opiates (2%)" (American Psychiatric Association [APA], 2013, p. 515). Further, individuals with military service in Vietnam who developed addiction to opioids such as heroin showed 90% recovery rates upon return to the United States, yet, it is suggested due to cross-addiction vulnerabilities, many veterans in opiate recovery "experienced increased rates of alcohol or amphetamine use disorder as well as increased suicidality" (APA, 2013, p. 543). Claudia Black and Patrick Carnes, both noted addiction specialists, add important thinking about many aspects of cross addiction and identified addiction interaction disorder as an overarching term encompassing cross-addiction (Black, 2010; Nino-de-Guzman, 2015). The new terminology, addiction interaction disorder (AID), leads the addiction counseling field in understanding a framework that includes the phenomenon of cross addiction, defined as one addiction replaced by another within a period of at least 3 months between the two separate addictive disorders (Black, 2010). Other patterns within AID, for example, include cross tolerance where multiple addictions are activated and is defined as follows: "First, both addictions get worse at the same time. Or, one addiction will replace another with little time between them" and for withdrawal management, "one addiction is used to blunt the withdrawal from another addiction" (Black, 2010, p. 3). Substantially more research is needed in order to better understand the many facets and complications of cross addiction, addictions interacting with other addictive patterns, and newer frameworks such as addiction interaction disorder. At this time, however, the *DSM-5* does not include such frameworks for better defining complications of substance use disorders in its diagnostic sections or in the *DSM-5* section on conditions for further study (APA, 2013).

Clearly, more research is needed to better understand cross-addiction patterns and susceptibility. However, it remains important for the counselor to highlight to clients the increased risks and vulnerabilities while recovering from a particular substance that other addicting substances may trigger a reactivation of addictive patterns with the newly used drug(s). Questions continue to grow regarding the addictive process and those questions include questions regarding cross addiction pertaining to process addictions.

In recent years with added knowledge about process addictions, new thinking has added the potential for other addictive processes to also be triggered after recovery is achieved in one addictive process. It is now thought that, for example, someone diagnosed with a moderate or severe alcohol use disorder might be at heightened risk for developing a gambling use disorder, if gambling activity might be started as a leisure pursuit, for example. Moreover, it is noted in the *DSM-5* that a stimulant use disorder puts individuals at risk for a gambling disorder (APA, 2013). Conversely, a process addiction might put one at greater risk for substance use disorders as noted in findings pertaining to gambling disorders: the *DSM-5* notes "gambling disorder may also occur prior to the onset of other mental disorders, especially anxiety disorders and substance use disorders" (APA, 2013, p. 589). Another example might involve someone who has suffered with health consequences of a sex addiction, achieved stable recovery, then suffered severe leg injuries from a major car crash and while prescribed an opiate such as OxyContin, began to develop symptoms of an opiate use disorder and also experienced a relapse back into the sexual addictive cycle. The preceding examples point out issues of concern and questions regarding cross addiction and why it is critically important for the counselor specializing in substance-related and other addictive disorders to be aware of cross-addiction complications from other addicting substances or processes.

Cross Addictions: Evidence-Based Knowledge and Substances

First, it is important to examine the current knowledge in the area of cross addiction to other substances of addiction. Is the client diagnosed with a severe heroin use disorder at a higher risk of developing a severe substance use disorder involving other addictive substances? Is the client who has had stable recovery for 5 years from a severe Xanax use disorder really at higher risk for developing a different substance use disorder if the client starts to have an occasional glass of wine with friends?

For a number of years the thinking by specialists has answered "yes" to all of the above. As scientific studies increase, it may help counselors be able to provide better answers to these questions though many questions remain and it can be quite confusing for both clients and counselors. Many clients are unprepared and unaware that substantial risks to develop cross addiction remain once a substance use disorder has developed. The counselor is well advised to help the client become more knowledgeable and aware of these heightened risks. With greater awareness of the brain's addictive process, it may help some clients to understand that the primary drug of addiction combined with the addictive process has damaged the brain, especially the pleasure and inhibitory centers. It seems logical, then, for the client to be provided this knowledge and that once that cycle has occurred, then any other euphoria-producing drug could then jeopardize one's recovery and add to the substances of addiction. However, few scientific studies tackle this major problem; cross addiction is poorly understood in terms of how many clients it affects and if there are known predictors that make some people more prone to cross addiction than others (Agrawal, Budney, & Lynskey, 2012).

One major study using national data pointed to problems with findings that showed not all clients in long-term recovery who used other drugs triggered the addictive cycle with use of a new drug (Lopez-Quintero et al., 2011). While this is one study, it is an important 2001–2002 national survey (National Epidemiological Survey of Alcohol and Related Conditions—NESARC) involving personal interviews that highlights mixed findings regarding cross addiction. It is of note that the findings showed a study sample of participants, age 18 and older, who indicated a history of and recovery from a substance use disorder: 6,937 individuals reported a nicotine use disorder, 4,781 individuals an alcohol use disorder, but a much smaller sample of only 530 reporting a cannabis use disorder and 408 reporting a cocaine use disorder (Lopez-Quintero et al., 2011). Major findings of this study showed a vast difference in ceasing substance use between the first year the substance use disorder began; for all four drugs the odds of quitting in the first year ranged from 3% for alcohol and nicotine, less than 5% for cannabis, and nearly 9% for cocaine. For overall lifetime cessation, the probabilities ranged from the lowest for nicotine cessation (83.7%), to almost 91% cessation probability for those addicted to alcohol, to approximately 97% for cannabis cessation, and finally 99.2% cessation of cocaine use (Lopez-Quintero et al., 2011). When looking at ages as a factor influencing cessation, or remission from the use disorder, "individuals in the youngest age group (18–29 years old) were less likely to remit from alcohol dependence and more likely to remit from cannabis dependence or cocaine dependence than individuals in the oldest age group (≥ 45 years old)" (Lopez-Quintero et al., 2011, p. 662). In addition, for all four of the substances studied, females were much more likely than males to stop use. When looking at cross addiction, while the study did not contain data on those who start another substance after ceasing use of one, the findings did indicate a pattern of decreased odds of cessation since "dependence on one substance tended to decrease the probability of remission on another substance" (Lopez-Quintero et al., 2011, p. 664). This finding particularly emphasizes the need for individuals once addicted to any one substance be made aware by the counselor of the reduced probability of remission when another substance is used. The authors attribute these problems as a result of brain changes and the ability of some particular drugs of abuse to more quickly trigger cross-addiction issues such as increased tolerance to other euphoria-producing drugs (cross tolerance) and cross sensitization (increased sensitivity to other euphoria-producing drugs). Conclusions by the authors underscore the remaining need for more evidence to better understand the brain's adaptations and vulnerabilities in recovery. Another study designed using national interviews from NESARC analyzed prescription drug use disorders and remission rates. Findings revealed an additional trend of remission at very high rates, exceeding 96%, with younger users stopping use on a more frequent basis (Blanco et al., 2013). In addition, additional research is needed to better understand this higher "quit rate" of youth in the areas of prescription drug use disorders since other studies show the opposite trend with increasing drug use as high school is completed and further education is pursued (Kirst, Mecredy, Borland, & Chaiton, 2014).

Further, it becomes critically important to help the client understand a difference between euphoria-producing drugs with addictive potential (since most drugs do not carry a bold labeling warning of the addictive potential) and those medications that are a part of medical care that do not carry a pronounced addictive potential. Different types of euphoria-producing illicit drugs such as marijuana, cocaine, or methamphetamine, for example, may be understood more clearly that any use is risky, especially given the illegal status of use of those drugs. However, understanding risk of use of pharmaceutical medications that a medical doctor has prescribed is far more challenging. Medications such as insulin for diabetes management or diltiazem hydrochloric, a calcium channel blocker for cardiac care management, are life-saving medications, yet they do not have addictive properties and are needed for health; these types of medications are vastly different from drugs that can increase risks of cross addiction. Yet, clearly use of some prescribed medications, especially for those in recovery, may be contraindicated. Many physicians may lack clear understanding of the addictive process and consequently in providing good medical care as their medical education emphasized, the triggering of the addictive process may begin with prescribing pain medications, such as opiates. The work of the knowledgeable counselor is critically important in helping clients have a better framework for understanding risks to their recovery. It may be helpful to educate the client, then, by using differing terms to help the client see a difference in risk potential. In clinical settings it can be explained that substances with addictive or abuse potential can be characterized as "drugs" whereas substances without addictive or abuse potential can be characterized as "medications" to help the client have clear terms that may reinforce risks. In addition, since pharmacology is not often known or understood by many counselors or clients, it can be daunting for clients to understand what prescription medications might then be best termed a drug. Pharmaceutical discoveries and new products are continually being introduced, making it even more challenging for the recovering individual to keep abreast of the changing landscape of pharmacology. In order to get expert help for clients, it may be helpful to encourage clients in recovery to speak with a pharmacist about the increased risks of cross addiction anytime a medication is prescribed. Pharmacists are often very knowledge about the addictive properties of any pharmaceutical product, and at times, are more informed about drug cautions than physicians. If a client is in doubt, it would be advisable to seek out more than one pharmacist with questions about the potential addictive risks of any prescription. Certain opiates or anxiety drugs, for instance, are extremely fast-acting and are euphoria-producing; these drugs have a very high potential for abuse and can place a recovering individual at increased risk for triggering the addictive response. It is recommended that in the treatment plan and relapse prevention planning, cross-addiction risks be addressed with the clients (Black, 2010). Other substances of use and the way other drugs are used, such as smoking and tobacco, may also trigger vulnerabilities to other drugs of abuse.

Interestingly, research is highlighting data showing smoking cigarettes might further increase the probabilities of continued use of cannabis as noted in research findings (Agrawal et al., 2012). It is thought that since smoking cigarettes involves smoking as the route of administration of the drug nicotine, smoking other drugs may increase the risk for triggering problematic use of cannabis (Agrawal et al., 2012). Minimal study has been conducted to examine the influence of route of administration and cross addiction. In other words, if my client's primary drug of addiction has been used by intranasal use (snorting), would any other use of an addictive substance by intranasal use make that particular other drug have greater potential for addiction in my client as compared to using a different route of administration, drinking alcohol, for instance? Questions like these remain since we have a minimal understanding of why some individuals struggle with cross addiction and others do not.

An additional counseling focus can occur when discussing cross addiction with clients. It is important to explore with clients what would influence them to consider using other addictive substances after achieving remission. There may be factors the client could examine that might highlight warning signs, such as talking in counseling sessions about using other addictive drugs that had not previously been problematic or beginning to date a person who uses drugs recreationally. Other factors such as psychological problems or environmental triggers may also compound the problem, and we will examine those factors with respect to relapse in the following chapter.

Box 12.1: Case Illustration of Julia, a Troubled Employee

Julia is a 33-year-old white female who lives in Chicago. Julia has been employed as a lawyer for the past 9 years and is on her way to making partner in her firm. Eight months ago, Julia was self-admitted to an inpatient rehabilitation unit. Per Julia's account, she had been referred to an employee assistance program (EAP) counselor following a "drunken debacle at a business lunch." Julia reports going to a business lunch with a partner in her firm and a prospective client. As was usual for their business luncheons, the three ordered a few bottles of wine; Julia was unable to remember how many glasses she personally had. In fact, she was unable to remember most of the luncheon following the initial meet and greets. The next day Julia woke to an e-mail from the human resources department stating she was required to attend counseling sessions with the firm's EAP counselor.

In Julia's initial session, the EAP counselor conducted several assessments, including a demographic questionnaire, the Beck Depression Inventory II (Beck, Steer, & Brown, 1996), the Beck Anxiety Inventory (Beck, 1993), and the Alcohol Use Disorders Identification Test (Babor, Higgins-Biddle, Saunders, & Monteiro, 2001). The EAP counselor described the tests and also Julia's results. Julia was surprised to hear that the results suggested she may be struggling some with anxiety as well as had a score that suggested concerns with her drinking. "But, I'm a lawyer; all of us that are not partnered yet are constantly concerned whether we will make partner or not. This is just normal. Not to mention I'm a woman—it is so much more difficult for us. And I mean, everyone drinks at business lunches, it's just the norm. If you don't drink, well, I just don't even know!" The counselor spent time talking with Julia and reflected her feelings of confusion and that this is a normal experience. She also helped her see her own concern, specifically with her blackouts. "I mean, it does help me calm down; there's nothing better than coming home after a 13-hour day and having a glass of wine. But you're right, I have woken up the next morning a couple times this past year and couldn't remember what had happened only to discover two empty wine bottles in the sink." Julia agreed to come for another appointment the next week.

The next week Julia came and was incredibly distraught. She had spoken to some of her close work friends and asked them what they thought about her drinking. She states that it was "so embarrassing to have them tell me the truth." Julia was awoken with awareness that although she previously understood her drinking to be on par with others, she was drinking much more than she believed. "I'm really scared; my dad was like this and people warned me, but I just never thought it would happen to me. What can I do?" The counselor listened and reflected Julia's concerns and desire for change. Because of the amount Julia was drinking, her experience with blackouts, and her high motivation

(Continued)

(Continued)

for change, the counselor recommended a 12-step-focused inpatient 28-day recovery program. The counselor explained the legal aspects of asking for a leave, and Julia felt ready to go. Five days later, Julia arrived at the facility and began an intense recovery program.

Julia was released from the treatment program 7 months ago, and she has been maintaining her sobriety and her recovery program. Julia has now contacted the same EAP counselor due to her family's concerns. Apparently, during her time in treatment Julia remembered how much she loved exercising, and was able to begin an exercise regimen again due to the on-site gym facility. She has been working out daily, sometimes in the morning and evening. "It's my new glass of wine! I love going home and rowing a 10k." The reason for her call was that her mom had come to her apartment and although they had plans to go to dinner, Julia was making her mother wait because she just had to finish her biking routine. Julia reported that her mother became very distraught and was yelling. "I never thought someone could be so upset by someone being healthy!" Julia said. Apparently, Julia's mom was concerned that Julia's exercising was interfering with their relationship. "She even brought up the fact that I was late for my nephews first birthday because I was at the gym," Julia explained. The counselor then discussed more of her mother's concerns with Julia. Julia states she commented on her drastic weight loss ("but doesn't that happen when you stop drinking?!"), her tardiness with family events, and her purchasing exercise equipment for her home and her office.

- As Julia's counselor, what are your main concerns?
- What do you think are some of Julia's treatment goals?
- As a counselor working in an addiction treatment facility, how might this issue been proactively dealt with?

Box 12.2: Death Rates Among Older Americans

In 2015, researchers noted a disturbing trend among older, white Americans showing a major increase in deaths at younger ages. As the data revealed, the rising death rates were primarily tied to substance-related patterns and suicide (Case & Deaton, 2015). Most alarming was the steep rise in deaths for older white Americans aged 50–64 due to substance misuse resulting in overdoses of alcohol, opioids, and prescription medications. Other findings noted increased dying stemming from substance-related medical problems such as liver disease (Case & Deaton, 2015; Kolata, 2015).

Cross Addictions: Evidence-Based Knowledge and Process Addictions

Minimal evidence-based research has examined process addictions and their role in cross addiction. Emerging scientific studies lack funding and resources to carefully conduct substantial research examining the evolving area of process addictions. At this time even including process addictions when defining the terms related to addictive disorders is relatively new. Smith (2012) explains more about cross addiction in the new American Society of Addiction Medicine (ASAM) definition that now addresses *both* substance and process addictions, and highlights the emphasis on repeated drug using or behaviors (processes) that can be addictive, which bring about brain changes and inability to successfully control those addictive behaviors or drug use. The inclusion of addictive processes is particularly important to highlight for clients while in treatment for a substance or process use disorder. His statement clearly emphasizes the risk for lack of control in further use of other drugs or processes that involve addictive behavior, for example, sex addiction. This important terminology can help the counselor share the definitions and clarify for the client the importance in being aware of vulnerabilities to other addictive patterns once in recovery from any substance or process disorder.

Next, it is important to briefly examine the emerging scientific literature pertaining to risks of cross addiction in substance and process addictions. A major study in South Korea involving 73,000 middle and high school students revealed data supporting the increased risk of cross addiction (Lee, Han, Kim, & Renshaw, 2013). The researchers noted a statistically significant high correlation between the severity of Internet use disorder with the severity of alcohol, nicotine, and other drug use disorders. In addition, their findings point to the accelerated risks of developing an Internet addiction disorder (IAD) with early use of substances (Lee et al., 2013).

Cross-Addiction Substance and Process Addictions

Emergence of Cross Addictions During Treatment and Recovery

Remission or early recovery from substance use disorders might also be compromised by a process addiction that becomes activated while in recovery from the substance(s). Addiction specialists theorize that the brain does not distinguish whether the dopaminergic rush seen in addictive patterns is stimulated by a chemical such as marijuana or a process such as placing a gambling bet. Many specialists believe that whatever triggers the addictive process, namely the brain's pleasure center and the faulty brain areas that govern controlling use, the recovering person is vulnerable to the newly introduced euphoriant, whether it is a chemical or a process. It may help the client while in treatment to underscore that the brain changes, neuroadaptation of the brain's circuitry, in addiction now leads to difficulty controlling the brain's response to other drugs or addictive processes. While controversy and opposing viewpoints exist with respect to cross addiction, process addiction, and vulnerabilities of recovering clients, it can be helpful to affirm for the client that they should anticipate conflicting viewpoints. However, for the client's best care, it can be helpful to provide them information that cross-addiction risks may jeopardize recovery so the client can make more informed choices with respect to future use of euphoria-producing, addictive processes. In helping the client consider their options and risks, it may be helpful to provide them with case examples. Many clients may believe once they have achieved abstinence from one process, such as Internet gaming, they are safe to engage in other behaviors such as gambling in a casino with no risks since casino gambling was never a prior issue. What the client new to recovery may not understand is how different effects may be experienced in new ways that may trigger new cross addictions. Since clients may not have experienced sobriety or abstinence for a sustained period, they may not be as aware of vulnerabilities. The counselor's role is therefore important to offer guidance and strategies in order for clients to better protect newly practiced recovery skills.

Skills in Action: Cross Addictions

Box 12.3: Case Illustration of Elizabeth/Eli, Current Intensive Outpatient Program Client

Elizabeth/Eli, a 25-year-old single female-to-male client, is in the third week of an intensive outpatient program. The major identifying issue related to substance use diagnoses is a primary diagnosis of a severe cocaine use disorder. However, in this past week in group counseling sessions, Elizabeth/Eli shared plans to develop more leisure activities in recovery including Internet gaming. The following is the transcript for the weekly individual session with Elizabeth's (Eli's) session:

Counselor (Dianne):	We closed our session last week as group members shared ideas for increased leisure activities while in recovery. I wondered about your ideas and would like to hear more.
Client (Elizabeth/Eli):	Umm, it's been a lot to think about. I've never really done much for fun that didn't include using. It's hard to know where to start.
Dianne:	You've wondered what fun is like without using.
Elizabeth/Eli:	I think I have some ideas, but it's all new to me.
Dianne:	You're concerned you may not know what you like.
Elizabeth/Eli:	Uhhhhhh, I've been getting high since I was 13, and most of my time in the last years has been *all* about getting and using. I don't even know what I'm good at anymore. I never had much of an athletic ability—never joined a team. But I really want to know—it's like a whole new world and, man, I could dream big.
Dianne:	You're surprised, excited, and afraid all at the same time when it comes to figuring out clean and sober fun.
Elizabeth/Eli:	Yeah, what if I don't know how? You know how bad that can be—I'm finally seeing how all my awful stuff I got involved in was so tied up with this brain/addiction thing. It's so much to take in—and maybe, just maybe, I can change. Maybe I'm not such a wreck of a human being.... I wanna know how to live, y'know, really live. Just the thought that I could actually go out and have fun, not high, it's sooooo wild and so hard to believe. But, what if, what if I blow it? What if I just don't know how to do this recovery stuff?

Dianne:	It's been a long time since you've been connected to the you that wasn't high or out figuring out how to get the next high. You're questioning trust in yourself.
Elizabeth/Eli:	So many changes and yeah, worried I may not make the best choices, since they've sucked so bad these last few years. And trusting me, ha, that's not even really ever been, has it? I don't even know how to do that.
Dianne:	On the one hand, you say you don't know how to build trust with yourself, yet, you are looking over lists of ideas you generated toward sober fun.
Elizabeth/Eli:	Wow! I did do that, didn't I? So I'm trying to learn to reach out and connect with others, you know, to get other input. I think it's a pretty good list—like I used to really like hiking, especially around the mountains here in our area. But that went away years ago; I'm not even sure how long it's been since I went out on any trail. . . . I miss that time out there. And I'm thinking something I can do indoors, like gaming. I haven't spent much time doing that, but lots of other people I've heard go on and on about how cool it is to be in an alternate universe and have avatars. That seems really cool.
Dianne:	You've started this discovery process with two things, one new idea and one you enjoyed a while back.
Elizabeth/Eli:	Yeah, it's something how I let go of something I thought was so much a part of me. I can't believe how I just stopped hiking. I used to do that every weekend—rain, snow, storms, it didn't matter. Now I don't even leave the streets. It's like, how did I let that go? Or now, I'm learning how I did not/could not see how my brain was being fed by this addiction and taking *me and my loves* away with it.
Dianne:	You're distressed when you see how much addiction has taken from you.
Elizabeth/Eli:	Ugh, yes!
Dianne:	I sense lots of emotions are right at the surface, and you look like you are clutching your sides.
Elizabeth/Eli:	Strong, strong feelings of regret—so much wasted. I want to make this work; I want my freedom back. Freedom to play and laugh, and of course, I want it all now—think that sounds like my all-or-nothing addiction talking?! And this new idea, gaming, getting lost in that world, sounds like so much fun.
Dianne:	As you talk about this new thing—gaming—your face looks tense but your words make it sound very inviting.
Elizabeth/Eli:	Hmm, I had not realized that; it just sounds so much like escaping all this day-to-day stuff. But then I don't know, I haven't done that before.
Dianne:	I hear lots of questions in your voice and words like "escape." What if I mentioned that a number of addiction counselors have worked with clients who have struggled with that escape they found in gaming—so much so that they believe they triggered a second addiction—to gaming? It might be important to explore how gaming can be an addictive process, putting your health and stable recovery in question.

(Continued)

(Continued)

Elizabeth/Eli: Something else I had not known or looked into; man, I could just get sideswiped by some other addicting thing and lose myself again—how do I avoid that?

Dianne: Looks like you just showed yourself how to go to others who understand addiction—asking how to enjoy sobriety and living, reviewing your plans by them, and being open to other's input, at least for these early months. As you said, it's learning a newer way of living now and taking new steps in recovery.

(Counselor and client close for the day. Counselor summarizes the session as well as goals for continuing to explore healthy recovery support ideas.)

Consider three additional creative ways you might approach the issue of Internet gaming and cross addiction with this client. (Hint: Create a handout? Produce a visual graphic depicting cross addiction? Other ideas?)

- How would you explain cross addiction to your client?
- How might you help the client examine these risks?
- What else might you want to highlight for the client?

Effective Interventions for Cross Addictions

Cognitive Behavior Therapy

Evidence-based approaches include the well-researched methods of cognitive behavioral therapy (CBT), where "anticipating likely problems and enhancing patients' self-control by helping them develop effective coping strategies" is key (NIDA, 2012, p. 48). Much of CBT includes "exploring the positive and negative consequences of continued drug use, self-monitoring to recognize cravings early and identify situations that might put one at risk for use, and developing strategies for coping with cravings" (NIDA, 2012, p. 48). Positive findings for CBT with Internet addiction (Young, 2007), sexual addiction (Birchard, 2015), and a number of other substance use disorders (NIDA, 2012) underscore the importance of utilizing the CBT approach for helping clients become aware of potential problems with other euphoria-producing drugs or behaviors that could increase risk for cross addiction. Clients can begin to list situations that enhance risks of euphoriant use in daily living, then develop written plans to lessen risks and increase help-seeking behaviors when the client might be prescribed opiates, for example, after a painful dental procedure. Listing alternative options could include inquiring of the dentist whether non-addicting medications might be able to be used instead. In summary, CBT techniques lend themselves to helping clients identify risky cross-addiction situations and can be a valuable tool for the addiction counselor.

Twelve-Step Facilitation

In searching for additional effective approaches with cross-addiction treatment, the Twelve-Step Facilitation (TSF) approach is prominent in many treatment settings. Those in recovery from an initial struggle with a cocaine use disorder, for example, may then discover that a sexual addiction was triggered while in recovery from the cocaine use disorder. The addiction counselor may develop a treatment plan in conjunction with the client that now includes support group work in Sex Addicts Anonymous (SAA) in addition to continued involvement in Cocaine Anonymous (CA). Clients can be presented with psychoeducation about the concept of cross addiction as important information to assist the client with a shame-based response to behaviors that the client may have believed was gone since they were in recovery from a substance addiction. Often clients experience shock, shame, anger, and confusion over recognition of the addictive patterns that emerged when in remission from a substance addiction. This increased awareness can help the client better accept the addictive process as a long-term vulnerability and thereby a chronic condition that warrants ongoing recovery awareness and vigilance to *both* addictive processes and other substances. Smith (2012) cautions that addiction is similar to other chronic diseases and clearly involves relapsing and remission cycles. When clients understand the broader scope of risks to recovery with other drugs or processes, the tools found in 12-step groups can thus be broadened for the client to find mutual support from others who experienced the devastating experiences from triggering an unexpected and unknown additional addiction. It is not uncommon for clients to be involved in multiple types of 12-step groups, such as Alcoholics Anonymous and Gamblers Anonymous, for example. While both groups use the same 12 steps as a foundation for mutual help, it is the key aspect of sharing strength, hope, and experiences unique to each addictive process that can be meaningful in the therapeutic presence of universality where one understands "I am not alone," and sharing in a 12-step group can profoundly foster connection to others who have not only experienced the pain of addiction but also the wisdom of recovering.

Interventions for Cross Addictions With Emerging Research Support

Mindfulness

Additional research into the benefits of mindfulness techniques suggests substantial resources and benefits for those in treatment for addictive disorders (Marcus & Zgierska, 2009). Techniques that are particularly useful focus on accepting disruptive thoughts in a nonjudgmental way without reacting negatively to harsh thoughts. Another benefit of mindfulness centers around a different response, acknowledging awareness to intrusive cravings, which also has a positive effect (Marcus & Zgierska, 2009). There are preliminary findings that encourage further research into mindfulness, especially as it pertains to cross addiction and beneficial ways to manage addiction risks and exposure to other drugs or euphoria-producing behaviors (Zgierska et al., 2009). In summary, counselors could provide more tools to clients as counselors become more proficient in mindfulness techniques.

Dialectal Behavior Therapy (DBT)

While solidly established in the 1990s as an evidence-based treatment approach for individuals diagnosed with borderline personality disorders or self-injurious and suicidal behaviors, dialectical behavior therapy (DBT) continues to be an emerging research area indicating DBT can be effective with individuals struggling with substance use disorders (Dimeoff & Linehan, 2008). It is not clear that cross-addiction issues have been measured with respect to DBT techniques, yet the approach involves a client focus on opposing threats to recovery. Use of other substances or processes to escape or experience a high (euphoria) can be reviewed with the client from the DBT perspective. Further research will help clarify the benefits of DBT with issues such as cross addiction with clients struggling with substance-related and addictive disorders (Dimeoff & Linehan, 2008). Other key areas of counseling that are pertinent to substance-related and addictive disorders includes comorbidity definitions and factors.

Comorbidity

As discussed in the previous section, additional conditions may have a substantial effect on substance use disorders. Considerable efforts in the last 20 years have improved care for comorbidities within the treatment spectrum of substance-related addictive disorders (Substance Abuse and Mental Health Administration [SAMHSA], 2005). Terminology such as comorbidity is often used to focus on additional health conditions that can co-occur simultaneously with active substance use disorders. In this section, comorbidity will be used to include additional conditions that may complicate a substance use or process disorder. A uniform definition for comorbidity remains a challenge, but recent attempts at developing an accurate definition have been put forth by Valderas and colleagues. At its basic level of understanding, comorbidity involves "the presence of more than 1 distinct condition in an individual" (Valderas, Starfield, Sibbald, Salisbury, & Roland, 2009, p. 357). In addition, four other characteristics should be considered (Valderas et al., 2009): first, the overall classification or lack of classification for various conditions involved; next, the importance of each of the various conditions; third, the time each condition has been present and the order in which each condition appeared; and lastly, the weighted burden of the illness or disease in conjunction with the individual's overall health or frailty in context of the person's social, cultural, economic, and environmental factors. This section will examine physical and emotional factors and comorbidities impacting a range of substance use issues.

At times a number of unhealthy physical conditions, comorbidities, are evident with addictive disorders. In the past, co-occurring physical conditions were often treated separately in the U.S. health care system, with minimal interface or coordination of care for the primary condition of the addictive disorder that was contributing to or exacerbating the physical condition(s). For a current example, endocarditis, a bacterial infection within the heart, can occur as one distinct condition directly related to another distinct condition of a severe opiate use disorder. Injecting opiates intravenously (directly into veins) can introduce bacteria into the bloodstream, which can then develop into endocarditis. This heart infection causes a life-threatening condition requiring major inpatient medical interventions within a hospital. It frequently involves a 3- to 6-week inpatient hospital course of treatment with intravenous antibiotic regimens. Once the individual is medically stable, greater physical mobility is possible. However, stabilized hospital patients being treated for endocarditis may complain about boredom and exhibit behavioral challenges, such as leaving the hospital unit without permission, drug-seeking behaviors, and other disruptive activities. When the comorbidities of endocarditis and a severe opiate use disorder are present, unfortunately hospitals are often not structured to simultaneously begin intensive addiction counseling with the patient. Few services for addiction treatment or substance-related counseling will be provided in any hospital medical unit in the United States during the many weeks the hospitalized patient is receiving medical care for endocarditis. At best, the hospitalized patient will be referred to an addiction treatment program upon discharge from the hospital. Currently, however, in the United States there is a promising future for individuals being treated within the health care system who are also struggling with comorbidities like mental or substance use disorders. Progressive developments within our medical system of care, often referred to as *integrated care*, are underway to greatly improve care of comorbid conditions.

Evidence-Based Practices and Comorbidities

Integrated care can best be defined in terms of both substance use disorders and other mental health issues in combination with medical care, often provided within the same clinic or health care setting. The U.S. Substance Abuse and Mental Health Services Administration (SAMHSA) specifies that individuals with mental and substance use disorders "may die decades earlier than the average person—mostly from untreated and preventable chronic illnesses like hypertension, diabetes, obesity, and cardiovascular disease that are aggravated by poor health habits such as inadequate physical activity, poor nutrition, smoking, and substance abuse" (SAMHSA, 2016a, p. 1). By some accounts at least six of every 10 clients seeking help for substance use disorders also are impacted by a diagnosable mental disorder, such as major depression (NIDA, 2012).

Integrated care utilizes a number of evidence-based, large-scale interventions that are both integrative in nature and provide greatly needed services (SAMHSA, 2014). Various settings and terminology are included in the implementation of integrated care as noted in Figure 12.1. One can understand the vast changes that are underway and particularly affecting how addiction and substance-related counseling is being provided (SAMHSA, 2005). There is a growing need for more skilled counselors, knowledgeable in substance-related and addictive disorders, who provide counseling within medical homes, primary care clinics, and hospital settings.

A large randomized clinical trial titled Primary Care Research in Substance Abuse and Mental Health for the Elderly (PRISM-E) particularly studied patterns of older

Figure 12.1 A Family Tree of Related Terms Used in Behavioral Health and Primary Care Integration

Illustration: A family tree of related terms used in behavioral health and primary care integration

Integrated Care
Tightly integrated, on-site teamwork with unified care plan as a standard approach to care for designated populations. Connotes organizational integration involving social and other services. "Attitudes" of integration: 1) Integrated treatments, 2) integrated program structure; 3) integrated system of programs, and 4) integrated payments. (Based on SAMHSA)

Shared Care
Predominately Canadian usage—PC and MH professionals (typically psychiatrists) working together in shared system and record, maintaining 1 treatment plan addressing all patient health needs (Kates et al, 1996; Kelly et al, 2011).

Integrated Primary Care or Primary Care Behavioral Health
Combines medical and BH services for problems patients bring to primary care, including stress-linked physical symptoms, health behaviors, MH or SA disorders. For any problem, they have come to the right place—"no wrong door" (Blount). BH professional used as a consultant to PC colleagues (Sabin & Borus, 2009; Haas & deGruy, 2004; Robinson & Reiter, 2007; Hunter et al., 2009).

Behavioral Health Care
An umbrella term for care that addresses any behavioral problems bearing on health, including MH and SA conditions, stress-linked physical symptoms, patient activation, and health behaviors. The job of all kinds of care settings, and done by clinicians and health coaches of various disciplines or training.

Mental Health Care
Care to help people with mental illnesses (or at risk)—to suffer less emotional pain and disability—and live healthier, longer, more productive lives. Done by a variety of caregivers in diverse public and private settings such as specialty MH, general medical, human services, and voluntary support networks. (Adapted from SAMHSA.)

Substance Abuse Care
Services, treatments, and supports to help people with addictions and substance abuse problems suffer less emotional pain, family and vocational disturbance, physical risks—and live healthier, longer, more productive lives. Done in specialty SA, general medical, human services, voluntary support networks, e.g., 12-step programs and peer counselors. (Adapted from SAMHSA.)

Patient-Centered Care
"The experience (to the extent the informed, individual patient desires it) of transparency, individualization, recognition, respect, dignity, and choice in all matters, without exception, related to one's person, circumstances, and relationships in health care"—or "nothing about me without me" (Berwick, 2011).

Collaborative Care
A general term for ongoing working relationships between clinicians, rather than a specific product or service (Doherty, McDaniel & Baird, 1996). Providers combine perspectives and skills to understand and identify problems and treatments, continually revising as needed to hit goals, e.g., in collaborative care of depression (Unützer et al, 2002).

Patient-Centered Medical Home
An approach to comprehensive primary care for children, youth and adults—a setting that facilitates partnerships between patients and their personal physicians, and when appropriate, the patient's family. Emphasizes care of populations, team care, whole person care—including behavioral health, care coordination, information tools, and business models needed to sustain the work. The goal is health, patient experience, and reduced cost (Joint Principles of PCMH, 2007).

Coordinated Care
The organization of patient care activities between two or more participants (including the patient) involved in care, to facilitate appropriate delivery of healthcare services. Organizing care involves the marshalling of personnel and other resources needed to carry out required care activities, and often managed by the exchange of information among participants responsible for different aspects of care" (AHRQ, 2007).

Co-Located Care
BH and PC providers (i.e. physicians, NPs) delivering care in same practice.
This denotes shared space to one extent or another, not a specific service or kind of collaboration (adapted from Blount, 2003).

Primary Care
Primary care is the provision of integrated, accessible health care services by clinicians who are accountable for addressing a large majority of personal health care needs, developing a sustained partnership with patients, and practicing in the context of family and community (Institute of Medicine, 1994).

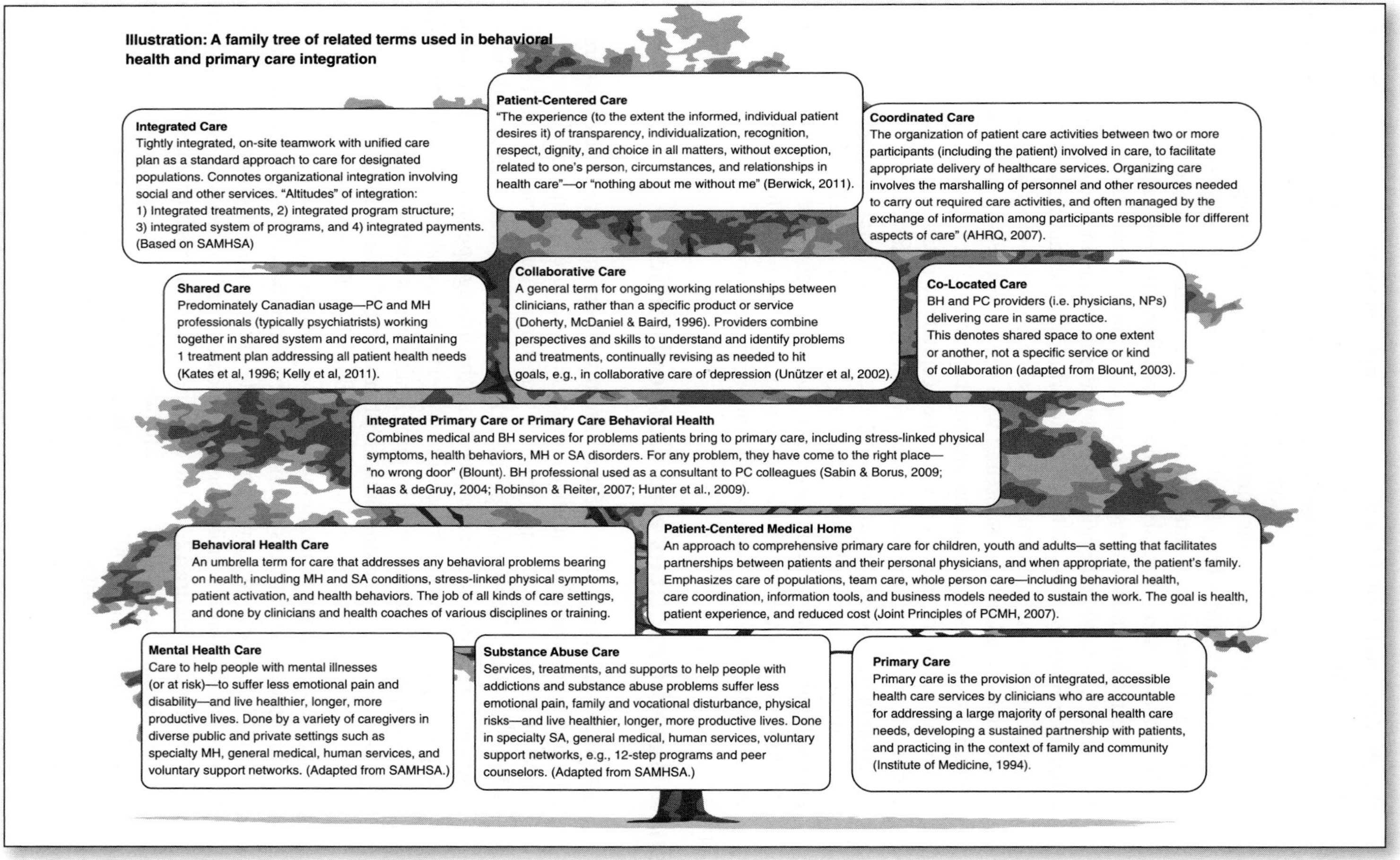

SOURCE: Peek & the National Integration Academy Council (2013).

adults who typically are less engaging in services by comparing two types of care: co-location of mental health and substance abuse services within primary care clinics, or enhanced referral to offsite mental health or substance abuse specialty clinics. Findings strongly supported the integrated care model, with nearly two-thirds of participants using the services offered leading to better engagement for older adults (over age 65) when counseling services were located within the primary physician offices as compared to the other study group, referral only, where less than half of the older adult participants used services when referred (Bartels et al., 2004). It is further important to note the benefits for older adults that the large majority of participating physicians cited: reducing harmful stigma that often limits clients from seeking counselors, improved communication between physicians and mental health/substance abuse specialists, and enhanced beneficial outcomes for the older participants (Gallo et al., 2004).

Box 12.4: Screening Older Adults for Risky Use in a Hospital Setting: Why Not Everyone?

As a doctoral counseling intern who conducts alcohol screening, brief intervention, and referral to treatment (SBIRT) for adults in an inpatient medical unit of a major general hospital in my area, I've learned that the best way to assess for substance use (aside from measuring levels in blood and urine) is through an open conversation. I've also learned that I can't determine who is at risk for substance use disorders or risky use simply by considering demographic factors. Although the popularized image of an addicted person might be someone who is young, as I've witnessed so often with hospitalized older adults whose health concerns are the direct result of their substance use, older adults are not immune to addiction or risky substance use. Detecting an alcohol use disorder or risky drinking behavior in an older adult can be difficult without deliberate assessment and a commitment to providing care that sidesteps common stereotypes. Imagine Mrs. Jones, an active 85-year-old female, who comes to the hospital following a fall in her home. Why do you think she fell? A scatter rug? A stroke? Peripheral neuropathy? What about her drinking patterns? Or would you presume that because of her age, falling is to be expected? Let's say Mrs. Jones drinks one 5-ounce glass of wine with dinner every Friday and Saturday night, well within the limits set by the National Institute for Health (NIH) for healthy adults 65 and older. This has been her habit for years, but a week ago, when Mrs. Jones hurt her wrist while gardening, her doctor prescribed a narcotic pain reliever. When she stood up from the dinner table last night, her glass of wine, combined with her pain medication, caused her to feel lightheaded, and she lost her balance and fell. Without an assessment of her drinking patterns, Mrs. Jones might never be aware of the connection between her otherwise low-risk behavior and her recent fall. Is Mrs. Jones living with an alcohol use disorder? It doesn't appear so. Is Mrs. Jones drinking at a level that could negatively impact her health? Well, as long as she is taking those pain pills, she certainly is. Regardless of their age, we owe it to *all* our clients and patients to assess for substance use disorders and risky use. Talking with our clients/patients about the health implications of drinking alcohol is one way we can better serve those for whom we have pledged to care.

Sara W. Bailey, MA, Doctoral Student, UNCG Counselor Education and Supervision, Greensboro, NC, specializes in conducting research in best practice and counseling older adults and individuals with substance use complications in a medical setting. Through a family foundation's sponsorship, she is beginning to examine best practice counseling older adults with substance use disorders who experience suicidal ideation or attempts leading to a hospital trauma admission.

The advent of integrated care, especially for the complex physical conditions that can accompany substance use disorders, is a major development in the way care is provided. At no time in the past has our field moved into a greater and more defined presence in health care, particularly co-locating screening and brief intervention substance abuse counselors into offices within primary care doctors' clinics. The value of this integrated, holistic approach lends itself to greater screening of other complicating conditions that thwart addiction recovery and thus, better coordination of services that can be more quickly provided once assessments reveal clarity of comorbidities that the client is struggling with.

Black (2010) highlights a number of comorbidities that are often associated with adverse childhood events (ACE) and major studies in the 1990s investigating the influence of adverse childhood events; major findings underscore substantial correlations of illness in adult life with adverse childhood experiences. As more adverse events are experienced by the growing child—like physical abuse, sexual abuse, or witnessing family violent events—the greater the incidence of comorbid complications, such as frequent headaches related to increased anxiety as a result of posttraumatic stress disorders with comorbid conditions, such as a severe alprazolam (Xanax) use disorder (Black, 2010). The effects of adverse childhood events can have a profound effect on the individual throughout the lifespan, from childhood to older age, especially related to substance use and comorbid psychiatric disorders. One such complication arising from a psychiatric comorbidity that can relate to childhood trauma involves suicidal thoughts, intents, or attempts.

In the United States, approximately every 15 seconds another person takes their own life by suicide (SAMHSA, 2016b). When examining suicide and substance use, alcohol is a particularly problematic substance. In layman's terms, adding alcohol, a central nervous system depressant, into an individual contemplating suicide is very much like adding gasoline to a fire. Pompili and colleagues (2010) conducted a thorough examination of suicide and alcohol use by researching all studies conducted to date with those key terms. Findings throughout extensive global research noted these highlights: Russian research noted a 60–120-fold increase of suicides for those with alcohol use disorders and psychiatric comorbidities when compared to drinkers without a psychiatric disorder; alcohol was present in 45% (Swedish) to nearly 30% (American) to 20% (Dutch) of autopsied suicide deaths; complicated trends were noted by the combination of depression and alcohol use disorders, found in 85% of 100 examined suicides; and, violence, including self-violence such as suicide, is often associated with alcohol use (Pompili et al., 2010). Conclusions by the researchers noted "alcohol use is neither a necessary nor sufficient condition for suicide, but may be regarded as a contributing factor" (Pompili et al., 2010, p. 1398). The findings highlighted "whereas suicidal behavior in youngsters is often impulsive and communicative, in older people it is often long-planned and involves highly lethal methods (Pompili et al., 2010, p. 1404). Screening and additional resources are noted in Figure 12.2. In conclusion, the authors emphasized the need for counselors to screen for the combined issues of alcohol use, depression, and suicidality. By far, alcohol is not the only substance or process that increases suicidal risks, so it is important for counselors to screen for any substance use in addition to suicidality.

Figure 12.2   Assessing Suicide Risk: Initial Tips for Counselors

What To Do If You Think a Person Is Having Suicidal Thoughts

You cannot predict death by suicide, but you can identify people who are at increased risk for suicidal behavior, take precautions, and refer them for effective treatment.

- **Ask** the person directly if he or she (1) is having suicidal thoughts/ideas, (2) has a plan to do so, and (3) has access to lethal means:

  - "Are you thinking about killing yourself?"

  - "Have you ever tried to hurt yourself before?"

  - "Do you think you might try to hurt yourself today?"

  - "Have you thought of ways that you might hurt yourself?"

  - "Do you have pills/weapons in the house?"

    - This *won't* increase the person's suicidal thoughts. It *will* give you information that indicates how strongly the person has thought about killing him- or herself.

- Take seriously all suicide threats and all suicide attempts. A past history of suicide attempts is one of the strongest risk factors for death by suicide.

- There is no evidence that "no-suicide contracts" prevent suicide. In fact, they may give counselors a false sense of reassurance.

- **Listen and look** for red flags for suicidal behavior, indicated by the mnemonic:

IS PATH WARM?

Ideation—Threatened or communicated
Substance abuse—Excessive or increased

Purposeless—No reasons for living
Anxiety—Agitation/Insomnia
Trapped—Feeling there is no way out
Hopelessness

Withdrawing—From friends, family, society
Anger (uncontrolled)—Rage, seeking revenge
Recklessness—Risky acts, unthinking
Mood changes (dramatic)

- **Act.**

  - If you think the person might harm him- or herself, do not leave the person alone.

  - Say, "I'm going to get you some help."

  - Call the National Suicide Prevention Lifeline, 1-800-273-TALK. You will be connected to the nearest available crisis center. Or...

  - Go to SAMHSA's Mental Health Services Locator (www.mentalhealth.samhsa.gov/databases/) or Substance Abuse Treatment Facility Locator (http://dasis3.samhsa.gov).

Assessing Suicide Risk: Initial Tips for Counselors

1-800-273-TALK (8255)

suicidepreventionlifeline.org

U.S. DEPARTMENT OF HEALTH AND HUMAN SERVICES
Substance Abuse and Mental Health Services Administration
www.samhsa.gov

Printed 2006 • Reprinted 2010
CMHS-SVP-0153

The study of care for psychiatric or mental health comorbidities in relation to care for substance use disorders is such an important area of focus that a major review of evidence-based studies was conducted reviewing 67 research-related contributions (Kelly, Daley, & Douaihy, 2012). With such a vast amount of information from these analyses, it may be helpful to first examine Table 12.1.

Table 12.1 Outcomes and Evidence-Based Approaches

Select Outcomes Using Various Approaches	Focus of Comorbidity in Related to Substance Use Disorder	Pharmacotherapy	Therapeutic Approach
Not indicated to improved substance-related symptoms; increased risks with side effects.	Clients with mood and anxiety	Antidepressants	Not the focus
Beneficial outcome to prescribe medication, especially clozapine, olanzapine, and rispiridone. Some evidence that clozapine shows effectiveness in reduction of alcohol, cocaine, and cannabis use.	Schizophrenia, especially when cannabis use contributes to psychosis	Second-generation psychotic medications	Not the focus
Improved therapeutic engagement and retention.	All	Not the focus	Motivational interviewing
Fewer cravings for cocaine, especially with use of olanzapine.	Psychosis and cocaine use disorder	Second-generation antipsychotic medications	Not the focus
Reduced psychosis and substance use.	Schizophrenia	Not the focus	Combination of MI, CBT, and family therapy
Intensive outpatient program showed more effectiveness for better cannabis recovery; mixed results regarding antidepressants benefiting reductions of cannabis use, especially in older teens with depressed mood.	Cannabis use and mood disorders	Antidepressants: SSRIs	Outpatient MI and CBT
Mixed findings; unclear if medications reduce cravings or substance use while stabilizing bipolar disorder. No benefit with cannabis reduction when divalproex, buproprion, lamotragine, gabapentin, or nefazadone were tried.	Bipolar disorder and cocaine or cannabis use	Mood-stabilizing medications, particularly lithium carbonate	Not the focus

Table based on selected outcomes reviewed in Kelly, Daley, & Douaihy, 2012.

Overall, continued research is needed to best identify unique combinations of approaches that work effectively to treat individuals with substance use disorders and a variety of mental disorders (Kelly, Daley, & Douaihy, 2012). It is clear that too few studies exist that adequately provide counselors with definitive approaches that are most effective. In general, the combination of CBT, MI, and TSF (Combined Behavioral Intervention) have been studied more extensively while other alternative approaches have very few studies to date (Kelly, Daley, & Douaihy, 2012). In conclusion, this chapter noted important overall findings highlighting the continued need to treat substance use disorders concurrently with other mental disorders to achieve the best outcomes. Thus, the addiction counselor can benefit from more specific professional development in the area of mental disorders as well as important opportunities to collaborate with addiction specialists who have strong backgrounds in understanding psychiatric medications that are often used in treating comorbidities. Counselors who continue to collaborate with specialists in psychiatry and addiction medicine are best prepared to advocate for clients.

Skills in Action: Comorbidity

Box 12.5: Case Illustration of Michael, Current Intensive Outpatient Program Client

Michael, a 31-year-old single male client is in the second week of outpatient counseling. The major identifying issue related to substance use diagnoses is a primary diagnosis of a severe alcohol use disorder. However, in this past week in counseling sessions, Michael shared he has had difficulty in the past with depressed mood, low energy levels, and lack of interest in hobbies or leisure activities. The following is the transcript for Michael's weekly individual session:

Counselor (Zia):	We closed our session last week with the top three goals you have for counseling. I wondered about your top goal and would like to hear more.
Client (Michael):	Yeah, I've thought a lot too about what I want from counseling. I keep going in circles. It's hard to know where to start. I mean, I do wanna get a handle on this drinking—it's time to make changes there, but I don't know what that will look like.
Zia:	You've pictured different views of how changing your drinking might look.
Michael:	I think I have some ideas and I can see I need to make changes, but it's all new and I'm not that good at coming up with goals.
Zia:	You're quite concerned.
Michael:	Yeah, uh, I get really down on myself; I've promised to stop cold turkey for a while. I try to stop, then that lasts maybe a coupla days—it's always harder than I thought or somebody's inviting me to stop for happy hour. I've also had some stuff in the past where

(Continued)

(Continued)

friends thought I was really depressed—just wouldn't go out with them, didn't look forward to much of anything, and just "no go"—I even saw my family doctor who started me on some kind of antidepressant. I took it for a few days but didn't see any changes; beer did more for me than those pills, I think.

Zia: Thinking of what you most want in counseling has brought up concerns around drinking changes, and maybe some questions you even have about being depressed at times.

Michael: Yeah, what if I have some deep depression? Can I even make changes in my drinking? Is that why I drink? I mean, I want to change; I see how the drinking messes me up too much lately—it's just walking around in a fog half the time. Either I'm hungover or ready for work to be over so I can go out to the bar, or heck, even kick back at home and drink a few . . . or maybe even a lot.

Zia: I have a few items that might help us begin to look at how much of what's going on with you—you seem to really be trying to figure out where to start.

The counselor provides additional screening tools for depressed mood (Patient Health Questionnaire [PHQ]-9) and alcohol use (AUDIT), and then tallies screening results and begins the process of reviewing the screening results with the client to help provide further input for this client's goal development.

- If you were the counselor, how worried would you be about this client following through with counseling?
- How interested in his screening results do you imagine that he will be?
- What would you most want him to know at the end of the session if his screening score clearly indicates he is at severe risk for an alcohol use disorder but has a very low screening score on his depression screen?
- Would you refer him further for a psychiatric evaluation? Why or why not?

Experiential Skills Learning Activities

1. Practice additional screening tools. First, as a learning exercise, locate the PHQ-9. Retrieve from http://www.cqaimh.org/pdf/tool_phq9.pdf or http://www.apa.org/pi/about/publications/caregivers/practice-settings/assessment/tools/patient-health.aspx

   Next, practice introducing the PHQ-9 to a peer who is portraying a client. Then, ask the nine questions in the PHQ-9 screen; follow the directions for scoring the PHQ-9, decide how you will share the results (look at the two websites for insights into the scoring guidelines), and practice going over the results with your role-play client.

Finally, each time you practice administering the PHQ-9, record your practice sessions and make notes to yourself, your peers, or your instructor about important insights you gained. Discuss with your instructor how you would proceed with various scoring results, especially if any suicidal thoughts or indicators are present.

2. Look in your area for a psychiatrist, psychologist, or other licensed mental health clinician who also specializes in working with clients with substance use disorders. Contact at least one of the professionals and inquire if you could interview them by phone. If so, develop at least five questions that pertain to comorbidities. You might want to ask how they define comorbidities. Or, how important is it to be aware of comorbidities? What are the most frequent comorbidities the professional treats? And, lastly, how do they collaborate with other addiction specialists such as addiction counselors?

RESOURCES FOR FURTHER LEARNING

Websites

Adverse Childhood Events Research: http://www.acestudy.org

The Center for Quality Assessment and Improvement in Mental Health (CQAIMH; Harvard University, Tufts Medical School, and Tufts–New England Medical Center: http://www.cqaimh.org

Suicide Prevention: http://www.integration.samhsa.gov/clinical-practice/suicide-prevention

Other Resources

NIDA DrugPubs Research Dissemination Center. NIDA publications and treatment materials are available from this information source. Staff provide assistance in English and Spanish and have TTY/TDD capability. Phone: 877-NIDA-NIH (877-643-2644); TTY/TDD: 240-645-0228; fax: 240-645-0227; e-mail: drugpubs@nida.nih.gov; Website: http://drugpubs.drugabuse.gov.

The National Registry of Evidence-based Programs and Practices (NREPP). This database of interventions for the prevention and treatment of mental and substance use disorders is maintained by SAMHSA and can be accessed at http://nrepp.samhsa.gov.

SAMHSA's Store has a wide range of products, including manuals, brochures, videos, and other publications. Phone: 800-487-4889; Website: http://store.samhsa.gov.

The National Institute of Justice. As the research agency of the U.S. Department of Justice, the National Institute of Justice (NIJ) supports research, evaluation, and demonstration programs relating to drug abuse in the context of crime and the criminal justice system. For information, including a wealth of publications, contact the National Criminal Justice Reference Service at 800-851-3420 or 301-519-5500; or visit http://nij.gov.

Clinical Trials. For more information on federally and privately supported clinical trials, please visit http://clinicaltrials.gov.

Box 12.6: Comorbidity Search Tip

National Registry of Evidence-based Programs and Practices (NREPP) Search Tip! To find programs related to comorbidities, use the advanced search options and include special populations such as "comorbidity" and/or "dual diagnosis." In addition, you may search under setting for "mental illness," and/or "co-occurring disorders."

REFERENCES

Agrawal, A., Budney, A. J., & Lynskey, M. T. (2012). The co-occurring use and misuse of cannabis and tobacco: A review. *Journal of Addiction, 107,* 1221–1233. doi:10.1111/j.1360-0443.2012.03837

American Psychiatric Association. (2013). *Diagnostic and statistical manual of mental disorders* (5th ed.). Arlington, VA: American Psychiatric Publishing.

Babor, T. F., Higgins-Biddle, J. C., Saunders, J. B., & Monteiro, M. G. (2001). *The Alcohol Use Disorders Identification Test: Guidelines for use in primary care* (2nd ed.). Published by the Department of Mental Health and Substance Dependence, World Health Organization. http://whqlibdoc.who.int/hq/2001/WHO_MSD_MSB_01.6a.pdf

Bartels, S. J., Coakley, E. H., Zubritsky, C., Ware, J. H., Miles, K. M., Areán, P. A., . . . Levkoff, S. E. (2004). Improving access to geriatric mental health services: A randomized trial comparing treatment engagement with integrated versus enhanced referral care for depression, anxiety, and at-risk alcohol use. *American Journal of Psychiatry, 161,* 1455–1462.

Beck, A. T. (1993). *Beck Anxiety Inventory.* New York, NY: Pearson.

Beck, A.T., Steer, R. A., & Brown, G. K. (1996). *Beck Depression Inventory II.* New York, NY: Pearson. Retrieved from http://www.pearsonclinical.com/psychology/products/100000159/beck-depression-inventoryii-bdi-ii.html

Birchard, T. (2015). *CBT for compulsive sexual behavior.* New York, NY: Routledge.

Black, C. (2010, April). *The addictive family with Claudia Black Ph.D. NASW – WV Chapter.* Retrieved from http://www.naswwv.org/dmgnt_files/Claudia%20Black%20Keynote%20Handouts.pdf

Blanco, C., Secades-Villa, R., Garcia-Rodriguez, O., Labrador-Mendez, M., Wang, S., & Schwartz, R. P. (2013). Probability and predictors of remission from life-time prescription drug use disorders: Results from the National Epidemiologic Survey on Alcohol and Related Conditions. *Journal of Psychiatric Research, 47,* 42–49. doi:10.1016/jpsychires.2012.08.019

Case, A., & Deaton, A. (2015). Rising morbidity and mortality in midlife among white non-Hispanic Americans in the 21st century. *PNAS, 112,* 15078–15083. http://www.pnas.org/cgi/doi/10.1073/pnas.1518393112

Dimeoff, L. A., & Linehan, M. M. (2008, June). Dialectical behavior therapy for substance abusers. *Addiction Science & Clinical Practice, 4,* 39–47.

Gallo, J. J., Zubritsky, C., Maxwell, J., Nazar, M., Bognar, H. R., Quijano, L. M., . . . Levkoff, S. E. (2004). Primary care clinicians evaluate integrated and referral models of behavioral health care for older adults: Results from a multisite effectiveness trial (PRISM-E). *Annals of Family Medicine, 2,* 305–309. doi:10.1370/amfm.116

Kelly, T. M., Daley, D. C., & Douaihy, A. B. (2012). Treatment of substance abusing patients with comorbid psychiatric disorders. *Addictive Behaviors, 37*, 11–24. doi:10.1016/j.addbeh.2011.09.010

Kirst M., Mecredy, G., Borland, T., & Chaiton, M. (2014). Predictors of substance use among young adults transitioning away from high school: A narrative review. *Substance Use Misuse, 49*, 1795–807. doi:10.3109/108260 84.2014.933240. Epub July 17, 2014.

Kolata, G. (2015, November). Death rates rising for middle-aged white Americans, study finds. *New York Times.*

Lee, Y. S., Han, D. H., Kim, S. M., & Renshaw, P. F. (2013). Substance abuse precedes Internet addiction. *Journal of Addictive Behaviors, 38*, 2022–2025. doi:10.1016/j.addbeh.2012.12.024

Lopez-Quintero, C., Hasin, D. S., Cobos, J. P., Pines, A., Wang, S., Grant, B. F., & Blanco, C. (2011). Probability and predictors of remission from lifetime nicotine, alcohol, cannabis, or cocaine dependence: Results from the National Epidemiologic Survey on Alcohol and Related Conditions. *Addiction, 106*, 657–669. doi:10.1111/ j.1360-0443.2010.03194x

Marcus, M. T., & Zgierska, A. (2009). Mindfulness-based therapies for substance use disorders: Part 1 (Editorial) *Substance Abuse, 30*(4), 263. doi:10.1080/08897070903250027

National Institute on Drug Abuse (NIDA). (2012). *Principles of Drug Addiction Treatment* (3rd ed.). Retrieved from https://www.drugabuse.gov/sites/default/files/podat_1.pdf

Nino-de-Guzman, I. (2015, November). *Addiction interaction disorder.* Retrieved from http://www.gentlepath meadows.com/blog/item/46-addiction-interaction-disorder

Peek, C. J., and the National Integration Academy Council. (2013). *Executive summary—Lexicon for behavioral health and primary care integration: Concepts and definitions developed by expert consensus.* AHRQ Publication No.13- IP001-1-EF. Rockville, MD: Agency for Healthcare Research and Quality. Retrieved from http://integrationacademy.ahrq.gov/sites/default/files/Lexicon_ExecSummary.pdf

Pompili, M., Serafini, G., Innamorati, M., Dominici, G., Ferracuti, S., Kotzalidis, G. D., . . . Lester, D. (2010). Suicidal behavior and alcohol abuse. *International Journal of Environmental Research and Public Health, 7(4)*, 1392–1431. http://doi.org/10.3390/ijerph7041392

Smith, D. E. (2012). The process addictions and the new ASAM definition of addiction. *Journal of Psychoactive Drugs, 44*(1), 1–4. doi:10.1080/02791072.2012.662105

Substance Abuse and Mental Health Services Administration (SAMHSA). (2005). *Substance abuse treatment for persons with co-occurring disorders. Treatment Improvement Protocol (TIP) Series, No. 42.* HHS Publication No. (SMA) 133992. Rockville, MD: Author.

Substance Abuse and Mental Health Services Administration (SAMHSA). (2014). *Trauma-informed care in behavioral health services. Treatment Improvement Protocol (TIP) Series 57.* HHS Publication No. (SMA) 14-4816. Rockville, MD: Author.

Substance Abuse and Mental Health Services Administration (SAMHSA). (2016a). *What is integrated care?* Retrieved from http://www.integration.samhsa.gov/about-us/what-is-integrated-care

Substance Abuse and Mental Health Services Administration (SAMHSA). (2016b). Risk assessment suicide prevention wallet card. Retrieved from http://suicidepreventionlifeline.org/wp-content/uploads/2016/09/ risk-assessment-suicide-prevention-lifeline-wallet-card.pdf

Valderas, J. M., Starfield, B., Sibbald, B., Salisbury, C., & Roland, M. (2009). Defining comorbidity: Implications for understanding health and health services. *Annals of Family Medicine, 7*, 357–363. doi:10.1370/afm.983

Young, K. S. (2007). Cognitive behavior therapy with Internet addicts: Treatment outcomes and implications, *CyberPsychology & Behavior, 10*(5), 671–679. doi:10.1089/cpb.2007.9971

Zgierska, A., Rabago, D., Chawla, N., Kushner, K., Koehler, R., & Marlatt, A. (2009). Mindfulness meditation for substance use disorders: a systematic review. *Substance Abuse, 30*, 266–294. doi:10.1080/08897070903250019

13

Continuing Care and Relapse Prevention

❖

LEARNING OBJECTIVES

The learner will be able to

- describe the continuing care level of addiction counseling and its importance to the full spectrum of substance or process-related counseling;
- describe at least two evidence-based approaches to use in counseling individuals to prevent relapse;
- define trauma-informed counseling in continuing care; and
- provide a description of one evidence-based approach for addressing relapse issues.

Knowledge

In this chapter, the level of care that is often at the far end of the spectrum—continuing care—will be reviewed. At times, great attention is given to the intensive phase of addiction-related counseling. Much effort may be expended to help get people into the intensive level of care, such as at a residential or an intensive outpatient program. Often the keen focus is to help clients complete the intensive level of care over a 4- to 6-week time period. However, in the continuing care phase of treatment, often occurring after completion of the intensive level of care and usually over a 12- to 24-week period of time, less focus is given. In truth, for many clients, this continuing level of care is perhaps the most important. And too often, it is the least emphasized. Clients and loved ones may mistakenly believe that the hardest part is over; the intensive phase is completed successfully, and many are relieved and hopeful that the worst is over. Learning about change and gaining new insights into the tools of recovery is vastly different from implementing changes and applying newly gained recovery tools in the fumbling and often awkward ways of learning any new set of skills. Yet, our field repeatedly reiterates that relapse is common; some even add that addiction is a disease of relapse. Why then, does this level of care, the continuing care phase, get minimized? How do we change to better stress the critical importance of the continuing care phase? Important questions and approaches will be reviewed further in this chapter addressing continuing care and relapse.

Prevalence and Scope of Relapse

Indicators of Relapse: Assessing Risk Factors

One of the primary indicators emerging as a substantial contributor to relapse risk involves trauma-related complications. Collectively, our world has changed in our aware-ness of trauma, what in the past was considered abnormal. Now, "with the attacks of September 11, 2001, and other acts of terror, the wars in Iraq and Afghanistan, disastrous hurricanes on the Gulf Coast, and sexual abuse scandals, trauma has moved to the forefront of national consciousness" (Substance Abuse and Mental Health Services Administration [SAMHSA], 2014, p. 8). A person in early recovery may have unrecognized trauma-in-duced symptoms that can impair strides toward recovery. Since the late 1990s, increasing attention has been developing in trauma-informed counseling (TIC) approaches. In the work of continuing care and relapse prevention for those in counseling for substance use or process addiction disorders, the trauma-informed counseling knowledge and awareness is growing in importance. A study conducted in the 1990s, the National Comorbidity Study, provided groundbreaking data that helped shape new thinking about the prevalence of trauma. Findings revealed that in one's lifetime, trauma was not rare. In fact, the study showed patterns of lifetime experiences of trauma for 61% of men and 51% of women; these may include witnessing one or more acts of violence, being impacted by a natural disaster, or being involved in a life-threatening accident (SAMHSA, 2014).

The connection between traumatic events and an increase in risky substance use is clearer. It is now known that people who report experiencing trauma are at higher risk for substance use disorders (SAMHSA, 2014). Particularly since the traumatic events of 9/11 in New York City, more research attention has explored the lasting effects of trauma as it relates to substance use. Rates of use for alcohol, cigarettes, and marijuana among a number of those individuals who used those particular substances were shown to increase for the first 2–6 months following 9/11 (SAMHSA, 2014). Studies, for exam-ple, of recovering heroin or cocaine addicts found a high rate of relapse among those with fewer than 6 months of recovery (SAMHSA, 2014). It is not clear, however, which classifications of substances (sedatives, stimulants, opiates, etc.) are favored more than others in response to traumatic events. In addition, more research is needed to under-stand the connection between trauma-related disorders, such as posttraumatic stress disorder (PTSD), acute stress disorder, and substance-related and addictive disorders. Newer evidence also examines the physical biology and neurobiology of trauma.

Findings indicate biological changes in conjunction with PTSD and substance use disorders. Trauma-related biological discoveries show the limbic system functions differently (perhaps aggravating sleep disruptions and nightmares), major changes in the activity and cortisol levels within the adrenal system (possibly related to the hyper-arousal or overactive startle reflexes), and imbalances of both arousal and naturally occurring pain-relieving neurotransmitters (SAMHSA, 2014). The case study below typifies a trauma-related biological response.

Box 13.1: Case Illustration of Kimi, PTSD, and SUD

Kimi is a 35-year-old Native American woman who was group raped at the age of 16 on her walk home from a suburban high school. She recounts how her entire life changed on that day: "I never felt safe being alone after the rape. I used to enjoy walking everywhere. Afterward, I couldn't tolerate the fear that would arise when I walked in the neighborhood. It didn't matter whether I was alone or with friends—every sound that I heard would throw me into a state of fear. I felt like the same thing was going to happen again. It's gotten better with time, but I often feel as if I'm sitting on a tree limb waiting for it to break. I have a hard time relaxing. I can easily get startled if a leaf blows across my path or if my children scream while playing in the yard. The best way I can describe how I experience life is by comparing it to watching a scary, suspenseful movie—anxiously waiting for something to happen, palms sweating, heart pounding, on the edge of your chair."

SOURCE: Substance Abuse and Mental Health Services Administration, 2014.

As is illustrated in Kimi's case, if she also developed a substance use disorder complicated by self-medicating her anxious fears, it is easier to understand how PTSD symptoms could wreak havoc in recovery, especially during the continuing care phase. When the intensive treatment counseling goes from 3–5 days per week and normally decreases to one continuing care group session per week, this can be a dramatic change in supportive counseling. Relapse risks are especially present in the continuing care phase. It is often when newly learned coping skills are tested on a frequent basis and after the structured and supportive intensive phase of substance or process addiction treatment has been completed. During this phase of continuing care, the PTSD symptoms can create challenges for taking each step in recovery. Imagine Kimi from the case above, if she were being asked to attend 12-step meetings in her community and her only means of transport was by walking just a few blocks to the meeting; how might that impact her continuing care plan? Added to the stressors of walking to a meeting might include her community 12-step meeting being comprised mostly of men. As an addiction counselor, it would be easy to understand how she would have substantial difficulty completing the most basic steps that would be important in her recovery. Without a trauma-informed approach to her care, especially in the continuing care phase, Kimi's recovery might not be able to achieve stability. Her relapse risk would be substantially heightened due to trauma-related complications. It is this informed awareness that trauma-informed counseling seeks to address; it is this trauma-informed counseling that can be particularly important during the continuing care phase to reduce relapse.

First, it may be important to provide a working definition of trauma. According to SAMHSA's Trauma and Justice Strategic Initiative, "trauma results from an event, series of events, or set of circumstances that is experienced by an individual as physically or emotionally harmful or threatening and that has lasting adverse effects on the individual's functioning and physical, social, emotional, or spiritual well-being" (SAMHSA, 2014, p. 28). Both authors of this textbook have conducted TIC in hospital trauma centers with severely injured patients. The following list, although not all-inclusive, includes many examples of types of trauma our clients experienced to bring them into the hospital. Intentional trauma is what is referred to, and often is the most violent injury both physically and emotionally when someone intentionally injures another. Many types of intentional injuries occur while a person is engaging in risky substance use, and trauma-informed counseling is critical for helping address the trauma response as well as connect the role of substances or processes to possible health changes often prompted by a near-death injury when working with TIC. Intentional trauma examples include the following:

- Burning someone's home, car, or belongings with the intent of burn injuries inflicted on another (arson).
- Attempted or completed homicide using various mechanisms of injury such as guns, knives, blunt objects such as wooden bats, vehicles, being shoved from a dangerous level or moving car, sharp objects such as broken glass, drug overdoses, or poisoning (including domestic violence).
- Assaults meant to injure but without homicidal intent, most injuries sustained in hand-to-hand fighting.
- Sexual assaults or abuse.
- Terrorist attacks.

Non-intentional trauma can occur as a result of accidents or natural disasters and may include motor vehicle crashes, including any wheeled vehicle such as mopeds, bicycles, dirt bikes, all-terrain vehicles, and motorcycles; airplane crashes or other flying mechanisms such as paragliders; falls including falls from heights (trees, billboards, scoreboards, balconies, rooftops, chimneys, hunting stands, ladders) or falls from standing (down steps, off porches or decks, off sidewalks, over furniture, pets, rugs, books); and, lastly, floods, hurricanes, wind damage, tornado, lightning strike, electrocution, mud or landslide, blizzard, or avalanche. Once the counselor has a better understanding of the scope of trauma and its definition, it can be helpful to examine the recommendations for providing trauma-informed counseling. It is very important to underscore that TIC is not a separate approach to counseling; rather, it is *adjunctive*. TIC blends well with any of the continuing care and relapse prevention counseling approaches by adding a comprehensive element to client care. In general, three overall elements should be included in all TIC: first, recognition that trauma affects many individuals, families, and communities—it is not a rarity; second, a better understanding of how trauma affects all involved (counselors, clients, administrators, agencies, etc.); and, third, taking action to incorporate TIC (SAMHSA, 2014). Here are more specific components for incorporating TIC in continuing care and relapse prevention programs:

1. Increase trauma awareness and a working knowledge of trauma-related complications impacting recovery and addictive disorders.

2. Review and select at least two trauma screening tools that have multicultural sensitivity with respect to age, gender, sexual identity, race, and ethnicity, for example.

3. Develop appropriate counseling interventions that may include collaboration with trauma specialists; provide psychoeducation about trauma and responses to trauma that can include drug seeking to self-medicate, or risky substance or process use (binges: shopping, eating, drinking, etc.); provide grounding techniques in case clients exhibit distressed reactions to trauma awareness; and include trauma-focused strategies within client's continuing care plan.

4. Attend to retraumatization issues, especially in group continuing care counseling settings where traumatic experiences may be shared without understanding the full trauma history of clients. Include staff in retraumatization awareness, as counselor's traumatic histories may become activated; as noted, "decrease the inadvertent retraumatization that can occur from implementing standard organizational policies, procedures, and interventions with individuals, including clients and staff, who have experienced trauma or are exposed to secondary trauma" (SAMHSA, 2014, p. 26).

For those who want to do more in-depth design of an agency in TIC, the reader is encouraged to consult the *TIP 57* downloadable guidebook (SAMHSA, 2014), which provides comprehensive material to help administrators incorporate TIC into an agency or clinic.

Box 13.2: Case Illustration of JanNisha

JanNisha is a beginning counselor, working toward licensure in her first job as a counselor in a substance-related addictive treatment center aptly called New Start. JanNisha is the continuing care counselor and has a group counseling session once per week for 90 minutes over a 12-week time period. At times, clients will request additional individual sessions on a weekly basis as a part of the services New Start offers. One of her continuing care clients, Jeff, requests additional individual sessions. In the first individual session with Jeff, he shares that he has recently had several bothersome nightmares about his older sister. He talks about how the dreams remind him of their difficult childhood and how much they relied on each other for safety from their violent father who suffered from a severe alcohol use disorder. Jeff talks about how he is committed to sobriety now that he sees he has what he calls the "terminal disease of alcoholism" just like his father. He quickly adds that he swore to his sister he would never be like his father and never let his drinking get out of control. Now at age 52, he says, he sees how wrong he has been all these years. JanNisha has provided several opportunities for group members to share similar promises that were made as children growing up in homes where one or more parent/caregiver struggled with an addictive disorder, thereby providing an important sense of universality; Jeff knows he is not alone.

JanNisha is incorporating more trauma-informed counseling tools; the first step, her trauma-informed awareness, is heightened. She has now heard Jeff share several times about current nightmares, difficulty sleeping, and increased sense of foreboding regarding his older sister. She has already talked with her trauma-informed counseling supervisor and plans to take the next steps in a trauma-informed counseling approach, which involve screening Jeff for trauma-related concerns. JanNisha explains to Jeff that there may be some of his current symptoms that might tie in to ways he learned to manage past traumatic events, like growing up with a violent father. She offers to go over a screening tool that may help both of them look at how those past ways of coping might be important in his early stages of recovery. He will be able to see results, and she emphasizes that the screening is not about getting a diagnosis but rather looking at current ways of dealing with life stressors that may be tied to past coping with traumatic events. Jeff expresses a strong interest in going forward with the screening tool JanNisha described. Rather than administering the screening with Jeff completing the tool using a paper and pencil format, JanNisha chooses to administer the screening in an interview format. This gives her more insight into Jeff's nonverbal communication for each item as well as how he chooses to answer each item.

In lieu of providing one specific screen, a representative example from the *Treatment Improvement Protocol 57*, Appendix D–Screening and Assessment Instruments is reprinted here (see Table 13.1). For a few of the screens, if a cost is involved for purchasing the screening instrument, the cost is indicated in the description. Many addiction-oriented agencies and centers have limited funding, so those screening tools in the public domain may have greater utility. As seen, a specific trauma–addiction scale designed for use with individuals receiving counseling for addictive disorders is not available at this time. More screening tools specific to the relapse prevention issues are needed.

Understanding the Importance of Continuing Care to Prevent Relapse

As Furr, Johnson, and Goodall (2015) noted in a study regarding the effects of grief and loss while counseling individuals with substance use disorders, the continuing care level of counseling included in the study was designed to offer supportive counseling to maximize recovery with a need to prevent relapse. It is important to note that a majority of the participants in the study had multiple, prior episodes of substance-related addiction treatment and thus, had a history of relapse (Furr et al., 2015). Loss can be considered traumatic for a number of individuals, and in this study loss history

Table 13.1	Distressing Event Questionnaire (DEQ)
Domains:	Posttraumatic stress disorder (PTSD) for multiple events
Timeframe:	Lifetime
Response format:	Self-administered
Format of administration:	Structured
Number of items:	35
Completion time:	10–15 minutes
Qualifications to administer:	Contact Edward Kubany, PhD
How to obtain scale:	Contact Edward Kubany, PhD
Cost or public domain:	Contact Edward Kubany, PhD
Psychometrics:	Population sampled: veterans, battered women Reliability: inter-item r = .93, test-retest = .95; validity: Pearson's r reliability coefficient = .83 (with Penn Inventory, Pearson's r reliability coefficient = .76 (with Beck Depression Inventory)
Author(s):	Edward Kubany, Mary Beth Leisen, Aaron S. Kaplan, Martin P. Kelly
Contact:	Edward Kubany, PhD, National Center for PTSD, Pacific Islands Division, Department of Veterans Affairs, Suite 307 Honolulu, HI
Relevant citations:	Kubany, E. S., Leisen, M. B., Kaplan, A. S., & Kelly, M. P. (2000). Validation of a brief measure of posttraumatic stress disorder: The distressing event questionnaire (DEQ). *Psychological Assessment, 12*, 197–209.

SOURCE: TIP 57, 2014. Appendix D: Screening and Assessment Instruments.

was deemed substantial. The researchers found the following upon questioning participants about losses:

> The top five losses reported by participants were: death of someone special (77.6%), financial losses (76.5%), loss of substance use (75.8%), witnessed violence (74.2%), and loss of cognitive functioning (73.5%). (Furr et al., 2015)

With such substantial loss history reported by the majority of participants, the importance of addressing loss is underscored for helping clients decrease the incidence of relapse. Continuing care can be an important level of care for the counselor to monitor issues, such as traumatic loss that may be thwarting progress toward recovery. In the continuing care phase, the counselor is tasked with checking in with clients to determine how successful clients are in applying recovery tools in everyday living challenges and successes. With sessions occurring ordinarily only once per week, the client will have many opportunities between sessions to try out new coping tools, new emotional responses, repairing intimacy if in a committed relationship or make new decisions about beginning new romantic relationships, start different routines, share in recovery-oriented support meetings, meet others in recovery, navigate returning to work and family settings, and facing many new challenges without turning back to using substances or addictive processes. In the critical months following intensive treatment, it is often the most vulnerable time for the newly recovering person to test how the use of recovery-oriented tools actually works. It can also be the time when those new to recovery learn more about where to get stuck and how to cope when progress is halted.

In the continuing care phase of care, it is also an important time for clients to assess their recovery support system, such as family, employer, social, cultural, spiritual, and wellness networks. For clients who have robust support systems that are intact, the continuing care phase will often result in continuing progress toward recovery. For clients who have extremely fragile or damaged support systems, the recovery efforts may suffer. Clients can find themselves asking more questions about the *why* of recovery. Emotions of loneliness and rejection can make the long days between weekly continuing care sessions seem overwhelming. Special planning and engagement to strengthen support can mediate and help build a new support system. In the mutual-help groups, there are structures to help the person new to recovery begin to build a sober and process/drug-free network. In the Twelve-Step Facilitation (TSF) model, the addiction counselor can review the important contacts between temporary (or permanent) sponsors, offset confusion about the expectations of sponsorship and relationships with members of 12-step or similar groups, and try to help the client identify and select a "home" group that best mirrors the client's age, gender, cultural identity, and recovery goals, and helps the client feel more at home.

At times, in continuing care sessions, family issues emerge that can indeed overwhelm newfound sobriety with powerful emotions. As a beginning counselor, this first author learned quickly about the power of family distress in the continuing care phase. Too soon many clients wanted to do in-depth counseling to quickly repair decades of addiction-related pain and damage. As a new counselor, it was so easy to join with the client to think intensive family therapy could begin in the second month of sobriety. Clinical supervision, fortunately, provided more clarity about realistic goals for the early months of sobriety. First, clients can identify goals of repairing loving relationships, yet it is important that timing be reviewed. In continuing care, it is clear that clients are beginning to get practice with new coping skills while resisting use of old coping skills, namely using drugs or processes to cope/escape. It is a delicate balance to honor the progress clients are making while, as a counselor, not leading the client (and loved ones) to tackle deep emotions and wounds that can engulf the fragile and beginning use of coping skills. The goal, then, of the continuing care addiction counselor is to individualize goal-setting related to family repair. It is not uncommon for deeper family therapy to begin later, possibly after 6 months of sustained recovery progress. Another important consideration may need to include reminders to the continuing care counselor to refer the family to a counselor who specializes in family therapy and addiction issues.

Box 13.3: Aftercare as an Essential Element for Successful Recovery

Recovery from the disease of addiction is rarely a smooth and seamless journey. Relapse rates are high enough to fuel the fears of skeptics who argue that there is no point in investing the funds, the time, or the hope for recovery. But before professional counselors reach the same conclusions, it is important to stay objective enough to recognize two critical variables: the quality of primary treatment and the quality of aftercare.

An accreditation surveyor once remarked, "If you've seen one treatment, you've seen one treatment center." As a surveyor, he had literally delved deep into all aspects of operations, leadership, clinical services, facilities, and safety of hundreds of treatment programs around the United States. He saw vast differences between them. Some programs operate with essentially no formally educated staff, relying almost exclusively on the application of 12-step facilitation as the framework for teaching patients how to utilize that model of recovery to sustain abstinence. Others are committed to utilizing evidence-based models of care; multidisciplinary teams of highly educated, credentialed professionals; and an array of traditional, experiential, and pharmacologic tools to achieve as much as possible while patients have 24/7 support. Ironically, programs that meet both of those extreme examples can achieve lasting or fleeting results. Perhaps the biggest differences, though, come from the quality of effective aftercare or continuing care planning and the degree of commitment from the patient to follow the plan.

Dr. Kevin McCauley, a former flight surgeon and highly renowned recovery advocate, argues that "the most important moment of inpatient treatment for addiction is the *first hour after discharge*." It is in that juncture from the safety and security of a primary residential environment back into everyday life that their risk to relapse is at its peak. Frankly, *anyone* can stay clean and sober in a residential treatment environment. In most cases, there is no opportunity to even have access to substances while in treatment, but immediately after discharge, all of that changes.

In our practice, we provide an array of aftercare supports that include clinically supported sober living, ongoing individual therapy, Gorski-CENAPS relapse prevention groups, breathalyzer and drug test monitoring, recovery coaching, recovery support groups, family support groups, medication reviews, and coordination of care with other providers. Some clients have participated in the development of a very comprehensive aftercare plan that is provided to us. Others have participated in the plan's development, but the primary treatment center fails to provide them or us a copy of the plan. Still others were never encouraged to develop an aftercare plan at all.

Ironically, the number of programs dedicated to meeting the aftercare needs of those in early recovery pale by comparison to the number of primary residential treatment and outpatient programs offering an alternative to residential treatment. In assessing the unmet needs in our region, we identified a need for pretreatment services, including formal intervention, and aftercare services. Ninety-five percent of the dedicated long-term aftercare we provide is focused on the needs of young adults and monitored professionals. Young adults have the greatest risk for destroying their *own* lives and the lives of their families if recovery cannot be sustained. Licensed professionals, on the other hand, pose the greatest risk for destroying the lives of *others* if recovery cannot be sustained.

Young adults often began abusing substances in their early teens and thus lack the maturity and coping skills necessary to sustain recovery without a tremendous amount of support. Some primary residential programs dedicated to serving young adults include sober living in 100% of aftercare plans. In our sober living program, we observe that most young adults present developmentally as very immature. Prefrontal cortex development is incomplete anyway, and their development has been further compromised by substance use during those critical adolescent years. Many have never learned how to wash their own clothes, load a dishwasher, sweep a floor, or dust. They have little or no experience managing their finances, interviewing for jobs, or even utilizing e-mail for correspondence with professionals. With executive functioning further compromised by post-acute withdrawal symptoms, these young adults need help developing even the most basic of functional life skills as well as strong support to manage cravings, conquer social anxieties that complicate integration into the recovery community, and manage symptoms of co-occurring disorders.

Licensed professionals have achieved great success as physicians, dentists, pharmacists, airline pilots, nurses, and attorneys. Virtually all of them have all the functional life skills they need, but if they are not able to sustain abstinence, they may unintentionally threaten the lives entrusted to them. Licensing boards in most states opt to establish separate monitoring organizations charged with the responsibility of monitoring the professionals' compliance with certain requirements intended to protect public safety. In our experience providing long-term relapse prevention to these bright, capable, responsible "high flyers," inflated egos and intellectualization and other forms of denial continue to interfere with a full engagement in recovery. But their fear of economic insecurity and loss of livelihood provide sufficient motivation for them to comply with requirements of the monitoring board. While monitoring boards require compliance, they hope that those who comply experience true recovery.

Whether the person in early recovery is a 20-year-old high school dropout, a 25-year-old law student, or a 40-year-old neurosurgeon, there are certain aftercare resources that dramatically improve the likelihood of achieving a sustained recovery for all of them. While the young adult may be highly proficient with a videogame controller and the surgeon may be highly proficient with a scalpel, both are learning new information and skills they will need to live full lives in recovery from the disease of addiction. Residential programs are like drivers' education programs that teach a new driver how to drive and give them the first few lessons behind the wheel. In contrast, aftercare programs like ours are there to help counsel, monitor, support, and encourage that new driver to apply everything they've learned in that first year of supervised practice.

It has been our experience that Dr. Kevin McCauley's recommendations are appropriate for virtually everyone in their first year of recovery. In his white paper titled *Ten Tips for the First Year of Recovery*, Dr. McCauley advocates that, whenever possible, the best opportunity to help establish a strong foundation for sustainable recovery includes the following:

- Residential treatment for a minimum of 4 weeks
- Immediate engagement in a formalized aftercare plan that begins on the day of discharge and admission to a pre-assigned outpatient treatment program
- Sober living environment for a minimum of 4 weeks after residential treatment
- Daily engagement in recovery support groups for a minimum of 3 months after residential treatment

(Continued)

(Continued)

- A relapse plan in place prior to discharge from residential treatment
- Testing to verify abstinence, typically
- Return to duty in fulfillment of primary responsibilities such as work, parenting, school, and so on as soon as safely possible
- Regular visits with an addictionologist for a minimum of 1 year
- Prescription(s) for non-addicting medication to treat depression, anxiety, insomnia, cravings, or mood swings causing distress significant enough to lead to relapse
- Regular opportunities for sober fun

These are the aftercare elements that are often mandated for professionals—the subgroup of the recovery community that has the lowest rates of relapse and the highest rates of sustained recovery. It makes perfect sense that—if these are the circumstances that are necessary for high-functioning, fully mature, and highly supported individuals to achieve sustainable recovery, young adults and others with fewer natural and community supports would need at least the same level of care.

Practices and agencies like ours have a chance to witness just how hard the first 6–12 months of recovery can be for young adults. We support them through their struggles with knowing how to make friends, have sober fun, deal with "unanesthetized" emotional pain, legal charges, debt or tax problems, and the wreckage of damaged relationships with the people they love the most. In our work with licensed professionals, we support them while they learn how to tolerate the loss of their right to practice for months or even years, loss of income, damage to their reputations, possible malpractice suits, legal charges, and problems with getting re-credentialed and re-approved for insurance panels and malpractice coverage.

But make no mistake! Supporting those in the first couple of years of recovery is not for the faint of heart. We also have a ringside seat for relapses, overdoses, and other forms of self-sabotage. We administer naloxone, make 911 calls, discharge using residents to protect those who are compliant with all the sober living rules, and comfort parents who are becoming more and more afraid and hopeless when self-sabotage continues. We comfort brilliant professionals as they discover that it's almost impossible to get even the most mindless minimum wage job, cope with possible non-recoverable cognitive damage that may bring an end to their career even if they do meet all their monitoring requirements, or determine how to move forward if they are victims of reputation assassination by a colleague or partner. But if those things happen with all of the support we provide, you can better believe that families and friends have the same ringside seat and are *far less-equipped* to help when the going gets tough.

And yet it is a huge privilege to be a part of the solution for young adults reconciling with their families, restoring their hope and confidence in themselves, and beginning to finally realize their potential. It is equally gratifying to be a part of the solution for recovering professionals returning to safe practice with a new humility, a renewed commitment to the reason they chose their profession in the first place, and tremendous appreciation for those who have supported them through the trials of suspended practice.

Not only is there tremendous need for dedicated aftercare programs, there are also tremendous entrepreneurial opportunities for addiction professionals. Addiction professionals have great opportunities to cultivate partnerships with residential treatment centers, professional monitoring organizations, collegiate recovery communities, drug courts, and professional recovery advocates that can identify aftercare needs in your own community or region.

SOURCE: Ginny Mills, MA, LCAS, LPCS, CCS, is the founder of Full Life Counseling, in Winston Salem, North Carolina.

Evidence-Based Practices

A variety of approaches to relapse prevention have been introduced in the care of addictive disorders. This section will examine select approaches used in relapse prevention. Even with evidence-based approaches that demonstrate effectiveness, addictive disorders remain challenging when faced with relapse. More research and relapse prevention approaches that are easily adaptable for various ages across the lifespan are needed. Our field benefits from continued efforts to prevent relapse. It remains a life-threatening condition since not all of our clients who relapse are able to live through the return to using. The addiction counselor is well served by continuing to research and gain skills in relapse prevention.

Box 13.4: Tips for Searching for Evidence-Based Programs

National Registry of Evidence-based Programs and Practices (NREPP) Search Tip! To find programs related to relapse, use the advanced search options and include special populations such as "relapse youth" and/or "relapse adults." In addition, you may search under setting for "relapse prevention" and/or "relapse," and any of the various options on the NREPP website.

Mindfulness

Important tools using mindfulness as a recovery aid are emerging as a safe and beneficial component in relapse prevention (Zgierska et al., 2009). Research studies, however, lack more uniformity to rise to the level of endorsement that is unequivocal. In other words, compared to stringent research found in testing pharmaceutical products and deemed a therapeutic intervention, the design of research to study mindfulness as a clear and definitive benefit to prevent relapse has not been met (Zgierska et al., 2009). Nor is it clear whether mindfulness approaches have certain benefit for some substances and not others (Zgierska et al., 2009), different age groups and not others, or other multicultural considerations. The research using mindfulness techniques to prevent process addiction relapse is minimal and also has some of the same robust research design needs before counselors can provide clear and consistent "manualized" ways of utilizing mindfulness techniques to prevent relapse. As such, it is often recommended that mindfulness techniques be taught during the intensive phase of care and emphasized during the continuing care phase to reduce relapse risks with the understanding that mindfulness approaches have considerable variation.

Medication-Assisted Treatment (MAT)

Medication-assisted treatment (MAT) is another important tool that can be used in relapse prevention. It is an evolving area, and there is no one medication that has been found to prevent relapse. Medications used currently may work better for one type of abstinence plan than others. Physicians, especially those trained in addiction medicine, are key when MAT is used. Continuing care counselors need to confer with any physician prescribing MAT to aid in relapse prevention in order to understand the goals of MAT and that those goals align with the counseling goals. MAT is more accepted as a part of the options available to help prevent relapse, but at times there may be mixed opinions about the use of any other medications with recovery as the central goal. Communication with the client and practitioners involved in the client's care plan can ensure better clarity and coordinated activity. Current patterns of prescribing medications that can help reduce cravings and therefore enhance relapse prevention are lower than expected (SAMHSA & National Institute on Alcohol Abuse and Alcoholism [NIAAA], 2015). It is clear from data analyses that only a very small percentage (less than 6%) of the approximately 18 million individuals who met diagnostic criteria for an alcohol use disorder even receive treatment for the use disorder. However, physicians who specialize in addiction medicine are recommending that for those individuals having "one or more heavy drinking days in the past year (or who has an AUDIT score greater than 8)" should be assessed for MAT (SAMHSA & NIAAA, 2015, p. 7). Another highly recommended component of MAT includes "some type of counseling, and it is recommended that all patients for whom these medications are prescribed receive at least brief counseling" (SAMHSA & NIAAA, 2015, p. 11). It is noteworthy to highlight a lack of evidence, however, for the effectiveness of MAT for adolescents, nor is any Food and Drug Administration (FDA) approval given for MAT for anyone under the age of 18 (SAMHSA & NIAAA, 2015); considerably more research is needed before any young people are considered for MAT. For older adults, MAT is noted to be increasingly viewed as an effective and safe resource for older adults (SAMHSA & NIAAA, 2015).

Relapse Prevention Therapy (RPT)

Specific identification of triggers to use or return to addictive behaviors in the case of process addictions is a key component of relapse prevention therapy (RPT). With better identification, the counselor and client can then develop a plan to recognize cues and change old response patterns by developing and practicing new behaviors to avoid cues to reactivate the addictive using patterns. RPT is provided to help clients better anticipate and be prepared for alternative behaviors to reduce slips and prevent relapsing. RPT is also been shown to provide integrated care when caring for comorbidities is also part of the relapse prevention goals (SAMHSA, 2005). RPT, as developed by Marlatt and Gordon in 1985 as referenced in the *Treatment Improvement Protocol (TIP) 42* (2005), consists of five main areas: Assessment (potential relapse issues are assessed); Insight and Awareness are increased to help the client understand the process of relapse; Coping Skills Training; Cognitive Strategies; and lastly, changes involving one's Lifestyle. Preparing clients for emergency plans that are written for the "what if" possibilities, for example, "what if I am tempted to stop at a bar?" Or "what if I find myself at an outing and see my old dealer?" Or "what if I stop going to my continuing care group sessions?" By preplanning some of the possible scenarios, it can provide clients with concrete steps to take to quickly seek help; seeking help is one of the best strategies to reduce the damage and danger when a relapse occurs. RPT has been shown to have particular effectiveness since its development in the 1980s.

Recovery Communities

Therapeutic communities (TC) are an additional resource for long-term continuing care and relapse prevention, are often provided in a residential setting, and may involve stays up to 1 year (SAMHSA, 2005). Therapeutic communities have been in existence for decades and are often recommended for individuals who have had severe and recurring relapse episodes. Much has been written about TC for the treatment of individuals with substance use disorders. Often, TC has been a major resource for those whose addictive illness has left them with fragmented family, work, and home life. Studies from the 1980s and on indicate beneficial outcomes for those completing TC (SAMHSA, 2005).

In summary, a number of resources and approaches are available for the addiction counselor to utilize in continuing care phases of treatment with goals toward relapse prevention. Additional evidence-based models are being developed, and the NREPP lists a number of available manualized relapse prevention models that demonstrate effectiveness. For a number of clients, the counseling received in the continuing care phase is a major aspect in the full spectrum of care. Counselors are encouraged to continue to review outcome studies and research effective approaches to relapse prevention as more addiction specialists strive to better understand how to reduce relapses and enhance sustained recovery in order for our clients to achieve their fullest human potential.

Box 13.5: Case Illustration of Charles, Current Continuing Care Challenges

Charles, a 65-year-old widow, is in the sixth week of a 12-week continuing care program. The major identifying issue related to substance use diagnoses is a primary diagnosis of a severe opiate use disorder. Charles is mandated by his licensure board, the state medical board, to complete this phase of continuing care with another 2–4 years of continued follow-up. However, in this past week in the weekly counseling group session, Charles shared his new list to identify triggers that might jeopardize his recovery. The following is the transcript for the weekly individual session following the group session:

(Continued)

(Continued)

Counselor (Lea):	You listed a number of triggers that you have become aware of and have concerns about. I wondered about the top five triggers and would like to hear more.
Client (Charles):	Some list, isn't it? Let's see—the top five will take a few minutes...(after several minutes passes) I think these ones I circled are my top concerns. It's hard to know where to start.
Lea:	You've wondered what triggers are the most concerning—and keep in mind those top five may change again in the next hour. This is a beginning to help you look at triggers and plans to address them.
Charles:	I am worried most about going back to my office, back to my desk, and back to the prescription pad.
Lea:	You're concerned about that particular trigger—I can see you tense up considerably.
Charles:	Exactly, my hands start sweating.
Lea:	It's triggering a physical reaction. Let's stop and focus on your breathing just now, practice some of the mindful breathwork that you learned in your intensive phase of treatment. (Again, letting time pass while the client practices mindful breathwork to regain calming resources.)
Charles:	I'm back to feeling more centered and calmer.
Lea:	It's important to you to know when to practice the calming breathwork.
Charles:	It's taking lots of practice, but yes, I find when I focus on that one moment and breathe deeply, I can regain more balance. It helps.
Lea:	I see you went to the top trigger; I'd like to invite you to look at the fifth one on the list. Maybe starting with that one will help guide you toward the harder ones after more practice.
Charles:	Ha! You helped me see that pattern I get into. You know, in medical school and all these years, it's still such a competitive thing with me. I didn't realize even that can be a trigger for my addictive patterns. I guess I can add that one too!
Lea:	You've started this discovery process and are beginning to see this as an ongoing learning— letting in more of that one day at a time mindset may give you more freedom to accept this healing process.
Charles:	So many helpful reminders...okay, so trigger number 5 on my list: it's the one about being so tired at the end of the day.
Lea:	And I'm wondering about some of the possible ways you can anticipate changing that, just looking at this next week and studying to see how much warning you may have that you are pushing your energy level to the tired zone.
Charles:	Hmm, almost like doing a case review—starting to look at how it all begins to start.

Lea:	I see you smiling and notice your breathing seems calm.
Charles:	Yeah, I am really curious about figuring out earlier signs of when I'm headed for overdoing it and getting way too tired.
Lea:	And writing notes about those discoveries this week may lead you to learn how to change that pattern somewhat during this week.
Charles:	I can write down more of how that usually unfolds.
Lea:	As you are thinking and writing, it also may be helpful to think about times when you were successful at pacing your day when it did not lead to overdoing it or being too tired. I'm wondering when you were able to do that; what did you do to get that to happen? We can review your notes in our next week's session.
Charles:	So, focus on this fifth trigger. I keep seeing how this addiction has played with my mind—always driven, always pushing to go straight to the hardest and push to the limit. It's so amazing to see that more clearly now and to really get to work on different choices.

(Counselor and client close this session. Counselor summarizes the session as well as goals for continuing to explore healthy relapse prevention goals and actions.)

Consider three additional creative ways you might approach the issue of identifying triggers and relapse prevention with this client. (Hint: Create a checklist? Produce a visual graphic depicting how triggers can trip the recovering person? Other ideas?)

- How would you explain relapse to your client?
- How might you help the client examine these relapse risks?
- What else might you want to highlight prevention planning for the client?

Skills in Action

Experiential Skills Learning Activities

1. Explore treatment centers in your area that have relapse prevention material in their information. Call or visit at least two of the centers and get more specifics on how they approach relapse prevention. Find out what the continuing care phase looks like in their program, or if not available, why not? If possible, inquire about shadowing or interviewing one of the continuing care counselors or a counselor specializing in relapse prevention. Make a list of questions to learn more about the approach used, whether medication-assisted treatment is available, what the relapse rates are like for clients in their program, and why do they believe the rates are such.

2. Search for a professional development opportunity (online or in person) that specifically is about relapse prevention. Make a goal sheet after the training to include additional training you identified to increase your relapse prevention knowledge and skills.

Box 13.5: Another NREPP Search Tip

National Registry of Evidence-based Programs and Practices (NREPP) Search Tip! To find programs related to relapse prevention programs, use the advanced search options and search for "continuing care."

REFERENCES

Furr, S. R., Johnson, W. D., & Goodall, C. S. (2015). Grief and recovery: The prevalence of grief and loss in substance abuse treatment. *Journal of Addictions and Offender Counseling, 36,* 43–56.

Substance Abuse and Mental Health Services Administration (SAMHSA). (2005). *Substance abuse treatment for persons with co-occurring disorders. Treatment Improvement Protocol (TIP) Series, No. 42.* HHS Publication No. (SMA) 133992. Rockville, MD: Author.

Substance Abuse and Mental Health Services Administration (SAMHSA). (2014). *Trauma-informed care in behavioral health services. Treatment Improvement Protocol (TIP) Series 57.* HHS Publication No. (SMA) 14-4816. Rockville, MD: Author.

Substance Abuse and Mental Health Services Administration and National Institute on Alcohol Abuse and Alcoholism. (2015). *Medication for the treatment of alcohol use disorder: A brief guide.* HHS Publication No. (SMA) 15-4907. Rockville, MD: Substance Abuse and Mental Health Services Administration.

Zgierska, A., Rabago, D., Chawla, N., Kushner, K., Koehler, R., & Marlatt, A. (2009). Mindfulness meditation for substance use disorders: A systematic review. *Substance Abuse, 30,* 266–294. doi:10.1080/08897070903250019.

14

Future Directions for Evidence-Based Addictions Counseling Research

Upon completion of reading this chapter and completing the suggested activities, the learner will be able to

- identify the biopsychosocial model of client case conceptualization;
- list advances in neuroscience research related to addictions counseling;
- describe at least two types of interventions using brain science; and
- apply the knowledge learned in a clinical case scenario.

Knowledge

Psychological Theory–Based Conceptualizations

Conceptualization is an important part of the clinical work for professional counselors working with clients who may be at different points on the addiction spectrum. Case conceptualization is the application of theoretical concepts to a client's story, in order to gain insight as to how the client has ended up where he or she is today. In addition, conceptualization helps inform treatment planning, a process that occurs for all clients we encounter.

Traditional case conceptualization of addictive disorders has used psychological theories, just as counselors apply these theories to any other mental health concern. For example, a client working from the person-centered theoretical framework of Carl Rogers (1957, 1961) will focus on fostering a genuine relationship in which the client can come to be their authentic selves. A counselor working from the cognitive behavioral framework (Ellis, 1962) will help a client explore his or her cycle of thoughts, feelings, and behaviors along with the underlying cognitive schema and work to restructure for desired outcomes. A counselor working from the solution-focused framework of Steve de Shazer and Insoo Kim Berg (see De Jong & Berg, 2012) will assist clients with examining their past successes and considering how those could be applied to current struggles. This counselor may also help this client see that the solution to their concern was within them the whole time; they only needed the reflective mirror of the counselor to help see that.

These psychological theories have been applied time and time again to the addictive process. And there is a growing recognition that to best serve clients on the addiction spectrum we need to include attention to more than psychological theories. Research has demonstrated that addiction is a brain disease that affects the brain and behavior (Volkow, 2014). There are key neurological systems at play with the addictive cycle and, as we discussed in Chapter 3, we are continuing to learn more. At this point we not only have the psychological tools, but now we have added on a biological piece to this puzzle. This has caused a growing number of professional counselors to use a biopsychosocial model to inform their clinical work with clients.

Biopsychosocial Conceptualizations

The biopsychosocial model was first described by physician George Engel (1977), and he used the model to help describe certain medical concerns. As the model states, the main idea is that there are biological, psychological, and sociological components to presenting problems. For medical physicians this recognition helps to expand the framework beyond sole biology, and for professional counselors this helps expand beyond psychological and sociological concepts. There is not formula for clients of percentages for each of the three components, as this can serve as a guiding framework that can inform your work with each and every unique client.

In addition to the biopsychosocial model described by Engel (1977), some clinicians are choosing to add on a spiritual component as this is important for many clients. Hatala (2013) outlines how an integration of the spiritual aspect can be infused within the biopsychosocial model, to create a fully encompassing approach for mental health professionals.

The biopsychosocial (+ spiritual) model has important implications for treatment planning with clients on the addiction spectrum. The model helps counselors consider other variables they may need to attend to with clients. For example, a counselor may be working with a female client in her mid-20s who has come in with concerns about her alcohol consumption. In talking with the client, the counselor learns that the client is a child of divorce whose mother died in a car accident while intoxicated when the client was 7 years old. In addition, the client reports after a couple sessions that she was sexually assaulted five years previous while in college. By applying the biopsychosocial model to the client's story, the counselor can arrange the pieces of the client's story to the corresponding areas, helping organize and better prepare for treatment planning. The assault is both a medical/biological and psychological event. The client's family history helps us consider sociological variables and also biological, as a red flag is raised concerning the genetic risk for an alcohol use disorder from the mother. By acknowledging the different components and organizing, the counselor can be sure to attend to each in the treatment plan. A treatment plan solely focused on one of the areas would be incomplete and although may relieve symptoms temporarily, may not help a client fully recover.

Neuroscience and the Brain

An area that many counselors are starting to look at to embrace the biological aspects of mental health concerns is neuroscience. Neuroscience is concerned with the human brain, and all that lies within. Some estimates state that we use a very small portion of what our brains are actually capable of, and in fact, a recent popular movie and television show were even based on the story of a medical drug that helped users expand this capacity (*Limitless*). Although these shows were based in fiction, it is surprising to find out how little we do know about the human brain. In April 2015 President Barack Obama launched the BRAIN Initiative, an innovative partnership between numerous federal and nonfederal partners. BRAIN is an acronym for Brain Research through Advancing Innovative Neurotechnologies (National Institutes of Health, 2016). This initiative specifically sets aside funding for grants in order to help scientists and the public learn more about the brain, and ultimately to ameliorate some of the concerns attributed to brain disease (of which addiction is recognized). There are professional counselors who specialize in addictions that are using the information that we are learning about the brain to improve their clinical work with clients, and in addition, there are counselors who are actively involved in neuroscience research.

Box 14.1: Technological Applications for Mindfulness

The United States Department of Veterans Affairs has published a free application for smartphones and tablets, titled "Mindfulness Coach." The app is free in the Apple IOS store, and has educational information, mindfulness practices, and a tracker to monitor one's mindfulness practice.

Another free technological application for mindfulness meditation is titled "Calm." In this app, users can complete a variety of different guided meditation programs of different time lengths and also track their progress.

Not only are these apps useful within the clinical counseling practice, they may be beneficial for counselor self-care!

Box 14.2: A Counselor's Personal Reflection of Neuroscience Addiction Research

Three sisters are walking along the river and they see small children in the water. The first sister jumps in and says to the other sisters, "Come help me get the children out of the river." The second sister says, "No, we need to teach them how to swim." The third sister continues walking up the stream and her sisters inquire, "Where are you going?" The third sister replies, "I am going to go up the stream and tell whoever is putting these children in the water to stop." – Native American Story

This story is representative of how I see incorporating neural imaging in my addiction work. I see the signs and symptoms of addiction and want to help my client achieve recovery (i.e., First Sister). I provide clients psychoeducational resources to understand how addiction is established, maintained, and treated, and provide a safe, unconditional environment for the client to process (i.e., Second Sister). I investigate brain activation in individuals who abuse substances to determine neurobiological markers and what type of counseling and interventions alter the parts of the brain involved in addiction (i.e., Third Sister).

There have been numerous neural imaging studies completed that show the connection between specific brain regions and drug taking/intoxication and withdrawal behaviors (e.g., prefrontal cortex, nucleus accumbens, ventral tegmental). There has also been significant research to establish and verify evidence-based practices. However, the high relapse statistics for our clients persist. So, it seemed crucial to me as a clinician and researcher to have evidence if the treatments I am using are effective. Neural imaging provides this impartial data. fMRI technology allows me to see if the parts of the brain related to resilience and recovery are being engaged and activated by my counseling interventions.

Now, it never occurred to me in my graduate studies that I would actually be working with neuroscientists and scanning brains! The passion to ensure our clients are receiving the best care possible led me to reaching out to neuroscientists to collaborate. Yes, I was intimidated at the beginning! However, I have learned that we, as professional counselors, provide a unique perspective regarding research in this area. We can actually use our clinical knowledge to inform how studies are developed, implemented, and how the results are interpreted. We have expertise and knowledge that can move this research forward! Currently, I am co-principal investigator with Dr. Gina Forster (neuroscientist) on a project to investigate how neural functioning in adult children of alcoholics (ACoA) relates to cognitive performance and psychological health in those with and without current hazardous alcohol use. The information gained from this pilot study will be the foundation to apply for additional funding that will involve research testing interventions for at-risk ACoA. So, this idea I had as a student is now coming to fruition as a professional! I am honored to be a representative of the counseling profession in addiction neuroscience research.

SOURCE: Kathleen Brown-Rice. Kathleen Brown-Rice, PhD, LPC, LMHP, LCAS, QMHP, CAC, ACS, NCC, is assistant professor of counselor education and member of the Center for Brain and Behavior Research at the University of South Dakota.

An Expanding Definition of Addiction: Behavioral/Process Addictions

The latest release of the *Diagnostic and Statistical Manual of Mental Disorders* (*DSM*) from the American Psychiatric Association (APA) included some substantial revisions to the Substance Use Disorder chapter. One of these revisions was the recognition of the first behavioral/process addiction: gambling use disorder (APA, 2013). Although gambling disorder had previously been in the *DSM*, it was not classified as an addictive disorder, but with research highlighting the similarities to substance disorders it was reclassified (APA, 2013). In addition to gambling disorder, the APA (2013) has included Internet gaming disorder, and non-suicidal self-injury in the Conditions for Future Study section, a preliminary step for recognition as a disorder.

The formal recognition of behavioral/process addictions was an important step in a variety of ways. Not only does this recognition help validate client experiences, but it also helps to conceptualize treatment more appropriately. As a profession, we will surely see an increase in research focusing on building an evidence base for the treatment of behavioral/process addictions, as it is a needed area of inquiry.

Evidence-Based Practices

Neurofeedback

Biofeedback is the process by which an individual learns how to alter his or her own physiological activity in order to improve health (Association for Applied Psychophysiology and Biofeedback, 2011). Neurofeedback is a type of biofeedback that specifically targets brain waves (Myers & Young, 2012). When participating in a neurofeedback session, electrodes are placed in various places of a client's head (e.g., earlobes, scalp); these electrodes relay real-time data about brainwave activity (Hammond, 2011). The brain wave bands visible are delta, theta, alpha, beta, and gamma rays (Hammond, 2011). When clients are able to see the brainwaves they are then able to have influence over them.

There are a few ways in which this relates to addictions counseling. Individuals with alcohol use disorders (and their children, commonly known as adult children of alcoholics) have been shown to have lower alpha and theta waves, and higher levels of beta waves (Hammond, 2011). These altered brain wave states have been shown even after long periods of abstinence. This knowledge is important for a few different reasons, one that it may inform etiology of the disordered use pattern. This also may help inform reasons for difficulty with relapse maintenance.

Research studies examining neurofeedback and addictions have produced important findings. Scott, Kaiser, Othmer, and Sideroff (as cited in Hammond, 2011) studied the influence of neurofeedback when added to an inpatient substance abuse program. Participants were randomized to either the treatment group or control group. Those in the treatment group received between 40 and 50 neurofeedback sessions, and findings suggest that those participants remained in therapy significant longer than the control group. In addition, upon follow-up 1 year later, 77% of participants in the treatment group were not using substances, compared to only 44% of control group participants.

In addition, Dehghani-Arani, Rostami, and Nadali (2013) conducted a study with 20 male participants who were receiving treatment for an opiate dependence disorder. Participants were enrolled in a medicine maintenance program (either methadone or buprenorphine) and were randomized to either the control or experimental group. Those in the experimental group received two months of 30-minute neurofeedback sessions. Overall, the findings of the Dehghani-Arani et al. study suggested that the added neurofeedback sessions helped reduce participant cravings to use and improved general mental health outcomes.

The research base of neurofeedback interventions for clients struggling with addictions has a lot of room to grow. The two studies cited above are certainly encouraging, yet both had small numbers of participants, a concern in generalizing results. Beyond the research limitations, there are many professional counselors that are excited about neurofeedback, particularly as we continue to learn more about the brain.

Box 14.3: The Excitement of Neurofeedback for the Counseling Profession

Recent years have seen a fundamental shift in the field of counseling. That shift was born out of the research of psycho-physiologists such as Bessel van der Kolk and Stephen Porges. We have come to understand the difference between a "top-down" approach, like cognitive behavioral therapy, in which changes to cognitions result in changes to mood and behaviors, and a "bottom-up" approach, like neurofeedback, in which physiological changes result in changes in cognitive states, and the effect of each on symptoms of trauma. At the same time, we have become increasingly more aware that trauma is much more common than we had once conceptualized it to be. The Center for Disease Control and Kaiser Permanente Adverse Childhood Experiences study and the argument for the developmental trauma disorder as a diagnostic category has brought that message home in a very strong way. As a clinician and professor in a graduate counseling program that focuses exclusively on preparing students to work with victims of all ages who have been impacted by trauma, I have been convinced that in order to effectively moderate and ameliorate the negative physical, emotional, and mental sequelae of trauma one needs to intervene on both an emotional and physiological level. Neurofeedback training allows clients to access more regulated brainwave states that calm the over-aroused nervous system and open doors for the processing of trauma.

In addition, neurofeedback holds promise relative to the treatment of substance abuse. First, we now have a better understanding of why some individuals with under-aroused or over-aroused nervous systems might be more susceptible to either depressant or stimulant addiction. Second, we now have an intervention that works on a physiological level that can help regulate a distressed nervous system and thereby reduce the impulse to use. The co-occurrence of addiction and trauma is also helped by neurofeedback as an intervention for substance use.

My initial introduction to neurofeedback was at a State counseling conference years ago. At the time I was told that the investment in equipment could run as high as many thousands of dollars. And yet I could not get the idea of pursuing training out of my mind. Since my initial exposure, the field has grown immensely. Equipment is now much more affordable and credentialing is possible through BCIA (Biofeedback Certification International Alliance). There are neurofeedback conferences as well as regional associations that support and advocate for neurofeedback training and awareness. In addition, I was surprised to find that advances in neurofeedback technology and research have resulted in a wide array of protocols and schools of thought, all of which have shown to be effective as treatment interventions in spite of their different approaches.

What excites me most about integrating neurofeedback into existing counseling and substance abuse treatment is the fact that neurofeedback allows clinicians to take a holistic approach to helping clients. Neurofeedback holds promise in treating anxiety and panic attacks, improving self-regulation, combatting depression, and in alleviating the symptoms of PTSD. Research on the effectiveness of neurofeedback continues, however, there is a solid body of existing research that confirms the benefits of neurofeedback. The VA currently uses neurofeedback as an intervention for PTSD, and my hope is that the acceptance of this life-changing treatment will continue to grow in the coming years.

SOURCE: Astra B. Czerny. Astra B. Czerny, PhD, LPC, NCC, DCC, is assistant professor at Philadelphia University.

Medication-Assisted Treatment (MAT) Efforts

Using medications for the treatment of addictions is not a new phenomenon. With the knowledge of the brain and neurotransmitters, medications can be developed that remove the ability of a user to have an altered state of consciousness (i.e., a user cannot become high). All medications used to assist treatment are intended to be one component of a comprehensive treatment plan; they are not intended for use in isolation.

Naltrexone

Naltrexone is a medication prescribed by a physician that can be used to help treat both alcohol use disorders as well as opioid disorders (Substance Abuse and Mental Health Services Administration [SAMHSA], 2016c). For both alcohol and opioids, naltrexone blocks the euphoric feelings (i.e., the high) associated with use. This blocking is achieved by binding to and blocking opioid receptors in the brain (SAMHSA, 2016c).

Methadone

Methadone is a well-known medication used to help individuals who have become addicted to heroin and/or narcotic pain medications (SAMHSA, 2015). Just like all other MATs, methadone is prescribed by a physician and must be obtained in a clinic certified by SAMHSA. Each methadone dose is tailored to the individual client and helps to reduce the symptoms of opioid withdrawal, which blocks the euphoria of other opioids (SAMHSA, 2015). Methadone can be an addictive substance, which is why the strict regulation is important.

Buprenorphine

Buprenorphine is prescribed by a physician as a part of a comprehensive treatment program (SAMHSA, 2016a). Buprenorphine is similar in nature to methadone, as it reduces the euphoria associated with opioid substances; however, it is available by prescription that can be obtained in a physician's office (SAMHSA, 2016a). This expands the access to the treatment; it may be much easier for someone to make an appointment with their primary care physician than it may be to overcome making an appointment at a methadone clinic, as the stigma surrounding substance use and addiction is still prevalent.

Naloxone

Naloxone is a medication that has seen an increase in popularity in recent years due to the opioid epidemic occurring in our country. Naloxone is a medication that can be administered in order to prevent a lethal overdose from an opioid (SAMHSA, 2016b). This medication blocks the opioid receptor sites and reverses the overdose as it is occurring (SAMHSA, 2016b). Naloxone is a prescription medication, although many first responders are carrying this medication in the event they encounter someone in distress. In addition, some treatment facilities are choosing to discharge individuals with a naloxone prescription in order to prevent future overdoses as you read in Chapter 10.

As previously mentioned, medication-assisted treatments are not a new phenomenon. These treatment modalities present an ever-present opportunity to conduct research, as through the years significant outcomes have been found. Of particular interest now is the influence that naloxone has not only on reducing death by overdose but any longer-term implications it may have. With the increasing use and availability of this medication, more research is needed to examine further-reaching implications.

Holistic Approaches

Holistic approaches refer to the infusion of mind, body, and spirit. In recent years, we have seen an increase of respect for these types of interventions. Much of this respect has come from an increase in scientific research being conducted, as well as individuals in respected positions acknowledging the role holistic approaches have had in their lives. One example is NBC News anchor Dan Harris, who had a panic attack during a live television broadcast. This experience led Harris to discover mindfulness, and further to author a book about living a healthier and happier life. Spirituality and mindfulness meditation are the two most commonly known holistic approaches, and those covered here.

Mindfulness Meditation

John Kabat-Zinn defines mindfulness as "the awareness that emerges through paying attention on purpose, in the present moment, and nonjudgmentally to the unfolding of experience moment by moment" (2003, p. 145). In other words mindfulness is "knowing what you are doing while you are doing it" (Kabat-Zinn, 2013, p. 16). Research has demonstrated positive results associated with infusing mindfulness meditation in treatment for a variety of medical and mental health concerns. Zgierska et al. (2009) conducted a systematic review of 22 research articles in order to examine the existing evidence base of mindfulness mediation therapies for addictive disorders. Of the randomized controlled trials, all reported positive results for the mindfulness meditation treatment arms (Zgierska et al., 2009). In addition, other studies that were not randomly controlled found a reduction of substance use overall (Zgierska et al., 2009). Marlatt and Chowla (2007) discuss how mindfulness and other forms of meditation can be skills utilized to extend treatment effects and reduce relapse. The appeal of integrating low-cost mindfulness into addictions treatment is exciting, yet Zgierska et al. caution that the research base is still maturing, and time will be needed to fully understand associated outcomes.

Research into mindfulness has blossomed in recent years, so much so that there is now an academic journal dedicated to the research and practice of mindfulness. This academic publication has been titled *Mindfulness*. In addition to the clinical realm, interest has blossomed among the general population. It is not unlikely that you will encounter a client in the future that has an interest in mindfulness, has heard about mindfulness and become intrigued, and may want to integrate some form of mindfulness into treatment. Not only are clinicians being trained, there are many technological applications available for use on personal smartphones.

Spirituality

According to Miller (2013), Carl Jung once wrote a letter to Bill W. (cofounder of Alcoholics Anonymous) that translated to "Spirits (alcohol) and spirituality seem to be mutually exclusive. They drive each other out" (p. 1258). There is a commonly known relationship between addiction and spirituality, particularly for anyone that has been to a 12-step-based meeting format (e.g., Alcoholics Anonymous, Narcotics Anonymous). Spirituality is often assumed to be the same as religion, yet the two are separate concepts. Mason, Deane, Kelly, and Crowe (2009) distinguish religiosity from spirituality as the first being an individual experience with institutional components, with spirituality solely consisting of an individual experience.

Of interest to many counselors are client perceptions related to the importance of spirituality. Arnold, Avants, Margolin, and Marcotte (2002) conducted a study with participants in a methadone-maintenance program. The authors surveyed 47 participants and found participants thought the addition of spirituality to treatment would be beneficial in a variety of ways (helpful in their recovery, reducing craving, and increasing hopefulness). In addition, focus groups were conducted with 21 participants who discussed a desire for interventions targeted to spirituality. The participants discussed the importance of using a broad definition of spirituality in order to attend to all varying belief and non-belief systems present in the participants.

In addition, in 2009, Mason et al. conducted a study of 77 males participating in addiction treatment. These authors examined the relationships between spirituality, religiosity, self-efficacy, and cravings to use. The authors found no relationship between religiosity and the other outcomes, yet did find an inverse relationship between spirituality and cravings to use; in other words, as spirituality increases, cravings to use decreases. In addition, Mason and colleagues found that self-efficacy mediated the relationship between spirituality and cravings, suggesting that spirituality may increase an individual's self-efficacy, allowing him or her to reduce his or her cravings to use. These are encouraging findings, particularly as they can help inform treatment interventions. Miller (2013) highlights that there is little time and expertise devoted to interventions targeting spirituality, beyond offering clients referrals to a 12-step program. Spirituality represents one facet of client culture, and attending to this is an ethically responsible way to practice.

Although holistic approaches are being recognized more and are undergoing more research, there are limitations with the literature base. One limitation, and often a common one, is that of smaller sample sizes. When you look above, the sample sizes of the studies are quite limited, so although the results are exciting, they need to be interpreted with caution. Another limitation is the lack of uniformity associated with holistic approaches, which makes rigorous studies difficult without manualizing the treatments. Not only are there numerous holistic approaches utilized as adjunctive treatments (e.g., yoga, acupuncture, reiki), but there is a great degree of variability among even the similar approaches. This is an area of inquiry that would benefit greatly from rigorous controlled trials.

Building Upon and Re-Examining Established Evidence-Based Models

Evaluating Research Methods

One of the biggest obstacles that professional counselors and addiction researchers face is that we are in the business of working with human beings who are ever changing. We have learned an incredible amount about ways to prevent, intervene, and treat individuals living on the addiction spectrum, yet the spectrum of addiction issues is alive and well in our society. Certainly, we know there is much more to be learned about this work.

One question is how best to study the addiction spectrum and associated interventions. Many will argue for the need for randomized controlled trials (RCTs) that have control groups as the gold standard. Yet, the Declaration of Helsinki (World Medical Association, 2008) prohibits using placebos (i.e., control groups) when there is a known treatment to test against, thus limiting control group studies. An argument can be made that the Declaration of Helsinki is in reference to the medical profession, and medications and placebo trials, and not to counseling interventions, yet is one then saying that we should not strive for the same high standards as the medical profession? Would it be ethical for an addictions researcher to withhold treatment to an individual in the sheer interest of having a control group? There is no easy answer to this question, as all ethical dilemmas are complex.

In order to alleviate some of this concern specifically to the ethics of control group RCTs, there are many researchers who utilize the wait-list control group method. Individuals who will be receiving treatment, but have not yet received it, are aligned as the control group in order to measure against the treatment group for outcomes. This is one answer to a complex problem. Research is a complex process, and you learn immensely throughout every study. You can read any research article of your choice, and you will see a "limitations" section in which the limitations of the study are addressed. This is where the authors will dictate concerns about the research, or cautions about interpretation of the data. This section is a great place to examine in order to learn from past research as to better inform future research.

Importance of Continued Research

Beyond the limitations of our research, we are continually learning more and more about the addiction spectrum and best ways to intervene. It is vital that research continue to occur. In order to conduct large-scale research, it is important to secure grants, and grant-funding sources publish research priorities on regular cycles, typically within the organization's strategic plan. These priorities are lists that help researchers consider the topics that are considered most needing of clear research evidence, and are therefore higher priority for funding initiatives.

Another important area to focus on is the counselors that are doing full-time clinical work. Although many counselors do not have the time to conduct a full research study, they can partner with researchers in order to examine treatment models. Full-time clinicians have a unique lens of being on the front lines with clients—in the trenches, here and now. Our hope is that if you are one of those professionals in the future, you consider ways you can use your clinical expertise to inform future research.

Skills in Action

Box 14.4: Case Illustration Demystifying Neuroscience for Clients

A key way in which neuroscience is used by professional counselors working with clients on the addiction spectrum is through psychoeducation. The below dialogue is between a professional addictions counselor (Jose) and his client (Sam). Sam has been coming to see Jose for individual counseling after her discharge from a 30-day residential treatment program for her marijuana addiction.

Jose (Counselor):	Hi, Sam, I'm glad to see you back.
Sam (Client):	Thanks.
Jose:	Tell me how the last week has been.
Sam:	Well, I guess it has been OK.
Jose:	Just, OK? (Sam nods her head.) Tell me more about what "OK" means for you.
Sam:	I mean, it's going fine. I went to work every day, did my thing, made it to my meetings, but it just doesn't seem like it's getting any easier.
Jose:	Not getting any easier . . .
Sam:	No, I just am ready for that awakening everyone keeps talking about. I'm ready for the cravings to end. Every night I get home from work and find myself looking for my bowl; I just want to take a hit. It's the only way I know how to relax.
Jose:	You are having a difficult time learning how to manage the cravings. (Sam says "yes.") Last week toward the end of our session I mentioned wanting to spend some time with you talking about the brain and how some of what you are experiencing may be explained that way.
Sam:	Yeah, I remember, and I remember I told you how bad I was at science (Sam giggles).
Jose:	Yes, I remember. And don't worry, what we're going to talk about does not require being a brain surgeon!
Sam:	Phfew!
Jose:	OK, so, Sam, you mentioned almost having a default response when you get home from work—that you find yourself looking for your bowl.
Sam:	Yeah, it's almost like I don't even have control! I just find myself looking all over my apartment. One time last week, it was almost as if I "woke up" when I was looking in my kitchen cupboards. Obviously I wasn't going to find anything since I got rid of it right before I left for treatment. And I don't know if it makes me sound like I'm crazy or not, but it was like I was in this fog, and the next thing I know I was looking in my coffee mug cupboard.

Jose:	I hear you saying that you were not in control with what was going on at that time. You defaulted back to one of your preset settings.
Sam:	Yes! How do I stop this?
Jose:	Well, first in order to stop it, how about I help explain it to you.
Sam:	OK.
Jose:	Like any complex machine, our brains are made up of many different parts. One type of part is neuropathways. Neuropathways sound really complex, but they are really just pathways, how brain information gets from one area to the next. These are kind of like highways and local roads. Following so far?
Sam:	Yeah, so far, so good.
Jose:	Great, so these neuropathways get established when we do things over and over. Just like when you come here to this office for your appointments. The first time you came here, you probably had to follow a map, but by now, you know the way to get here. Just like you know how to walk, or write, or type on your computer. These neuropathways were not always there, but now they are ingrained in your brain. The concrete has been laid, so to speak.
Sam:	OK, that makes sense. Well, I mean so far.
Jose:	When you think about you and your marijuana use, you have an established neuropathway. Your pathway is that you come home from work, grab your bowl, take a hit, and feel relaxed. Your brain knows how to do this. So when that pathway isn't available, you feel frustrated!
Sam:	Yes!
Jose:	It's like you are trying to drive down the road you always take to get to work, but now there is a road closure sign, but no detour signs. You need to develop your own detour, which is a lot to ask when you only know one way.
Sam:	Wow, that does make sense! So, how do I make the detour route?
Jose:	Well, that is what you and I can work on together. From brain research we know that this is possible—it is called neuroplasticity. If we say that one reason for you using is to feel relaxed, then what is another tool you use, or could use, that helps you feel relaxed?
Sam:	Hmm, I like to ride my bike, but I've had a flat tire for who knows how long.

Jose and Sam will now continue the session by exploring the alternatives Sam has for relaxation. Talking to clients about neuroscience and the brain does not have to be intimidating. Hopefully from the above demonstration you saw how a conversation may go, and how beneficial it can be to clients to demystify this big organ in our heads!

Experiential Skills Learning Activity

This exercise can be completed individually, with a partner, or in a small group. Download one of the apps referenced during the mindfulness section ("Mindfulness Coach" or "Calm") and select a program to complete. If someone in your group knows of an alternative mindfulness activity, you may use that. After completing the mindfulness exercise, reflect on the following questions, either individually or in your group:

- What was your experience?
- How might you use this in the future as a professional counselor?
- Are there any specific clients or client situations that you would recommend this type of intervention?

RESOURCES FOR FURTHER LEARNING

Websites

The Association for Applied Psychophysiology and Biofeedback, Inc.
http://www.aapb.org/i4a/pages/index.cfm?pageid=1

Biofeedback Certification International Alliance
http://www.bcia.org/i4a/pages/index.cfm?pageid=1

National Institutes for Health
http://www.nih.gov

Brain Research through Advancing Innovative Neurotechnologies Initiative
http://www.braininitiative.nih.gov/about/index.htm

University of Massachusetts Medical School Center for Mindfulness in Medicine, Health Care, and Society; Oasis Institute: Mindfulness-Based Professional Education and Training
http://www.umassmed.edu/cfm/training/

Books

Kabat-Zinn, J. (2013). *Full catastrophe living: Using the wisdom of your body and mind to face stress, pain, and illness.* New York, NY: Bantam.

Luke, C. (2016). *Neuroscience for counselors and therapists: Integrating the sciences of mind and brain.* Thousand Oaks, CA: Sage.

Academic Journal

Mindfulness
http://link.springer.com/journal/12671

Journal Article

Engel, G. L. (1980). The clinical application of the biopsychosocial model. *The American Journal of Psychiatry*, *137*(5), 535–544.

REFERENCES

American Psychiatric Association (APA). (2013). *Diagnostic and statistical manual of mental disorders* (5th ed.). Washington, DC: Author.

Arnold, R. M., Avants, S. K., Margolin, A., & Marcotte, D. (2002). Patient attitudes concerning the inclusion of spirituality into addiction treatment. *Journal of Substance Abuse Treatment*, *22*, 319–326.

Association for Applied Psychophysiology and Biofeedback. (2011). About biofeedback. Retrieved from http://www.aapb.org/i4a/pages/index.cfm?pageid=3463

Dehghani-Arani, F., Rostami, R., & Nadali, H. (2013). Neurofeedback training for opiate addiction: Improvement of mental health and craving. *Applied Psychophysiology and Biofeedback*, *38*, 133–141. doi:10.1007/s10484-013-9218-5

De Jong, P., & Berg, I. K. (2012). *Interviewing for solutions* (4th ed.). Belmont, CA: Brooks/Cole.

Ellis, A. (1962). *Reason and emotion in psychotherapy*. New York, NY: Citadel Press.

Engel, G. L. (1977). The need for a new medical model: A challenge for biomedicine. *Science*, *196*, 129–136.

Hammond, D. C. (2011). What is neurofeedback: An update. *Journal of Neurotherapy*, *15*, 305–336. doi:10.1080/10874208.2011.623090

Hatala, A. R. (2013). Towards a biopsychosocial-spiritual approach in health psychology: Exploring theoretical orientations and future directions. *Journal of Spirituality in Mental Health*, *15*(4), 256–276. doi:10.1080/19349637.2013.776448

Kabat-Zinn, J. (2003). Mindfulness-based interventions in context: Past, present, and future. *Clinical Psychology Science and Practice*, *10*(2), 144–156. doi:10.1093/clipsy.bpg016

Kabat-Zinn, J. (2013). *Full catastrophe living: Using the wisdom of your body and mind to face stress, pain, and illness*. New York, NY: Bantam.

Marlatt, G. A., & Chowla, N. (2007). Meditation and alcohol use. *Southern Medical Journal*, *100*(4), 451–453.

Mason, S. J., Deane, F. P., Kelly, P. J., & Crowe, T. P. (2009). Pilot study: Spirituality and religiosity. *Substance Use & Misuse*, *44*, 1926–1940. doi:10.3109/10826080802486723

Miller, W. R. (2013). Addiction and spirituality. *Substance Use & Misuse*, *48*, 1258–1259. doi:10.3109/10826084.2013.799024

Myers, J. E., & Young, J. S. (2012). Brain wave biofeedback: Benefits of integrating neurofeedback in counseling. *Journal of Counseling and Development*, *90*, 20–28.

National Institutes of Health. (2016). *What is the brain initiative?* Retrieved from http://www.braininitiative.nih.gov

Rogers, C. R. (1957). The necessary and sufficient conditions of therapeutic personality change. *Journal of Consulting Psychology*, *21*, 95–100.

Rogers, C. R. (1961). *On becoming a person: A therapist's view of psychology*. Boston, MA: Houghton Mifflin.

Substance Abuse and Mental Health Services Administration (SAMHSA). (2015). *Methadone*. Retrieved from http://www.samhsa.gov/medication-assisted-treatment/treatment/methadone

Substance Abuse and Mental Health Services Administration (SAMHSA). (2016a). *Buprenorphine*. Retrieved from http://www.samhsa.gov/medication-assisted-treatment/treatment/buprenorphine

Substance Abuse and Mental Health Services Administration (SAMHSA). (2016b). *Naloxone*. Retrieved from http://www.samhsa.gov/medication-assisted-treatment/treatment/naloxone

Substance Abuse and Mental Health Services Administration (SAMHSA). (2016c). *Naltrexone*. Retrieved from http://www.samhsa.gov/medication-assisted-treatment/treatment/naltrexone

Volkow, N. D. (2014). *How science has revolutionized the understanding of drug addiction.* Retrieved from https://www.drugabuse.gov/publications/drugs-brains-behavior-science-addiction/preface

World Medical Association. (2008). *World medical association declaration of Helsinki: Ethical principles for medical research involving human subjects.* Retrieved from http://www.wma.net/en/30publications/10policies/b3/17c.pdf

Zgierska, A., Rabago, D., Chawla, N., Kushner, K., Koehler, R., & Marlatt, A. (2009). Mindfulness meditation for substance use disorders: A systematic review. *Substance Abuse, 30*(4), 266–294. doi:10.80/08897070903250019

Index

Pages followed by b, f, or t indicate boxes, figures, or tables respectively.

About the Authors

Laura J. Veach, PhD, professor with a primary faculty appointment in the Department of Surgery-Trauma and a joint faculty appointment in Psychiatry/Behavioral Medicine at Wake Forest School of Medicine in Winston–Salem, North Carolina, is licensed in that state as a professional counselor (LPC), a clinical addiction specialist (LCAS), and is a certified clinical supervisor (CCS). Dr. Veach has her PhD in counselor education and supervision from the University of New Orleans. She serves as the Wake Forest Baptist Health director of counselor training in acute care services: surgery/trauma/ burns/medicine and specialized screening and counseling intervention research and trauma-informed counseling, with over 35 years of work in counseling and supervision, especially in counseling individuals impacted by substance use disorders.

In August 2007 she pioneered alcohol screening and brief counseling intervention services, research, and counselor training at Wake Forest Baptist Medical Level I Trauma Center. She served as co-principal investigator for a Robert Wood Johnson Foundation grant examining alcohol screening and brief counseling interventions in a prospective clinical trial comparing two counseling interventions. Recently, she received funding from the Childress Institute for Pediatric Trauma as principal investigator to conduct ATV safety interventions with pediatric trauma patients and also completed violence intervention research with violently injured youth in hospital trauma centers at Wake Forest and Carolinas Medical Center. In addition, she is a key care manager for an NIH-funded multicenter pragmatic trial examining intensive PTSD interventions in hospitalized trauma patients. She specializes in counseling individuals with addictive and substance-related use disorders, trauma-informed counseling in medical and integrated care settings, behavioral health consulting, and has over 20 publications. In previous counselor education tenured faculty appointments at Wake Forest University and University of North Carolina at Charlotte and in previous behavioral health administration work, she created innovative counselor and clinical addiction specialist training, externally funded graduate assistantships, and intensive outpatient addiction treatment programs with managed care services.

Dr. Veach served as the 2006 president of the International Association of Addictions and Offender Counseling (IAAOC). She was awarded the IAAOC Counselor Educator Award in March 2007, the Graduate Faculty Award for Excellence in Teaching at Wake Forest University in May 2007, and the national ACA Advocacy Award in March 2008. She cherishes spending time with her devoted partner and friend of more than 46 years, George, and amazing photographer and daughter, Alana, enjoying their shared vintage auto racing and travel pursuits in the United States.

Regina R. Moro currently serves as an assistant professor in the Department of Counselor Education at Boise State University in Boise, Idaho. She received her PhD in counseling from the University of North Carolina at Charlotte with an emphasis in multicultural counseling, received a graduate certificate from UNC Charlotte in substance abuse counseling, and an MS in community counseling from Syracuse University. Dr. Moro is licensed as a licensed professional counselor (ID), licensed mental health counselor (FL), a licensed clinical addictions specialist (NC), is an advanced certified alcohol/drug counselor (ID), and is a national certified counselor. Her clinical passion involves work with crisis and trauma, including a focus on addiction with individuals and families. Dr. Moro has held leadership positions in counseling organizations, most recently with the International Association of Addictions and Offender Counselors. She enjoys spending her free time enjoying the great outdoors with her partner, Ryan, and their rescue dog, Barkley.